SUICIDERS
VOLUME 1

LEE BERMEJO
writer & artist

MATT HOLLINGSWORTH
colorist

JARED K. FLETCHER
letterer

SUICIDERS created by
LEE BERMEJO

Will Dennis Jamie S. Rich Editors – Original Series Greg Lockard Associate Editor – Original Series
Jeb Woodard Group Editor – Collected Editions Scott Nybakken Editor – Collected Edition Sarabeth Kett Publication Design

Shelly Bond VP & Executive Editor – Vertigo

Diane Nelson President Dan DiDio and Jim Lee Co-Publishers Geoff Johns Chief Creative Officer
Amit Desai Senior VP – Marketing & Global Franchise Management Nairi Gardiner Senior VP – Finance
Sam Ades VP – Digital Marketing Bobbie Chase VP – Talent Development
Mark Chiarello Senior VP – Art, Design & Collected Editions John Cunningham VP – Content Strategy
Anne DePies VP – Strategy Planning & Reporting Don Falletti VP – Manufacturing Operations
Lawrence Ganem VP – Editorial Administration & Talent Relations Alison Gill Senior VP – Manufacturing & Operations
Hank Kanalz Senior VP – Editorial Strategy & Administration Jay Kogan VP – Legal Affairs
Derek Maddalena Senior VP – Sales & Business Development Jack Mahan VP – Business Affairs
Dan Miron VP – Sales Planning & Trade Development Nick Napolitano VP – Manufacturing Administration
Carol Roeder VP – Marketing Eddie Scannell VP – Mass Account & Digital Sales
Courtney Simmons Senior VP – Publicity & Communications Jim (Ski) Sokolowski VP – Comic Book Specialty & Newsstand Sales
Sandy Yi Senior VP – Global Franchise Management

Special Thanks to Valentina Testa.

SUICIDERS VOLUME 1

DC Comics, 4000 Warner Blvd., Burbank, CA 91522
A Warner Bros. Entertainment Company.
Printed in the USA. First Printing.
ISBN: 978-1-4012-4897-0

Library of Congress Cataloging-in-Publication date
Bermejo, Lee, author, illustrator.
   Suiciders / Lee Bermejo.
      pages cm
   ISBN 978-1-4012-4897-0 (v. 1 : hardback) 1. Los Angeles
(Calif.)—Comic books, strips, etc. 2. Graphic novels. I. Title.
PN6727.B424S85 2015
741.5'973—dc23
                                          2015033155

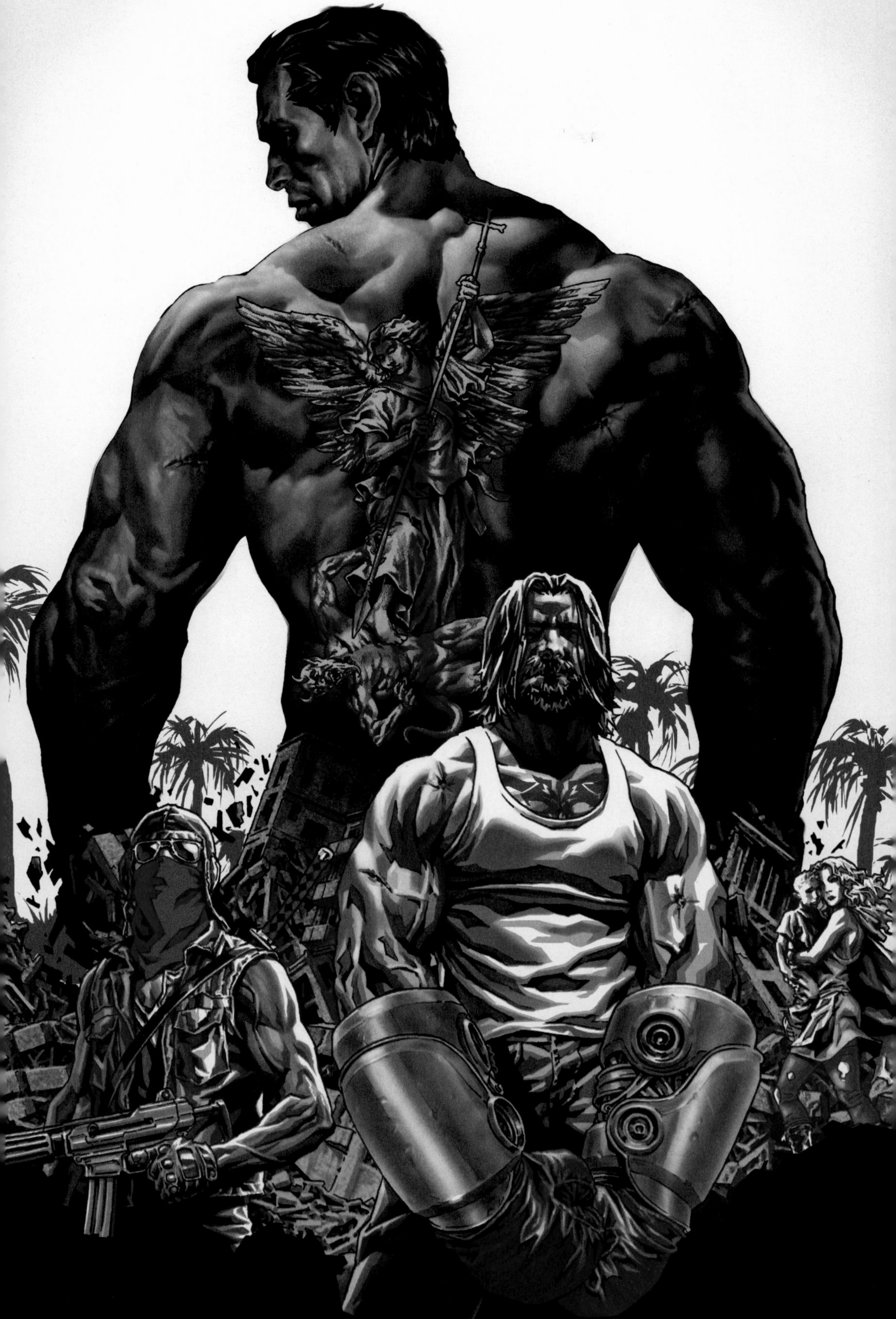

CHAPTER ONE:
THE BRUTALITY MALADY

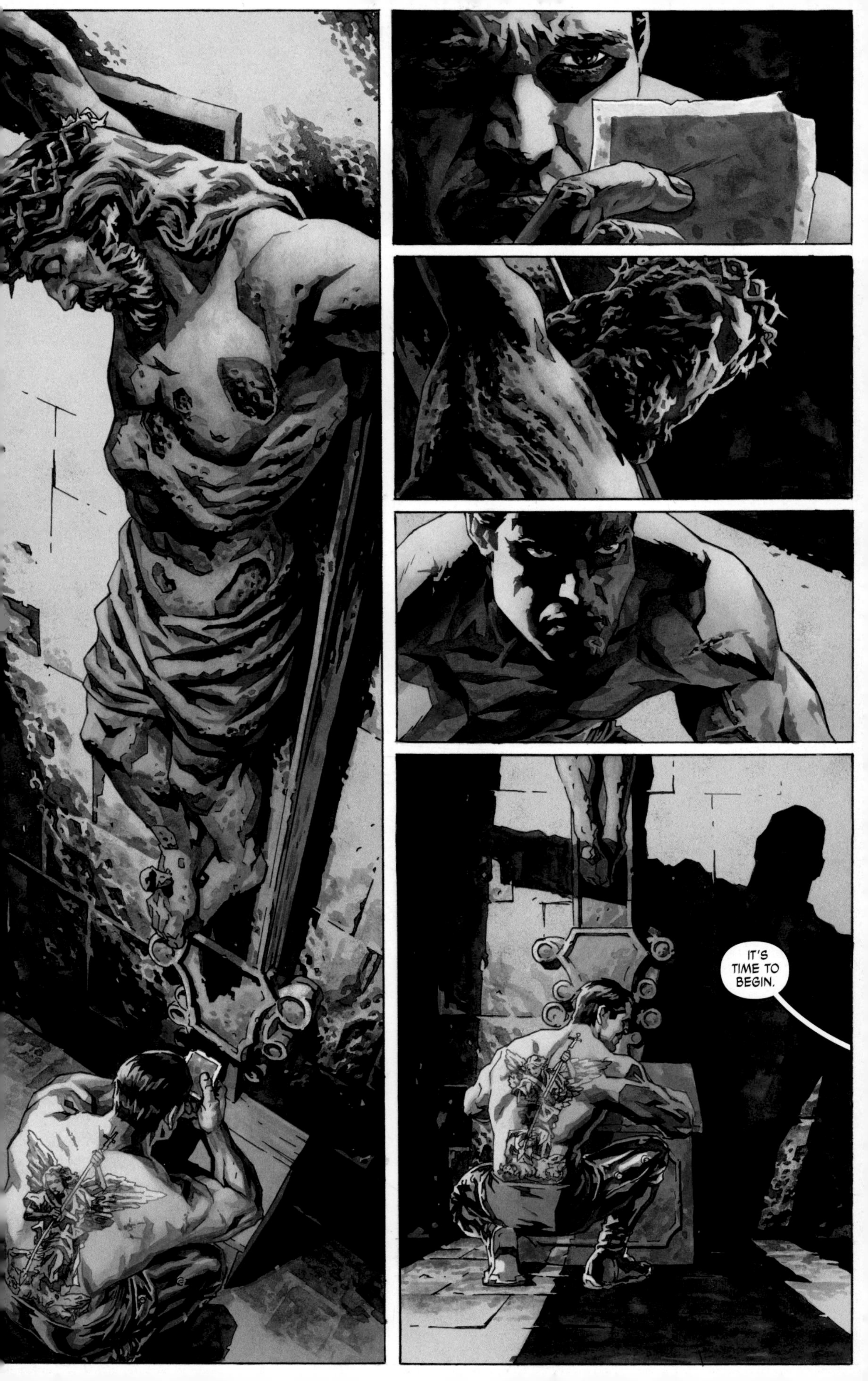
IT'S TIME TO BEGIN.

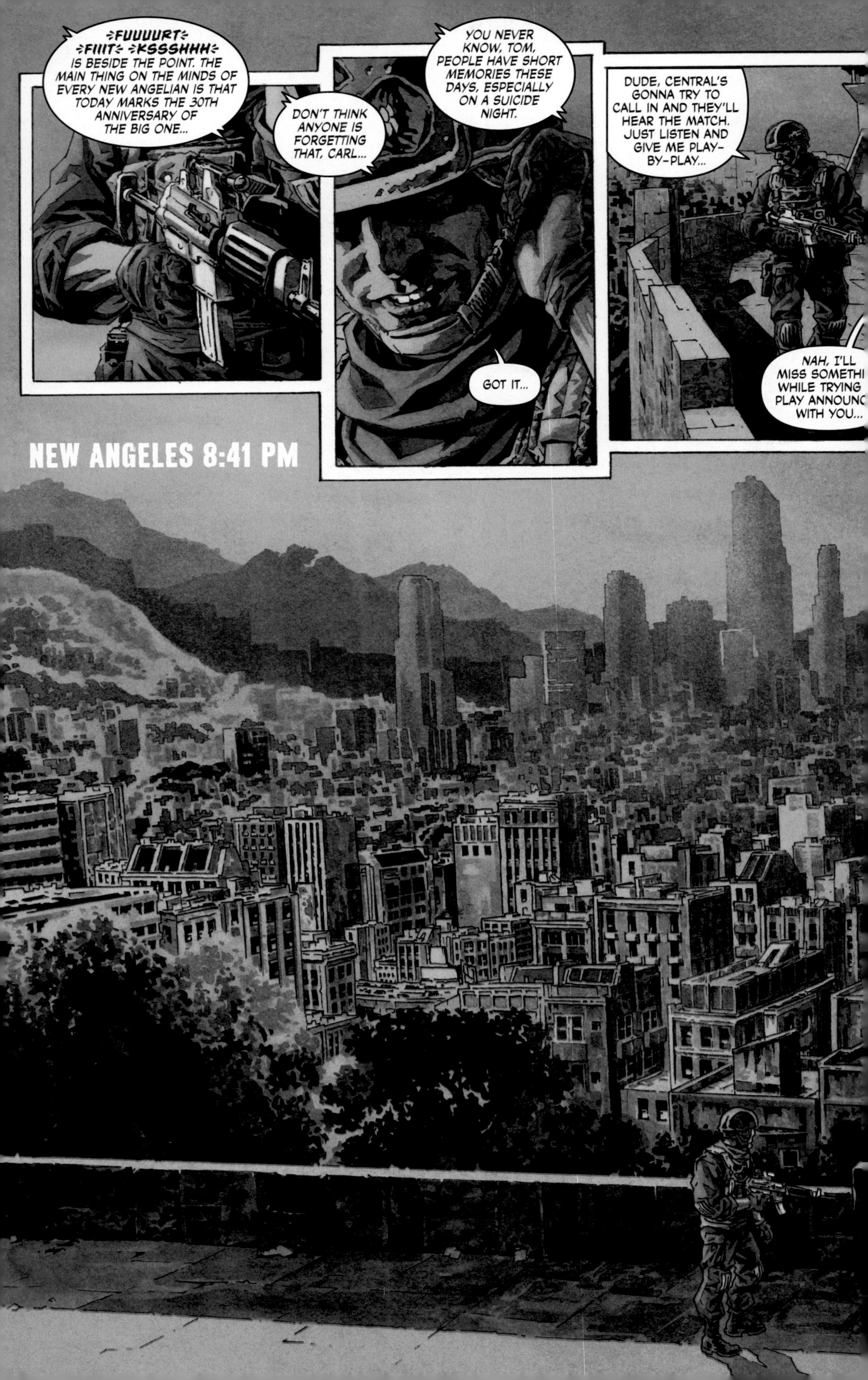

FUUUURT FIIIT KSSSHHH IS BESIDE THE POINT. THE MAIN THING ON THE MINDS OF EVERY NEW ANGELIAN IS THAT TODAY MARKS THE 30TH ANNIVERSARY OF THE BIG ONE...
DON'T THINK ANYONE IS FORGETTING THAT, CARL...
YOU NEVER KNOW, TOM, PEOPLE HAVE SHORT MEMORIES THESE DAYS, ESPECIALLY ON A SUICIDE NIGHT.
GOT IT...
DUDE, CENTRAL'S GONNA TRY TO CALL IN AND THEY'LL HEAR THE MATCH. JUST LISTEN AND GIVE ME PLAY-BY-PLAY...
NAH, I'LL MISS SOMETHI WHILE TRYING PLAY ANNOUNC WITH YOU...
NEW ANGELES 8:41 PM

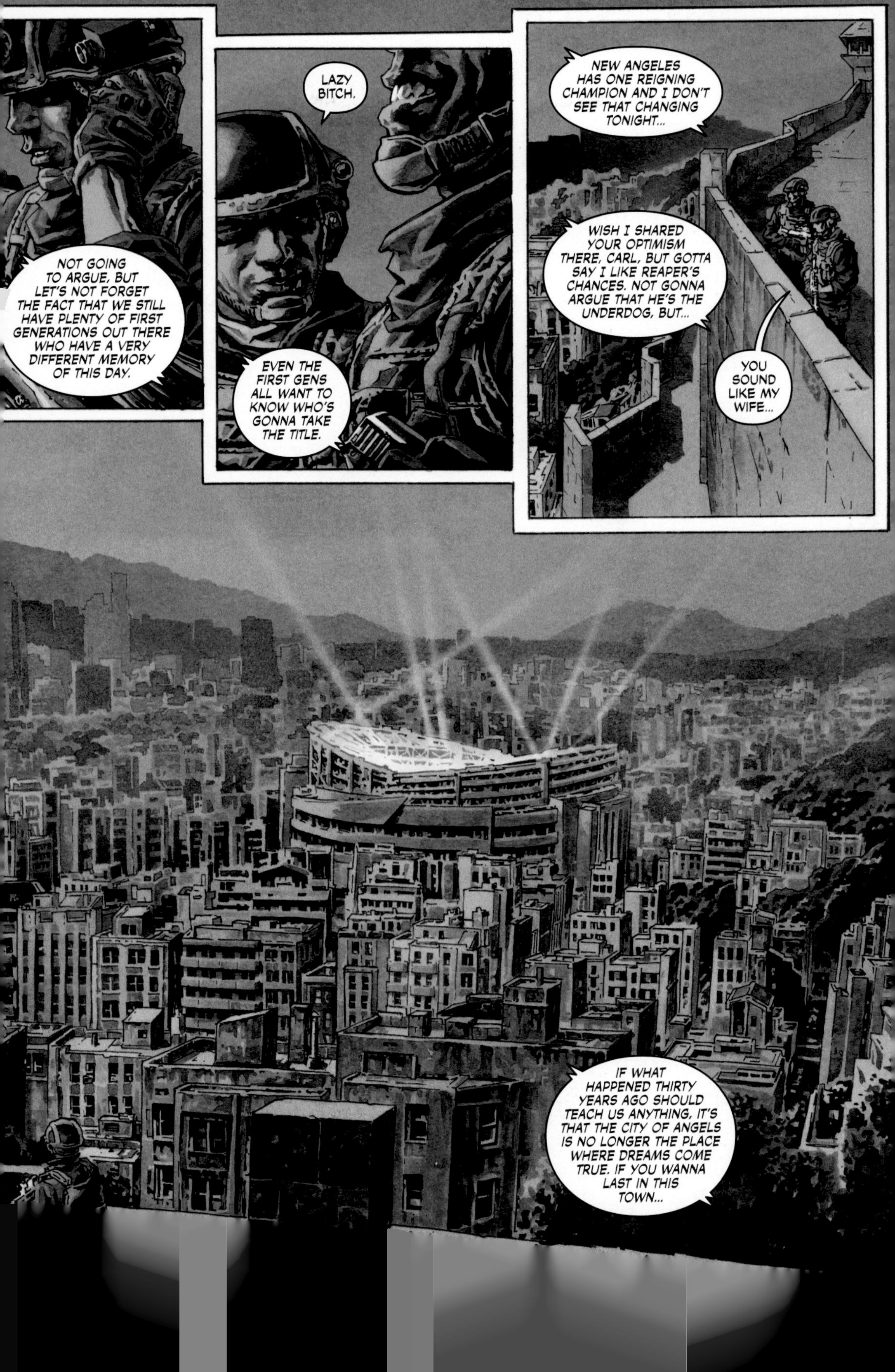
NOT GOING TO ARGUE, BUT LET'S NOT FORGET THE FACT THAT WE STILL HAVE PLENTY OF FIRST GENERATIONS OUT THERE WHO HAVE A VERY DIFFERENT MEMORY OF THIS DAY.
LAZY BITCH.
EVEN THE FIRST GENS ALL WANT TO KNOW WHO'S GONNA TAKE THE TITLE.
NEW ANGELES HAS ONE REIGNING CHAMPION AND I DON'T SEE THAT CHANGING TONIGHT...
WISH I SHARED YOUR OPTIMISM THERE, CARL, BUT GOTTA SAY I LIKE REAPER'S CHANCES. NOT GONNA ARGUE THAT HE'S THE UNDERDOG, BUT...
YOU SOUND LIKE MY WIFE...
IF WHAT HAPPENED THIRTY YEARS AGO SHOULD TEACH US ANYTHING, IT'S THAT THE CITY OF ANGELS IS NO LONGER THE PLACE WHERE DREAMS COME TRUE. IF YOU WANNA LAST IN THIS TOWN...

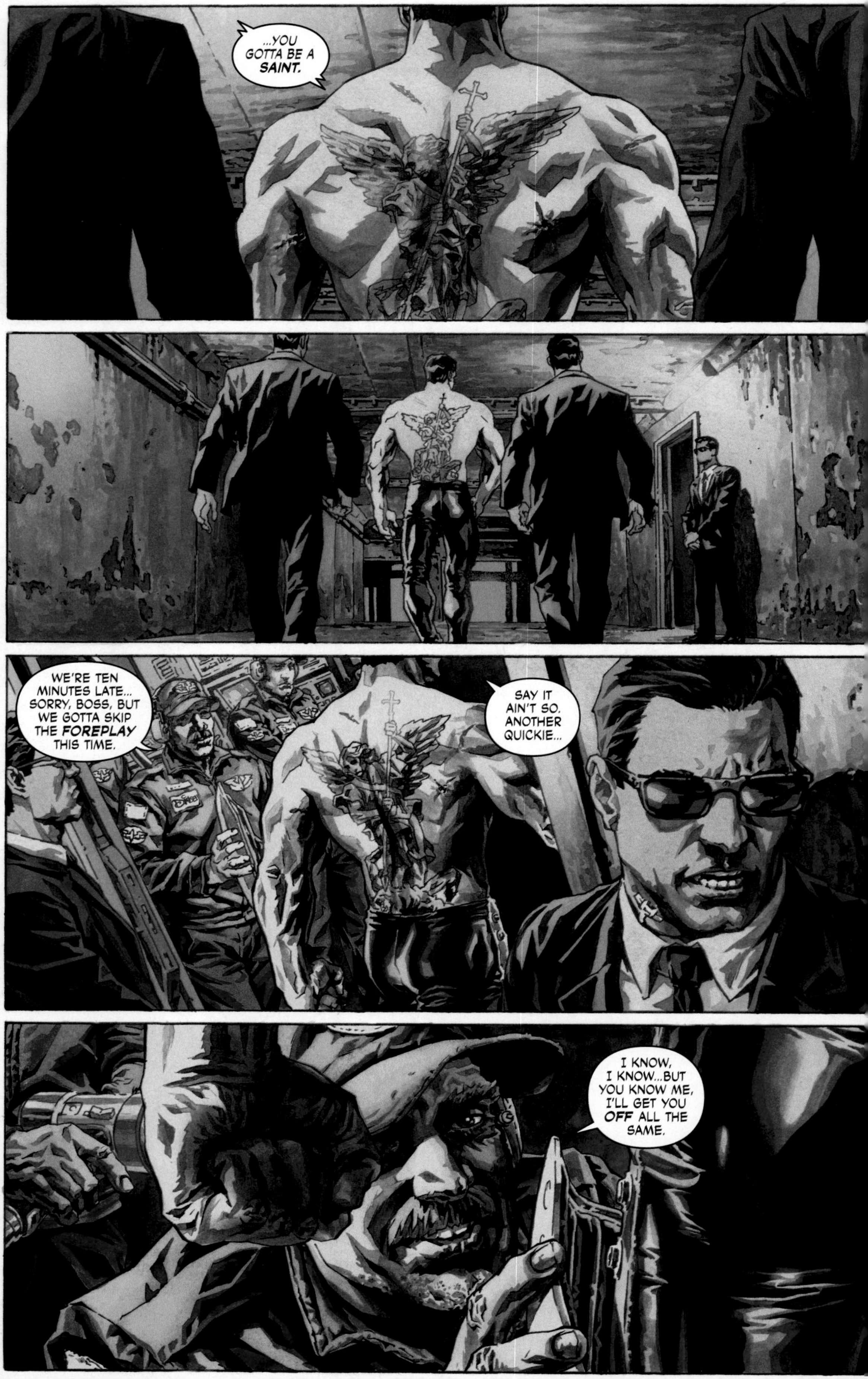
...YOU GOTTA BE A SAINT.
WE'RE TEN MINUTES LATE... SORRY, BOSS, BUT WE GOTTA SKIP THE FOREPLAY THIS TIME.
SAY IT AIN'T SO. ANOTHER QUICKIE...
I KNOW, I KNOW...BUT YOU KNOW ME, I'LL GET YOU OFF ALL THE SAME.

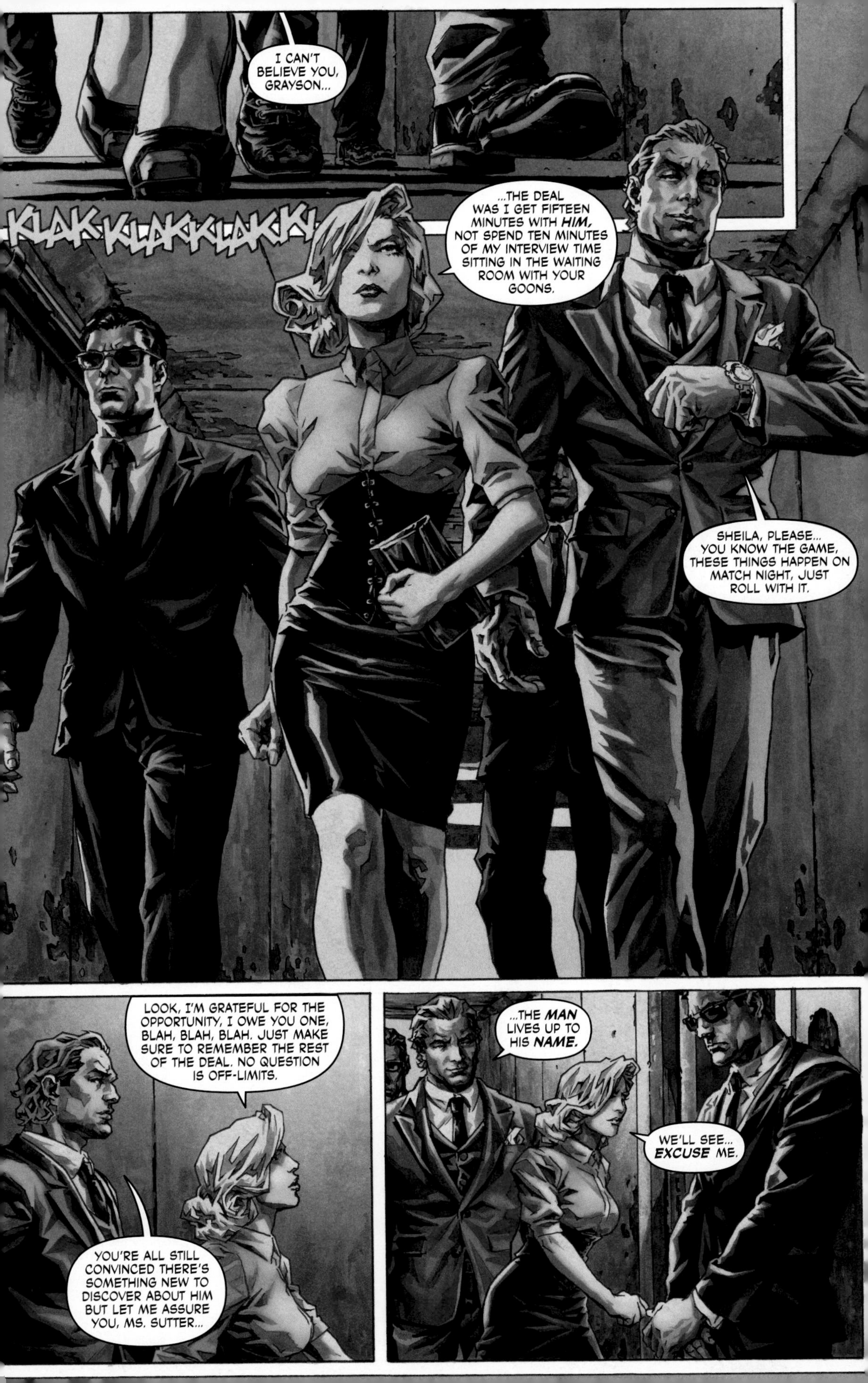
I CAN'T BELIEVE YOU, GRAYSON...
KLAK KLAK KLAK KLAK KLAK
...THE DEAL WAS I GET FIFTEEN MINUTES WITH *HIM,* NOT SPEND TEN MINUTES OF MY INTERVIEW TIME SITTING IN THE WAITING ROOM WITH YOUR GOONS.
SHEILA, PLEASE... YOU KNOW THE GAME, THESE THINGS HAPPEN ON MATCH NIGHT, JUST ROLL WITH IT.
LOOK, I'M GRATEFUL FOR THE OPPORTUNITY, I OWE YOU ONE, BLAH, BLAH, BLAH. JUST MAKE SURE TO REMEMBER THE REST OF THE DEAL. NO QUESTION IS OFF-LIMITS.
YOU'RE ALL STILL CONVINCED THERE'S SOMETHING NEW TO DISCOVER ABOUT HIM BUT LET ME ASSURE YOU, MS. SUTTER...
...THE *MAN* LIVES UP TO HIS *NAME.*
WE'LL SEE... *EXCUSE* ME.

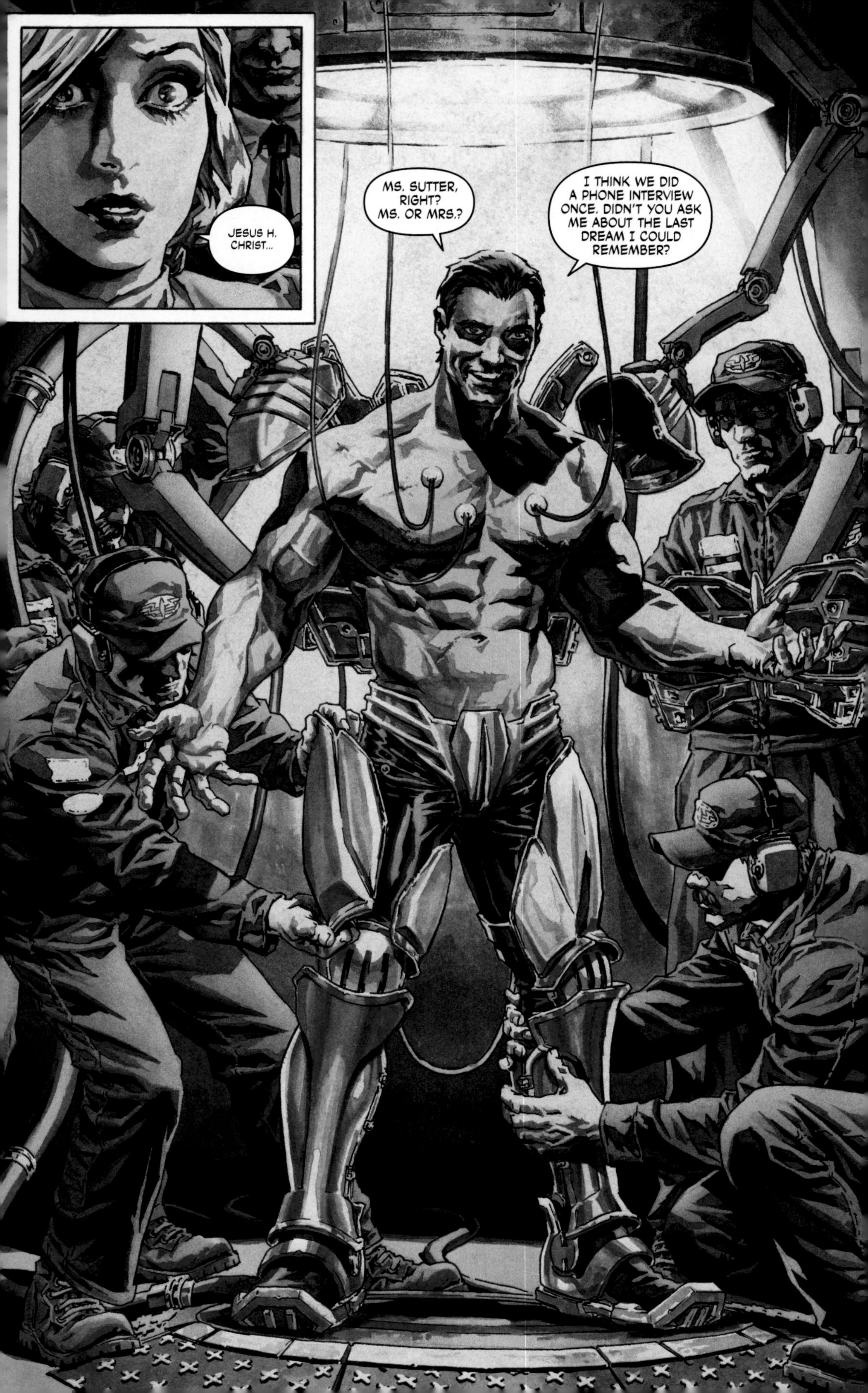
JESUS H. CHRIST...
MS. SUTTER, RIGHT? MS. OR MRS.?
I THINK WE DID A PHONE INTERVIEW ONCE. DIDN'T YOU ASK ME ABOUT THE LAST DREAM I COULD REMEMBER?

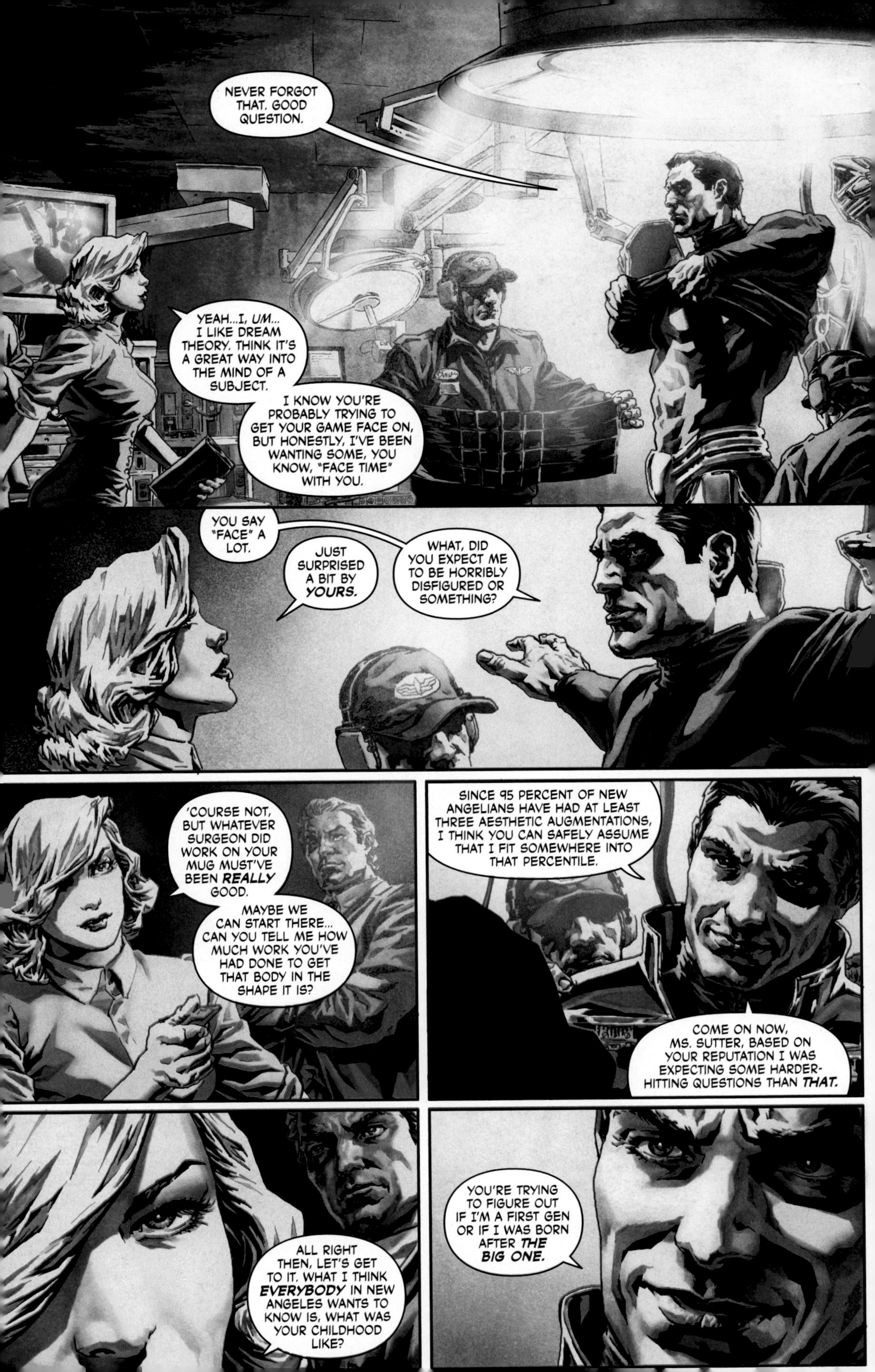
NEVER FORGOT THAT. GOOD QUESTION.
YEAH...I, *UM*... I LIKE DREAM THEORY. THINK IT'S A GREAT WAY INTO THE MIND OF A SUBJECT.
I KNOW YOU'RE PROBABLY TRYING TO GET YOUR GAME FACE ON, BUT HONESTLY, I'VE BEEN WANTING SOME, YOU KNOW, "FACE TIME" WITH YOU.
YOU SAY "FACE" A LOT.
JUST SURPRISED A BIT BY ***YOURS.***
WHAT, DID YOU EXPECT ME TO BE HORRIBLY DISFIGURED OR SOMETHING?
'COURSE NOT, BUT WHATEVER SURGEON DID WORK ON YOUR MUG MUST'VE BEEN ***REALLY*** GOOD.
MAYBE WE CAN START THERE... CAN YOU TELL ME HOW MUCH WORK YOU'VE HAD DONE TO GET THAT BODY IN THE SHAPE IT IS?
SINCE 95 PERCENT OF NEW ANGELIANS HAVE HAD AT LEAST THREE AESTHETIC AUGMENTATIONS, I THINK YOU CAN SAFELY ASSUME THAT I FIT SOMEWHERE INTO THAT PERCENTILE.
COME ON NOW, MS. SUTTER, BASED ON YOUR REPUTATION I WAS EXPECTING SOME HARDER-HITTING QUESTIONS THAN ***THAT.***
ALL RIGHT THEN, LET'S GET TO IT. WHAT I THINK ***EVERYBODY*** IN NEW ANGELES WANTS TO KNOW IS, WHAT WAS YOUR CHILDHOOD LIKE?
YOU'RE TRYING TO FIGURE OUT IF I'M A FIRST GEN OR IF I WAS BORN AFTER ***THE BIG ONE.***

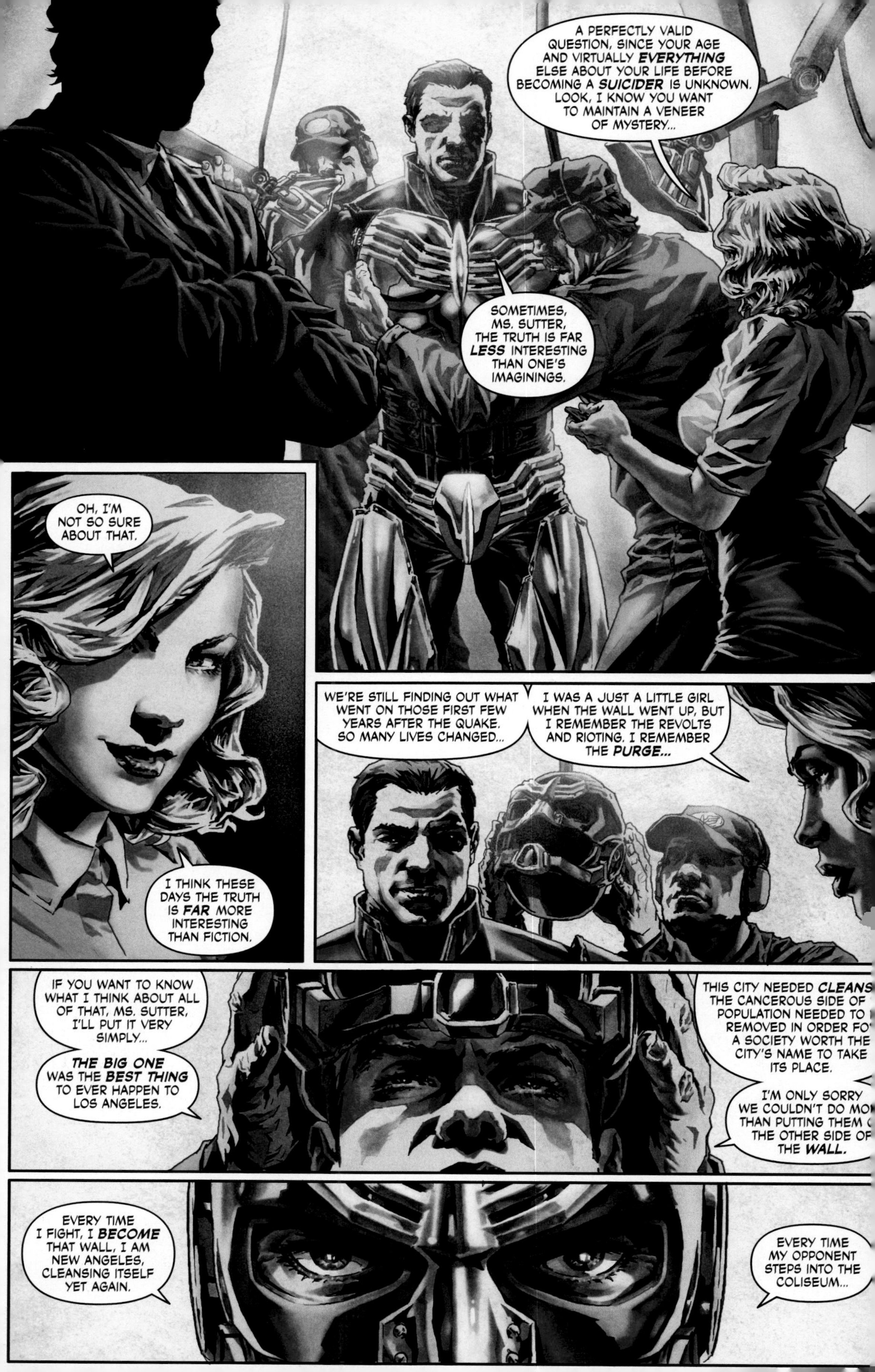
A PERFECTLY VALID QUESTION, SINCE YOUR AGE AND VIRTUALLY EVERYTHING ELSE ABOUT YOUR LIFE BEFORE BECOMING A SUICIDER IS UNKNOWN. LOOK, I KNOW YOU WANT TO MAINTAIN A VENEER OF MYSTERY...
SOMETIMES, MS. SUTTER, THE TRUTH IS FAR LESS INTERESTING THAN ONE'S IMAGININGS.
OH, I'M NOT SO SURE ABOUT THAT.
I THINK THESE DAYS THE TRUTH IS FAR MORE INTERESTING THAN FICTION.
WE'RE STILL FINDING OUT WHAT WENT ON THOSE FIRST FEW YEARS AFTER THE QUAKE. SO MANY LIVES CHANGED...
I WAS A JUST A LITTLE GIRL WHEN THE WALL WENT UP, BUT I REMEMBER THE REVOLTS AND RIOTING. I REMEMBER THE PURGE...
IF YOU WANT TO KNOW WHAT I THINK ABOUT ALL OF THAT, MS. SUTTER, I'LL PUT IT VERY SIMPLY...
THE BIG ONE WAS THE BEST THING TO EVER HAPPEN TO LOS ANGELES.
THIS CITY NEEDED CLEANS THE CANCEROUS SIDE OF POPULATION NEEDED TO REMOVED IN ORDER FO A SOCIETY WORTH THE CITY'S NAME TO TAKE ITS PLACE.
I'M ONLY SORRY WE COULDN'T DO MO THAN PUTTING THEM THE OTHER SIDE OF THE WALL.
EVERY TIME I FIGHT, I BECOME THAT WALL, I AM NEW ANGELES, CLEANSING ITSELF YET AGAIN.
EVERY TIME MY OPPONENT STEPS INTO THE COLISEUM...

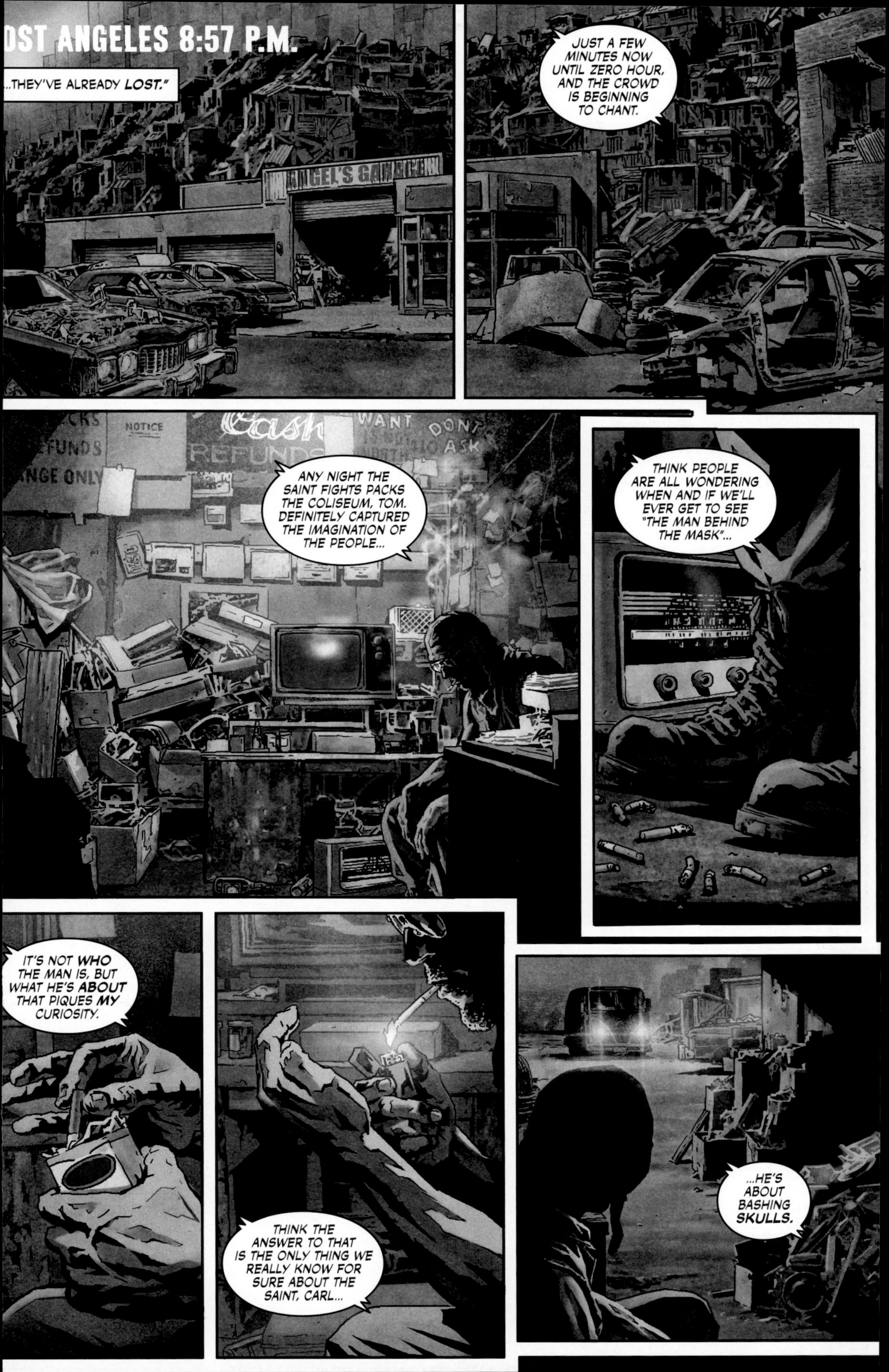
OST ANGELES 8:57 P.M.
...THEY'VE ALREADY LOST."
ANGEL'S GARAGE
JUST A FEW MINUTES NOW UNTIL ZERO HOUR, AND THE CROWD IS BEGINNING TO CHANT.
NOTICE
REFUNDS
ANGE ONLY
Cash
REFUNDS
DON'T ASK
ANY NIGHT THE SAINT FIGHTS PACKS THE COLISEUM, TOM. DEFINITELY CAPTURED THE IMAGINATION OF THE PEOPLE...
THINK PEOPLE ARE ALL WONDERING WHEN AND IF WE'LL EVER GET TO SEE "THE MAN BEHIND THE MASK"...
IT'S NOT WHO THE MAN IS, BUT WHAT HE'S ABOUT THAT PIQUES MY CURIOSITY.
THINK THE ANSWER TO THAT IS THE ONLY THING WE REALLY KNOW FOR SURE ABOUT THE SAINT, CARL...
...HE'S ABOUT BASHING SKULLS.

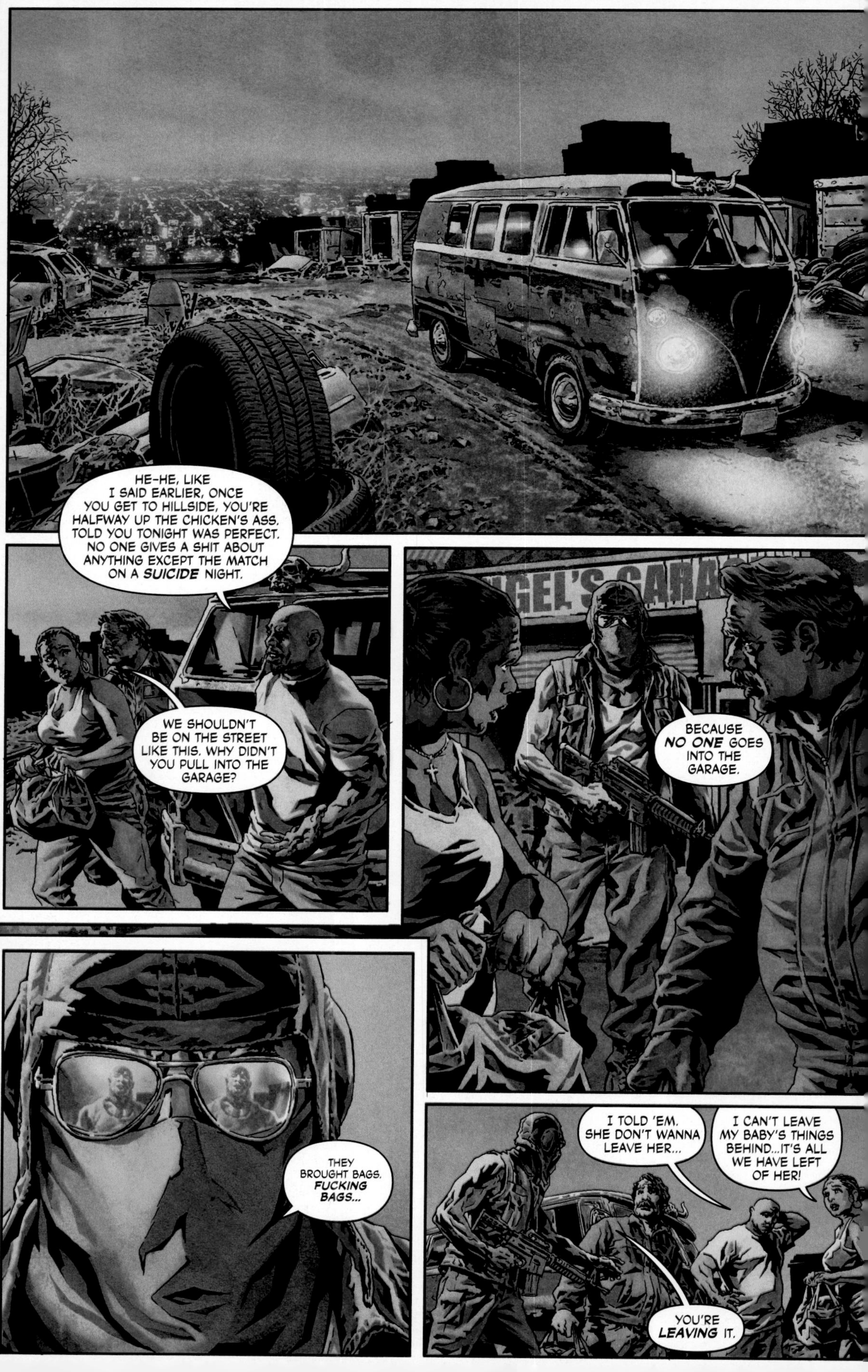
HE-HE, LIKE I SAID EARLIER, ONCE YOU GET TO HILLSIDE, YOU'RE HALFWAY UP THE CHICKEN'S ASS. TOLD YOU TONIGHT WAS PERFECT. NO ONE GIVES A SHIT ABOUT ANYTHING EXCEPT THE MATCH ON A SUICIDE NIGHT.
WE SHOULDN'T BE ON THE STREET LIKE THIS. WHY DIDN'T YOU PULL INTO THE GARAGE?
BECAUSE NO ONE GOES INTO THE GARAGE.
THEY BROUGHT BAGS. FUCKING BAGS...
I TOLD 'EM. SHE DON'T WANNA LEAVE HER...
I CAN'T LEAVE MY BABY'S THINGS BEHIND...IT'S ALL WE HAVE LEFT OF HER!
YOU'RE LEAVING IT.

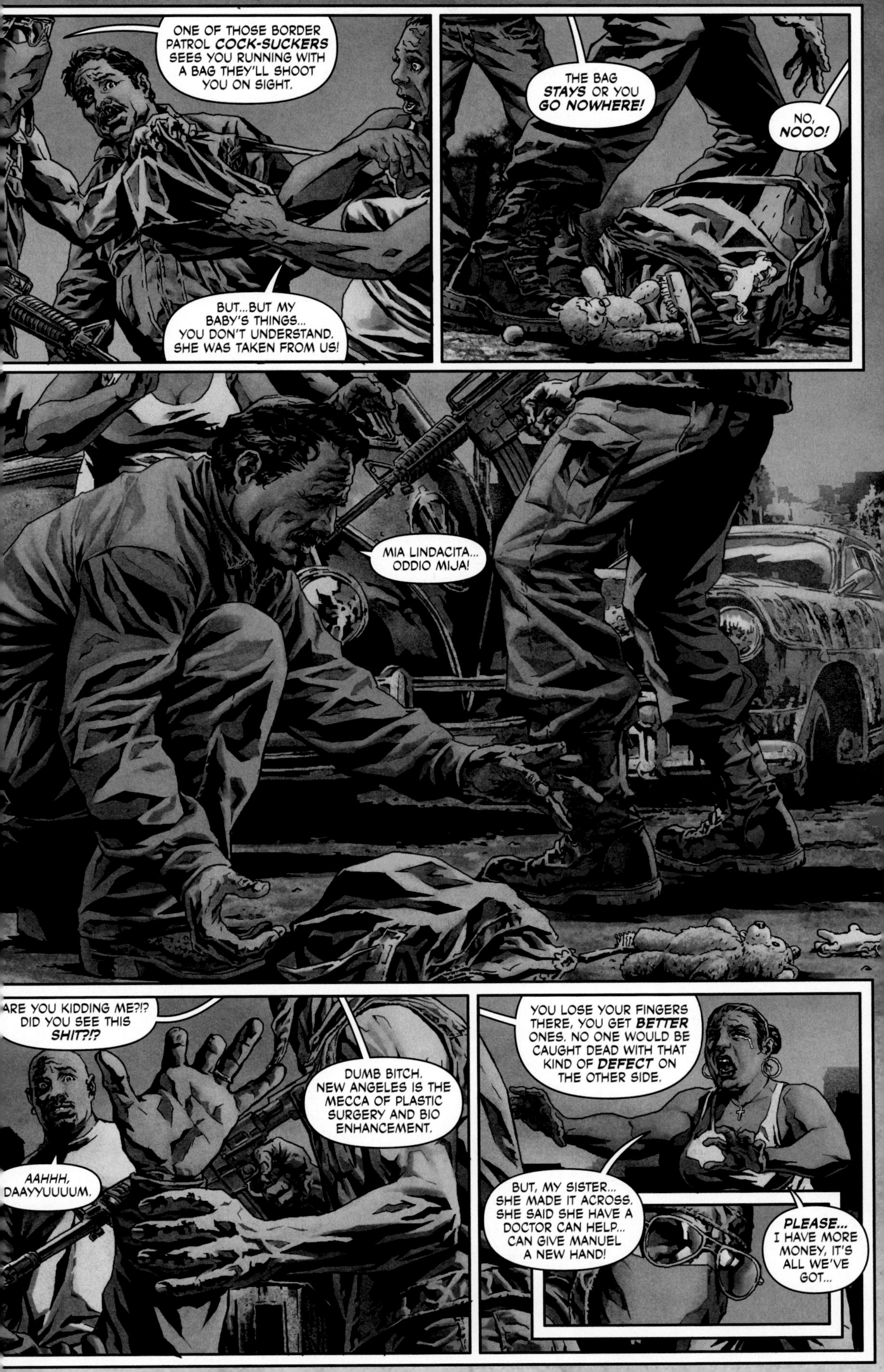

ONE OF THOSE BORDER PATROL *COCK-SUCKERS* SEES YOU RUNNING WITH A BAG THEY'LL SHOOT YOU ON SIGHT.
BUT...BUT MY BABY'S THINGS... YOU DON'T UNDERSTAND. SHE WAS TAKEN FROM US!
THE BAG *STAYS* OR YOU *GO NOWHERE!*
NO, *NOOO!*
MIA LINDACITA... ODDIO MIJA!
ARE YOU KIDDING ME?!? DID YOU SEE THIS *SHIT?!?*
AAHHH, DAAYYUUUUM.
DUMB BITCH. NEW ANGELES IS THE MECCA OF PLASTIC SURGERY AND BIO ENHANCEMENT.
YOU LOSE YOUR FINGERS THERE, YOU GET *BETTER* ONES. NO ONE WOULD BE CAUGHT DEAD WITH THAT KIND OF *DEFECT* ON THE OTHER SIDE.
BUT, MY SISTER... SHE MADE IT ACROSS. SHE SAID SHE HAVE A DOCTOR CAN HELP... CAN GIVE MANUEL A NEW HAND!
PLEASE... I HAVE MORE MONEY, IT'S ALL WE'VE GOT...

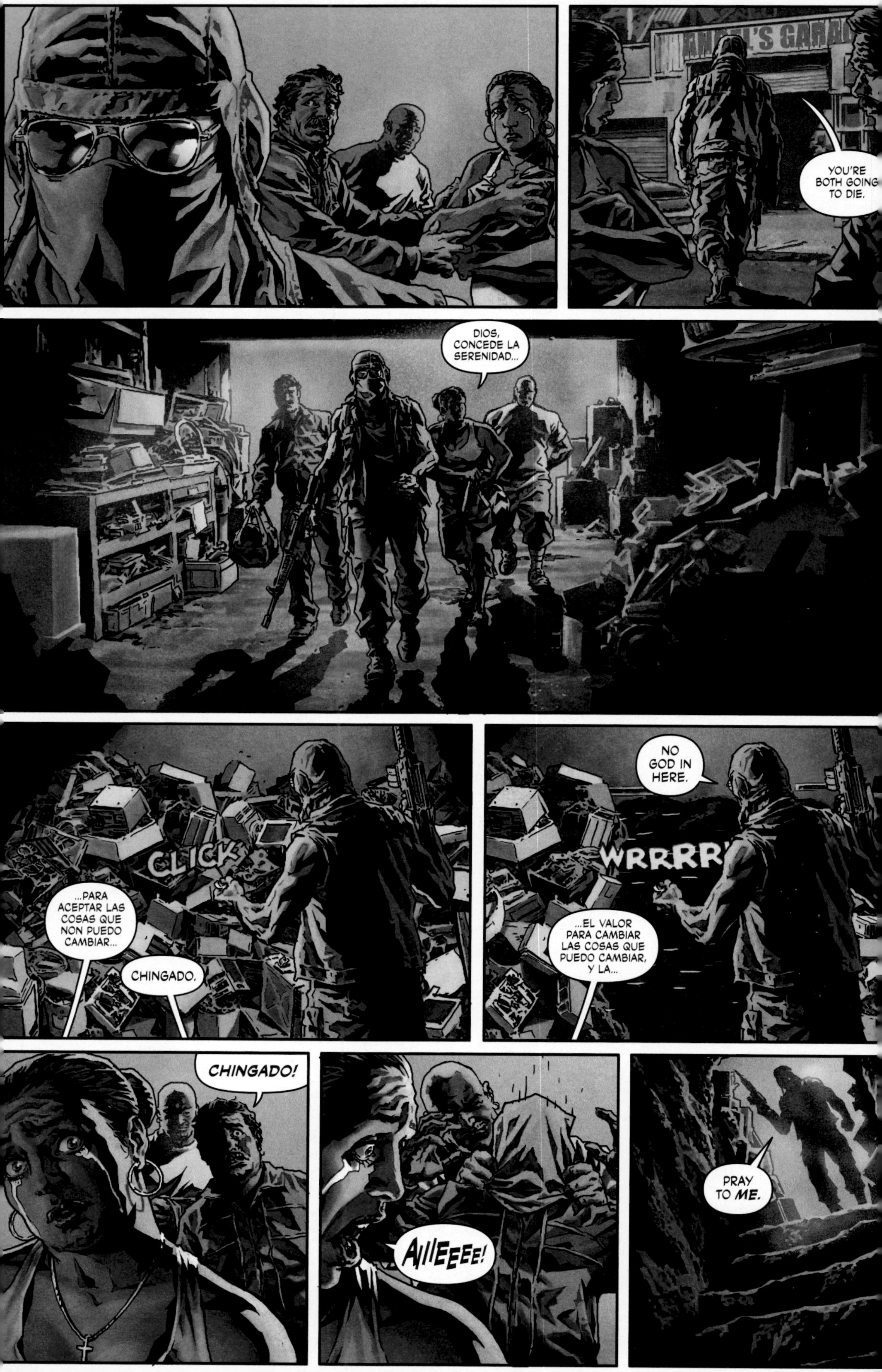
ANGEL'S GARAG
YOU'RE BOTH GOING TO DIE.
DIOS, CONCEDE LA SERENIDAD...
CLICK
...PARA ACEPTAR LAS COSAS QUE NON PUEDO CAMBIAR...
CHINGADO.
NO GOD IN HERE.
WRRRR
...EL VALOR PARA CAMBIAR LAS COSAS QUE PUEDO CAMBIAR, Y LA...
CHINGADO!
AIIIEEEE!
PRAY TO ME.

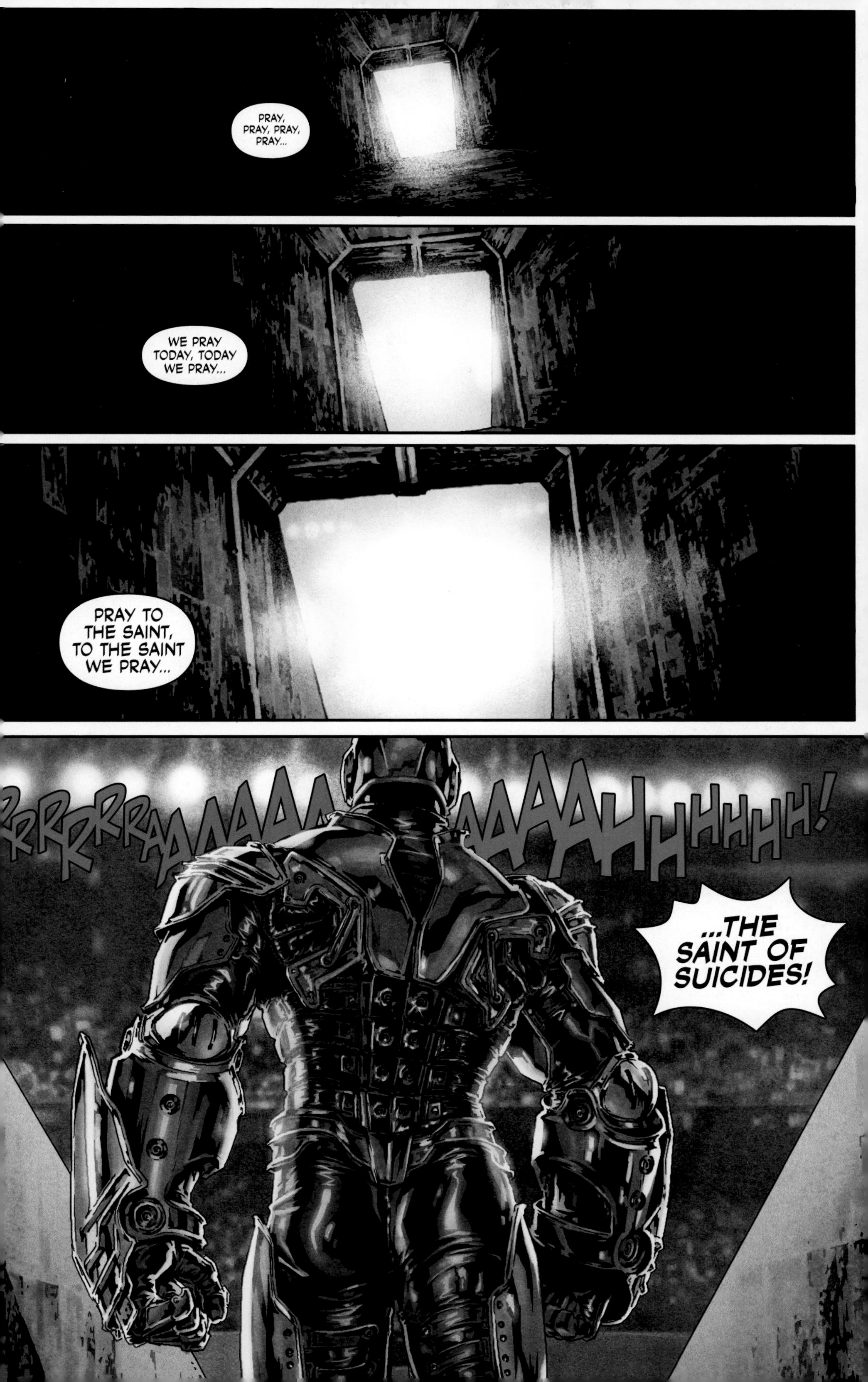
PRAY, PRAY, PRAY, PRAY...
WE PRAY TODAY, TODAY WE PRAY...
PRAY TO THE SAINT, TO THE SAINT WE PRAY...
RRRRRAAAAAAAAAAAAHHHHHHH!
...THE SAINT OF SUICIDES!

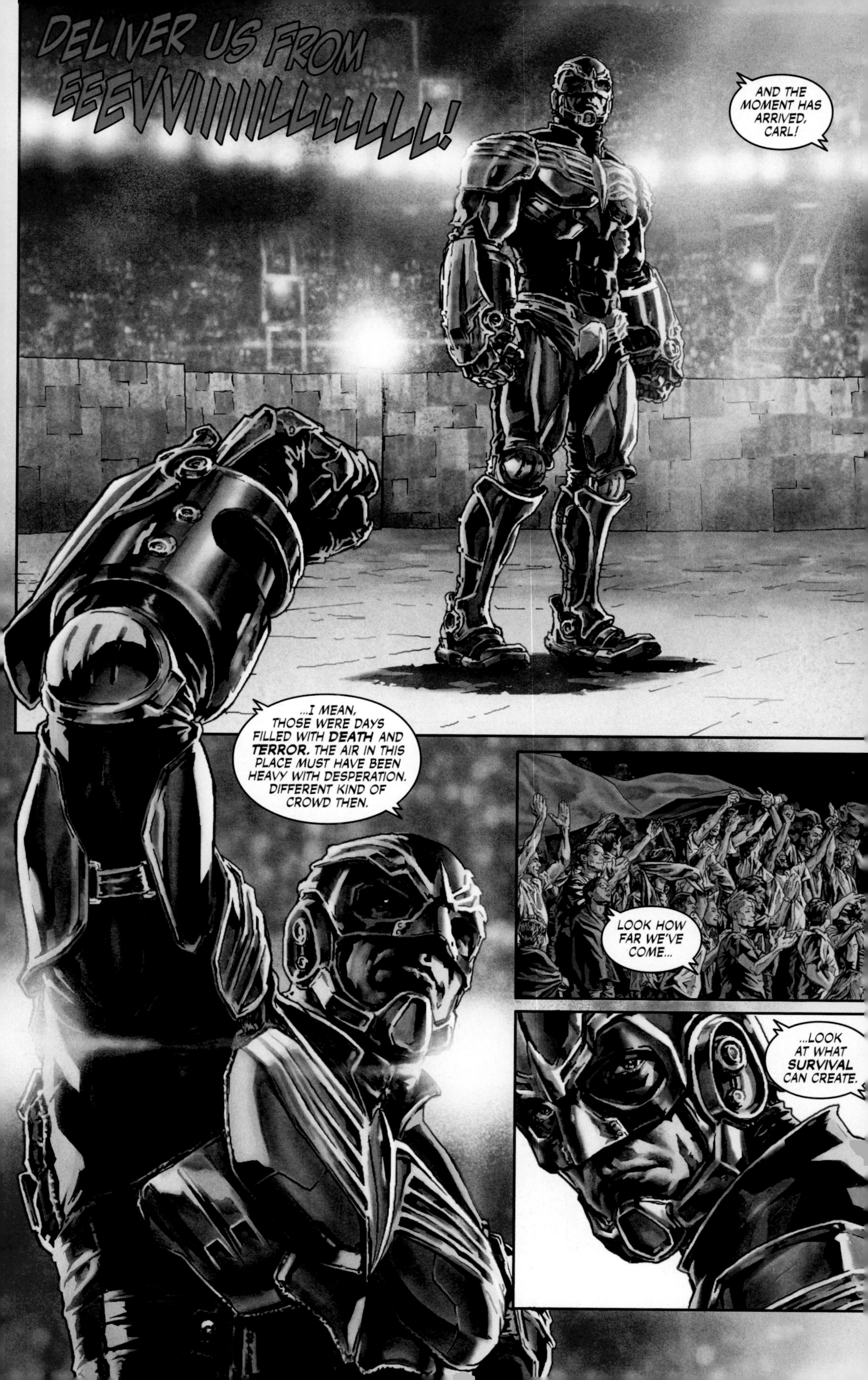
DELIVER US FROM EEEEVVIIIIIILLLLLLLL!
AND THE MOMENT HAS ARRIVED, CARL!
...I MEAN, THOSE WERE DAYS FILLED WITH DEATH AND TERROR. THE AIR IN THIS PLACE MUST HAVE BEEN HEAVY WITH DESPERATION. DIFFERENT KIND OF CROWD THEN.
LOOK HOW FAR WE'VE COME...
...LOOK AT WHAT SURVIVAL CAN CREATE.

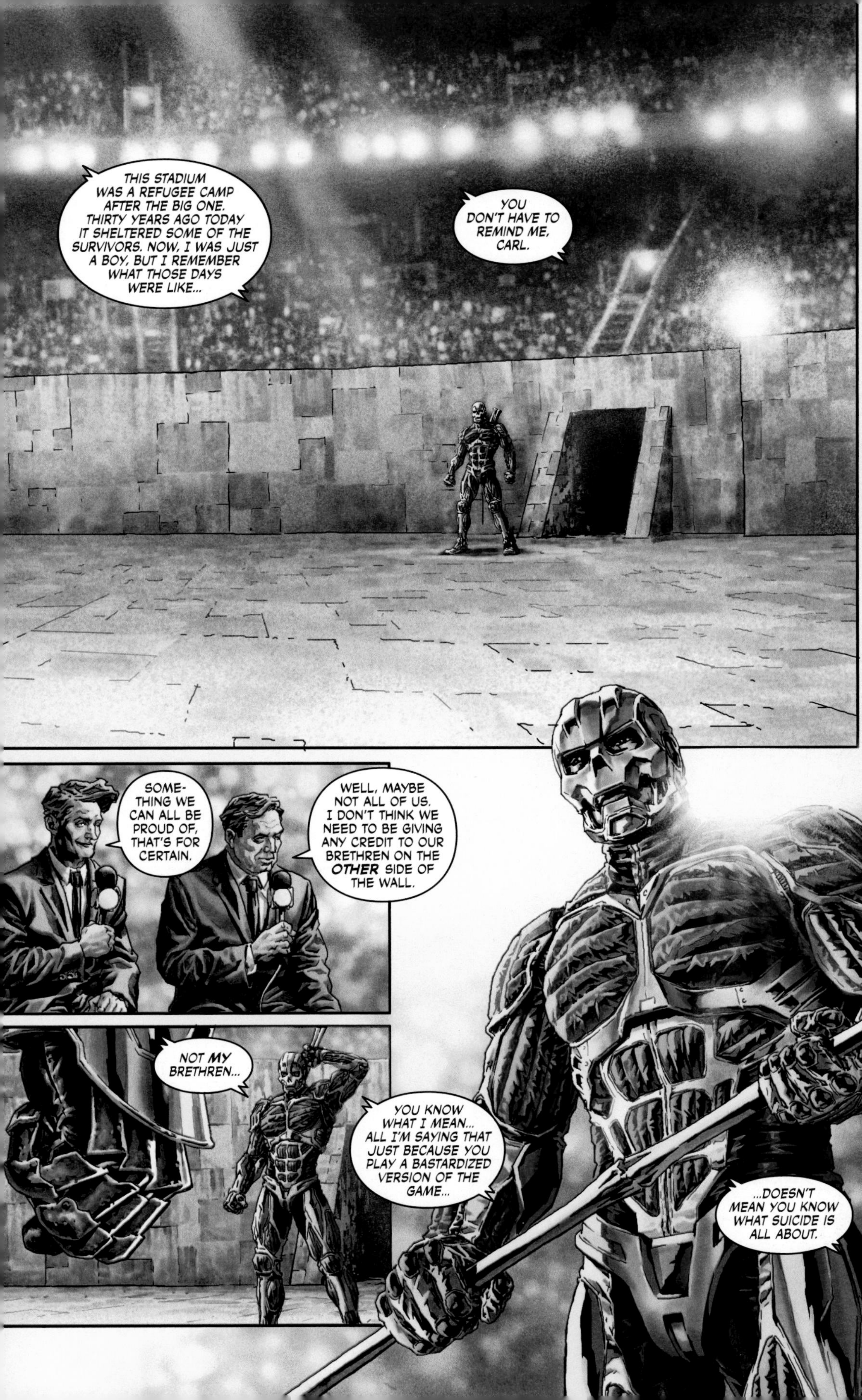
THIS STADIUM WAS A REFUGEE CAMP AFTER THE BIG ONE. THIRTY YEARS AGO TODAY IT SHELTERED SOME OF THE SURVIVORS. NOW, I WAS JUST A BOY, BUT I REMEMBER WHAT THOSE DAYS WERE LIKE...
YOU DON'T HAVE TO REMIND ME, CARL.
SOME-THING WE CAN ALL BE PROUD OF, THAT'S FOR CERTAIN.
WELL, MAYBE NOT ALL OF US. I DON'T THINK WE NEED TO BE GIVING ANY CREDIT TO OUR BRETHREN ON THE OTHER SIDE OF THE WALL.
NOT MY BRETHREN...
YOU KNOW WHAT I MEAN... ALL I'M SAYING THAT JUST BECAUSE YOU PLAY A BASTARDIZED VERSION OF THE GAME...
...DOESN'T MEAN YOU KNOW WHAT SUICIDE IS ALL ABOUT.

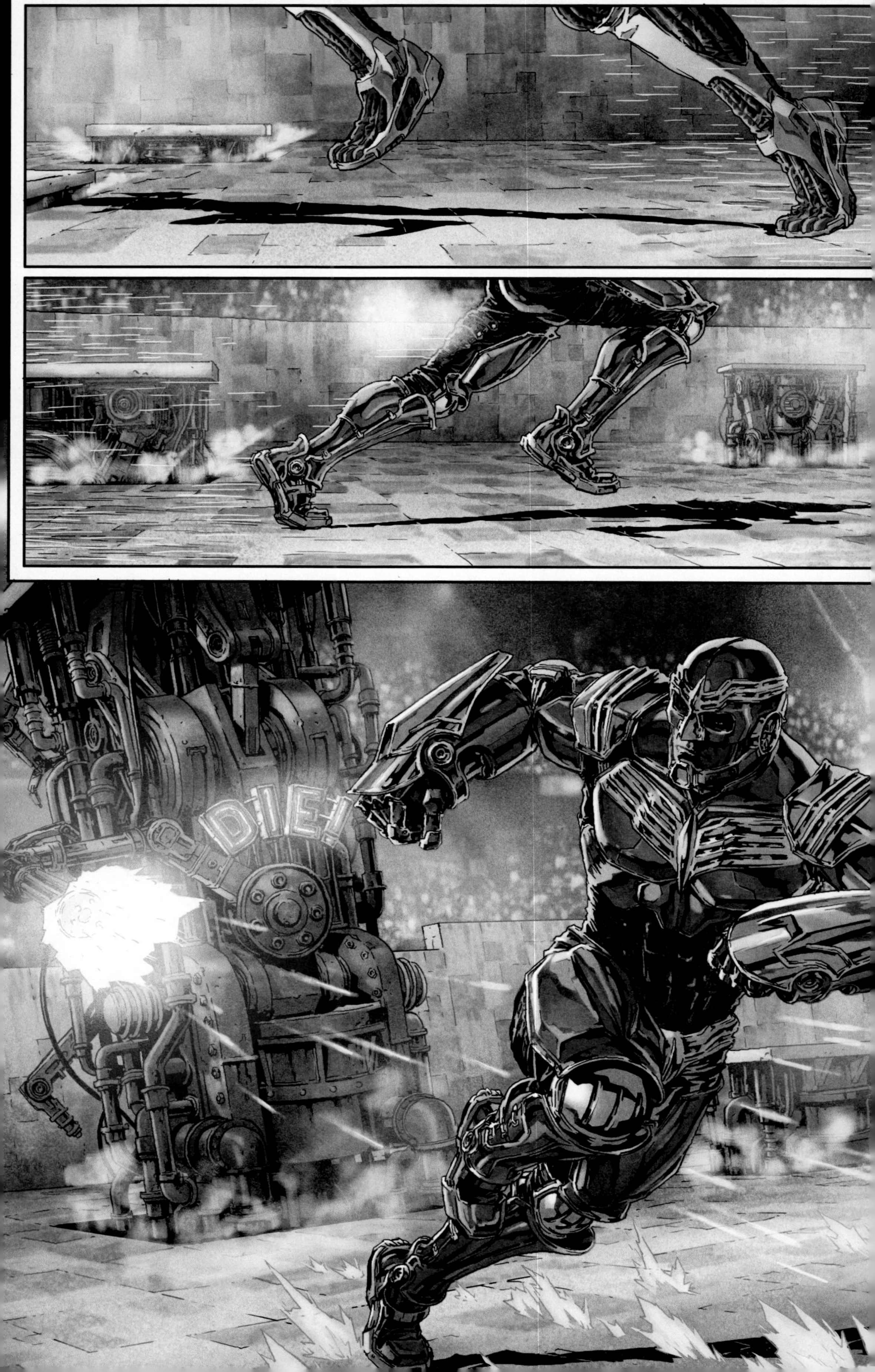
DIE!

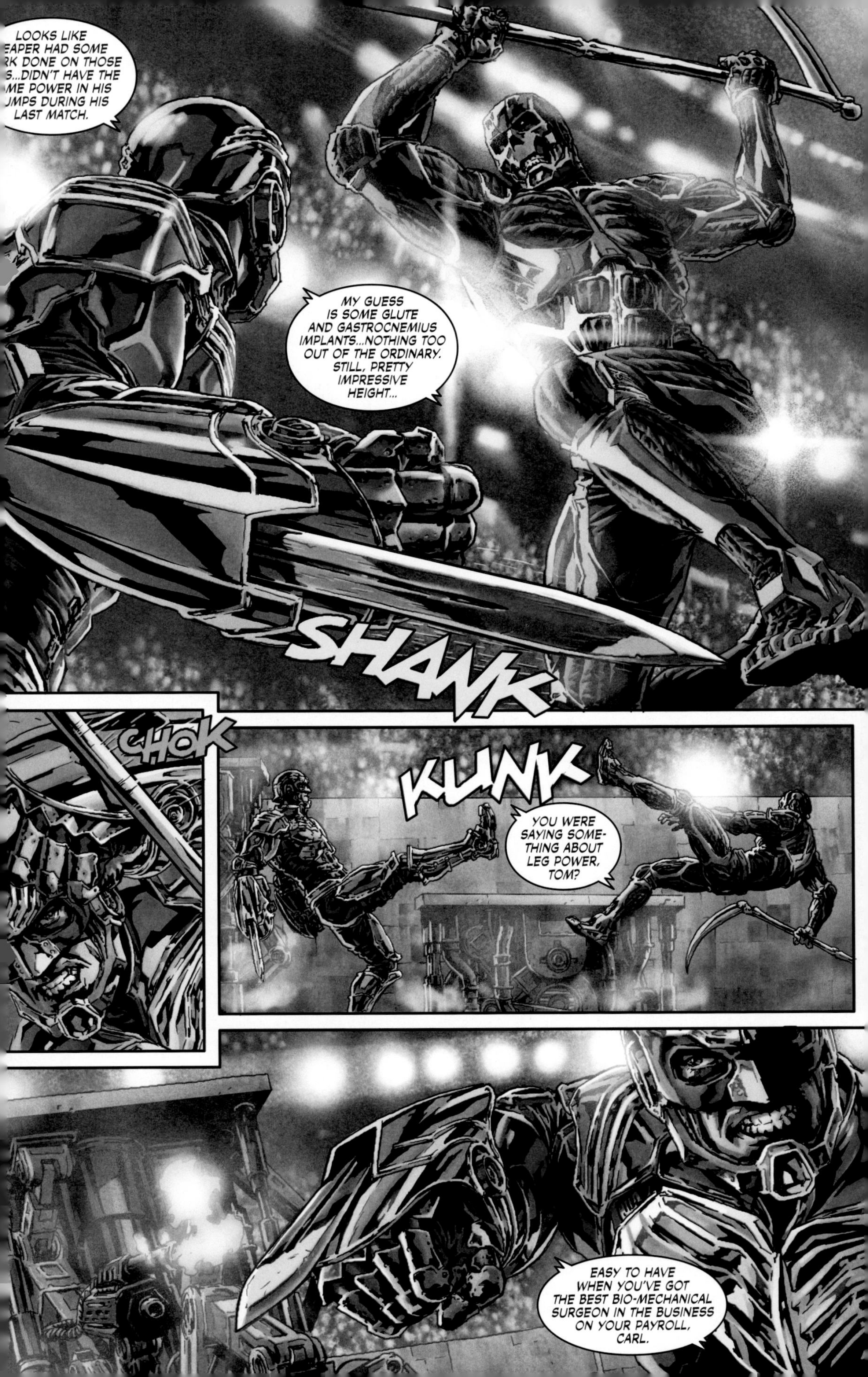
LOOKS LIKE EAPER HAD SOME RK DONE ON THOSE S...DIDN'T HAVE THE ME POWER IN HIS UMPS DURING HIS LAST MATCH.
MY GUESS IS SOME GLUTE AND GASTROCNEMIUS IMPLANTS...NOTHING TOO OUT OF THE ORDINARY. STILL, PRETTY IMPRESSIVE HEIGHT...
SHANK
CHOK
KUNK
YOU WERE SAYING SOME-THING ABOUT LEG POWER, TOM?
EASY TO HAVE WHEN YOU'VE GOT THE BEST BIO-MECHANICAL SURGEON IN THE BUSINESS ON YOUR PAYROLL, CARL.

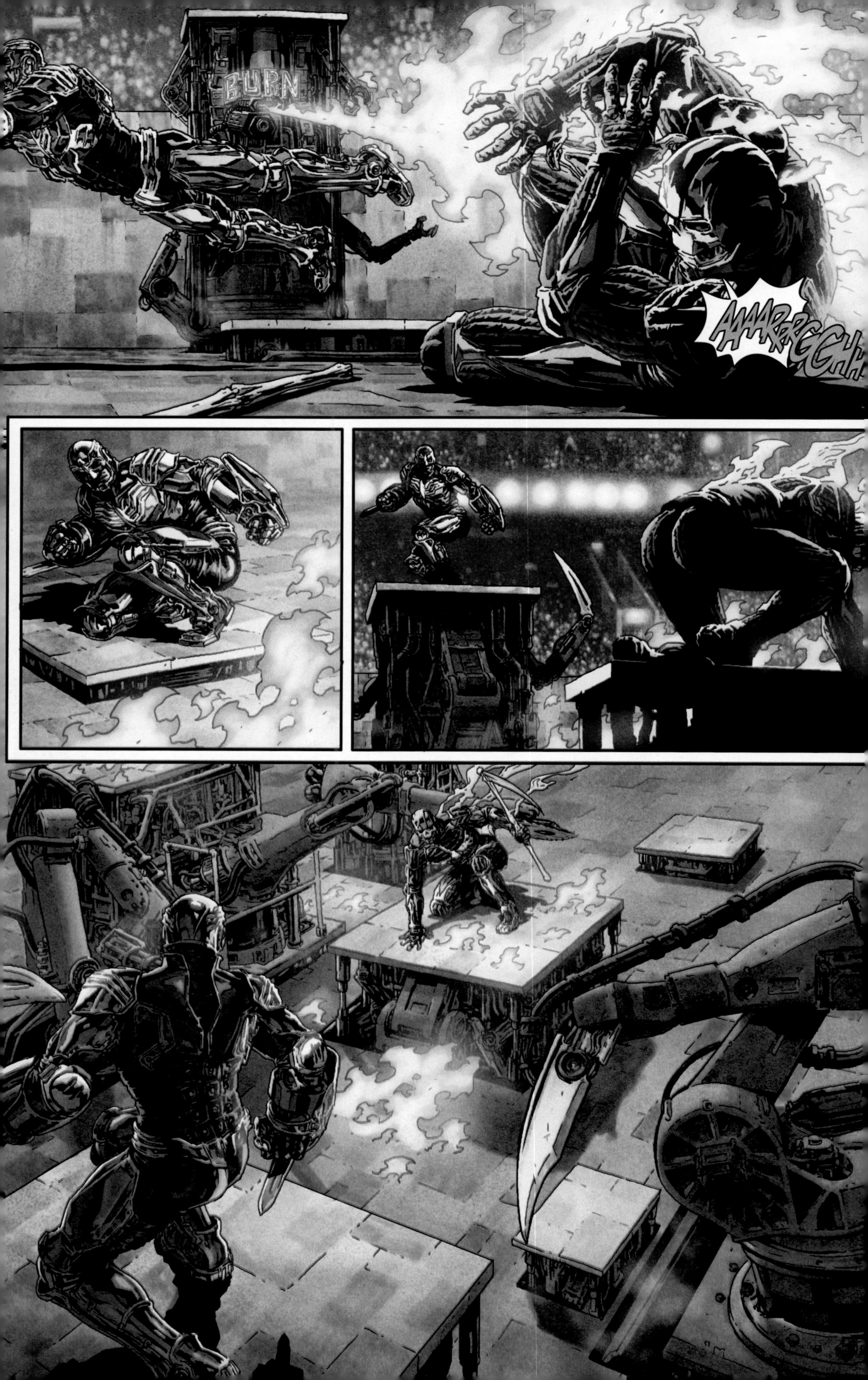
BURN
AAAARRRGGHH

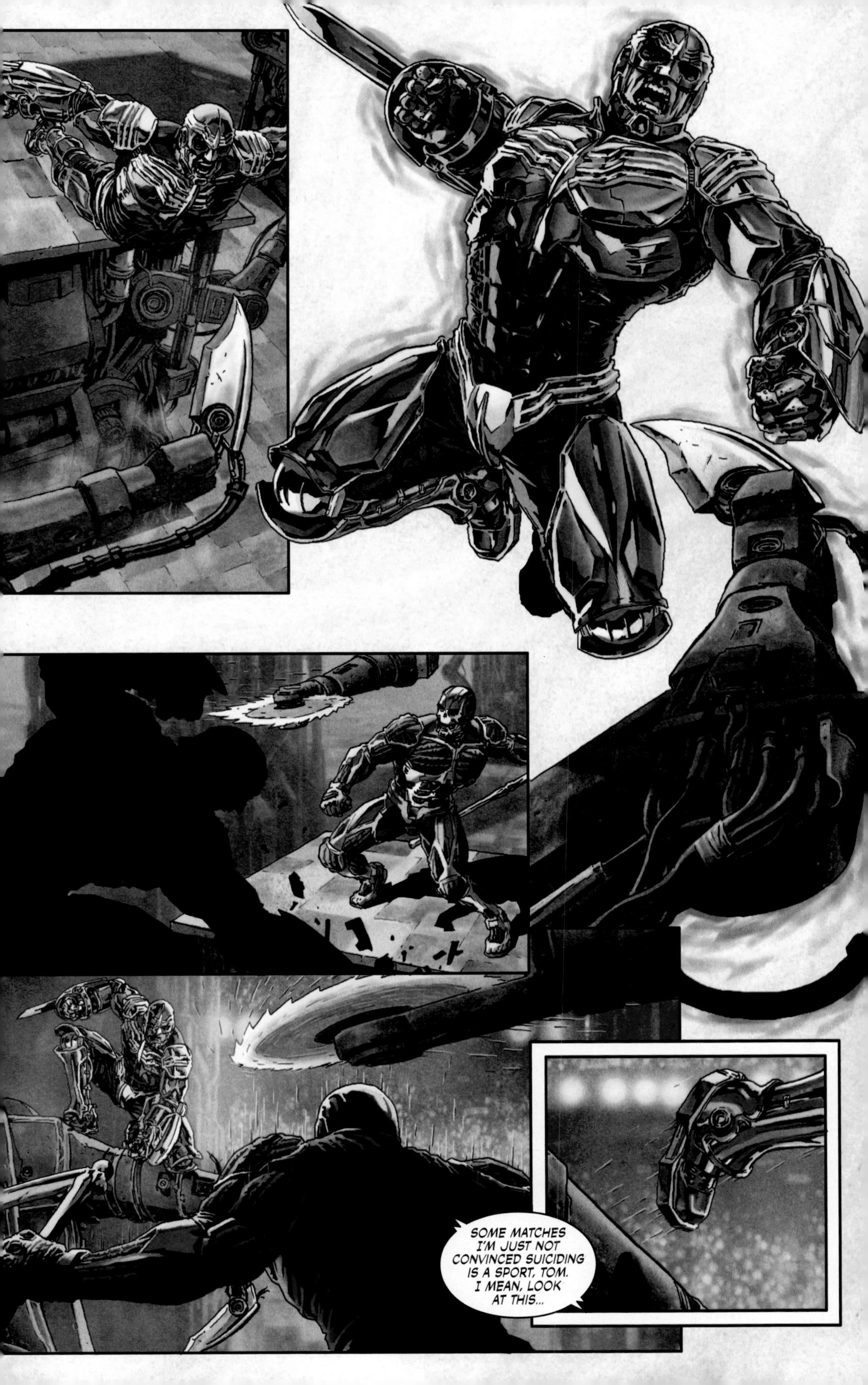
SOME MATCHES I'M JUST NOT CONVINCED SUICIDING IS A SPORT, TOM. I MEAN, LOOK AT THIS...

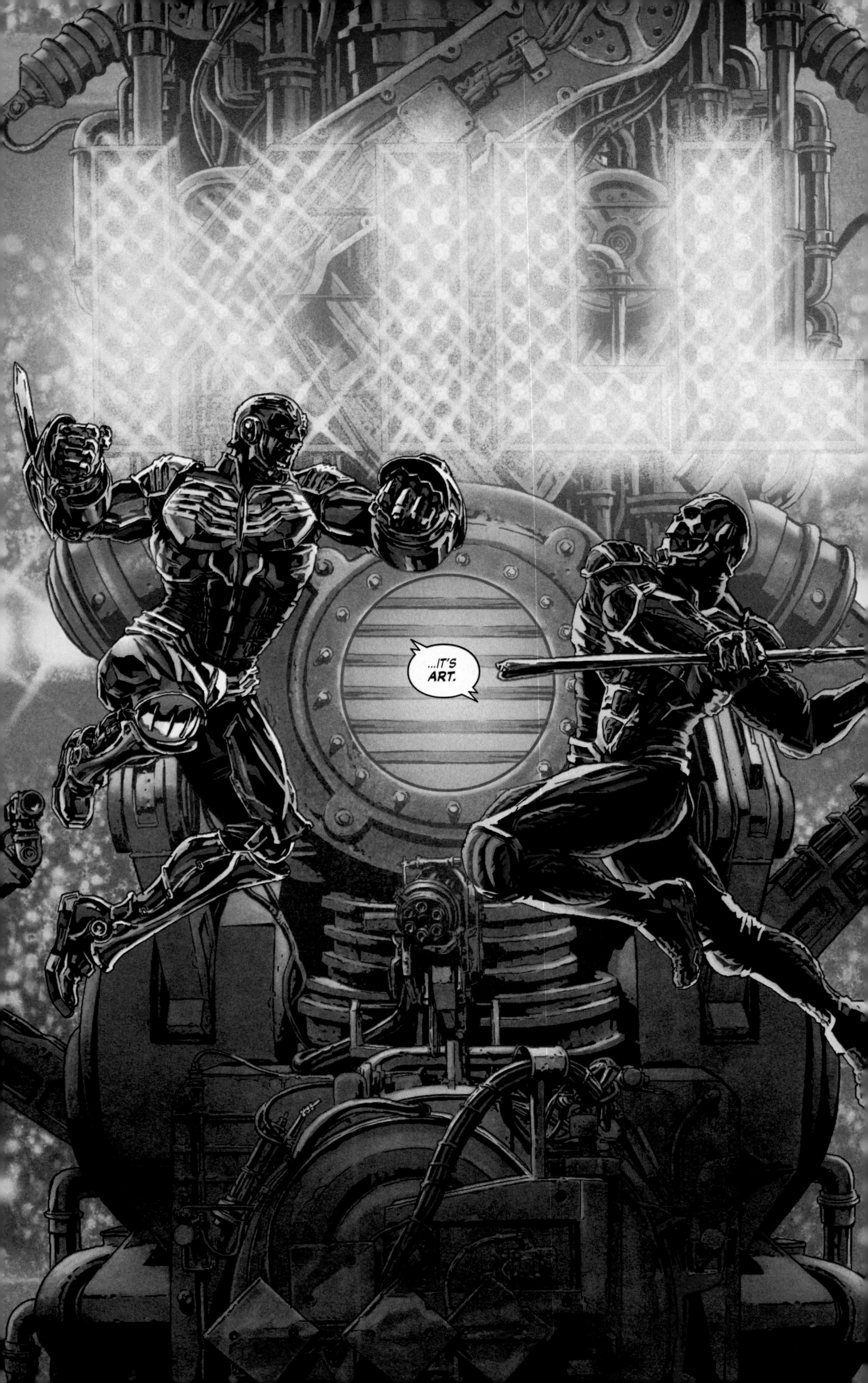
...IT'S ART.

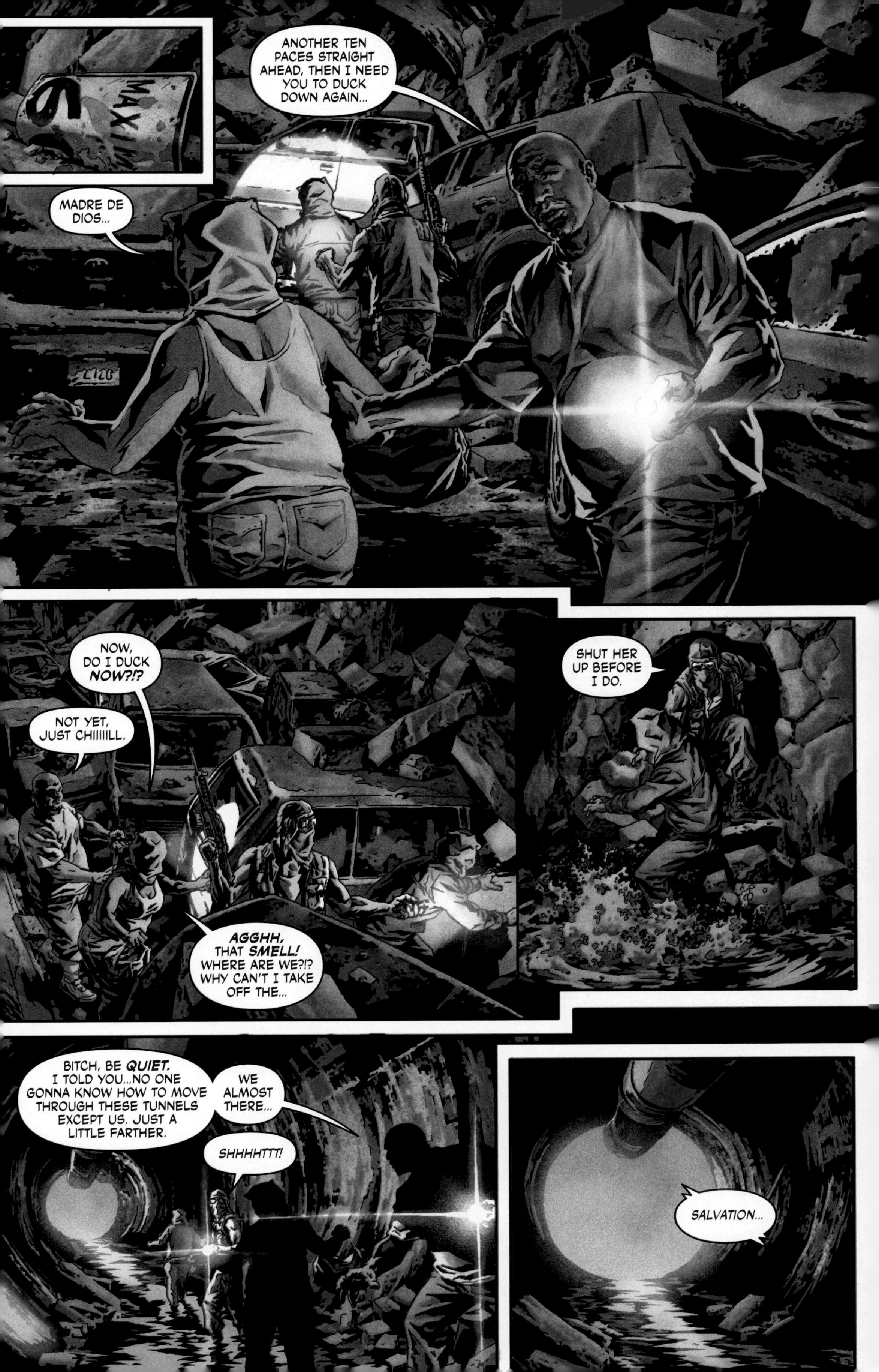
MAX
ANOTHER TEN PACES STRAIGHT AHEAD, THEN I NEED YOU TO DUCK DOWN AGAIN...
MADRE DE DIOS...
NOW, DO I DUCK *NOW?!?*
NOT YET, JUST CHIIIIILL.
AGGHH, THAT ***SMELL!*** WHERE ARE WE?!? WHY CAN'T I TAKE OFF THE...
SHUT HER UP BEFORE I DO.
BITCH, BE ***QUIET.*** I TOLD YOU...NO ONE GONNA KNOW HOW TO MOVE THROUGH THESE TUNNELS EXCEPT US. JUST A LITTLE FARTHER.
WE ALMOST THERE...
SHHHHTTT!
SALVATION...

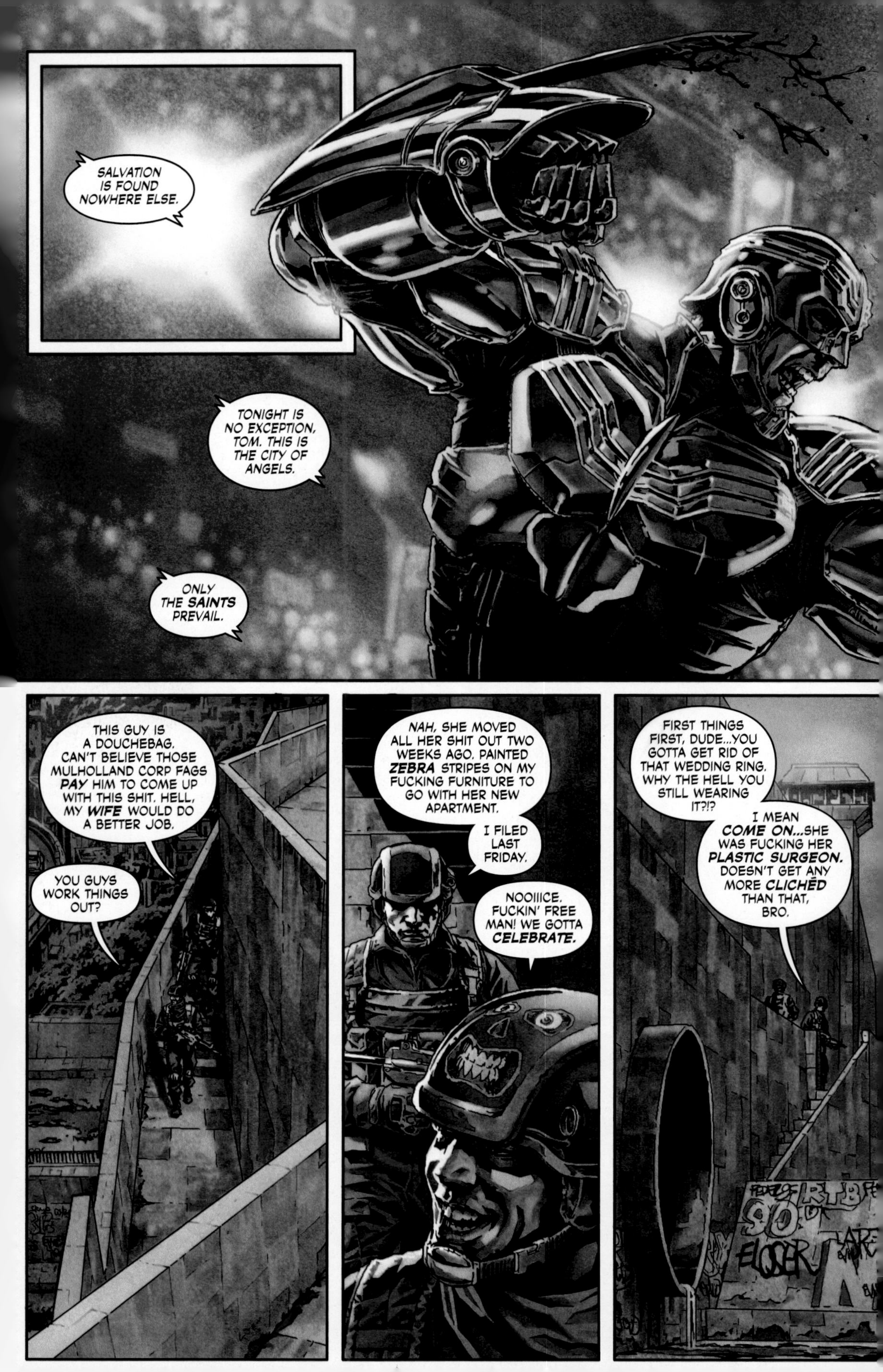
SALVATION IS FOUND NOWHERE ELSE.
TONIGHT IS NO EXCEPTION, TOM. THIS IS THE CITY OF ANGELS.
ONLY THE **SAINTS** PREVAIL.
THIS GUY IS A DOUCHEBAG. CAN'T BELIEVE THOSE MULHOLLAND CORP FAGS ***PAY*** HIM TO COME UP WITH THIS SHIT. HELL, MY ***WIFE*** WOULD DO A BETTER JOB.
YOU GUYS WORK THINGS OUT?
NAH, SHE MOVED ALL HER SHIT OUT TWO WEEKS AGO. PAINTED ***ZEBRA*** STRIPES ON MY FUCKING FURNITURE TO GO WITH HER NEW APARTMENT.
I FILED LAST FRIDAY.
NOOIIICE. FUCKIN' FREE MAN! WE GOTTA ***CELEBRATE.***
FIRST THINGS FIRST, DUDE...YOU GOTTA GET RID OF THAT WEDDING RING. WHY THE HELL YOU STILL WEARING IT?!?
I MEAN ***COME ON...***SHE WAS FUCKING HER ***PLASTIC SURGEON.*** DOESN'T GET ANY MORE ***CLICHÉD*** THAN THAT, BRO.

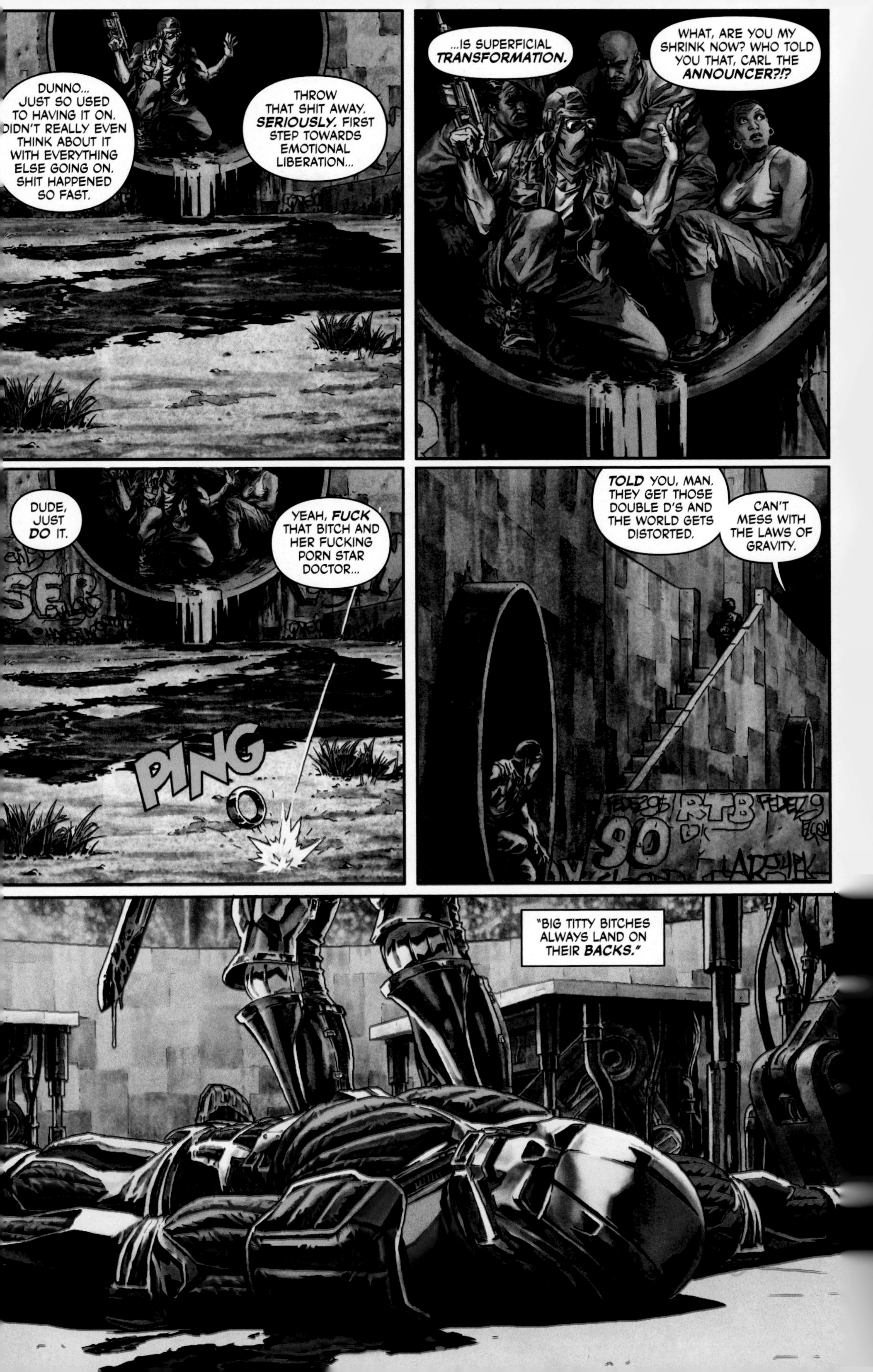
DUNNO... JUST SO USED TO HAVING IT ON. DIDN'T REALLY EVEN THINK ABOUT IT WITH EVERYTHING ELSE GOING ON. SHIT HAPPENED SO FAST.
THROW THAT SHIT AWAY. SERIOUSLY. FIRST STEP TOWARDS EMOTIONAL LIBERATION...
...IS SUPERFICIAL TRANSFORMATION.
WHAT, ARE YOU MY SHRINK NOW? WHO TOLD YOU THAT, CARL THE ANNOUNCER?!?
DUDE, JUST DO IT.
YEAH, FUCK THAT BITCH AND HER FUCKING PORN STAR DOCTOR...
PING
TOLD YOU, MAN. THEY GET THOSE DOUBLE D'S AND THE WORLD GETS DISTORTED.
CAN'T MESS WITH THE LAWS OF GRAVITY.
"BIG TITTY BITCHES ALWAYS LAND ON THEIR BACKS."

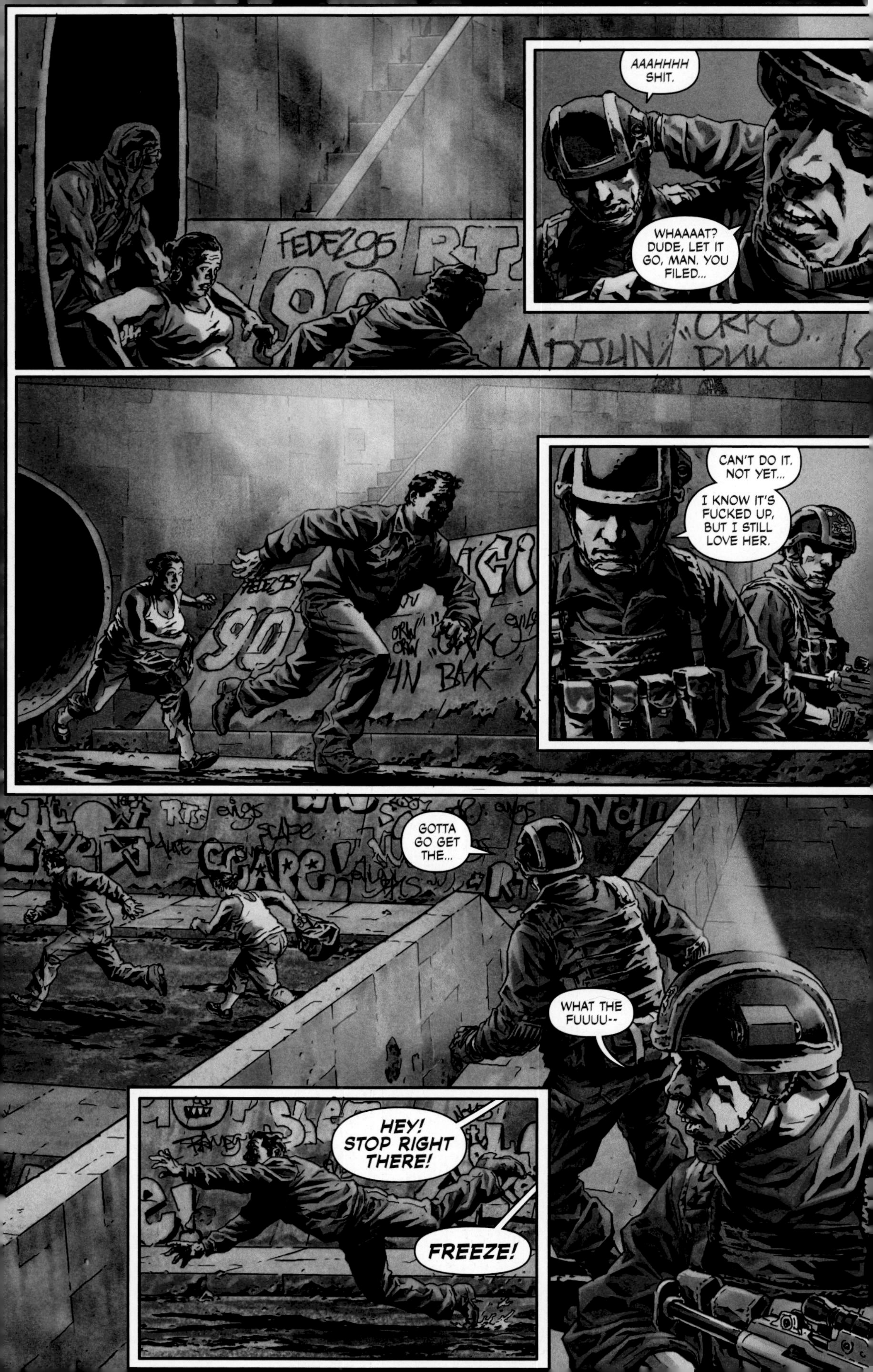
AAAHHHH SHIT.
WHAAAAT? DUDE, LET IT GO, MAN. YOU FILED...
CAN'T DO IT. NOT YET...
I KNOW IT'S FUCKED UP, BUT I STILL LOVE HER.
GOTTA GO GET THE...
WHAT THE FUUUU--
HEY! STOP RIGHT THERE!
FREEZE!

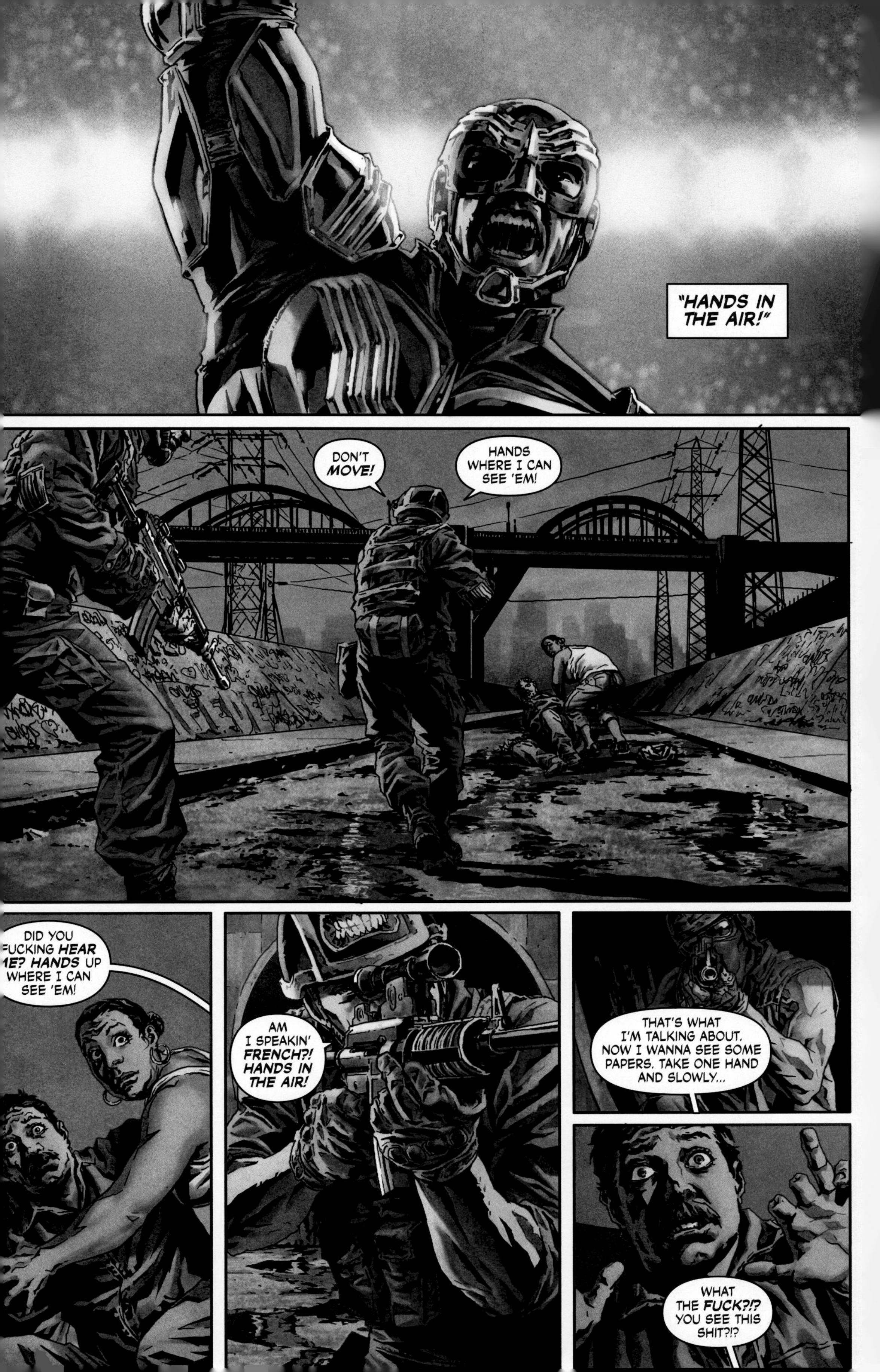
"HANDS IN THE AIR!"
DON'T MOVE!
HANDS WHERE I CAN SEE 'EM!
DID YOU FUCKING HEAR ME? HANDS UP WHERE I CAN SEE 'EM!
AM I SPEAKIN' FRENCH?! HANDS IN THE AIR!
THAT'S WHAT I'M TALKING ABOUT. NOW I WANNA SEE SOME PAPERS. TAKE ONE HAND AND SLOWLY...
WHAT THE FUCK?!? YOU SEE THIS SHIT?!?

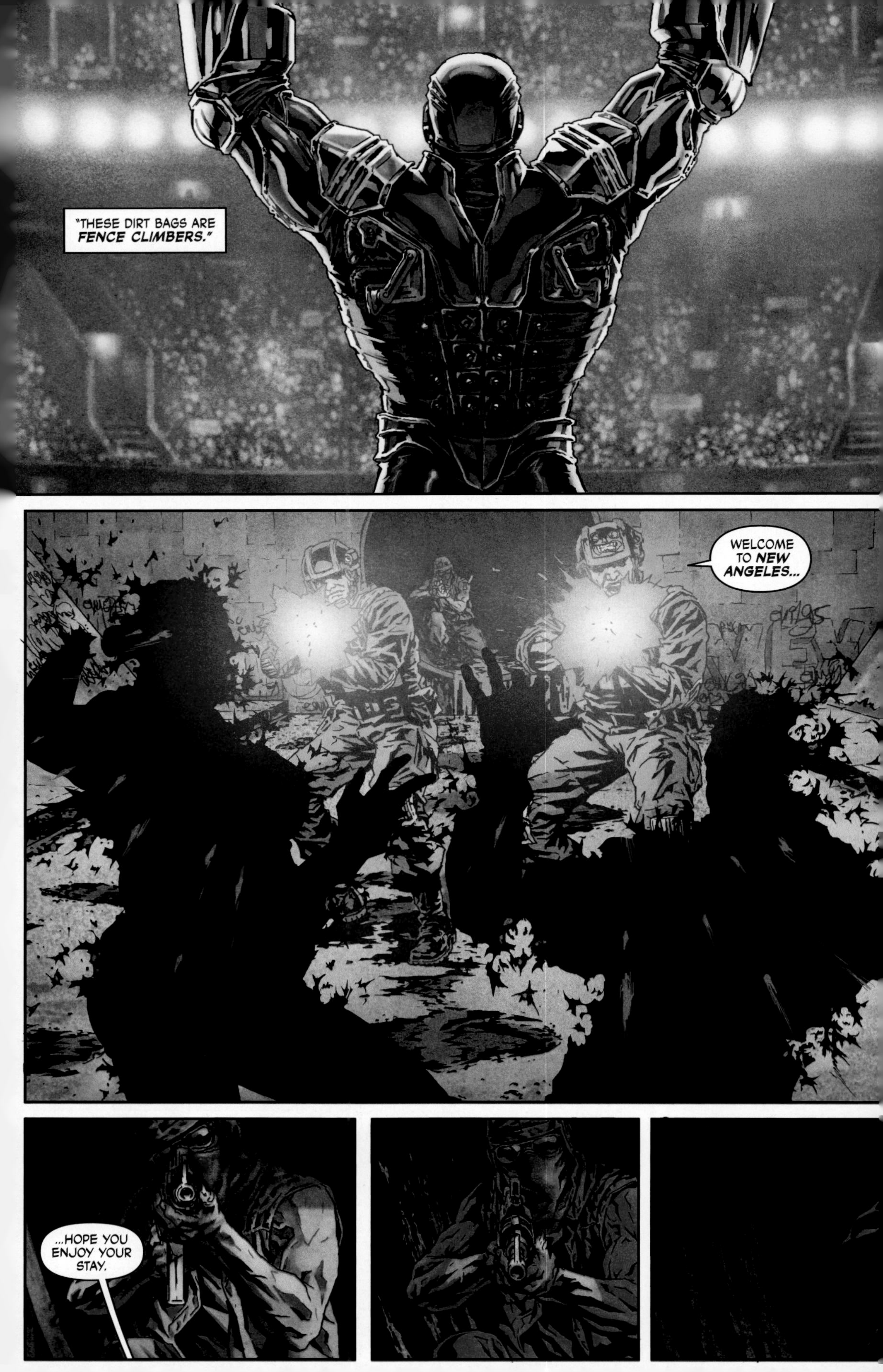
"THESE DIRT BAGS ARE FENCE CLIMBERS."
WELCOME TO NEW ANGELES...
...HOPE YOU ENJOY YOUR STAY.

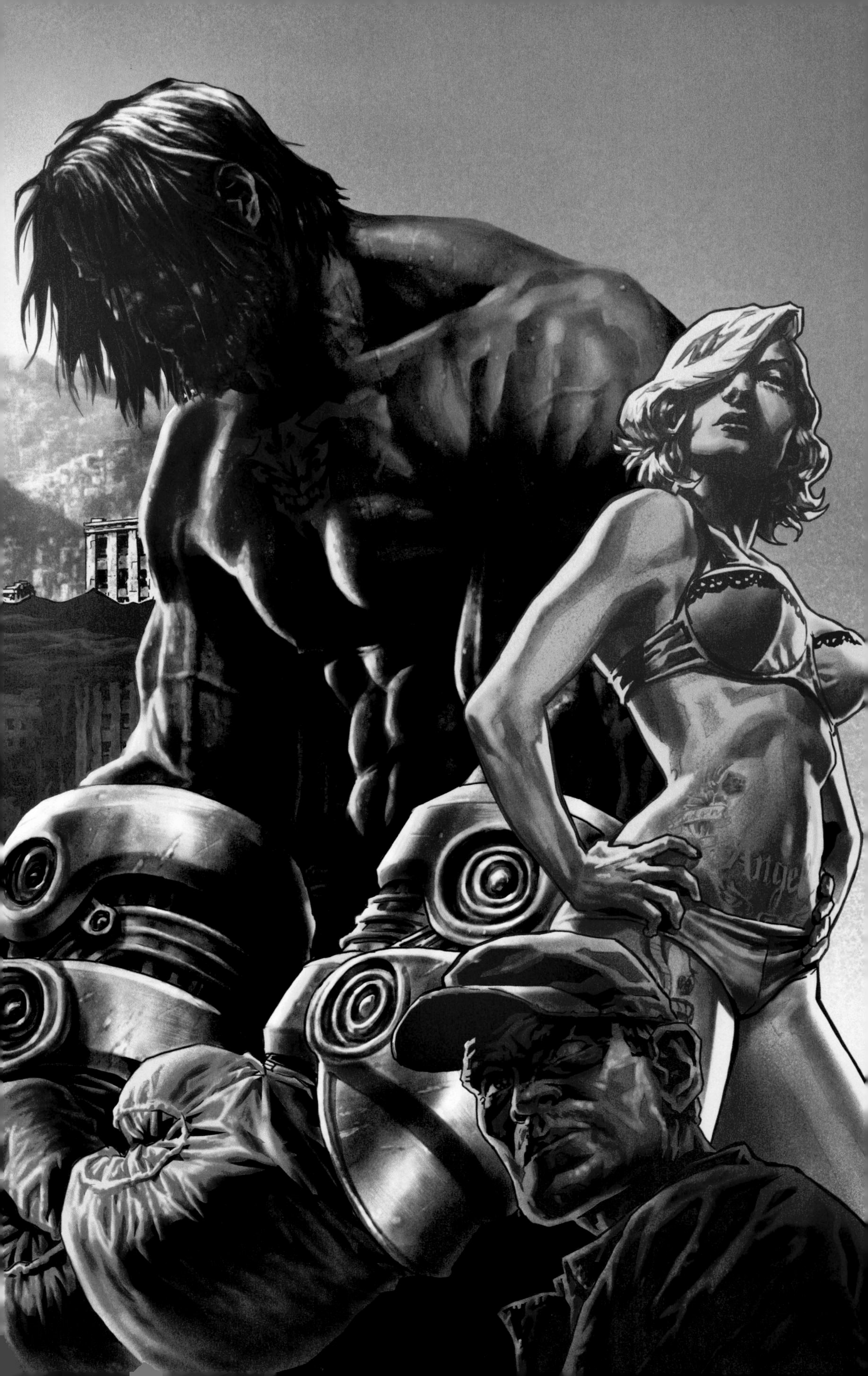
Angel

CHAPTER TWO:
STRANIERO

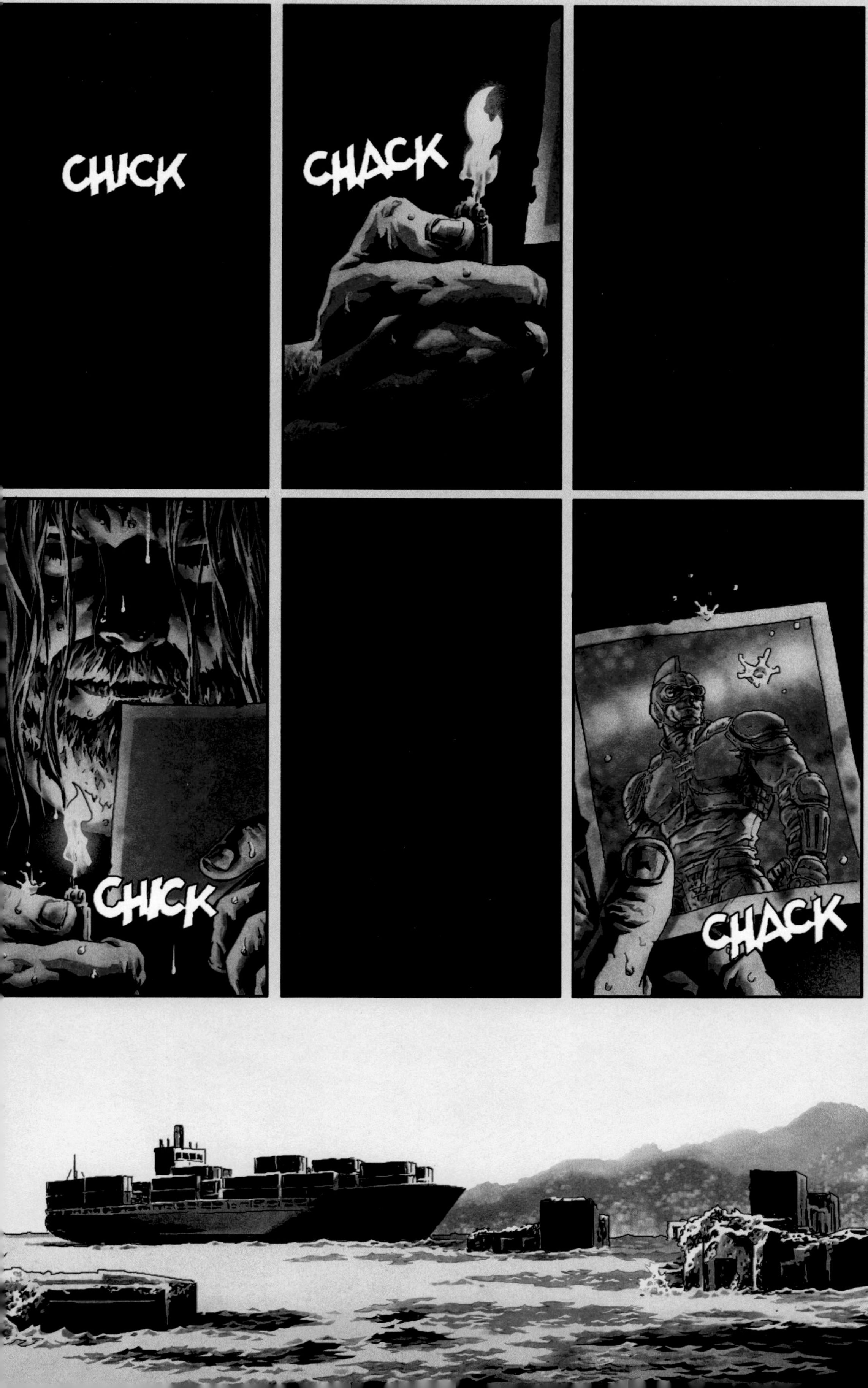
CHICK
CHACK
CHICK
CHACK

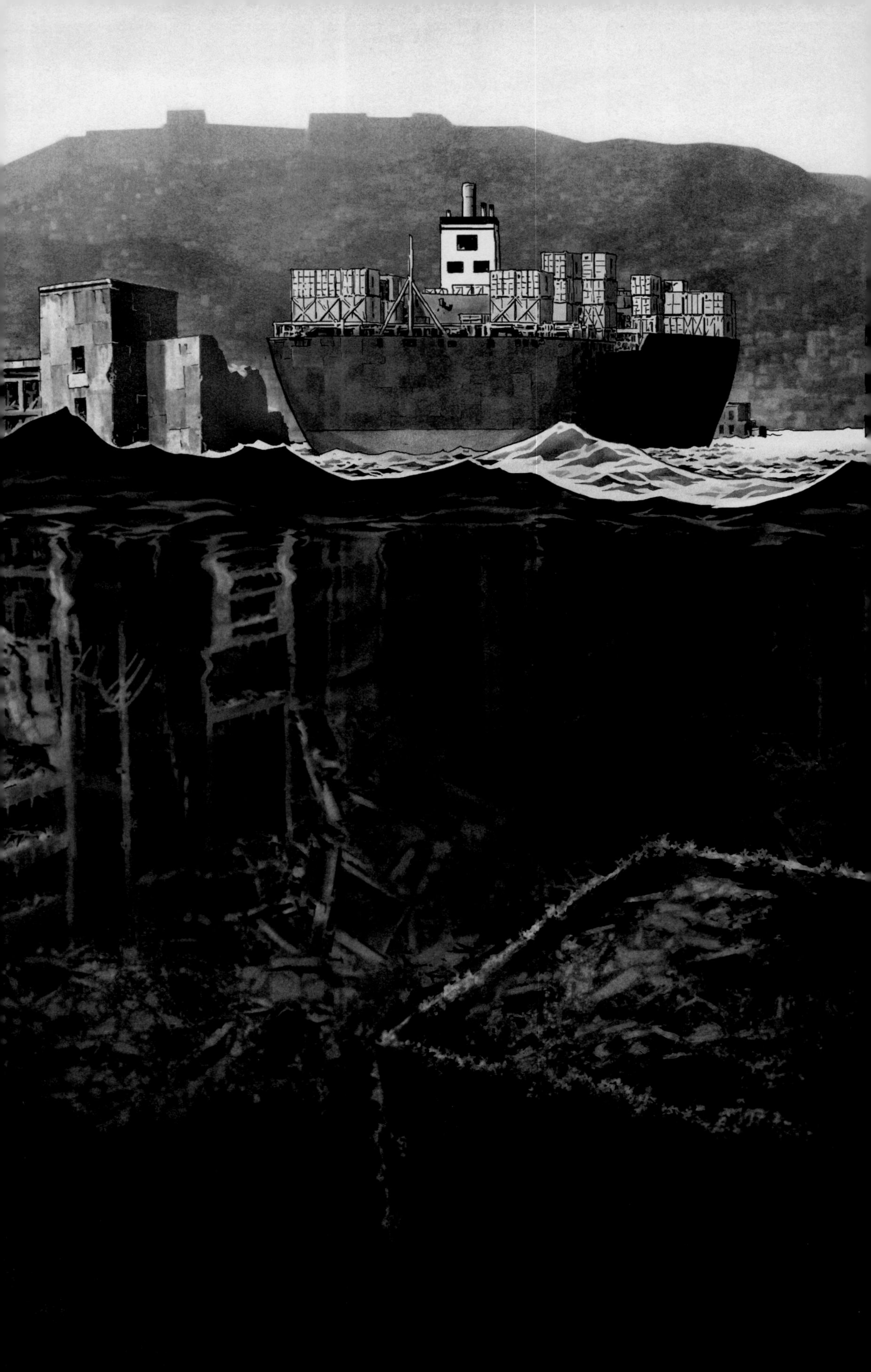

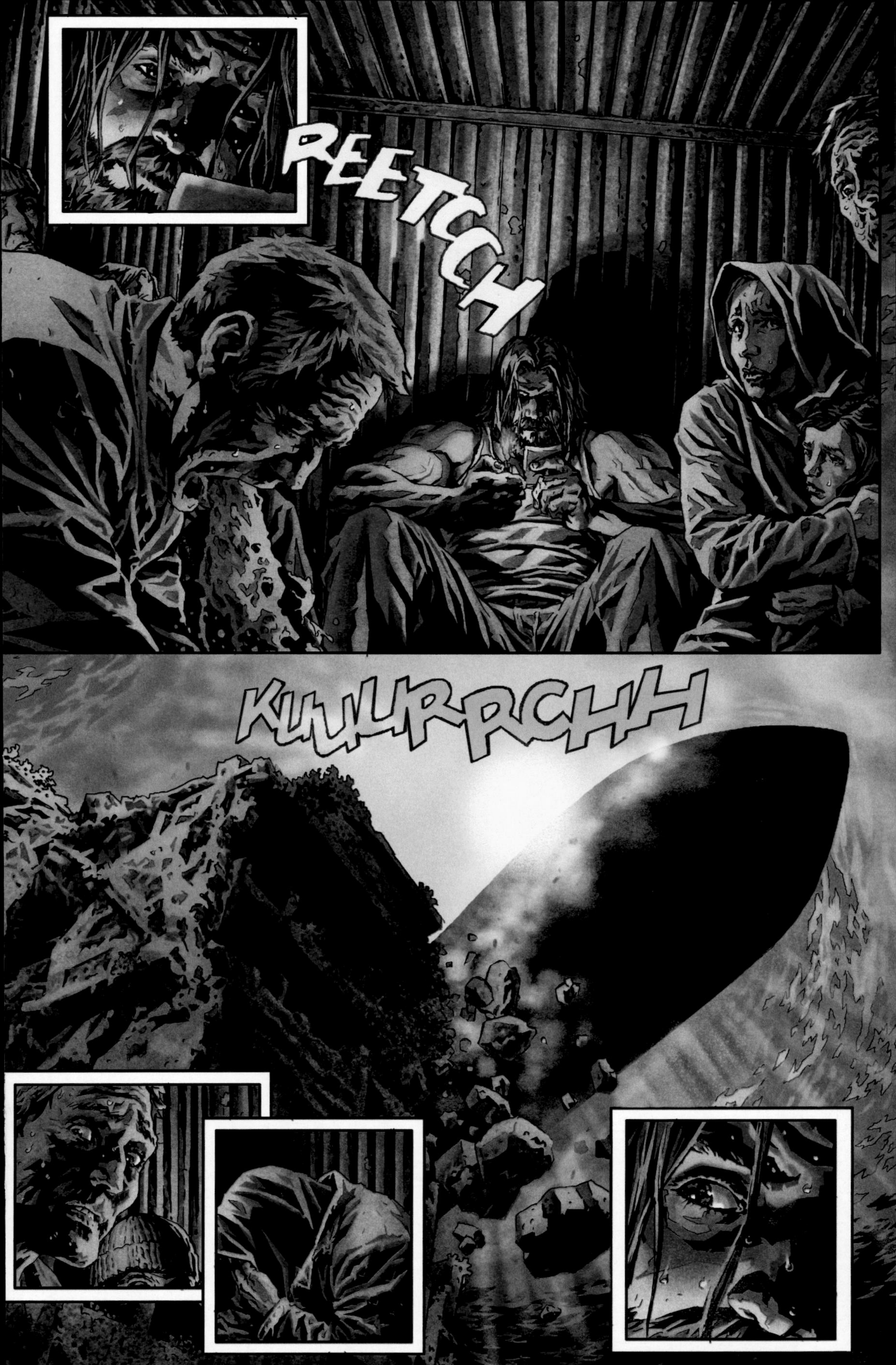
REETCH
KLUURRCHH

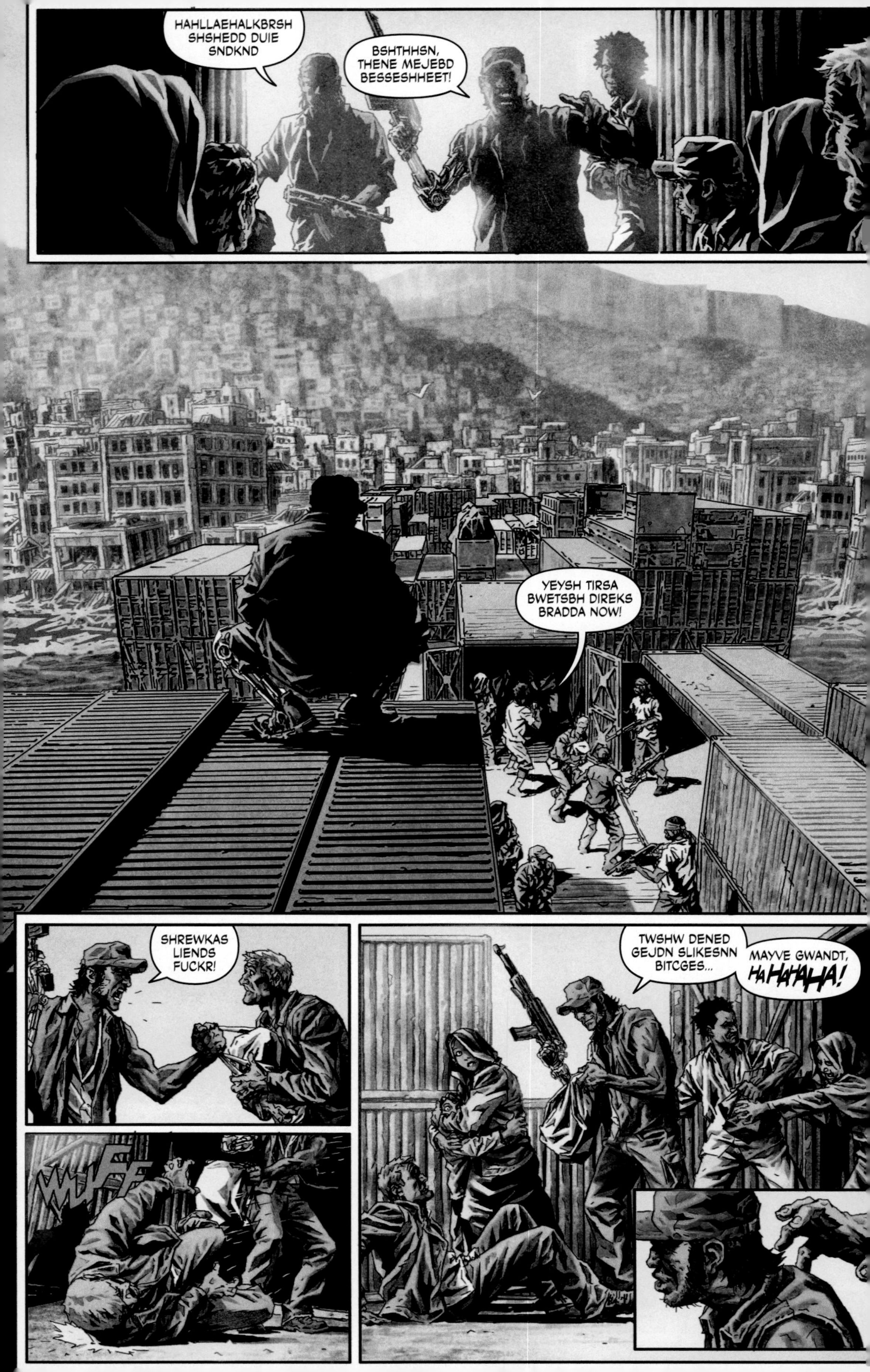
HAHLLAEHALKBRSH SHSHEDD DUIE SNDKND
BSHTHHSN, THENE MEJEBD BESSESHHEET!
YEYSH TIRSA BWETSBH DIREKS BRADDA NOW!
SHREWKAS LIENDS FUCKR!
WUFF
TWSHW DENED GEJDN SLIKESNN BITCGES...
MAYVE GWANDT, HA HA HAHA!

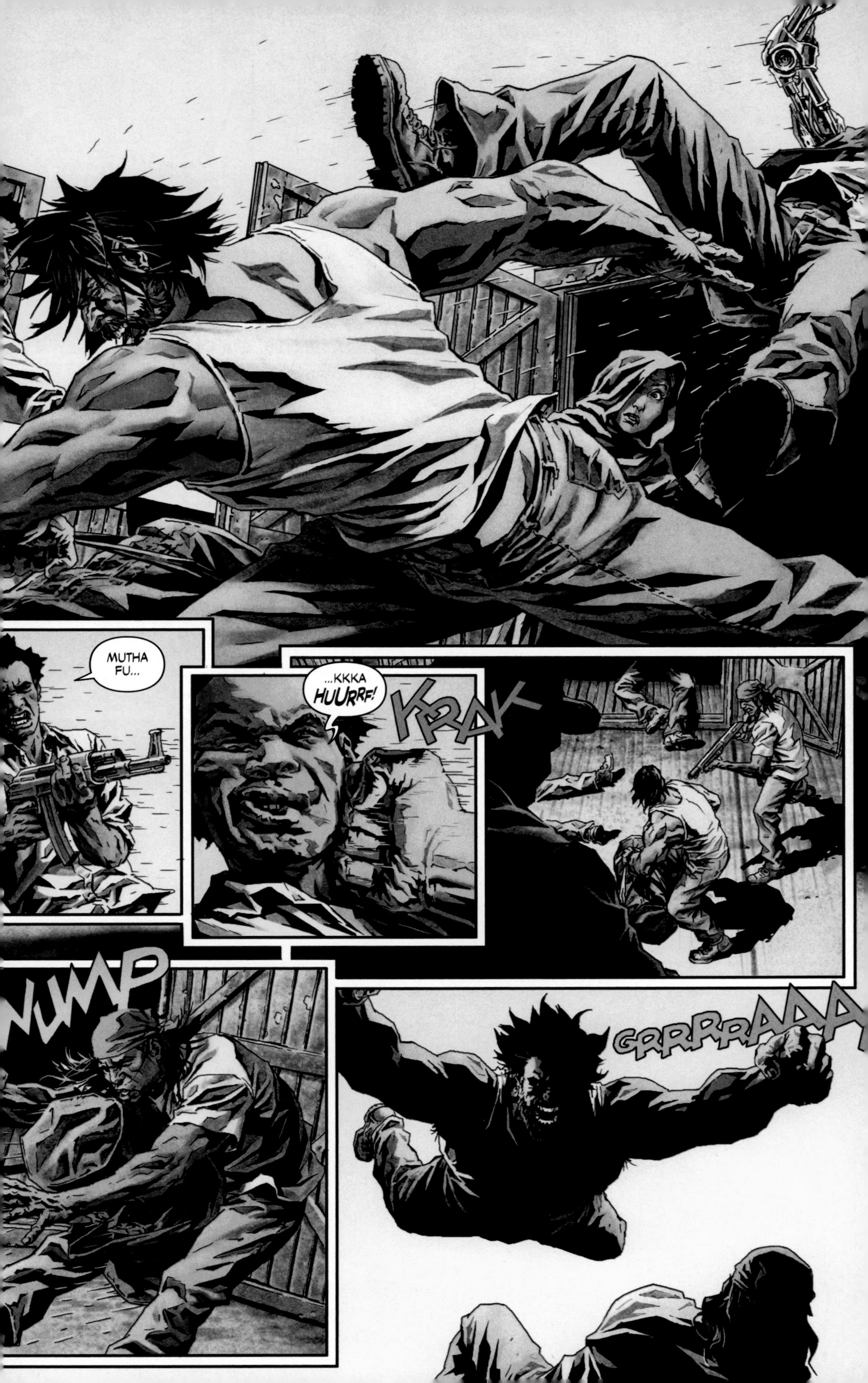
MUTHA FU...
...KKKA HUURRF!
KRAK
WUMP
GRRRRAAA

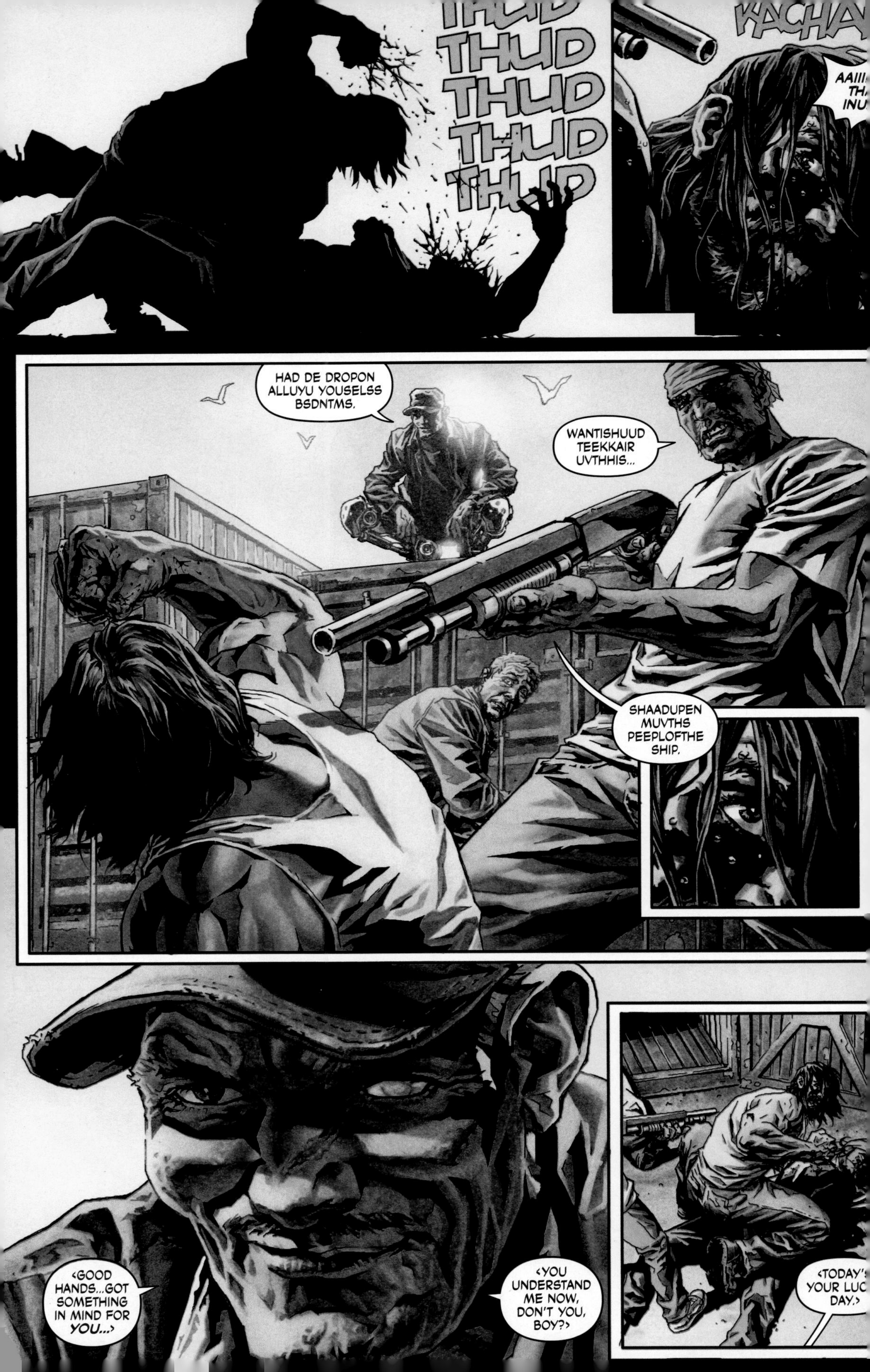
THUD
THUD
THUD
THUD
HAD DE DROPON ALLUYU YOUSELSS BSDNTMS.
WANTISHUUD TEEKKAIR UVTHHIS...
SHAADUPEN MUVTHS PEEPLOFTHE SHIP.
‹GOOD HANDS...GOT SOMETHING IN MIND FOR *YOU...*›
‹YOU UNDERSTAND ME NOW, DON'T YOU, BOY?›

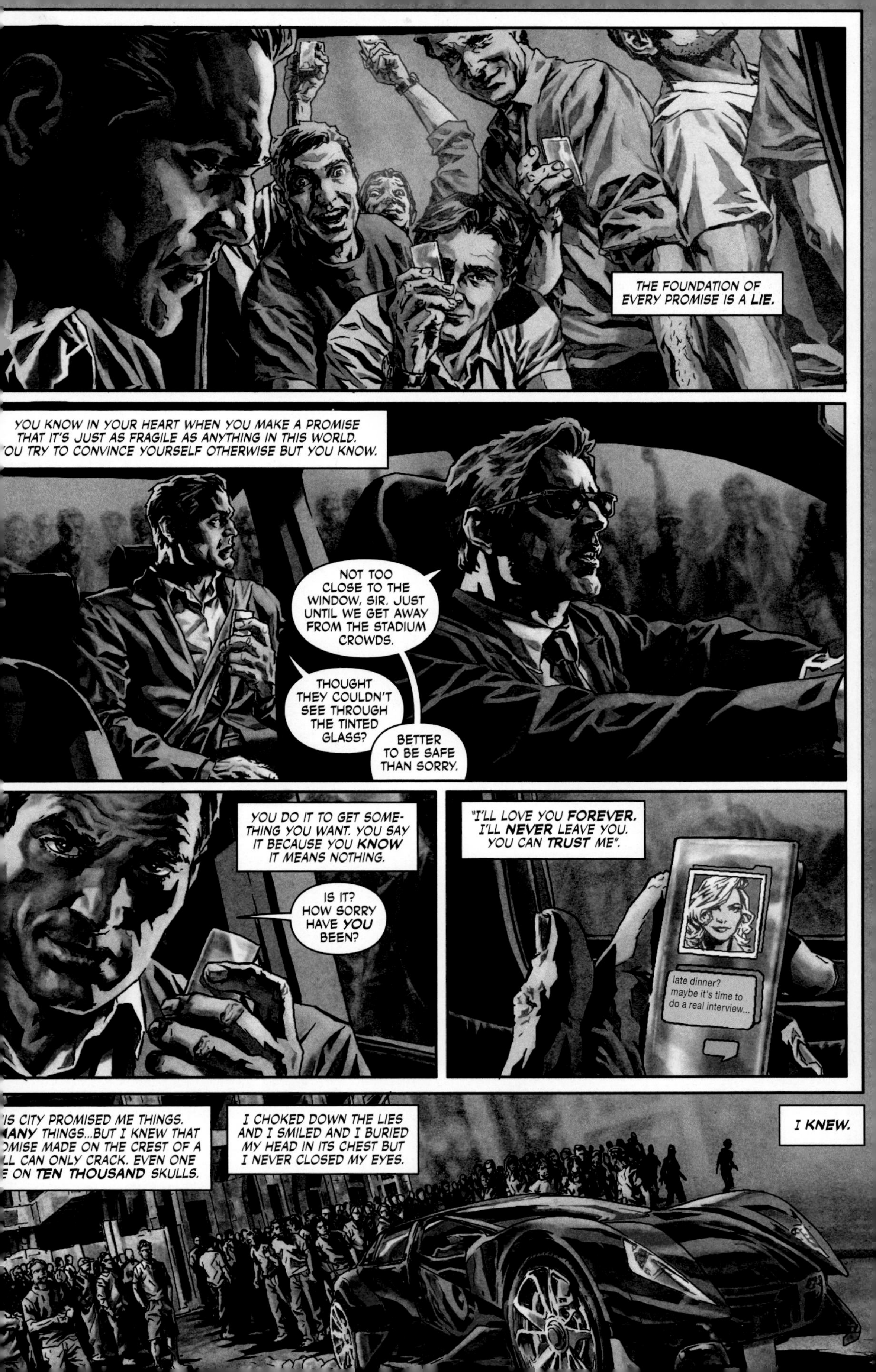
THE FOUNDATION OF EVERY PROMISE IS A LIE.
YOU KNOW IN YOUR HEART WHEN YOU MAKE A PROMISE THAT IT'S JUST AS FRAGILE AS ANYTHING IN THIS WORLD. OU TRY TO CONVINCE YOURSELF OTHERWISE BUT YOU KNOW.
NOT TOO CLOSE TO THE WINDOW, SIR. JUST UNTIL WE GET AWAY FROM THE STADIUM CROWDS.
THOUGHT THEY COULDN'T SEE THROUGH THE TINTED GLASS?
BETTER TO BE SAFE THAN SORRY.
YOU DO IT TO GET SOME-THING YOU WANT. YOU SAY IT BECAUSE YOU KNOW IT MEANS NOTHING.
IS IT? HOW SORRY HAVE YOU BEEN?
"I'LL LOVE YOU FOREVER. I'LL NEVER LEAVE YOU. YOU CAN TRUST ME".
late dinner? maybe it's time to do a real interview...
IS CITY PROMISED ME THINGS. MANY THINGS...BUT I KNEW THAT OMISE MADE ON THE CREST OF A LL CAN ONLY CRACK. EVEN ONE E ON TEN THOUSAND SKULLS.
I CHOKED DOWN THE LIES AND I SMILED AND I BURIED MY HEAD IN ITS CHEST BUT I NEVER CLOSED MY EYES.
I KNEW.

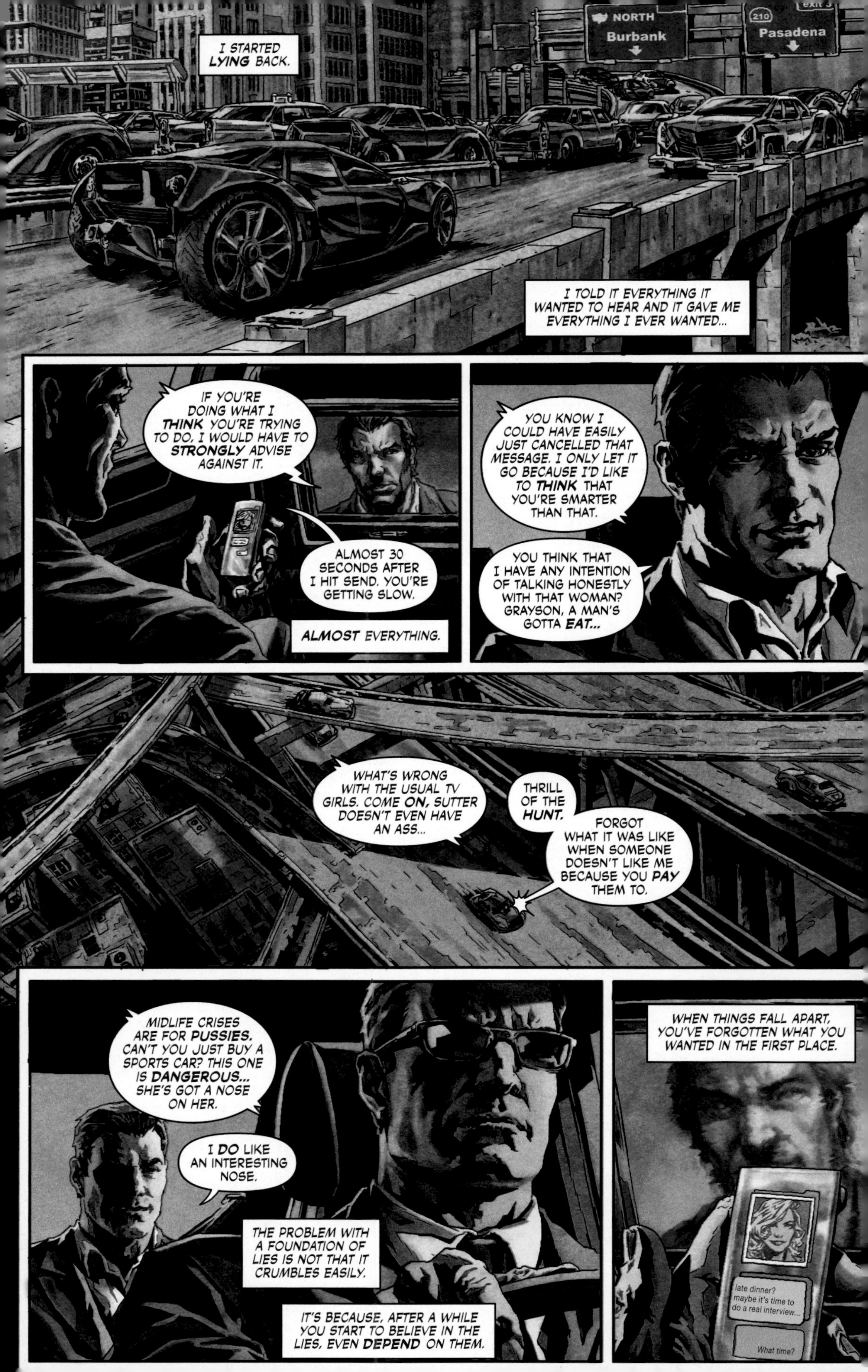

NORTH
Burbank
210
Pasadena
I STARTED LYING BACK.
I TOLD IT EVERYTHING IT WANTED TO HEAR AND IT GAVE ME EVERYTHING I EVER WANTED...
IF YOU'RE DOING WHAT I THINK YOU'RE TRYING TO DO, I WOULD HAVE TO STRONGLY ADVISE AGAINST IT.
ALMOST 30 SECONDS AFTER I HIT SEND. YOU'RE GETTING SLOW.
ALMOST EVERYTHING.
YOU KNOW I COULD HAVE EASILY JUST CANCELLED THAT MESSAGE. I ONLY LET IT GO BECAUSE I'D LIKE TO THINK THAT YOU'RE SMARTER THAN THAT.
YOU THINK THAT I HAVE ANY INTENTION OF TALKING HONESTLY WITH THAT WOMAN? GRAYSON, A MAN'S GOTTA EAT...
WHAT'S WRONG WITH THE USUAL TV GIRLS. COME ON, SUTTER DOESN'T EVEN HAVE AN ASS...
THRILL OF THE HUNT.
FORGOT WHAT IT WAS LIKE WHEN SOMEONE DOESN'T LIKE ME BECAUSE YOU PAY THEM TO.
MIDLIFE CRISES ARE FOR PUSSIES. CAN'T YOU JUST BUY A SPORTS CAR? THIS ONE IS DANGEROUS... SHE'S GOT A NOSE ON HER.
I DO LIKE AN INTERESTING NOSE.
THE PROBLEM WITH A FOUNDATION OF LIES IS NOT THAT IT CRUMBLES EASILY.
IT'S BECAUSE, AFTER A WHILE YOU START TO BELIEVE IN THE LIES, EVEN DEPEND ON THEM.
WHEN THINGS FALL APART, YOU'VE FORGOTTEN WHAT YOU WANTED IN THE FIRST PLACE.
late dinner? maybe it's time to do a real interview...
What time?

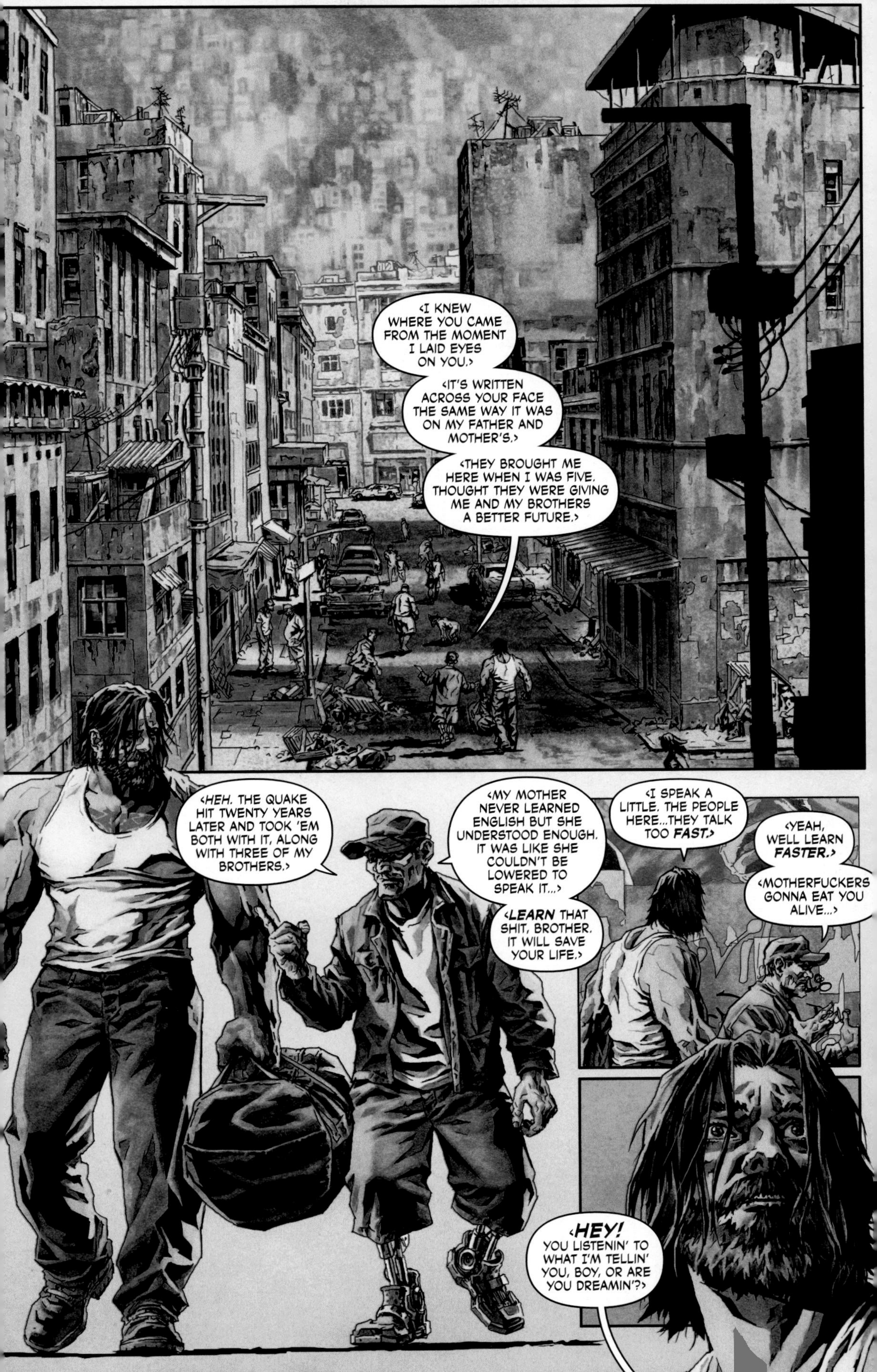
‹I KNEW WHERE YOU CAME FROM THE MOMENT I LAID EYES ON YOU.›
‹IT'S WRITTEN ACROSS YOUR FACE THE SAME WAY IT WAS ON MY FATHER AND MOTHER'S.›
‹THEY BROUGHT ME HERE WHEN I WAS FIVE. THOUGHT THEY WERE GIVING ME AND MY BROTHERS A BETTER FUTURE.›
‹*HEH.* THE QUAKE HIT TWENTY YEARS LATER AND TOOK 'EM BOTH WITH IT, ALONG WITH THREE OF MY BROTHERS.›
‹MY MOTHER NEVER LEARNED ENGLISH BUT SHE UNDERSTOOD ENOUGH. IT WAS LIKE SHE COULDN'T BE LOWERED TO SPEAK IT...›
‹***LEARN*** THAT SHIT, BROTHER. IT WILL SAVE YOUR LIFE.›
‹I SPEAK A LITTLE. THE PEOPLE HERE...THEY TALK TOO ***FAST.***›
‹YEAH, WELL LEARN ***FASTER.***›
‹MOTHERFUCKERS GONNA EAT YOU ALIVE...›
‹***HEY!*** YOU LISTENIN' TO WHAT I'M TELLIN' YOU, BOY, OR ARE YOU DREAMIN'?›

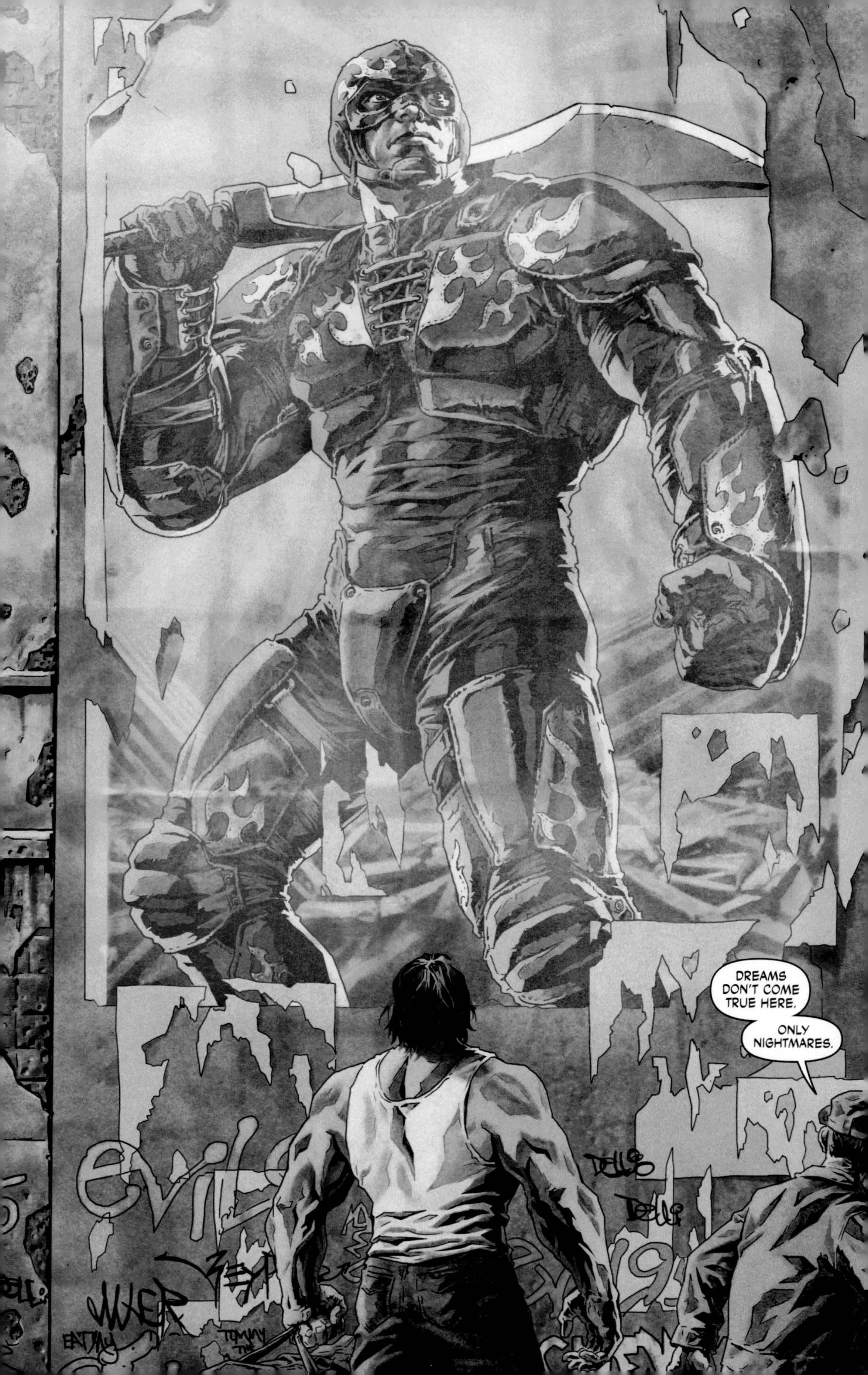
DREAMS DON'T COME TRUE HERE.
ONLY NIGHTMARES.

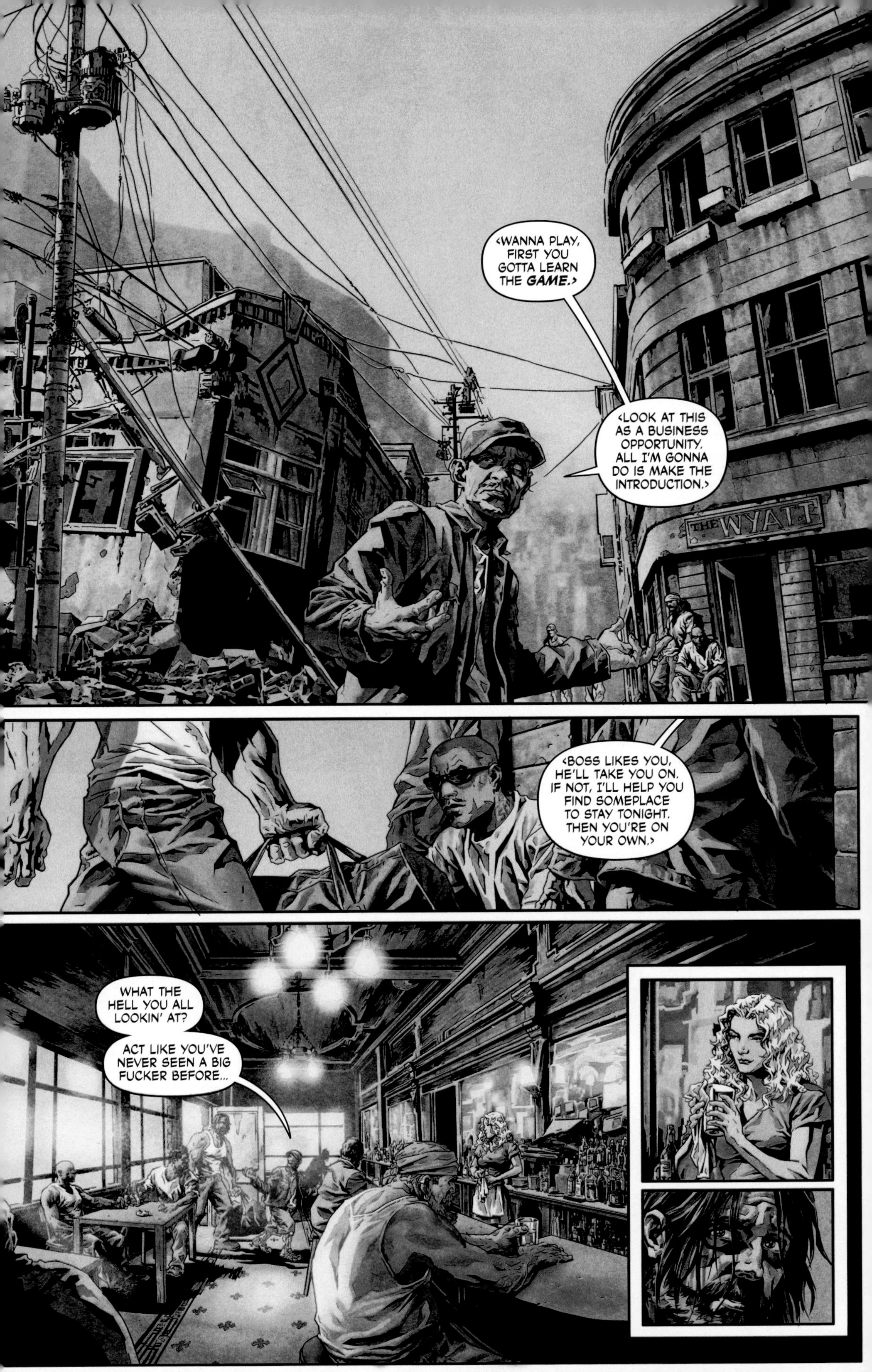

‹WANNA PLAY, FIRST YOU GOTTA LEARN THE ***GAME.***›
‹LOOK AT THIS AS A BUSINESS OPPORTUNITY. ALL I'M GONNA DO IS MAKE THE INTRODUCTION.›
THE WYATT
‹BOSS LIKES YOU, HE'LL TAKE YOU ON. IF NOT, I'LL HELP YOU FIND SOMEPLACE TO STAY TONIGHT. THEN YOU'RE ON YOUR OWN.›
WHAT THE HELL YOU ALL LOOKIN' AT?
ACT LIKE YOU'VE NEVER SEEN A BIG FUCKER BEFORE...

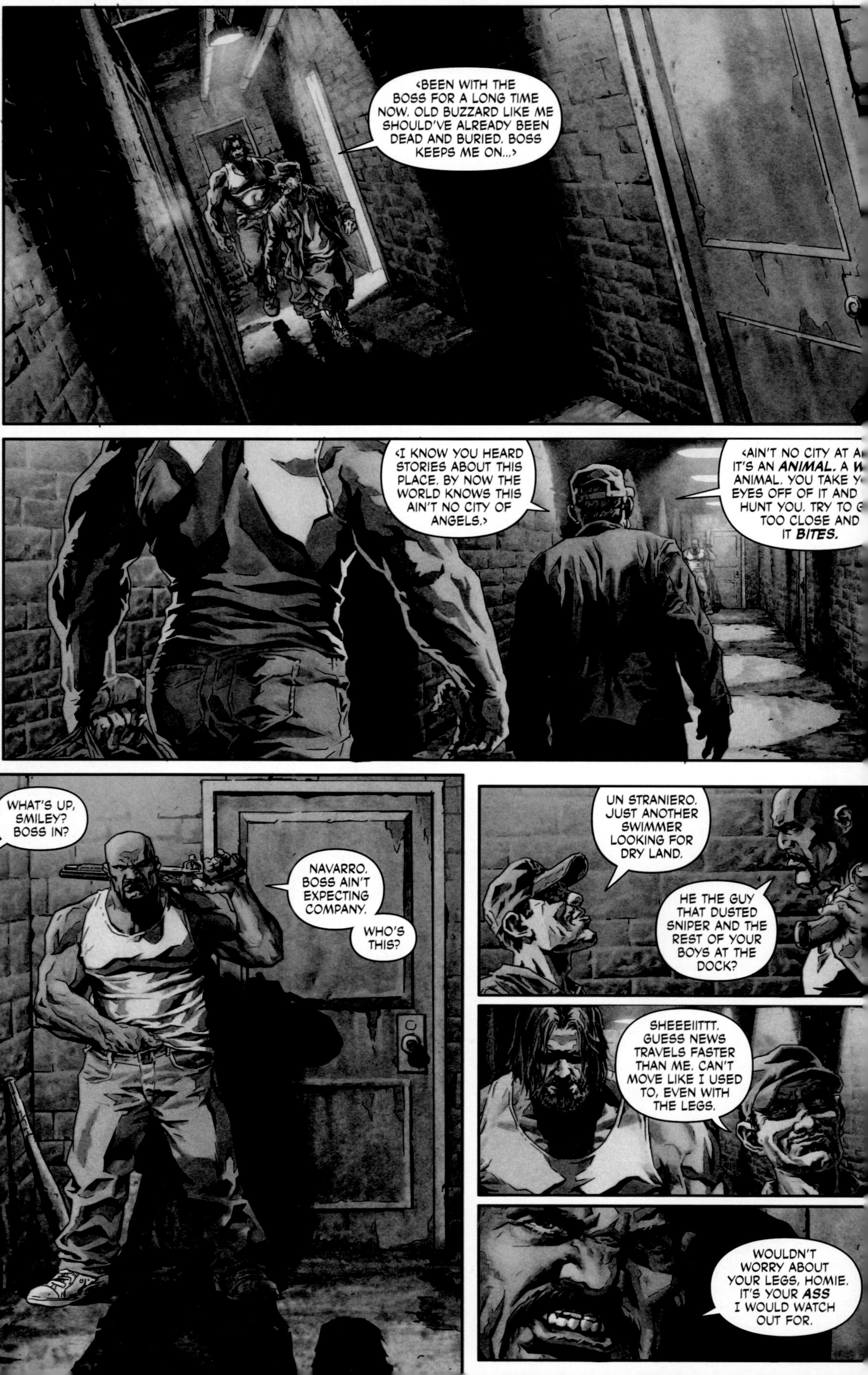
‹BEEN WITH THE BOSS FOR A LONG TIME NOW. OLD BUZZARD LIKE ME SHOULD'VE ALREADY BEEN DEAD AND BURIED. BOSS KEEPS ME ON...›
‹I KNOW YOU HEARD STORIES ABOUT THIS PLACE. BY NOW THE WORLD KNOWS THIS AIN'T NO CITY OF ANGELS.›
‹AIN'T NO CITY AT A
IT'S AN ANIMAL. A W
ANIMAL. YOU TAKE Y
EYES OFF OF IT AND
HUNT YOU. TRY TO G
TOO CLOSE AND
IT BITES.
WHAT'S UP, SMILEY? BOSS IN?
NAVARRO. BOSS AIN'T EXPECTING COMPANY.
WHO'S THIS?
UN STRANIERO. JUST ANOTHER SWIMMER LOOKING FOR DRY LAND.
HE THE GUY THAT DUSTED SNIPER AND THE REST OF YOUR BOYS AT THE DOCK?
SHEEEIITTT. GUESS NEWS TRAVELS FASTER THAN ME. CAN'T MOVE LIKE I USED TO, EVEN WITH THE LEGS.
WOULDN'T WORRY ABOUT YOUR LEGS, HOMIE. IT'S YOUR ASS I WOULD WATCH OUT FOR.

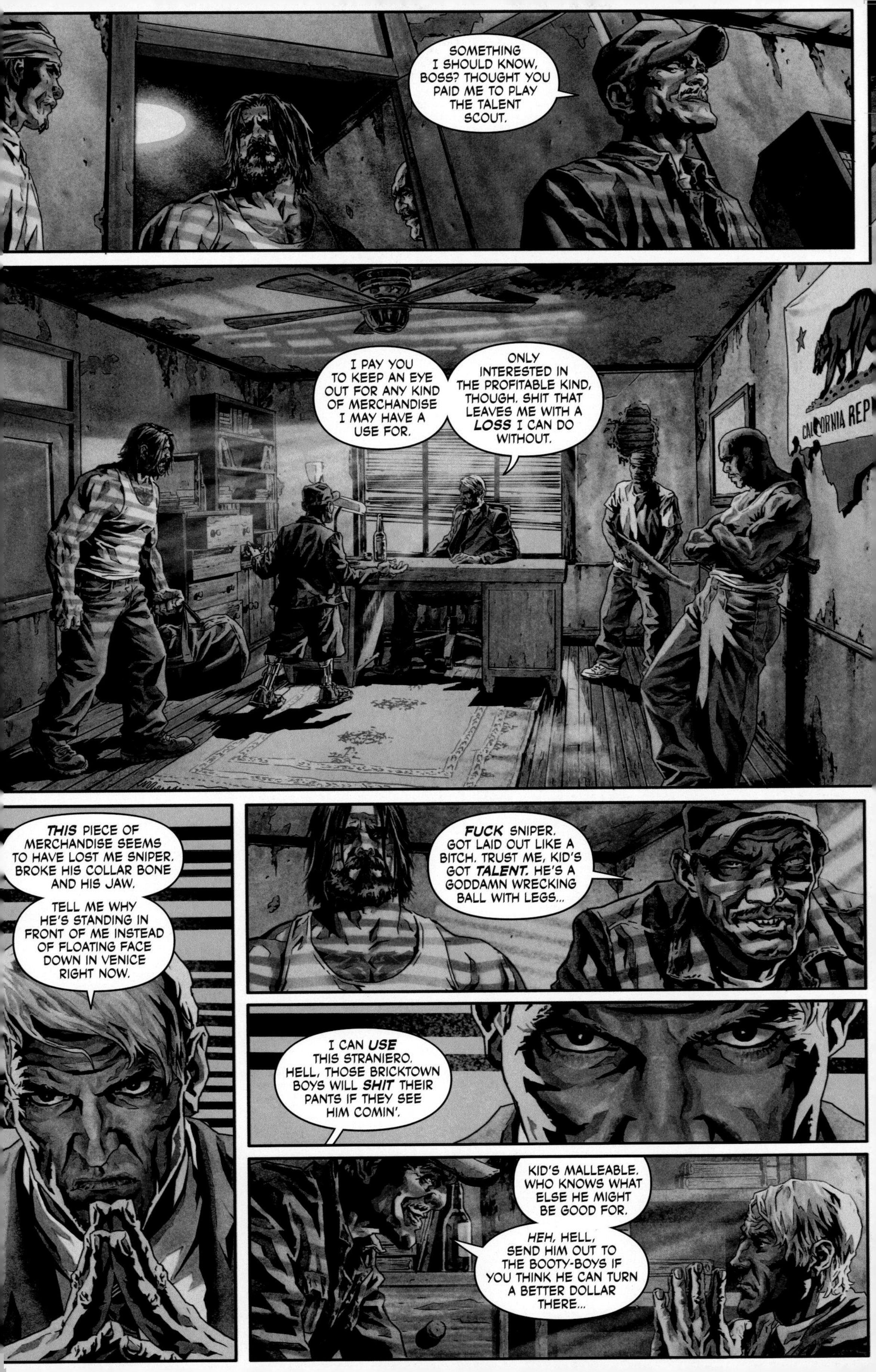
SOMETHING I SHOULD KNOW, BOSS? THOUGHT YOU PAID ME TO PLAY THE TALENT SCOUT.
I PAY YOU TO KEEP AN EYE OUT FOR ANY KIND OF MERCHANDISE I MAY HAVE A USE FOR.
ONLY INTERESTED IN THE PROFITABLE KIND, THOUGH. SHIT THAT LEAVES ME WITH A LOSS I CAN DO WITHOUT.
CALIFORNIA REP
THIS PIECE OF MERCHANDISE SEEMS TO HAVE LOST ME SNIPER. BROKE HIS COLLAR BONE AND HIS JAW.
TELL ME WHY HE'S STANDING IN FRONT OF ME INSTEAD OF FLOATING FACE DOWN IN VENICE RIGHT NOW.
FUCK SNIPER. GOT LAID OUT LIKE A BITCH. TRUST ME, KID'S GOT TALENT. HE'S A GODDAMN WRECKING BALL WITH LEGS...
I CAN USE THIS STRANIERO. HELL, THOSE BRICKTOWN BOYS WILL SHIT THEIR PANTS IF THEY SEE HIM COMIN'.
KID'S MALLEABLE. WHO KNOWS WHAT ELSE HE MIGHT BE GOOD FOR.
HEH, HELL, SEND HIM OUT TO THE BOOTY-BOYS IF YOU THINK HE CAN TURN A BETTER DOLLAR THERE...

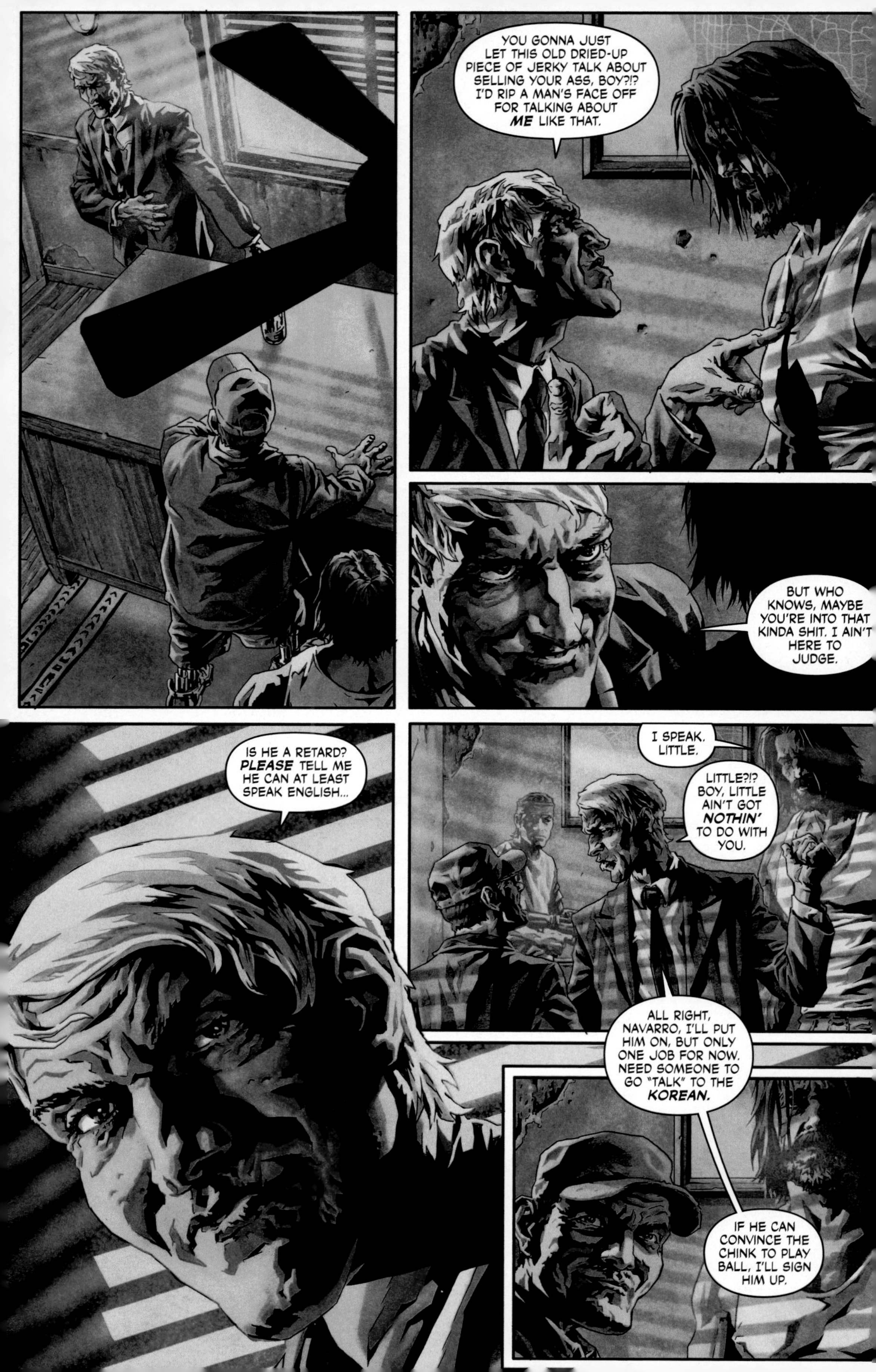
YOU GONNA JUST LET THIS OLD DRIED-UP PIECE OF JERKY TALK ABOUT SELLING YOUR ASS, BOY?!? I'D RIP A MAN'S FACE OFF FOR TALKING ABOUT *ME* LIKE THAT.
BUT WHO KNOWS, MAYBE YOU'RE INTO THAT KINDA SHIT. I AIN'T HERE TO JUDGE.
IS HE A RETARD? *PLEASE* TELL ME HE CAN AT LEAST SPEAK ENGLISH...
I SPEAK. LITTLE.
LITTLE?!? BOY, LITTLE AIN'T GOT *NOTHIN'* TO DO WITH YOU.
ALL RIGHT, NAVARRO, I'LL PUT HIM ON, BUT ONLY ONE JOB FOR NOW. NEED SOMEONE TO GO "TALK" TO THE *KOREAN.*
IF HE CAN CONVINCE THE CHINK TO PLAY BALL, I'LL SIGN HIM UP.

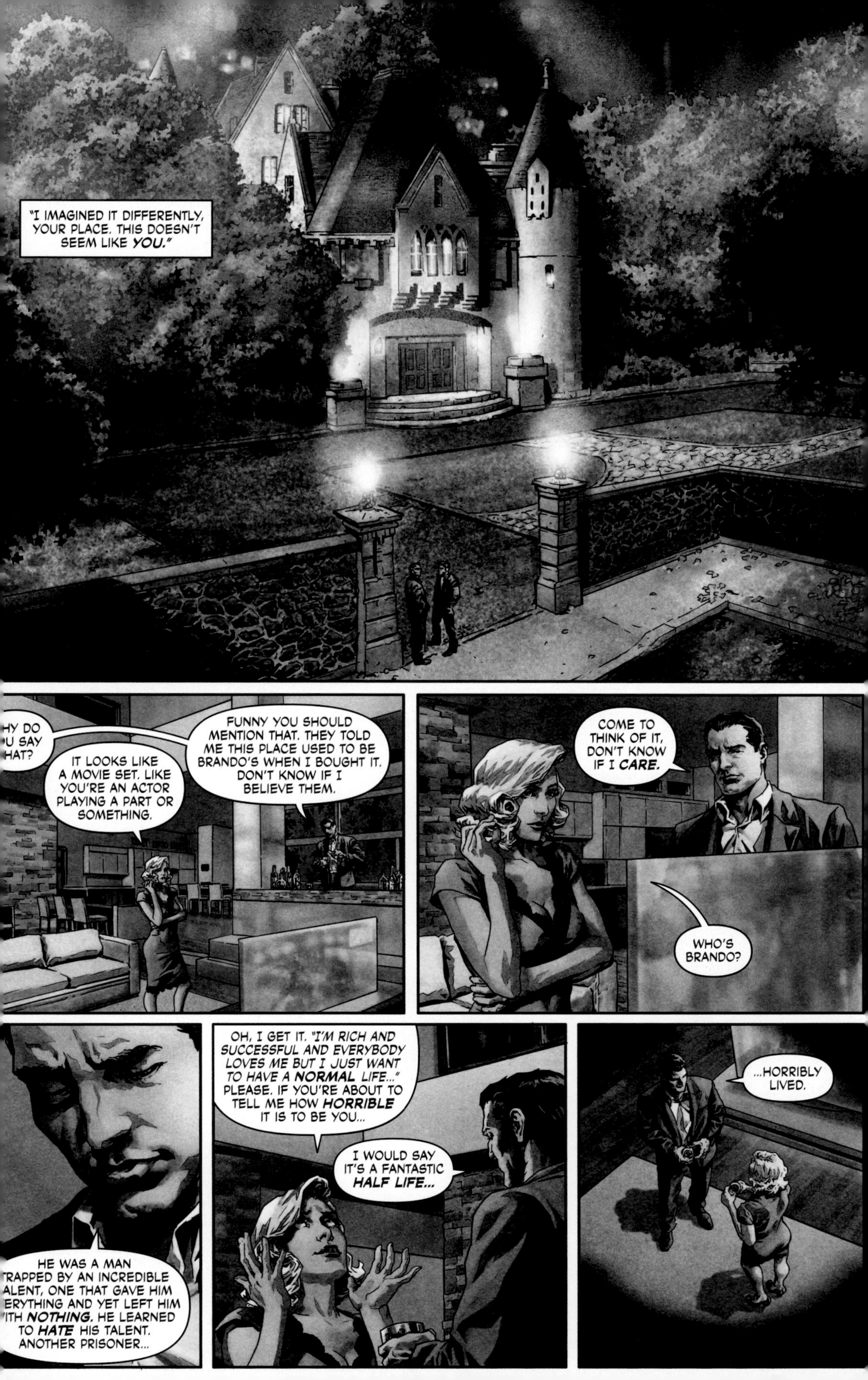

"I IMAGINED IT DIFFERENTLY, YOUR PLACE. THIS DOESN'T SEEM LIKE YOU."
HY DO
U SAY
HAT?
IT LOOKS LIKE A MOVIE SET. LIKE YOU'RE AN ACTOR PLAYING A PART OR SOMETHING.
FUNNY YOU SHOULD MENTION THAT. THEY TOLD ME THIS PLACE USED TO BE BRANDO'S WHEN I BOUGHT IT. DON'T KNOW IF I BELIEVE THEM.
COME TO THINK OF IT, DON'T KNOW IF I CARE.
WHO'S BRANDO?
HE WAS A MAN
RAPPED BY AN INCREDIBLE
ALENT, ONE THAT GAVE HIM
ERYTHING AND YET LEFT HIM
ITH NOTHING. HE LEARNED
TO HATE HIS TALENT.
ANOTHER PRISONER...
OH, I GET IT. "I'M RICH AND SUCCESSFUL AND EVERYBODY LOVES ME BUT I JUST WANT TO HAVE A NORMAL LIFE..." PLEASE. IF YOU'RE ABOUT TO TELL ME HOW HORRIBLE IT IS TO BE YOU...
I WOULD SAY IT'S A FANTASTIC HALF LIFE...
...HORRIBLY LIVED.

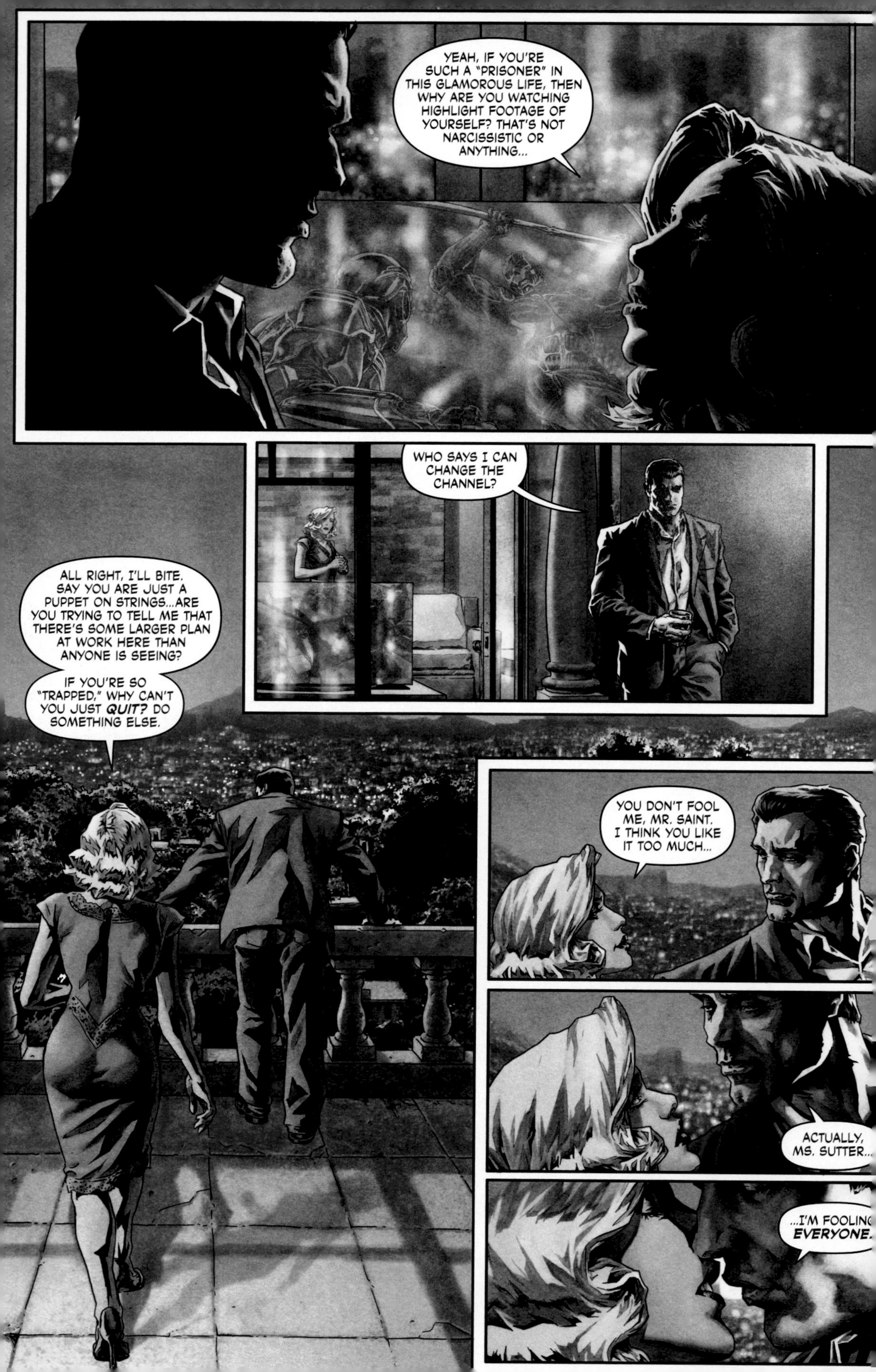
YEAH, IF YOU'RE SUCH A "PRISONER" IN THIS GLAMOROUS LIFE, THEN WHY ARE YOU WATCHING HIGHLIGHT FOOTAGE OF YOURSELF? THAT'S NOT NARCISSISTIC OR ANYTHING...
WHO SAYS I CAN CHANGE THE CHANNEL?
ALL RIGHT, I'LL BITE. SAY YOU ARE JUST A PUPPET ON STRINGS...ARE YOU TRYING TO TELL ME THAT THERE'S SOME LARGER PLAN AT WORK HERE THAN ANYONE IS SEEING?
IF YOU'RE SO "TRAPPED," WHY CAN'T YOU JUST QUIT? DO SOMETHING ELSE.
YOU DON'T FOOL ME, MR. SAINT. I THINK YOU LIKE IT TOO MUCH...
ACTUALLY, MS. SUTTER...
...I'M FOOLING EVERYONE.

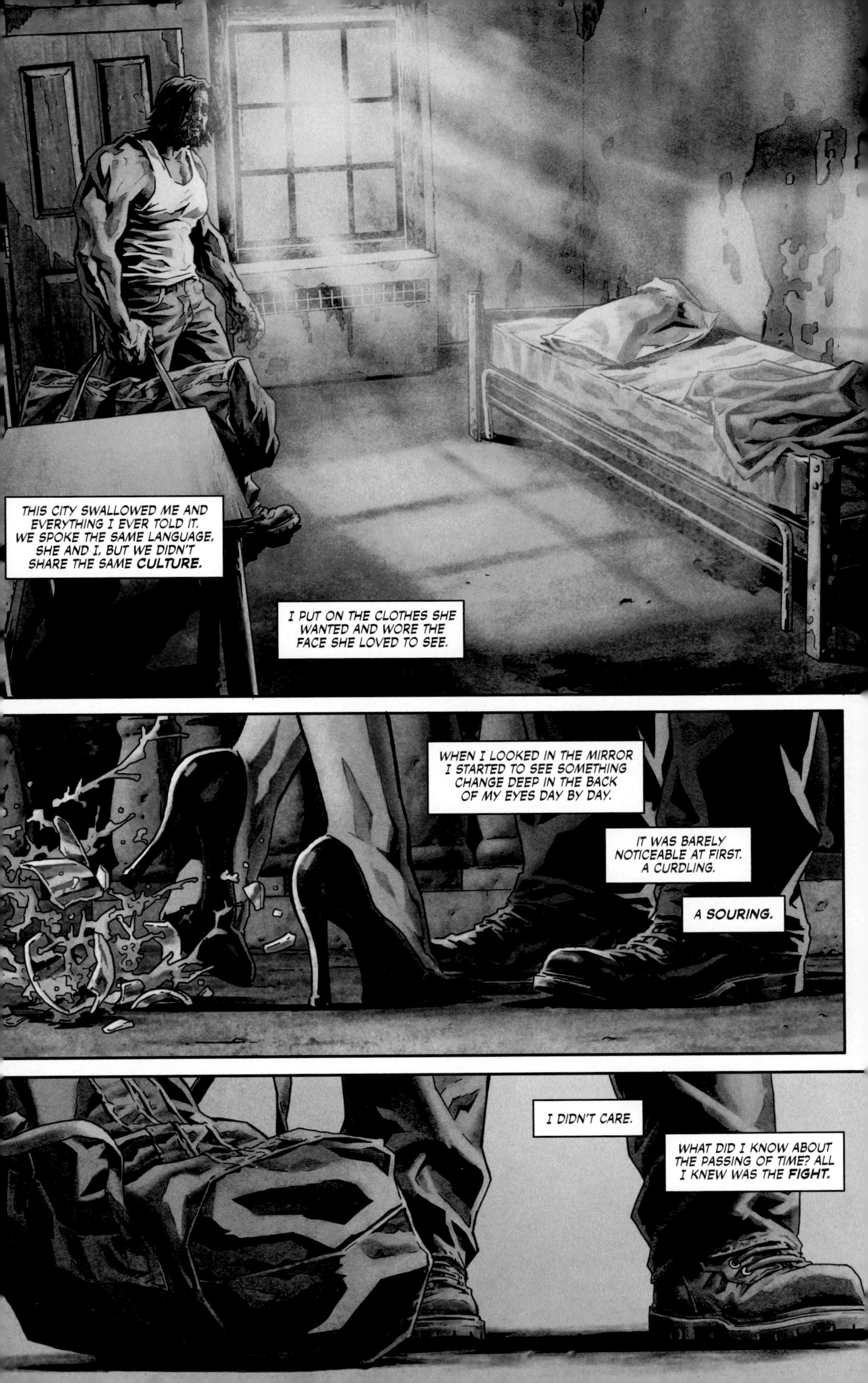
THIS CITY SWALLOWED ME AND EVERYTHING I EVER TOLD IT. WE SPOKE THE SAME LANGUAGE, SHE AND I, BUT WE DIDN'T SHARE THE SAME **CULTURE.**
I PUT ON THE CLOTHES SHE WANTED AND WORE THE FACE SHE LOVED TO SEE.
WHEN I LOOKED IN THE MIRROR I STARTED TO SEE SOMETHING CHANGE DEEP IN THE BACK OF MY EYES DAY BY DAY.
IT WAS BARELY NOTICEABLE AT FIRST. A CURDLING.
A **SOURING.**
I DIDN'T CARE.
WHAT DID I KNOW ABOUT THE PASSING OF TIME? ALL I KNEW WAS THE **FIGHT.**

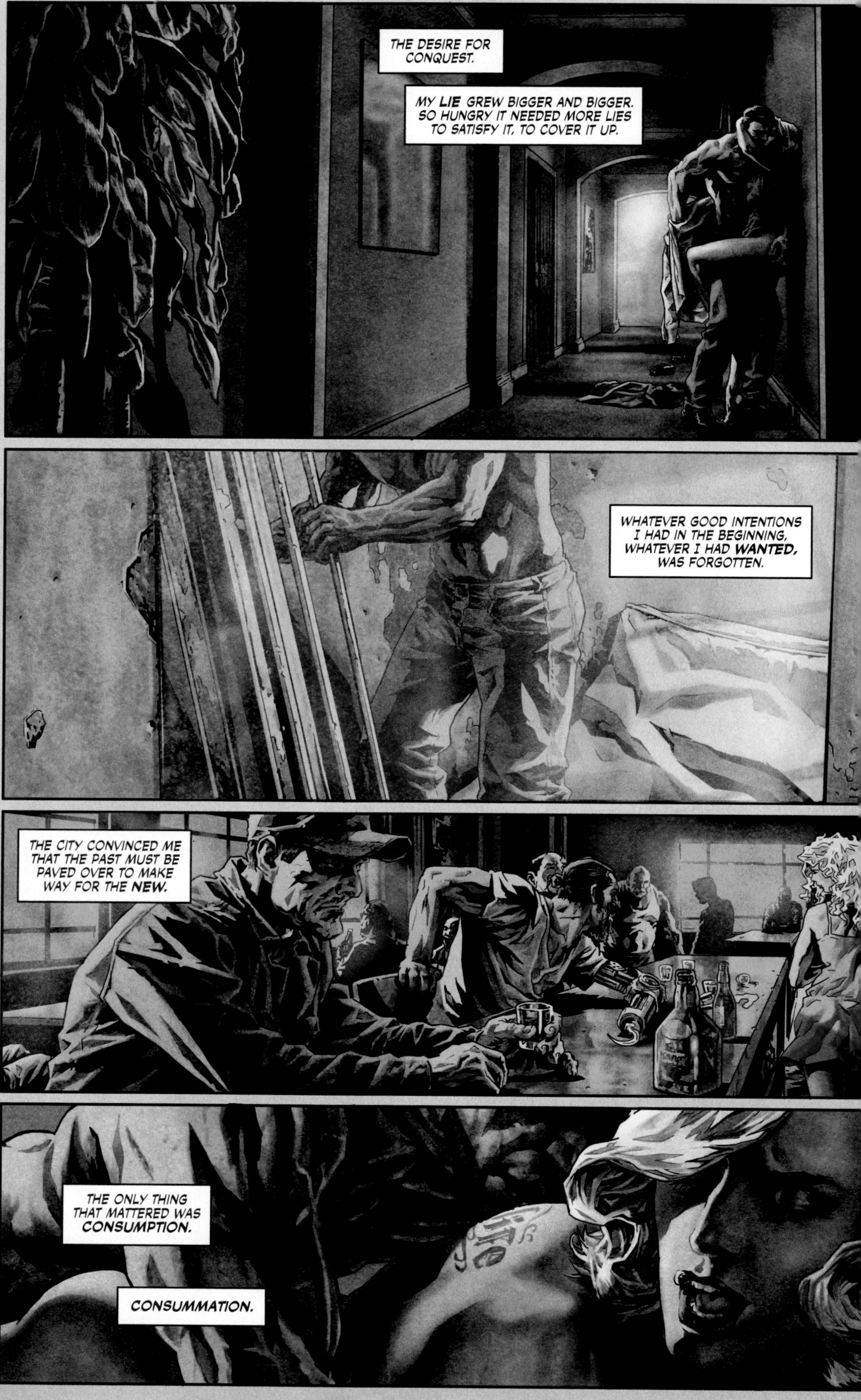
THE DESIRE FOR CONQUEST.
MY LIE GREW BIGGER AND BIGGER. SO HUNGRY IT NEEDED MORE LIES TO SATISFY IT, TO COVER IT UP.
WHATEVER GOOD INTENTIONS I HAD IN THE BEGINNING, WHATEVER I HAD WANTED, WAS FORGOTTEN.
THE CITY CONVINCED ME THAT THE PAST MUST BE PAVED OVER TO MAKE WAY FOR THE NEW.
THE ONLY THING THAT MATTERED WAS CONSUMPTION.
CONSUMMATION.

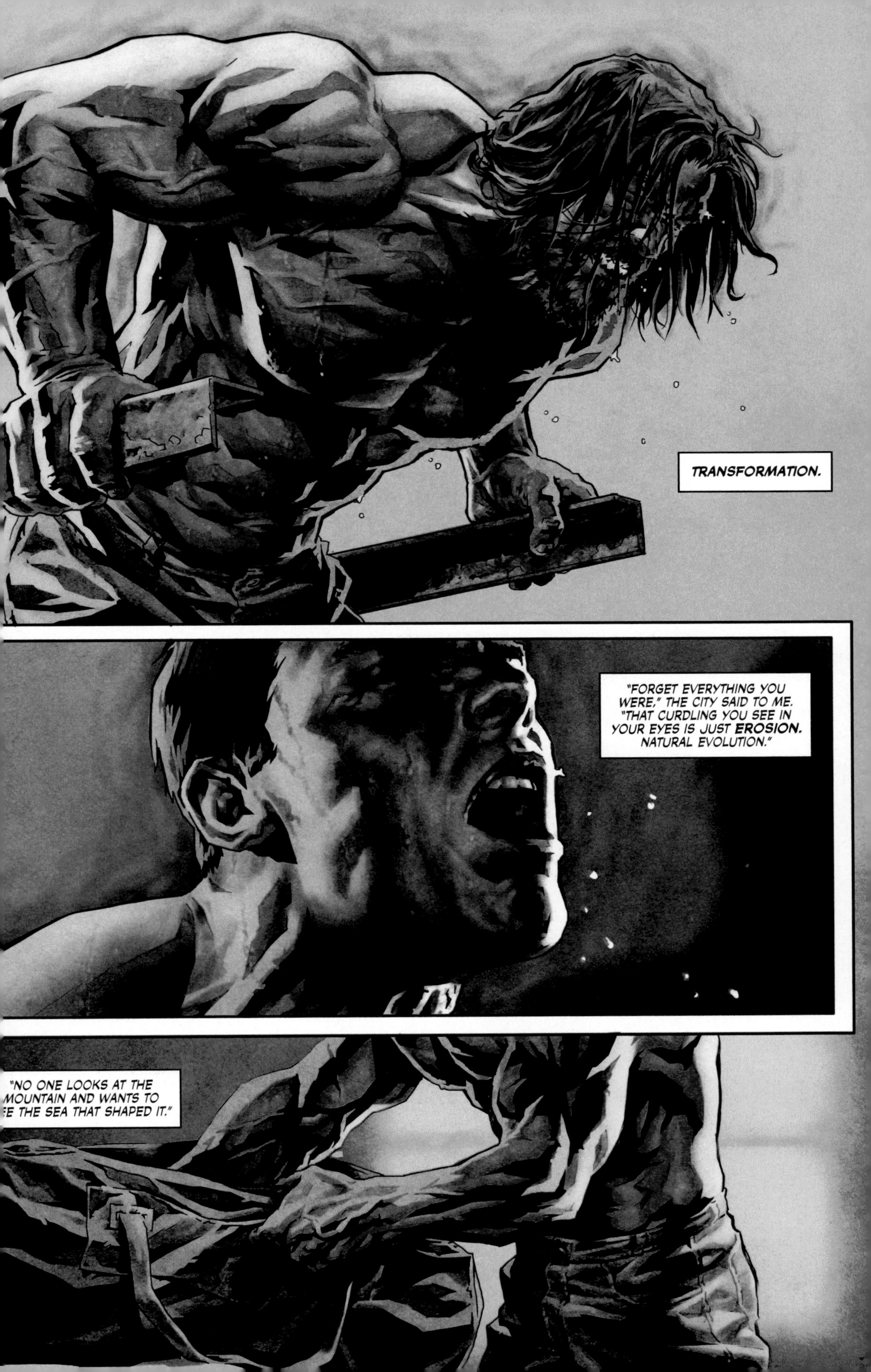
TRANSFORMATION.
"FORGET EVERYTHING YOU WERE," THE CITY SAID TO ME. "THAT CURDLING YOU SEE IN YOUR EYES IS JUST EROSION. NATURAL EVOLUTION."
"NO ONE LOOKS AT THE MOUNTAIN AND WANTS TO
E THE SEA THAT SHAPED IT."

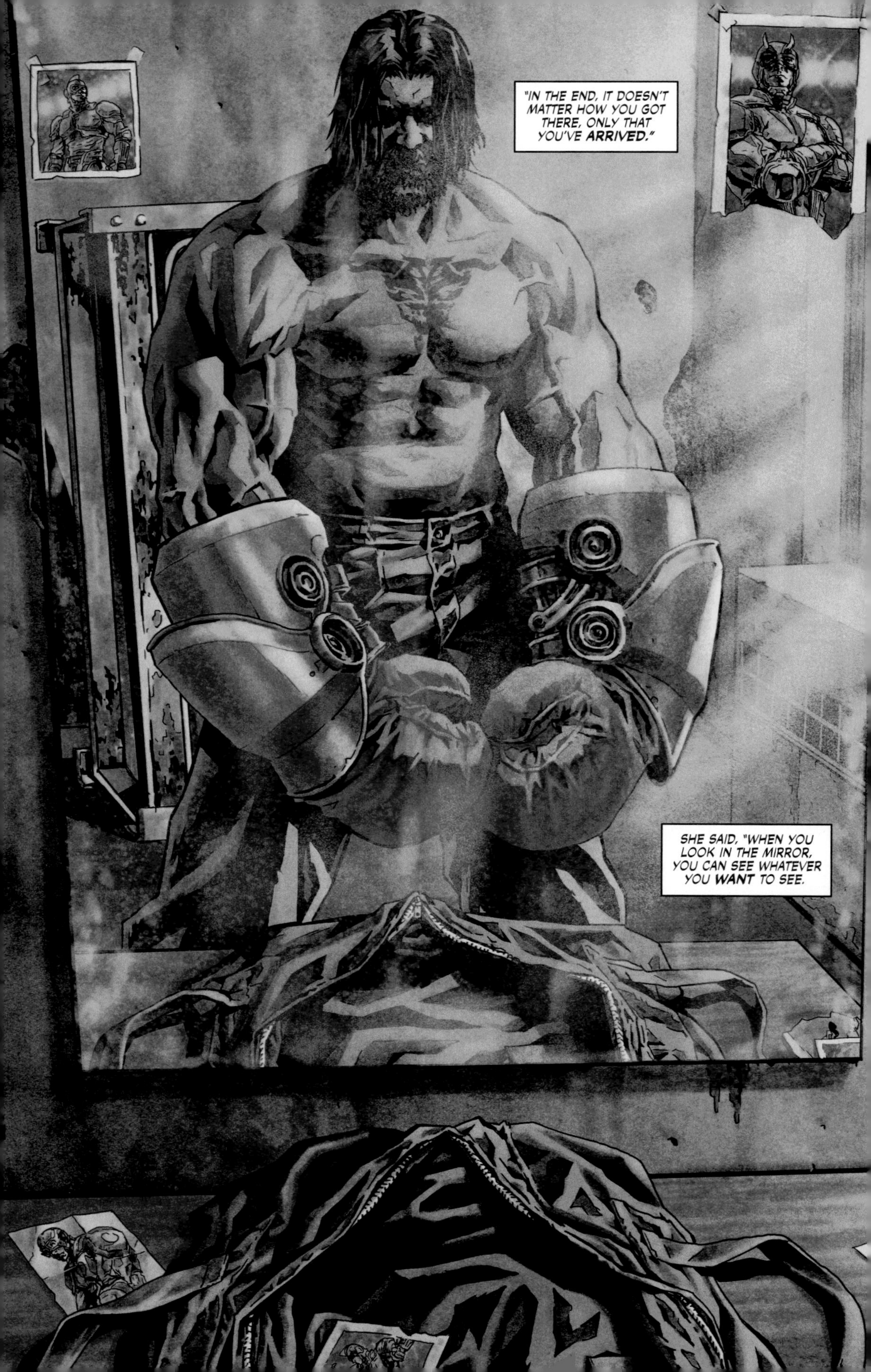
"IN THE END, IT DOESN'T MATTER HOW YOU GOT THERE, ONLY THAT YOU'VE ARRIVED."
SHE SAID, "WHEN YOU LOOK IN THE MIRROR, YOU CAN SEE WHATEVER YOU WANT TO SEE.

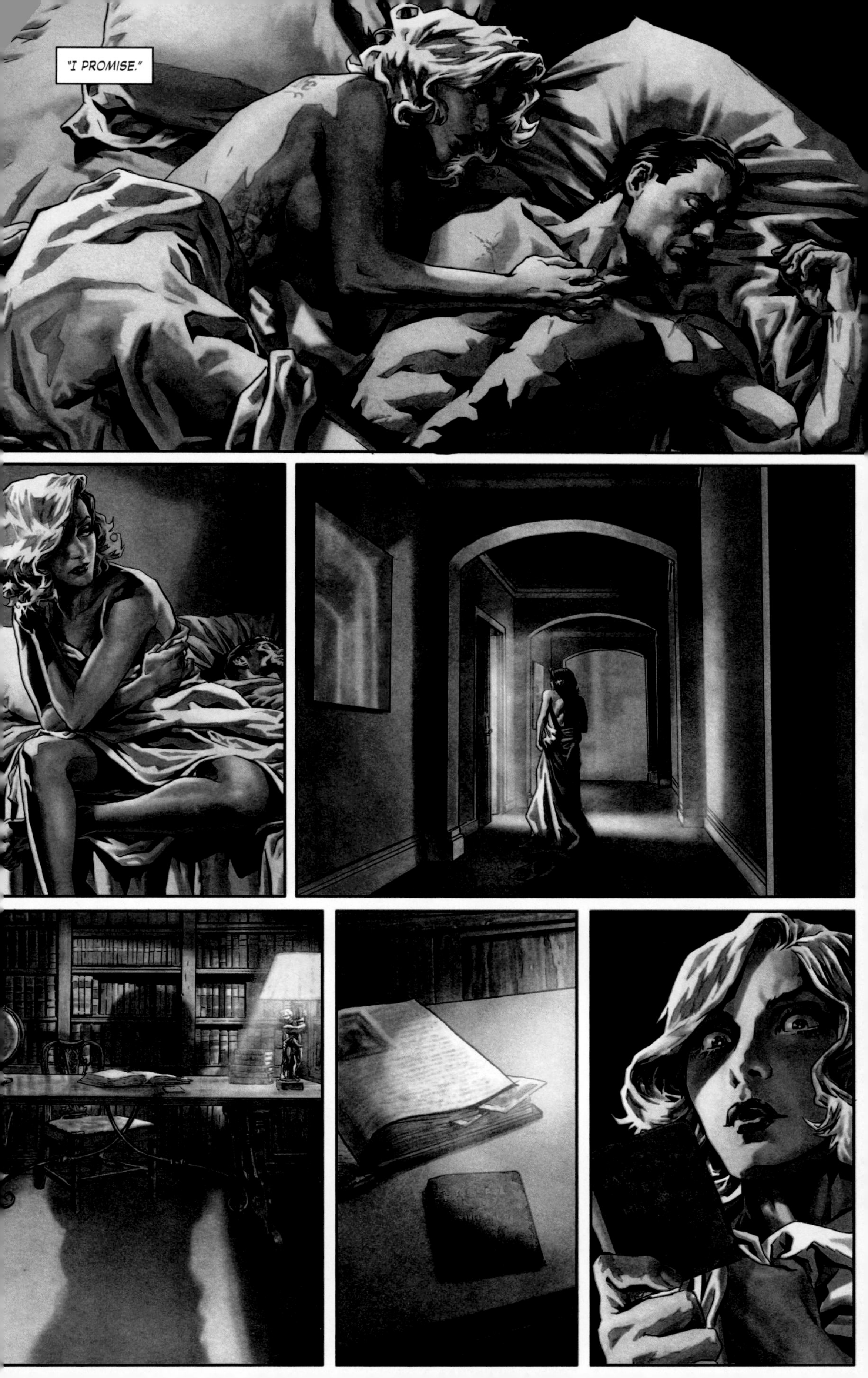
"I PROMISE."

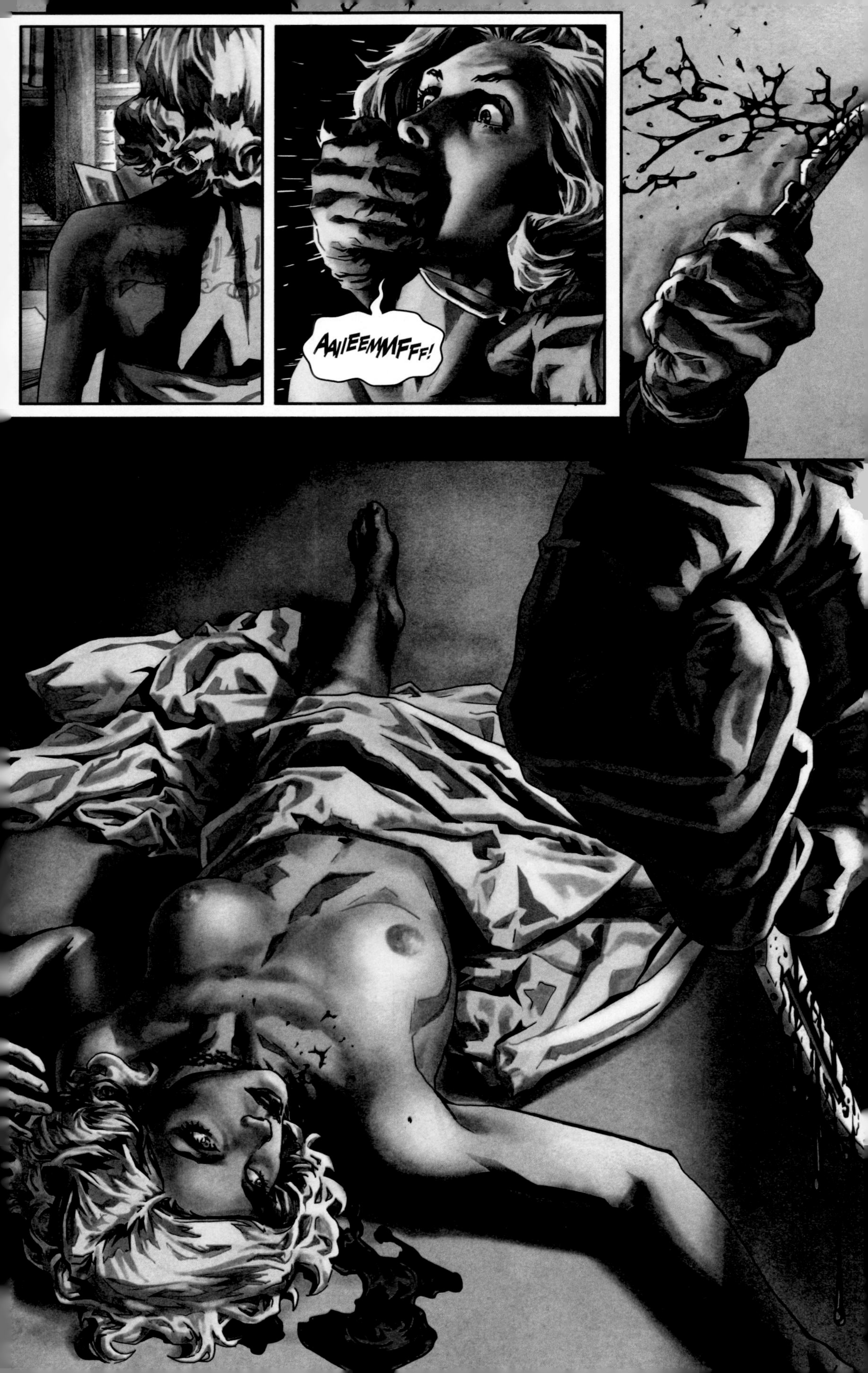
AAIIEEMMFFF!

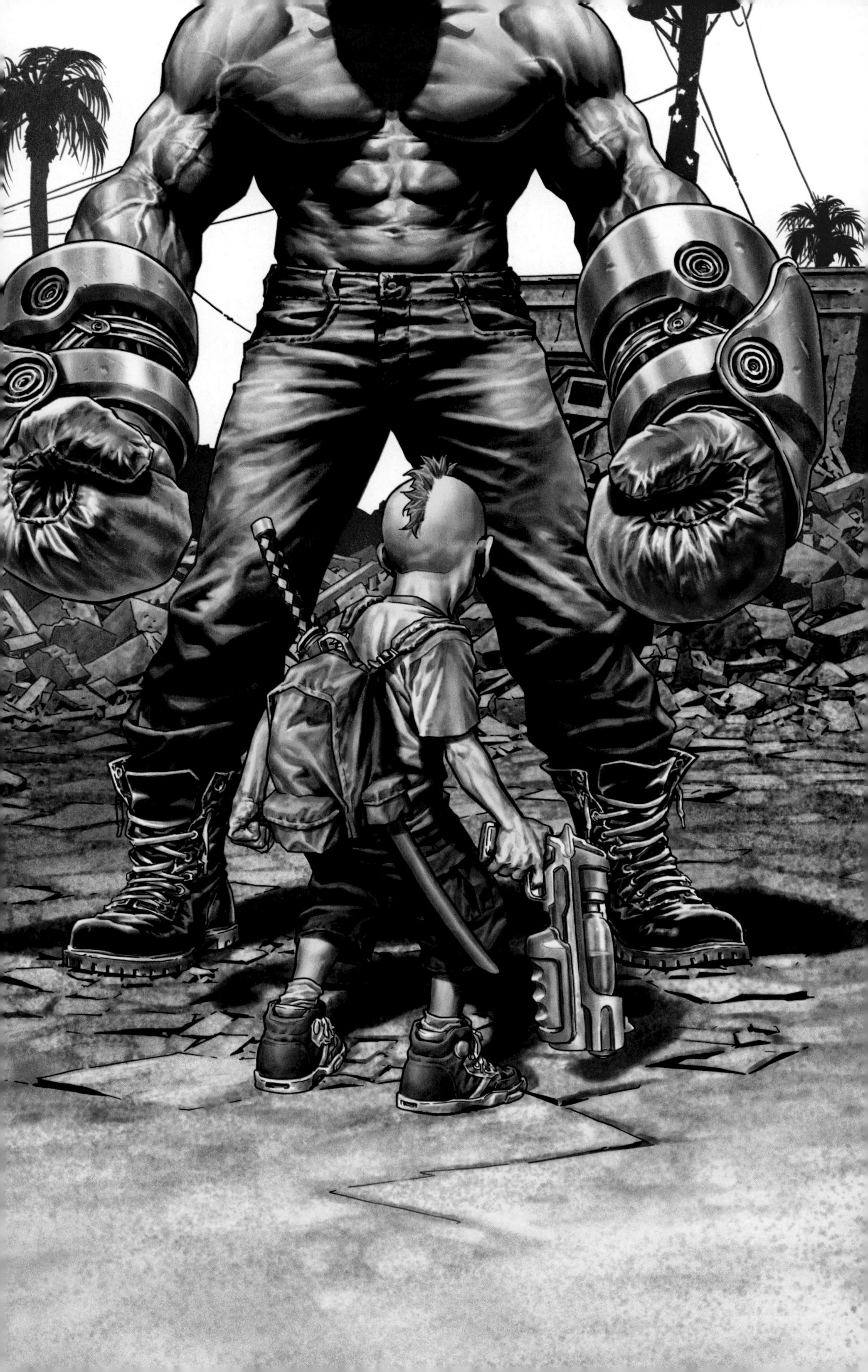

CHAPTER THREE:
THE DEEP HEIGHTS

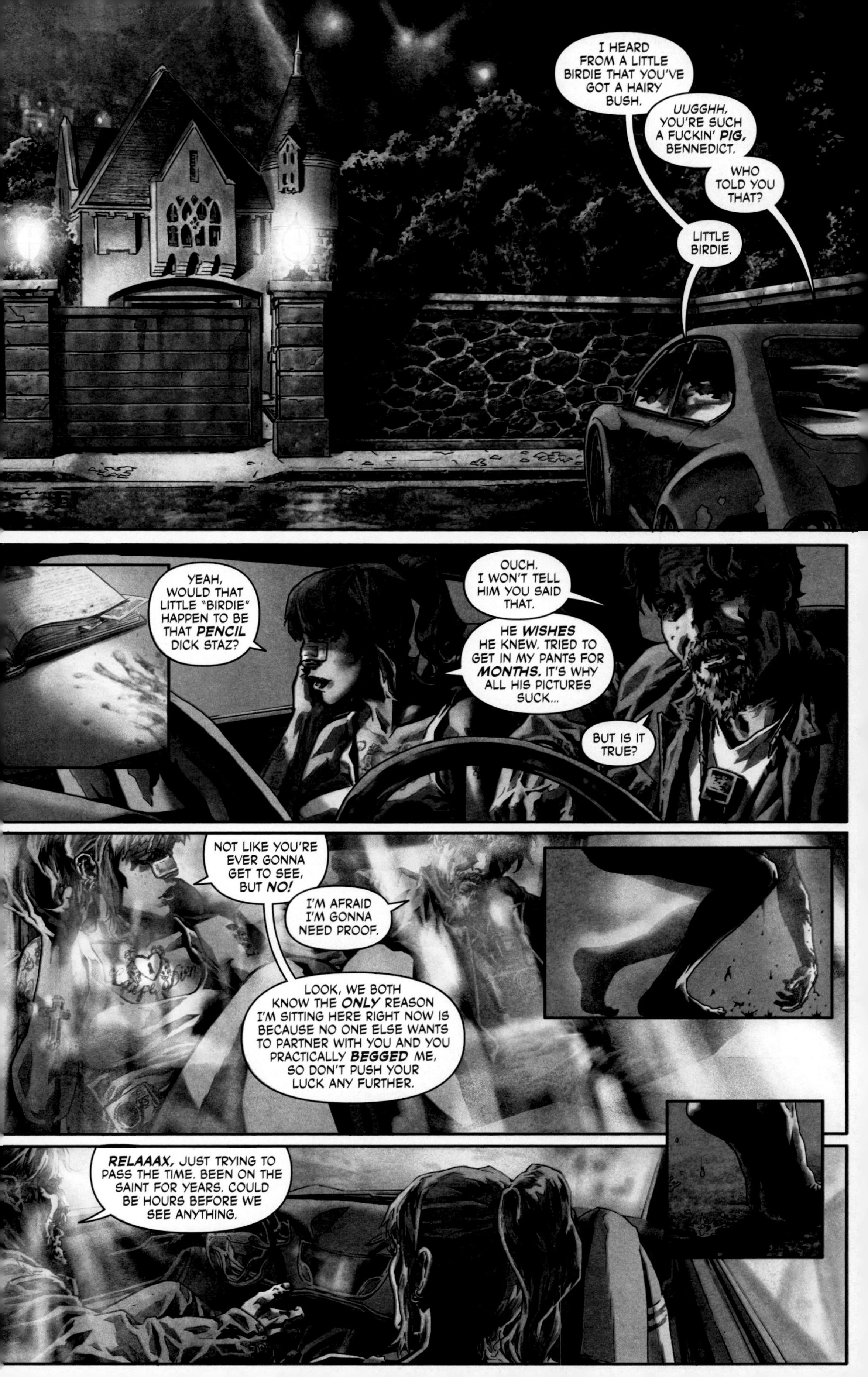
I HEARD FROM A LITTLE BIRDIE THAT YOU'VE GOT A HAIRY BUSH.
UUGGHH, YOU'RE SUCH A FUCKIN' PIG, BENNEDICT.
WHO TOLD YOU THAT?
LITTLE BIRDIE.
YEAH, WOULD THAT LITTLE "BIRDIE" HAPPEN TO BE THAT PENCIL DICK STAZ?
OUCH. I WON'T TELL HIM YOU SAID THAT.
HE WISHES HE KNEW. TRIED TO GET IN MY PANTS FOR MONTHS. IT'S WHY ALL HIS PICTURES SUCK...
BUT IS IT TRUE?
NOT LIKE YOU'RE EVER GONNA GET TO SEE, BUT NO!
I'M AFRAID I'M GONNA NEED PROOF.
LOOK, WE BOTH KNOW THE ONLY REASON I'M SITTING HERE RIGHT NOW IS BECAUSE NO ONE ELSE WANTS TO PARTNER WITH YOU AND YOU PRACTICALLY BEGGED ME, SO DON'T PUSH YOUR LUCK ANY FURTHER.
RELAAAX, JUST TRYING TO PASS THE TIME. BEEN ON THE SAINT FOR YEARS. COULD BE HOURS BEFORE WE SEE ANYTHING.

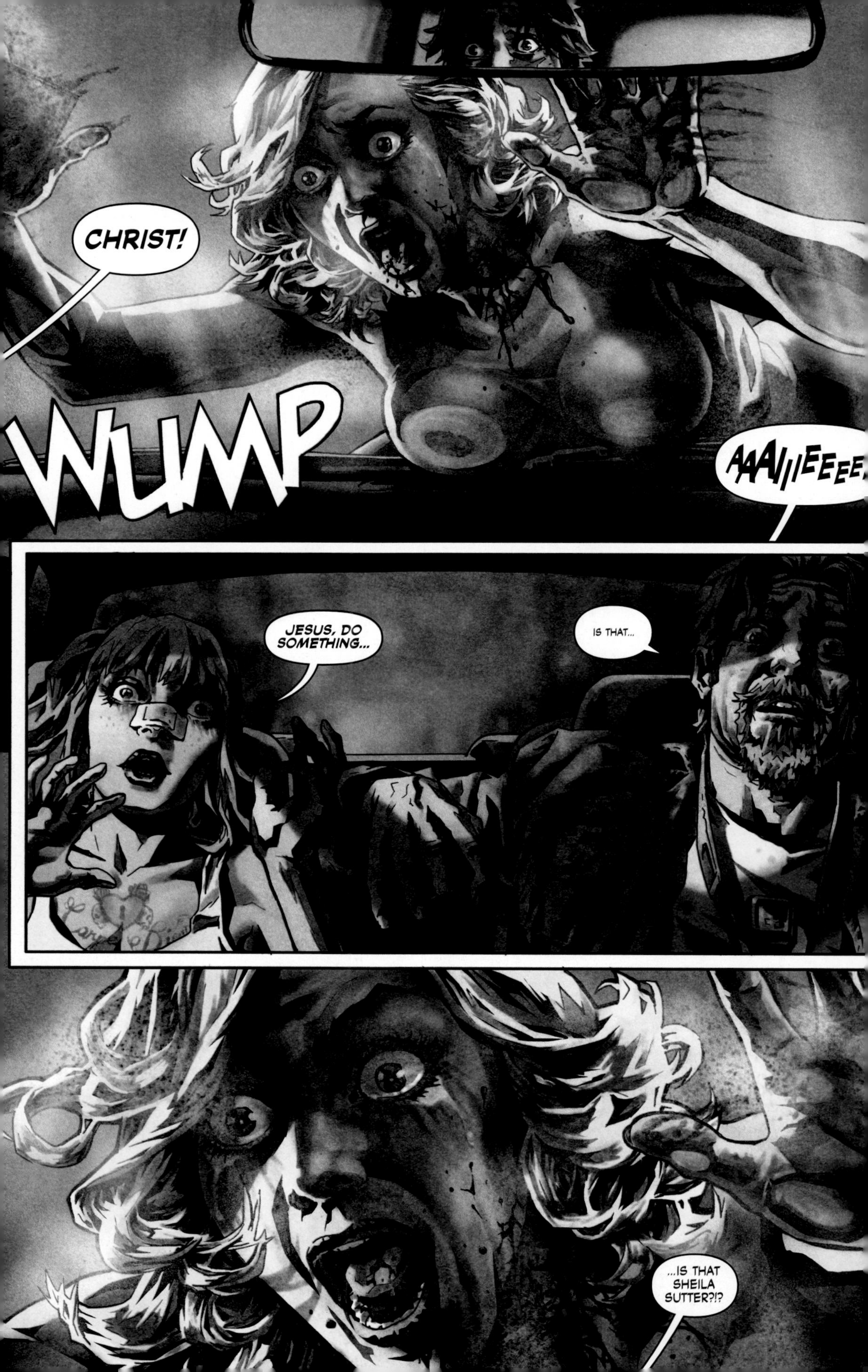
CHRIST!
WUMP
AAAIIIIEEEE
JESUS, DO SOMETHING...
IS THAT...
...IS THAT SHEILA SUTTER?!?

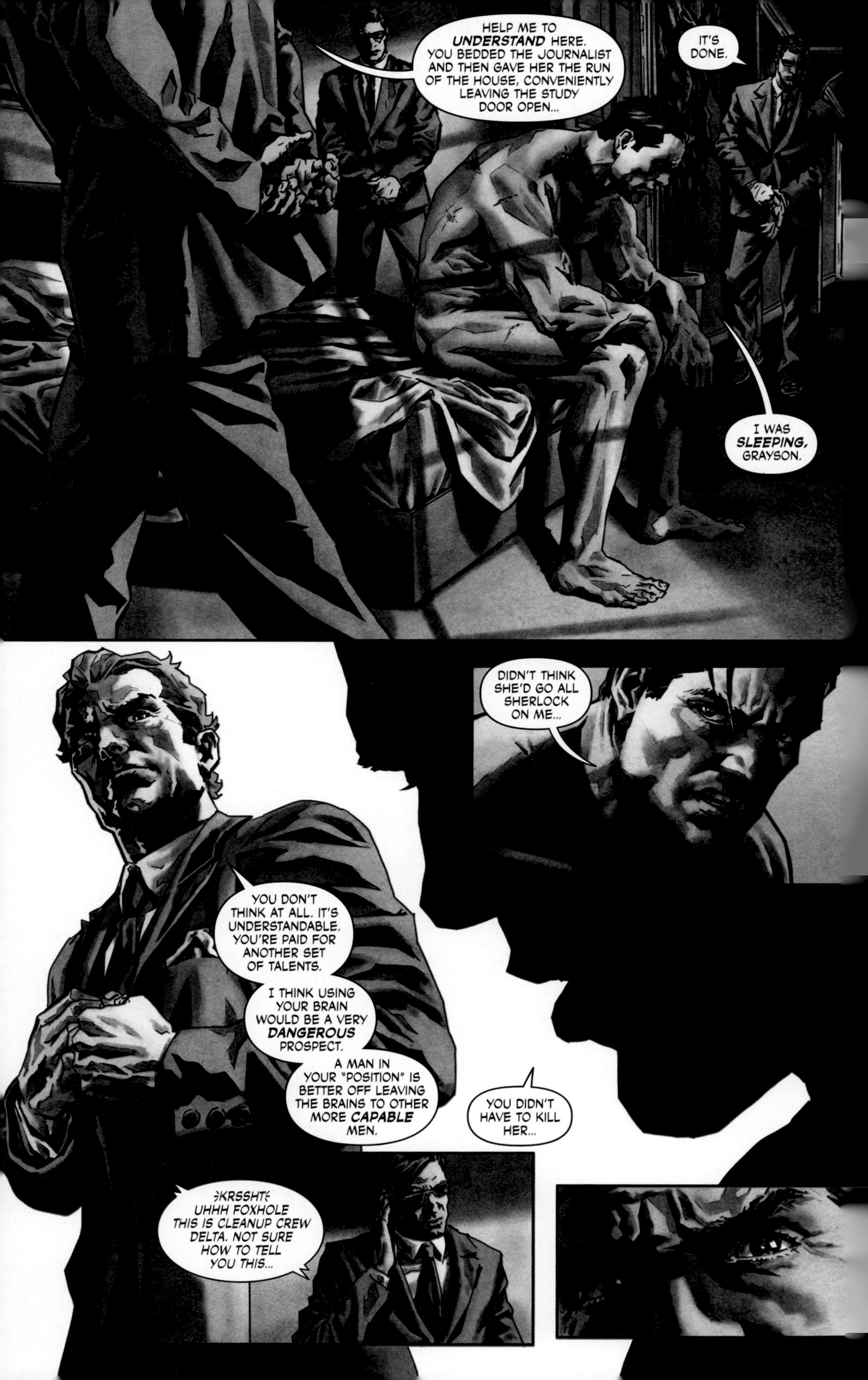
HELP ME TO UNDERSTAND HERE. YOU BEDDED THE JOURNALIST AND THEN GAVE HER THE RUN OF THE HOUSE, CONVENIENTLY LEAVING THE STUDY DOOR OPEN...
IT'S DONE.
I WAS SLEEPING, GRAYSON.
DIDN'T THINK SHE'D GO ALL SHERLOCK ON ME...
YOU DON'T THINK AT ALL. IT'S UNDERSTANDABLE. YOU'RE PAID FOR ANOTHER SET OF TALENTS.
I THINK USING YOUR BRAIN WOULD BE A VERY DANGEROUS PROSPECT.
A MAN IN YOUR "POSITION" IS BETTER OFF LEAVING THE BRAINS TO OTHER MORE CAPABLE MEN.
YOU DIDN'T HAVE TO KILL HER...
KRSSHT UHHH FOXHOLE THIS IS CLEANUP CREW DELTA. NOT SURE HOW TO TELL YOU THIS...

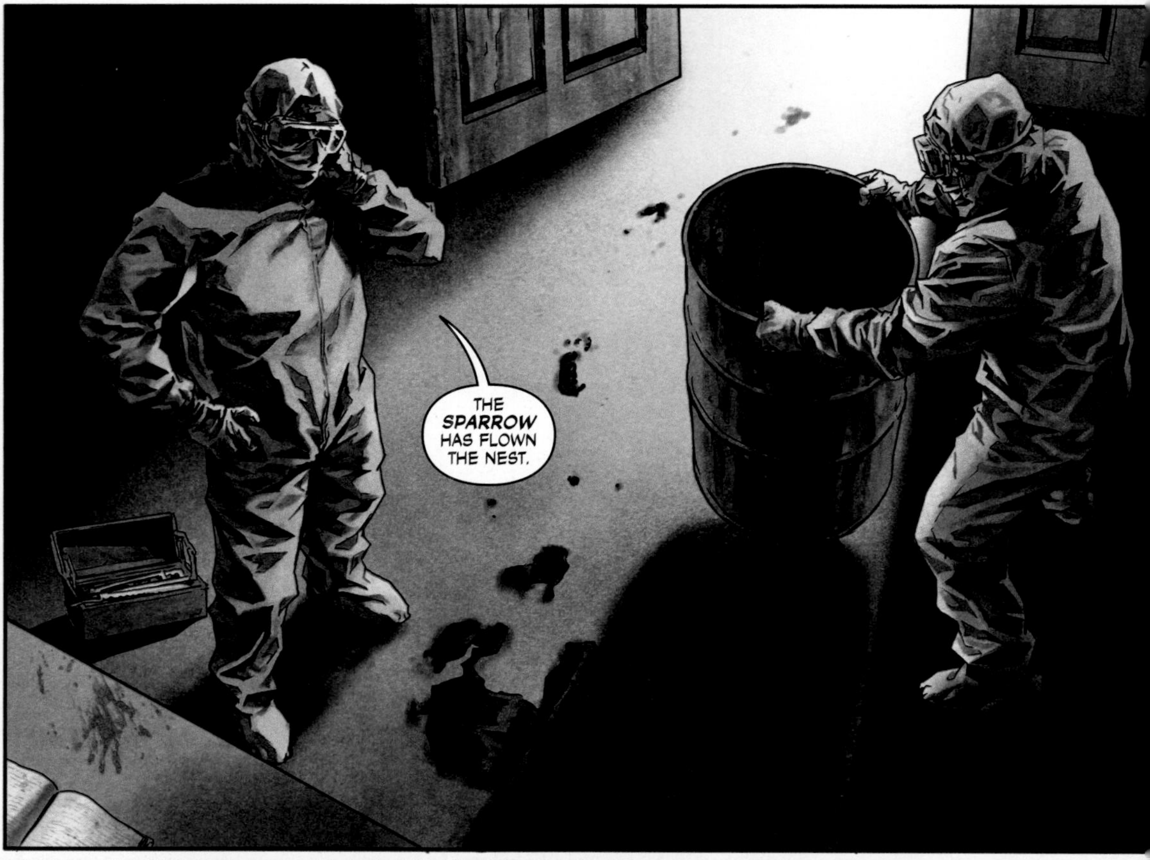
THE SPARROW HAS FLOWN THE NEST.

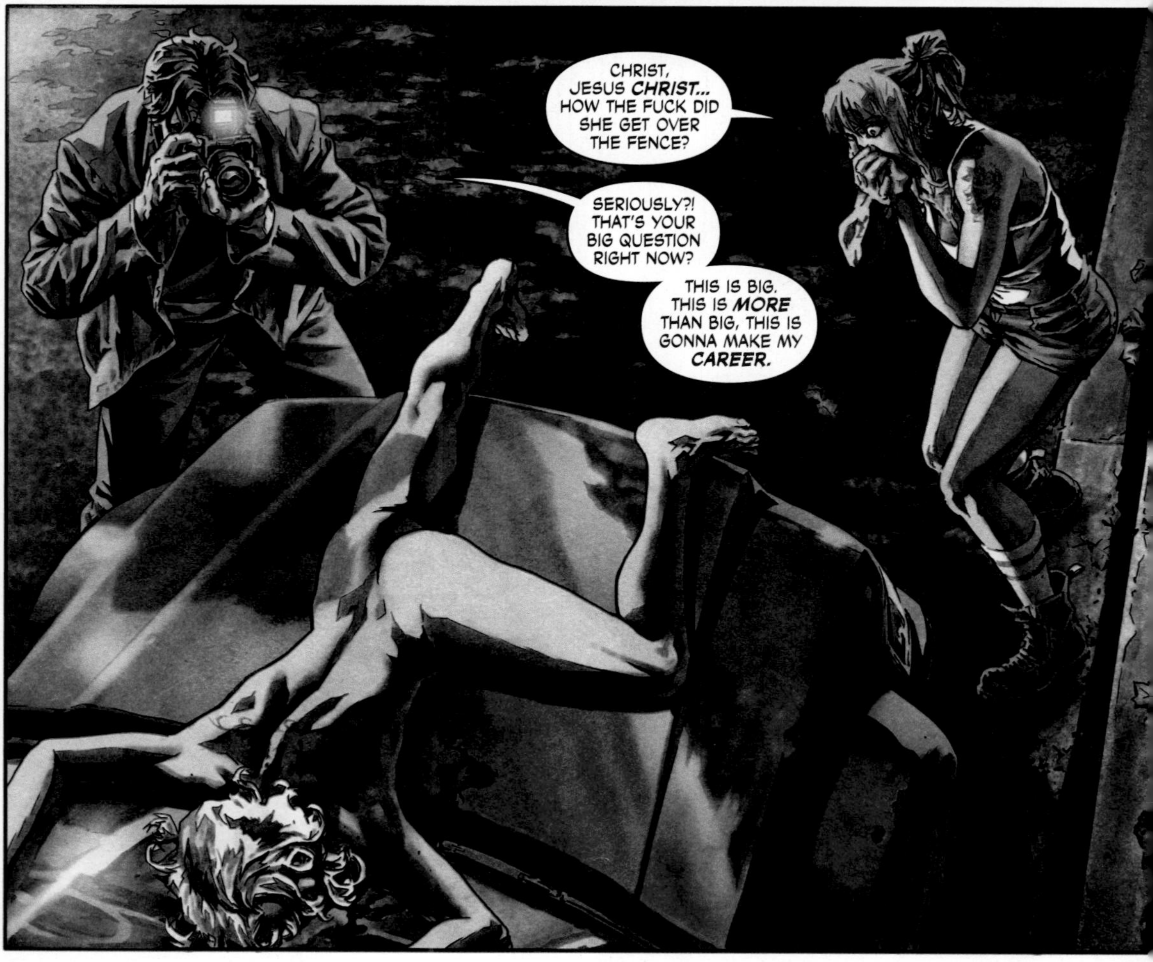
CHRIST, JESUS CHRIST... HOW THE FUCK DID SHE GET OVER THE FENCE?
SERIOUSLY?! THAT'S YOUR BIG QUESTION RIGHT NOW?
THIS IS BIG. THIS IS MORE THAN BIG, THIS IS GONNA MAKE MY CAREER.

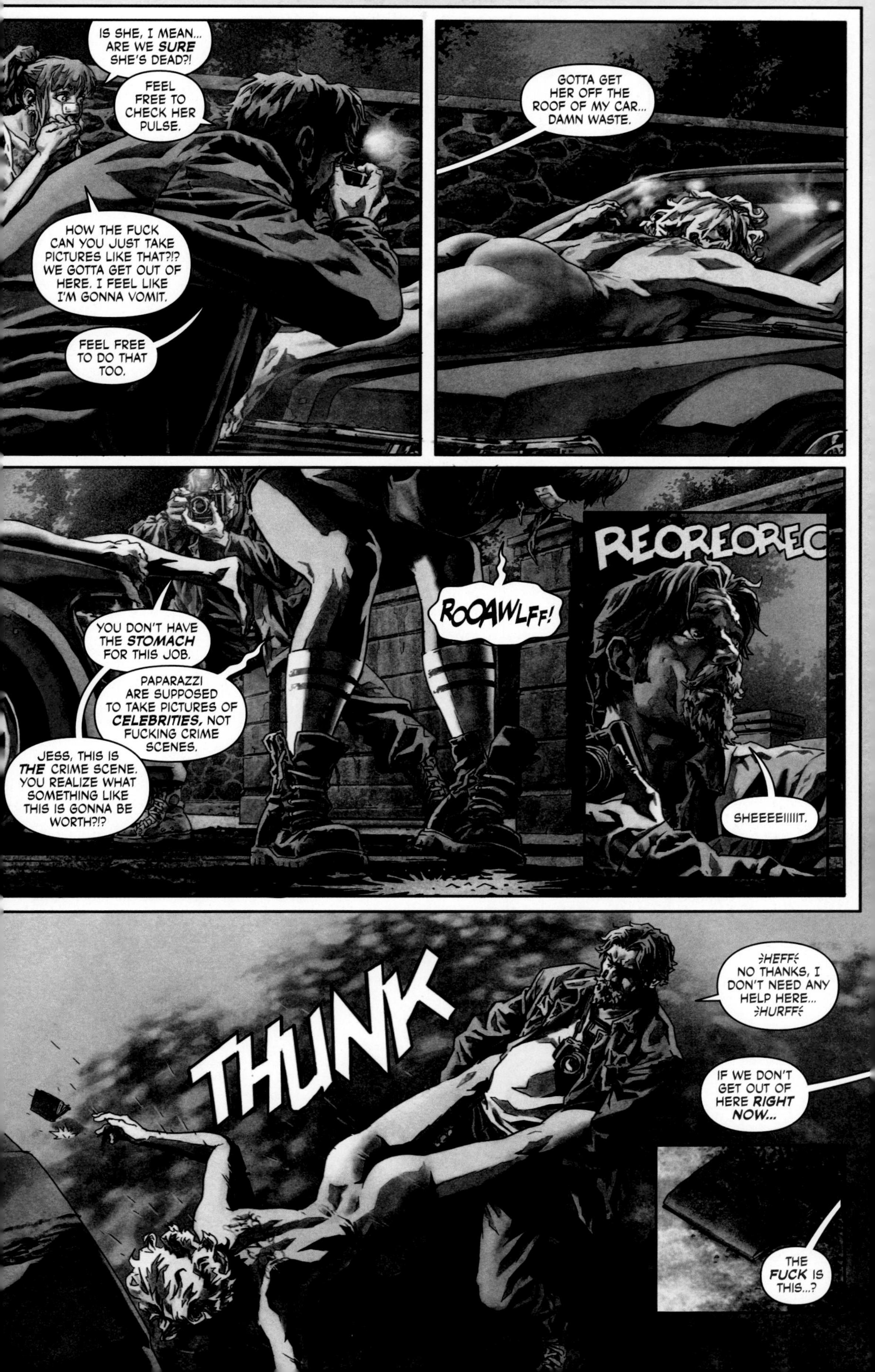
IS SHE, I MEAN... ARE WE SURE SHE'S DEAD?!
FEEL FREE TO CHECK HER PULSE.
HOW THE FUCK CAN YOU JUST TAKE PICTURES LIKE THAT?!? WE GOTTA GET OUT OF HERE. I FEEL LIKE I'M GONNA VOMIT.
FEEL FREE TO DO THAT TOO.
GOTTA GET HER OFF THE ROOF OF MY CAR... DAMN WASTE.
ROOAWLFF!
YOU DON'T HAVE THE STOMACH FOR THIS JOB.
PAPARAZZI ARE SUPPOSED TO TAKE PICTURES OF CELEBRITIES, NOT FUCKING CRIME SCENES.
JESS, THIS IS THE CRIME SCENE. YOU REALIZE WHAT SOMETHING LIKE THIS IS GONNA BE WORTH?!?
REORREOREC
SHEEEEIIIIIT.
THUNK
HEFF
NO THANKS, I DON'T NEED ANY HELP HERE...
HURFF
IF WE DON'T GET OUT OF HERE RIGHT NOW...
THE FUCK IS THIS...?

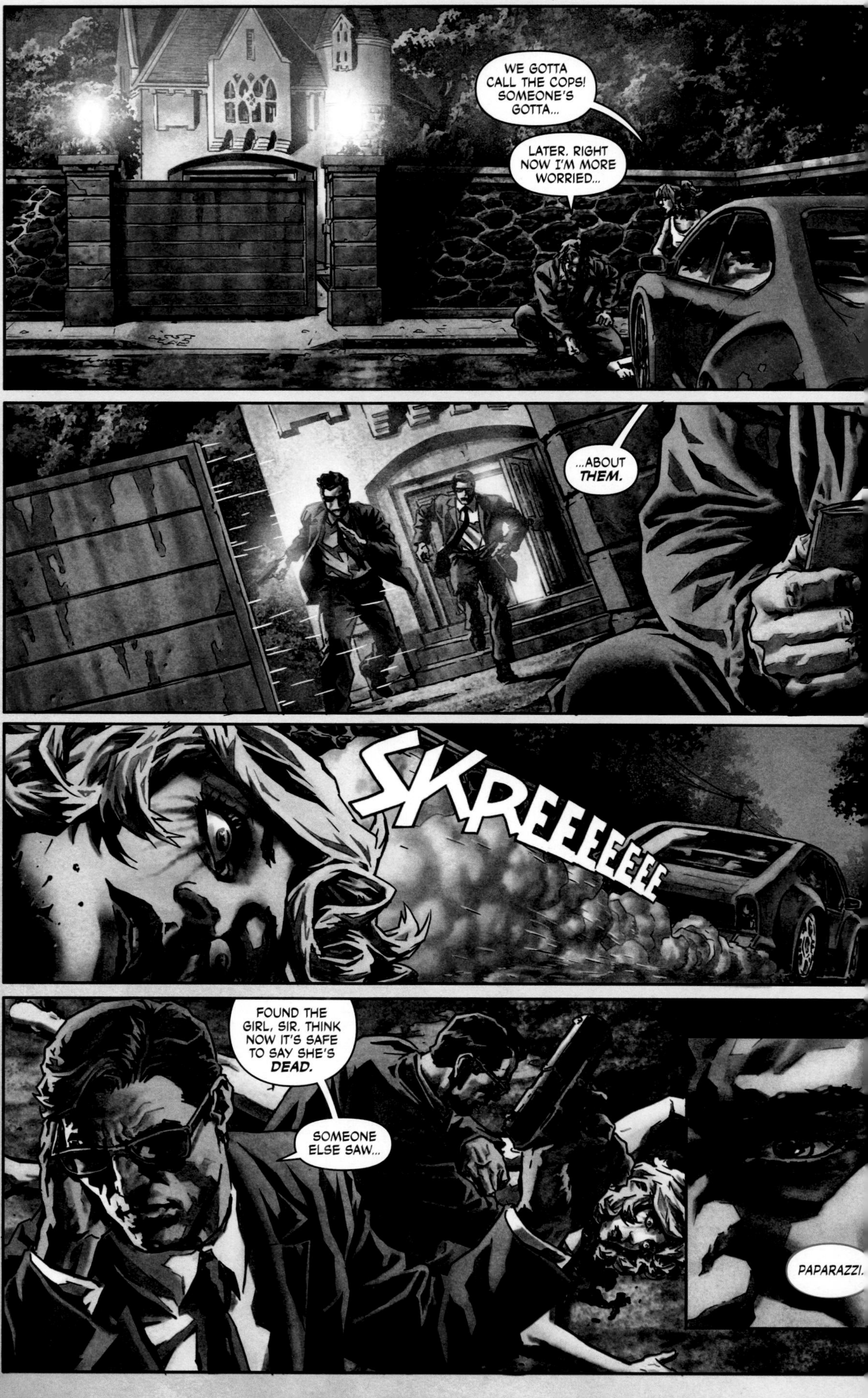
WE GOTTA CALL THE COPS! SOMEONE'S GOTTA...
LATER. RIGHT NOW I'M MORE WORRIED...
...ABOUT *THEM.*
SKREEEEEEE
FOUND THE GIRL, SIR. THINK NOW IT'S SAFE TO SAY SHE'S *DEAD.*
SOMEONE ELSE SAW...
PAPARAZZI.

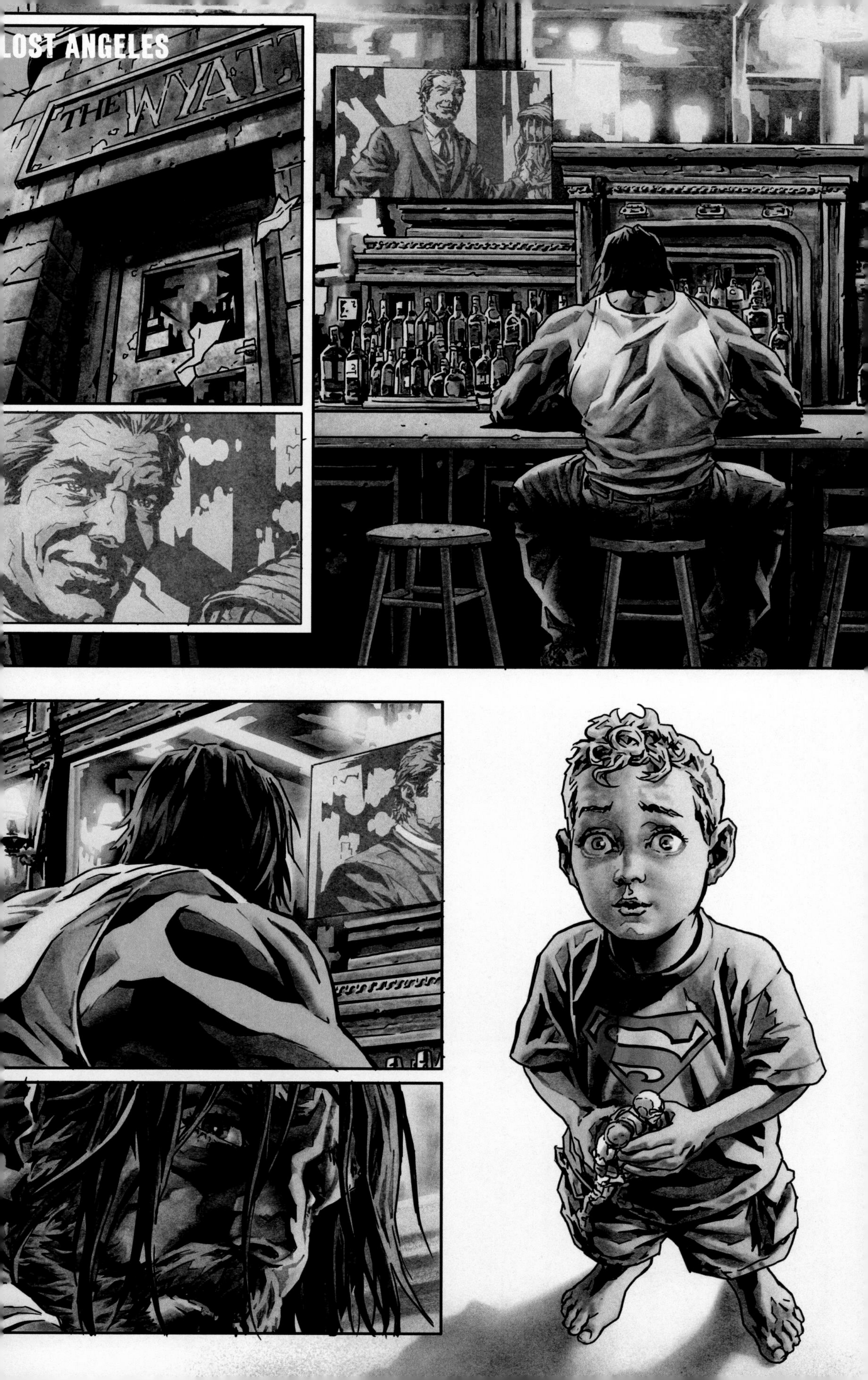
THE WYAT

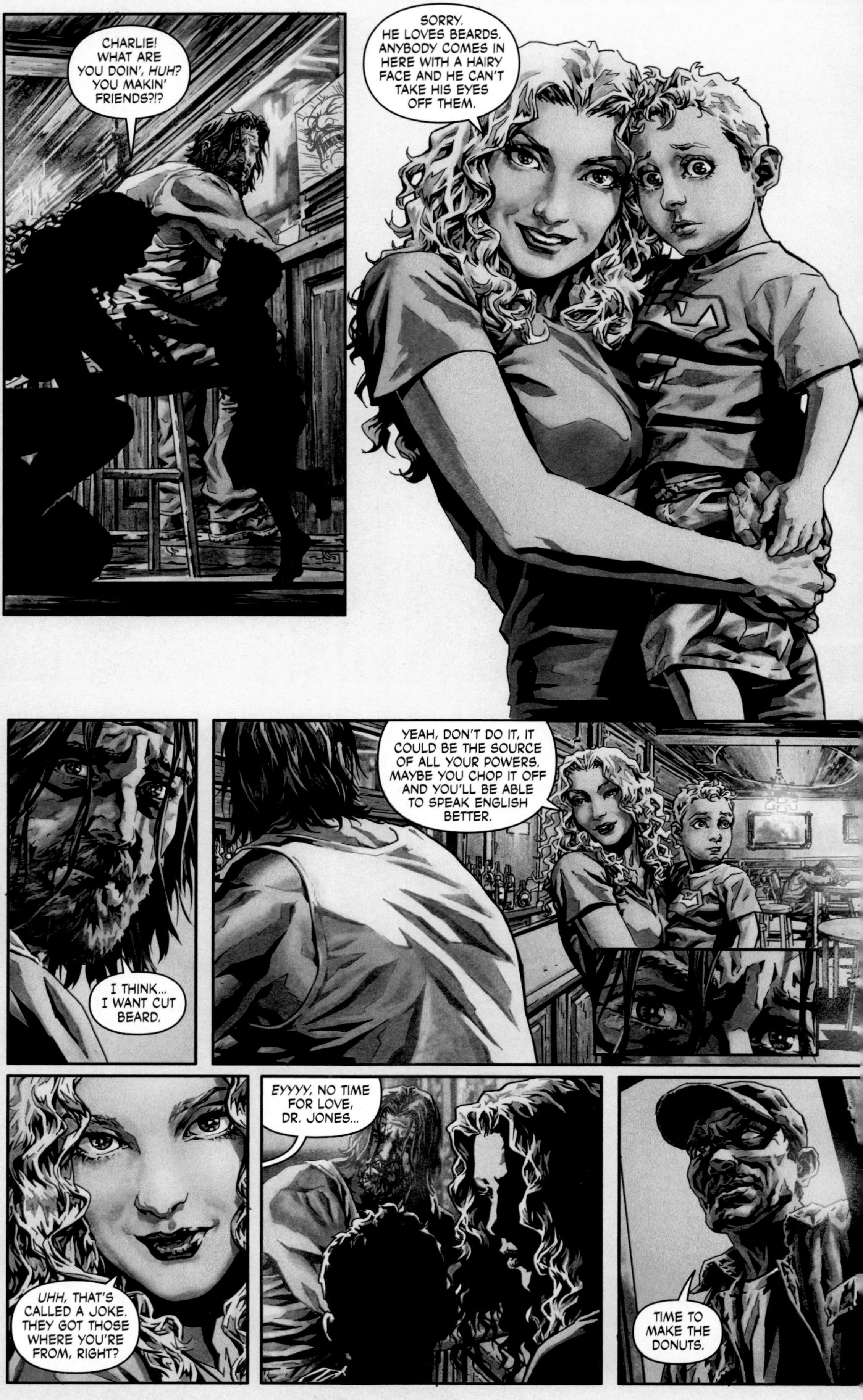
CHARLIE! WHAT ARE YOU DOIN', *HUH*? YOU MAKIN' FRIENDS?!?
SORRY. HE LOVES BEARDS. ANYBODY COMES IN HERE WITH A HAIRY FACE AND HE CAN'T TAKE HIS EYES OFF THEM.
I THINK... I WANT CUT BEARD.
YEAH, DON'T DO IT, IT COULD BE THE SOURCE OF ALL YOUR POWERS. MAYBE YOU CHOP IT OFF AND YOU'LL BE ABLE TO SPEAK ENGLISH BETTER.
UHH, THAT'S CALLED A JOKE. THEY GOT THOSE WHERE YOU'RE FROM, RIGHT?
EYYYY, NO TIME FOR LOVE, DR. JONES...
TIME TO MAKE THE DONUTS.

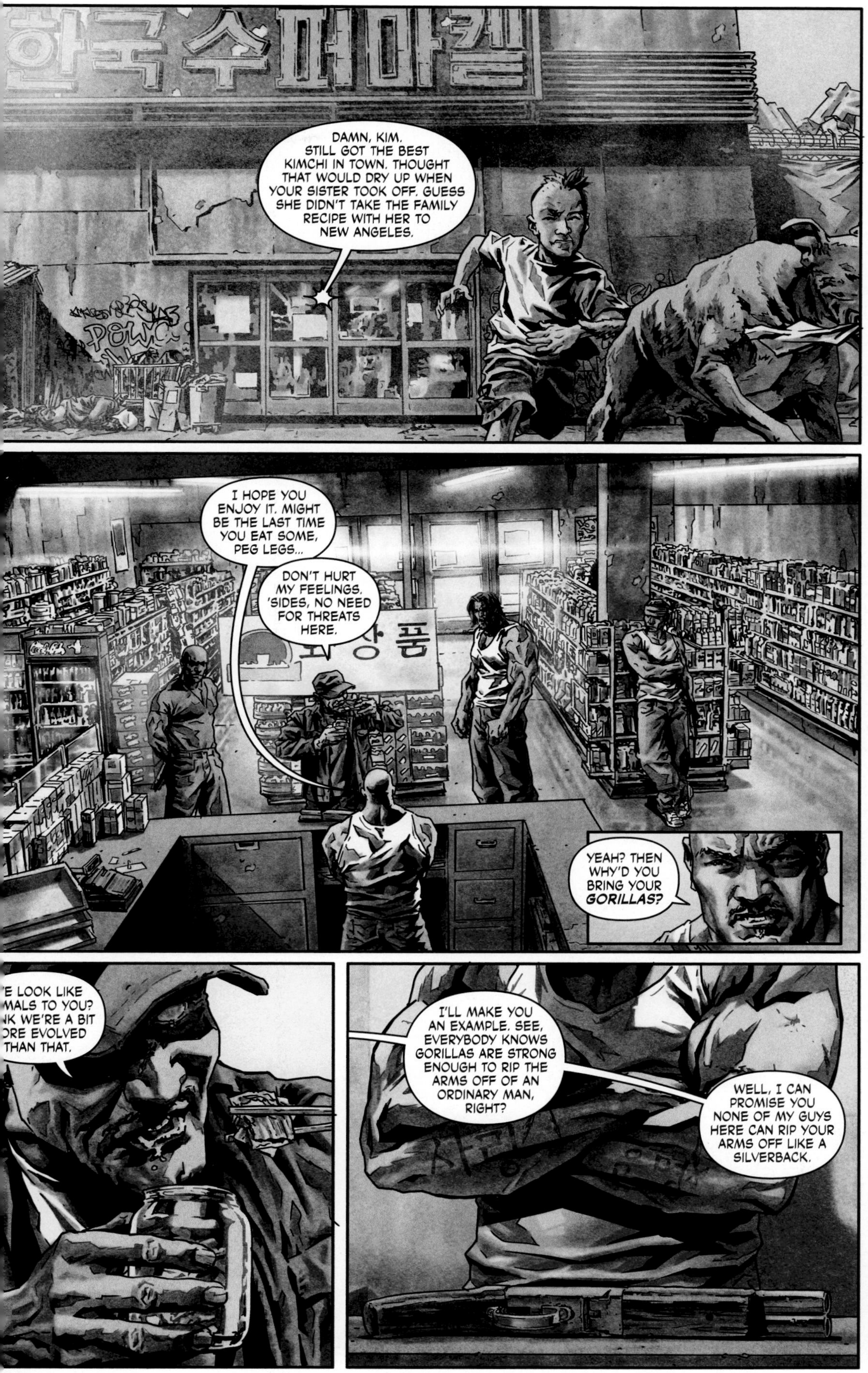
DAMN, KIM. STILL GOT THE BEST KIMCHI IN TOWN. THOUGHT THAT WOULD DRY UP WHEN YOUR SISTER TOOK OFF. GUESS SHE DIDN'T TAKE THE FAMILY RECIPE WITH HER TO NEW ANGELES.
I HOPE YOU ENJOY IT. MIGHT BE THE LAST TIME YOU EAT SOME, PEG LEGS...
DON'T HURT MY FEELINGS. 'SIDES, NO NEED FOR THREATS HERE.
YEAH? THEN WHY'D YOU BRING YOUR GORILLAS?
'E LOOK LIKE MALS TO YOU? NK WE'RE A BIT ORE EVOLVED THAN THAT.
I'LL MAKE YOU AN EXAMPLE. SEE, EVERYBODY KNOWS GORILLAS ARE STRONG ENOUGH TO RIP THE ARMS OFF OF AN ORDINARY MAN, RIGHT?
WELL, I CAN PROMISE YOU NONE OF MY GUYS HERE CAN RIP YOUR ARMS OFF LIKE A SILVERBACK.

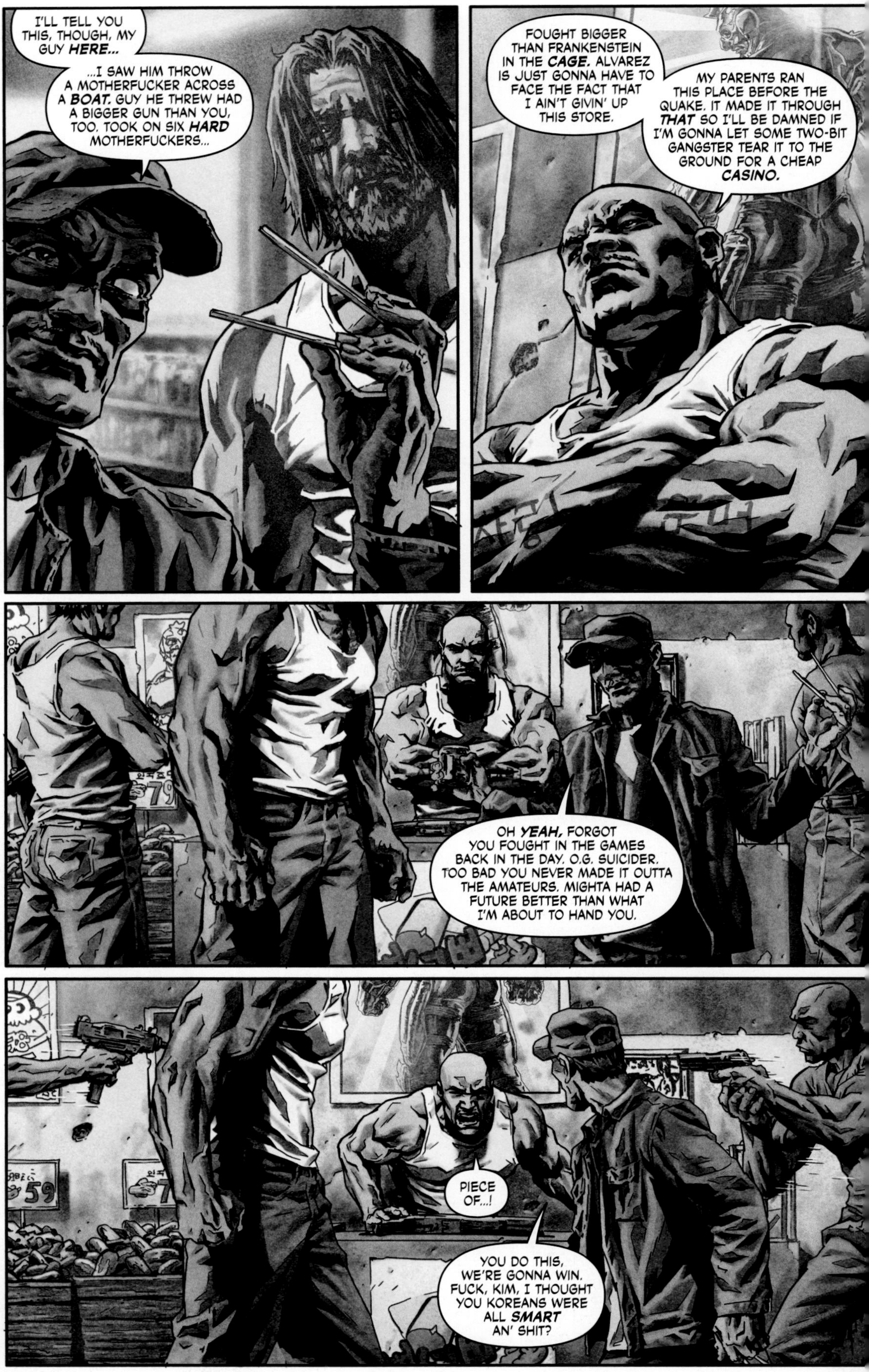
I'LL TELL YOU THIS, THOUGH, MY GUY HERE...
...I SAW HIM THROW A MOTHERFUCKER ACROSS A BOAT. GUY HE THREW HAD A BIGGER GUN THAN YOU, TOO. TOOK ON SIX HARD MOTHERFUCKERS...
FOUGHT BIGGER THAN FRANKENSTEIN IN THE CAGE. ALVAREZ IS JUST GONNA HAVE TO FACE THE FACT THAT I AIN'T GIVIN' UP THIS STORE.
MY PARENTS RAN THIS PLACE BEFORE THE QUAKE. IT MADE IT THROUGH THAT SO I'LL BE DAMNED IF I'M GONNA LET SOME TWO-BIT GANGSTER TEAR IT TO THE GROUND FOR A CHEAP CASINO.
OH YEAH, FORGOT YOU FOUGHT IN THE GAMES BACK IN THE DAY. O.G. SUICIDER. TOO BAD YOU NEVER MADE IT OUTTA THE AMATEURS. MIGHTA HAD A FUTURE BETTER THAN WHAT I'M ABOUT TO HAND YOU.
PIECE OF...!
YOU DO THIS, WE'RE GONNA WIN. FUCK, KIM, I THOUGHT YOU KOREANS WERE ALL SMART AN' SHIT?

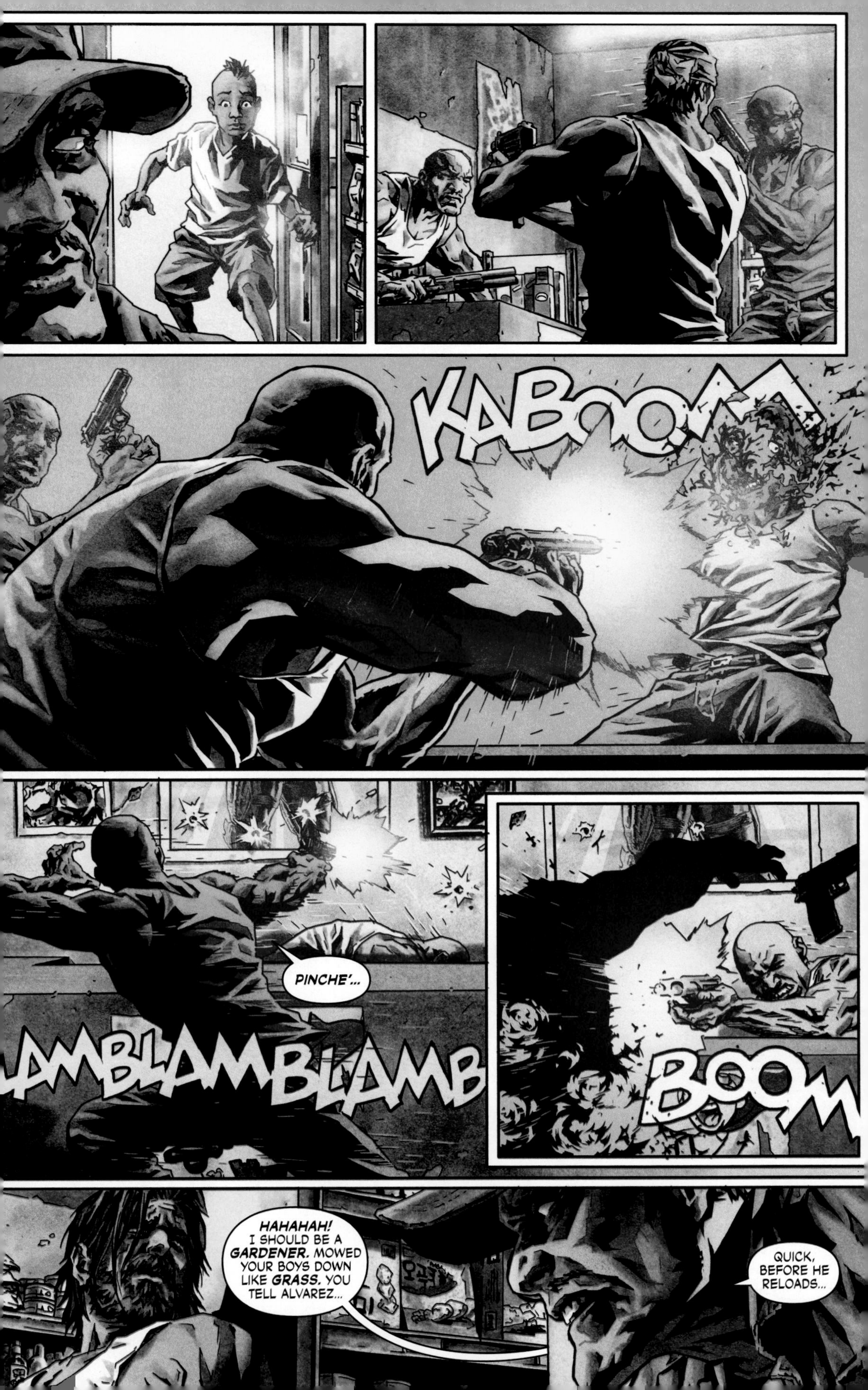
KABOOM
PINCHE'...
AMBLAMBLAMB
BOOM
HAHAHAH! I SHOULD BE A GARDENER. MOWED YOUR BOYS DOWN LIKE GRASS. YOU TELL ALVAREZ...
QUICK, BEFORE HE RELOADS...

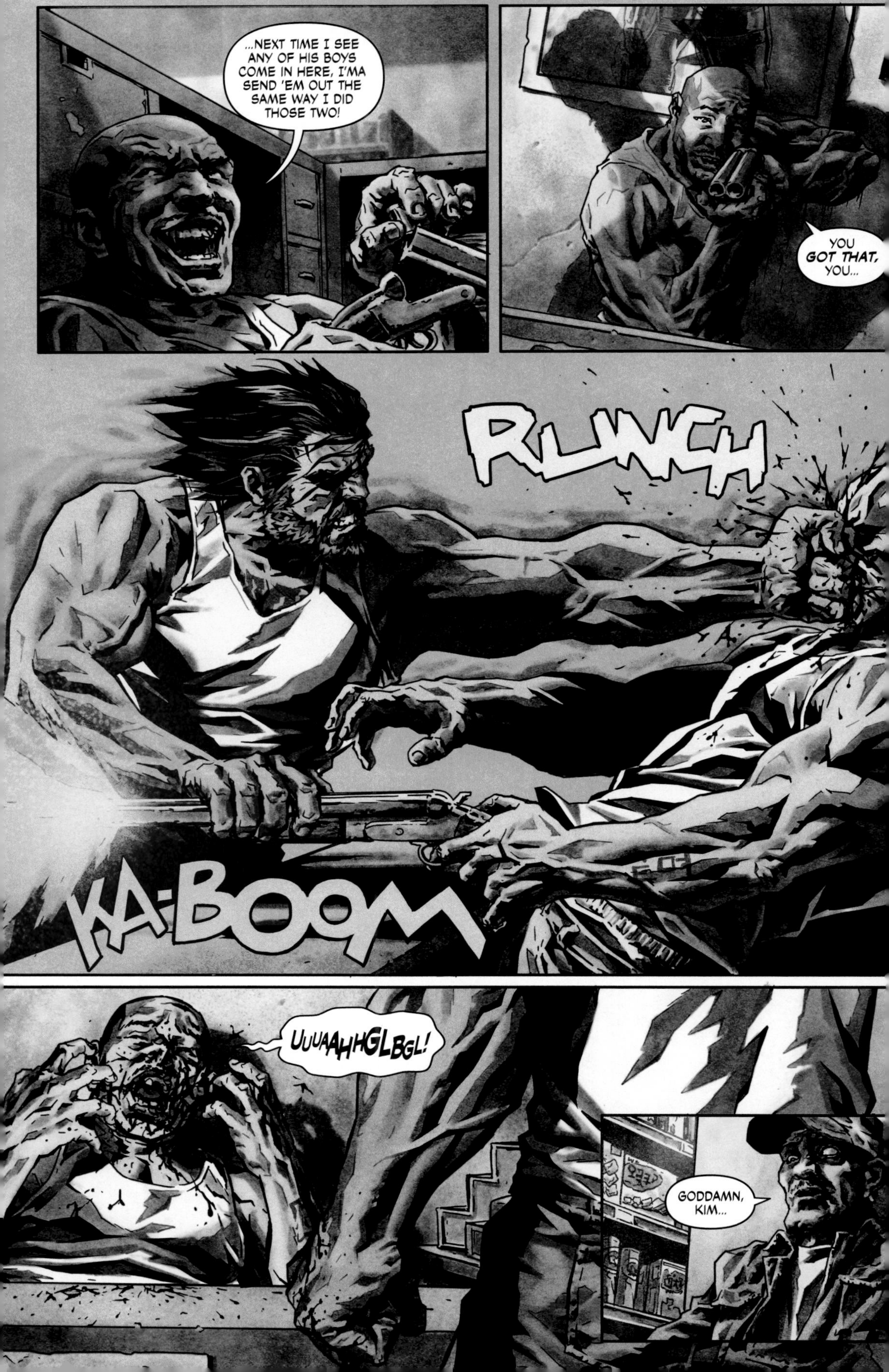
...NEXT TIME I SEE ANY OF HIS BOYS COME IN HERE, I'MA SEND 'EM OUT THE SAME WAY I DID THOSE TWO!
YOU GOT THAT, YOU...
RUNCH
KA-BOOM
UUUAAHHGLBGL!
GODDAMN, KIM...

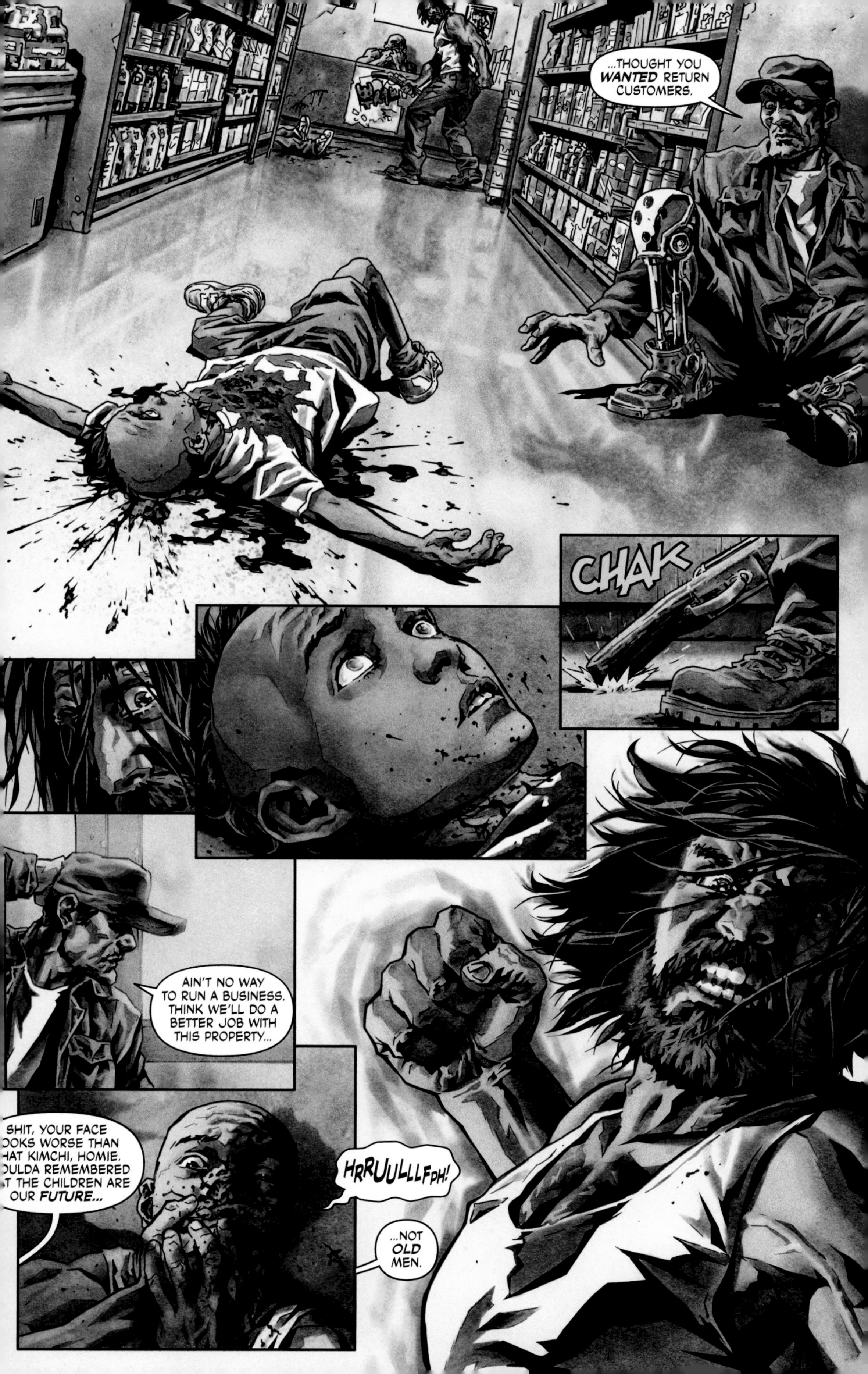
...THOUGHT YOU WANTED RETURN CUSTOMERS.
CHAK
AIN'T NO WAY TO RUN A BUSINESS. THINK WE'LL DO A BETTER JOB WITH THIS PROPERTY...
SHIT, YOUR FACE OOKS WORSE THAN HAT KIMCHI, HOMIE. OULDA REMEMBERED T THE CHILDREN ARE OUR FUTURE...
HRRUUULLLFPH!
...NOT OLD MEN.

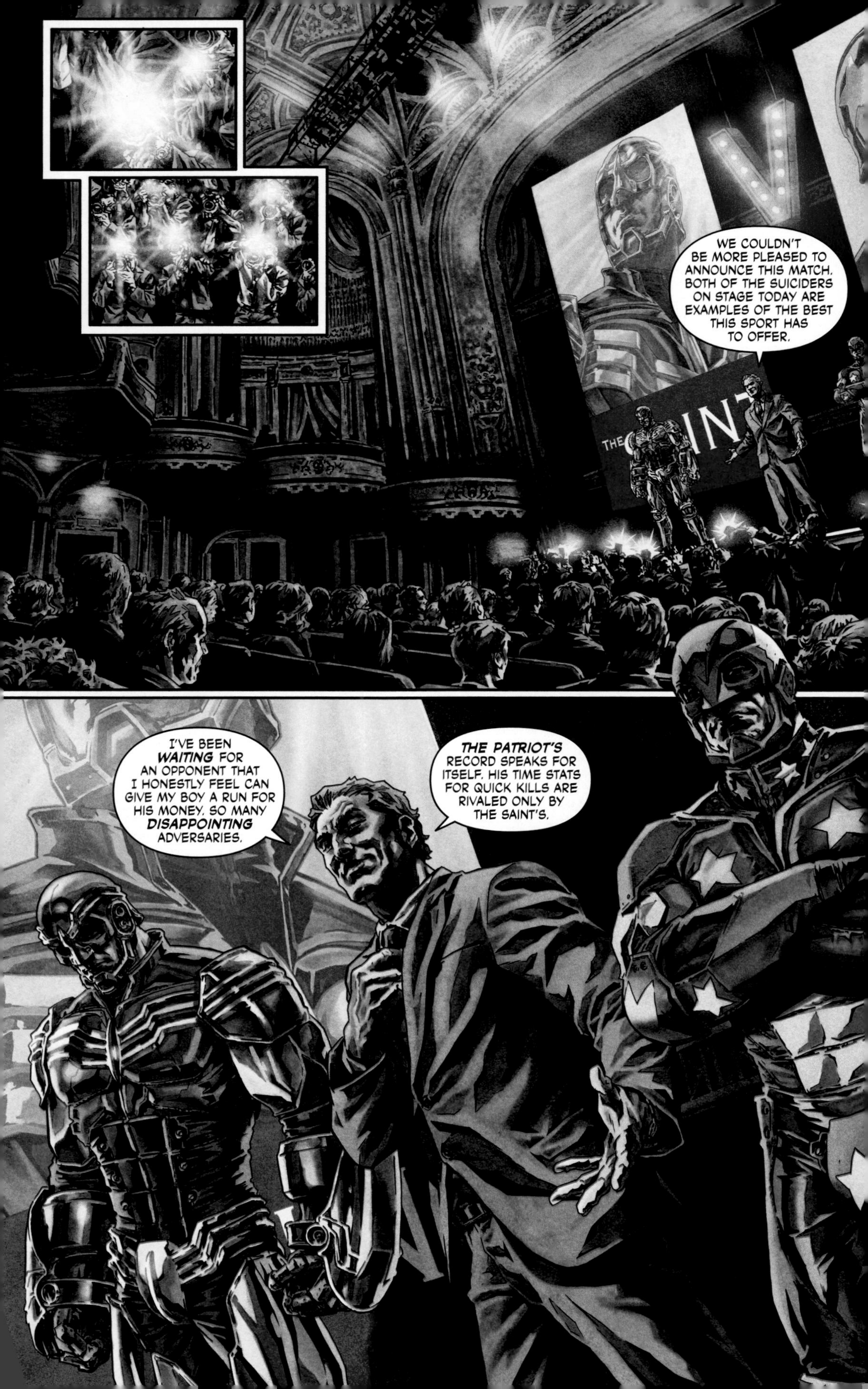
WE COULDN'T BE MORE PLEASED TO ANNOUNCE THIS MATCH. BOTH OF THE SUICIDERS ON STAGE TODAY ARE EXAMPLES OF THE BEST THIS SPORT HAS TO OFFER.
THE
I'VE BEEN *WAITING* FOR AN OPPONENT THAT I HONESTLY FEEL CAN GIVE MY BOY A RUN FOR HIS MONEY. SO MANY *DISAPPOINTING* ADVERSARIES.
THE PATRIOT'S RECORD SPEAKS FOR ITSELF. HIS TIME STATS FOR QUICK KILLS ARE RIVALED ONLY BY THE SAINT'S.

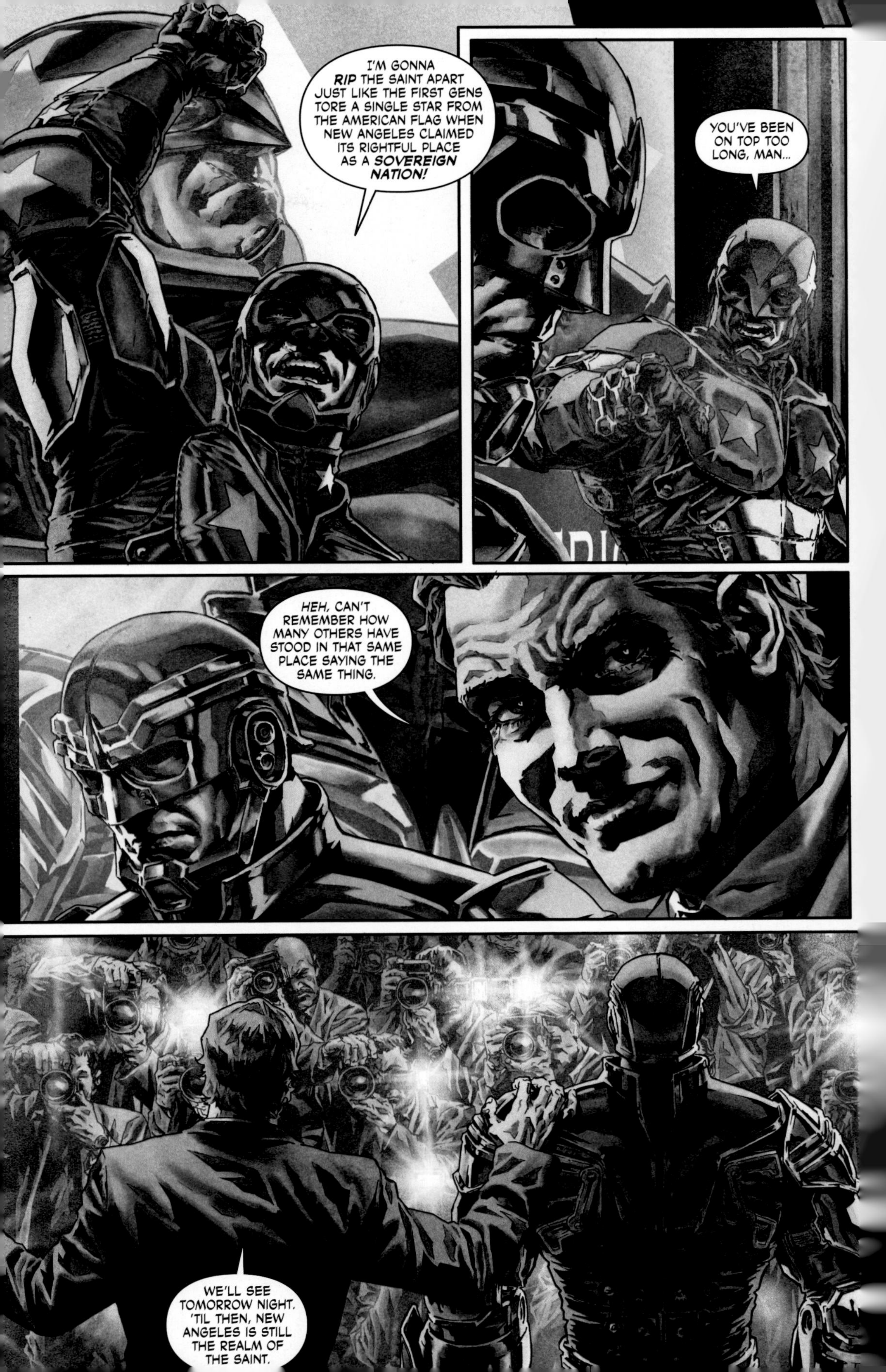
I'M GONNA RIP THE SAINT APART JUST LIKE THE FIRST GENS TORE A SINGLE STAR FROM THE AMERICAN FLAG WHEN NEW ANGELES CLAIMED ITS RIGHTFUL PLACE AS A SOVEREIGN NATION!
YOU'VE BEEN ON TOP TOO LONG, MAN...
HEH, CAN'T REMEMBER HOW MANY OTHERS HAVE STOOD IN THAT SAME PLACE SAYING THE SAME THING.
WE'LL SEE TOMORROW NIGHT. 'TIL THEN, NEW ANGELES IS STILL THE REALM OF THE SAINT.

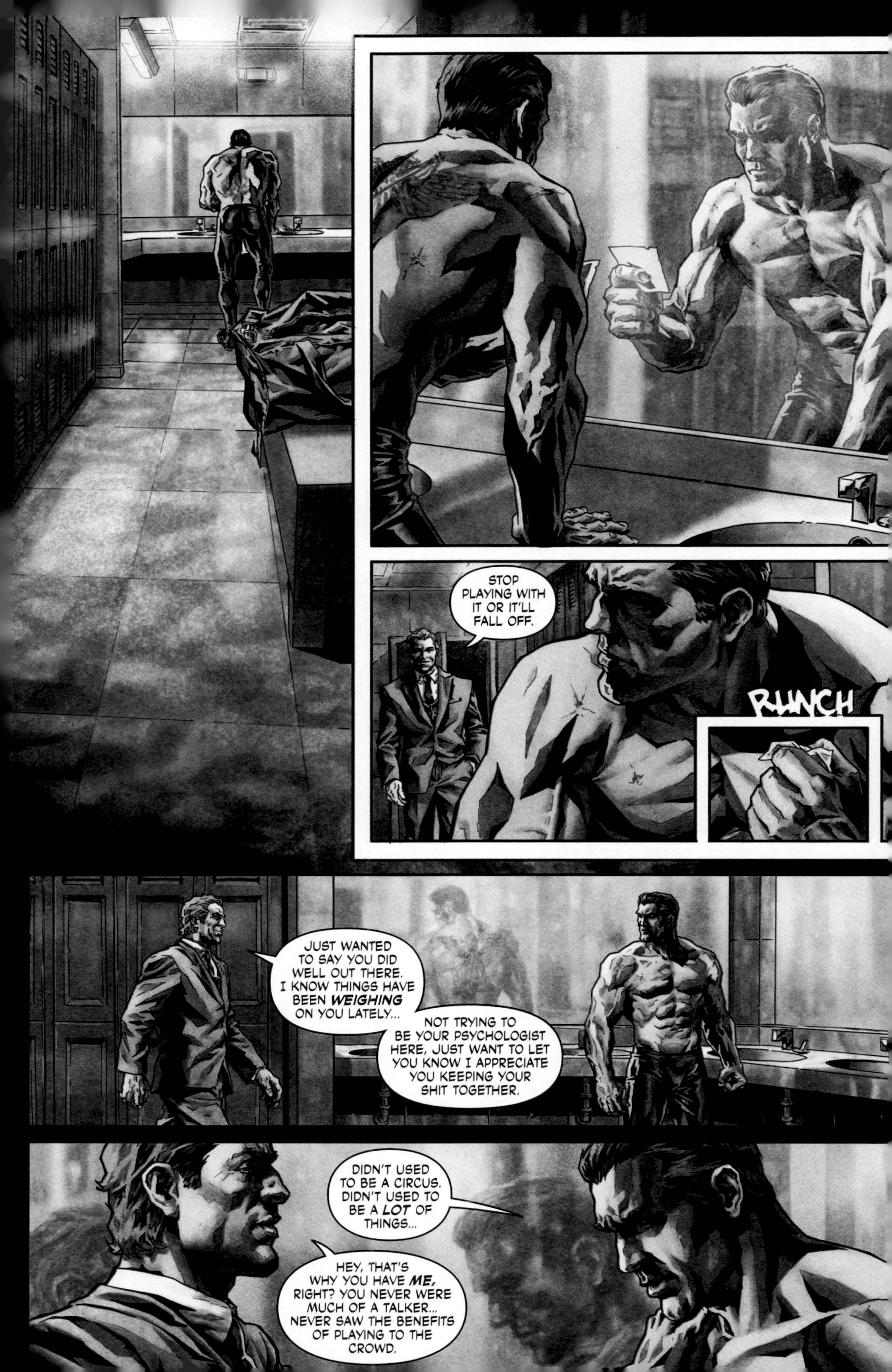
STOP PLAYING WITH IT OR IT'LL FALL OFF.
RUNCH
JUST WANTED TO SAY YOU DID WELL OUT THERE. I KNOW THINGS HAVE BEEN *WEIGHING* ON YOU LATELY...
NOT TRYING TO BE YOUR PSYCHOLOGIST HERE, JUST WANT TO LET YOU KNOW I APPRECIATE YOU KEEPING YOUR SHIT TOGETHER.
DIDN'T USED TO BE A CIRCUS. DIDN'T USED TO BE A *LOT* OF THINGS...
HEY, THAT'S WHY YOU HAVE *ME,* RIGHT? YOU NEVER WERE MUCH OF A TALKER... NEVER SAW THE BENEFITS OF PLAYING TO THE CROWD.

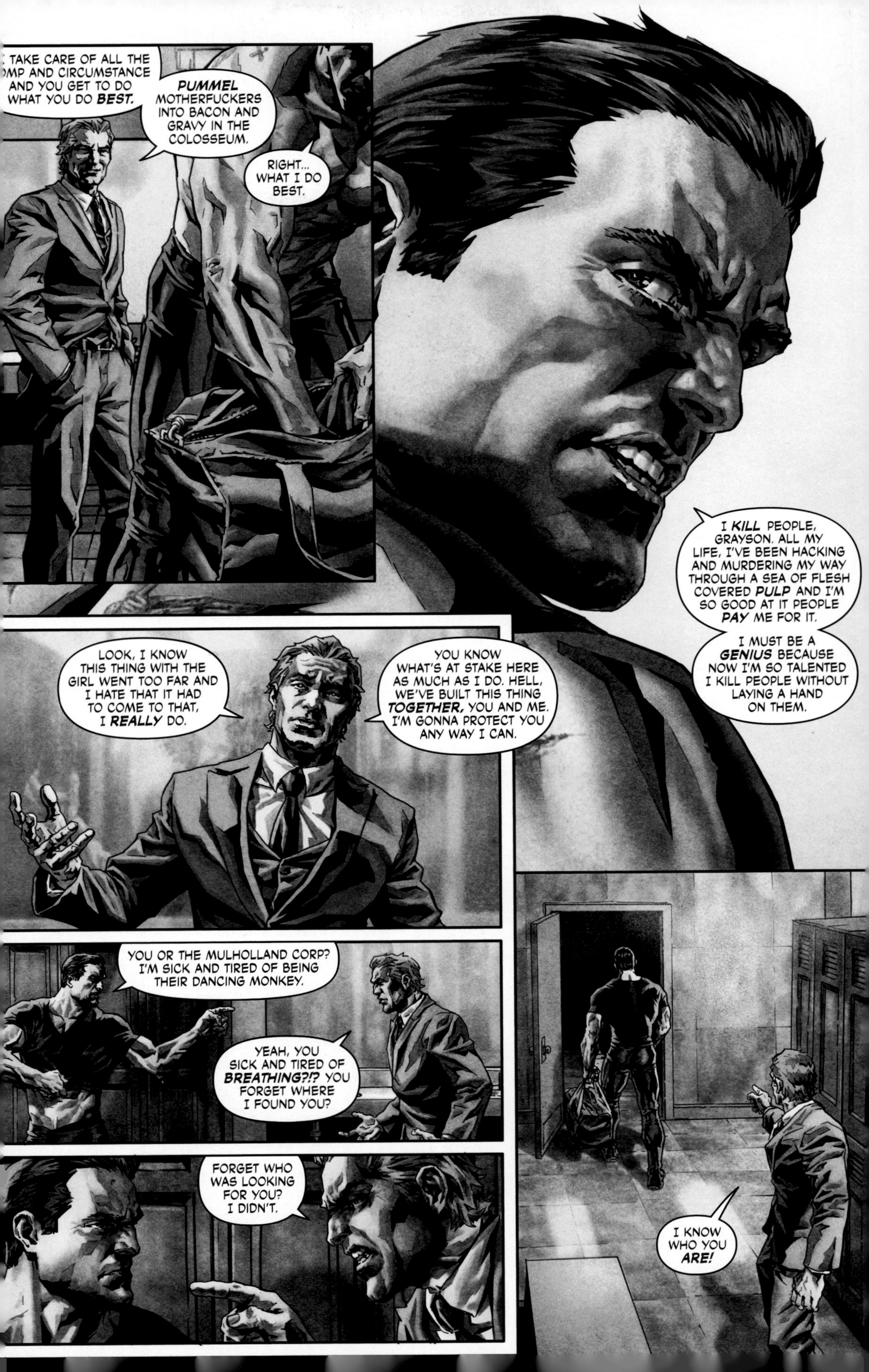

TAKE CARE OF ALL THE
OMP AND CIRCUMSTANCE
AND YOU GET TO DO
WHAT YOU DO BEST.
PUMMEL MOTHERFUCKERS INTO BACON AND GRAVY IN THE COLOSSEUM.
RIGHT... WHAT I DO BEST.
I KILL PEOPLE, GRAYSON. ALL MY LIFE, I'VE BEEN HACKING AND MURDERING MY WAY THROUGH A SEA OF FLESH COVERED PULP AND I'M SO GOOD AT IT PEOPLE PAY ME FOR IT.
I MUST BE A GENIUS BECAUSE NOW I'M SO TALENTED I KILL PEOPLE WITHOUT LAYING A HAND ON THEM.
LOOK, I KNOW THIS THING WITH THE GIRL WENT TOO FAR AND I HATE THAT IT HAD TO COME TO THAT, I REALLY DO.
YOU KNOW WHAT'S AT STAKE HERE AS MUCH AS I DO. HELL, WE'VE BUILT THIS THING TOGETHER, YOU AND ME. I'M GONNA PROTECT YOU ANY WAY I CAN.
YOU OR THE MULHOLLAND CORP? I'M SICK AND TIRED OF BEING THEIR DANCING MONKEY.
YEAH, YOU SICK AND TIRED OF BREATHING?!? YOU FORGET WHERE I FOUND YOU?
FORGET WHO WAS LOOKING FOR YOU? I DIDN'T.
I KNOW WHO YOU ARE!

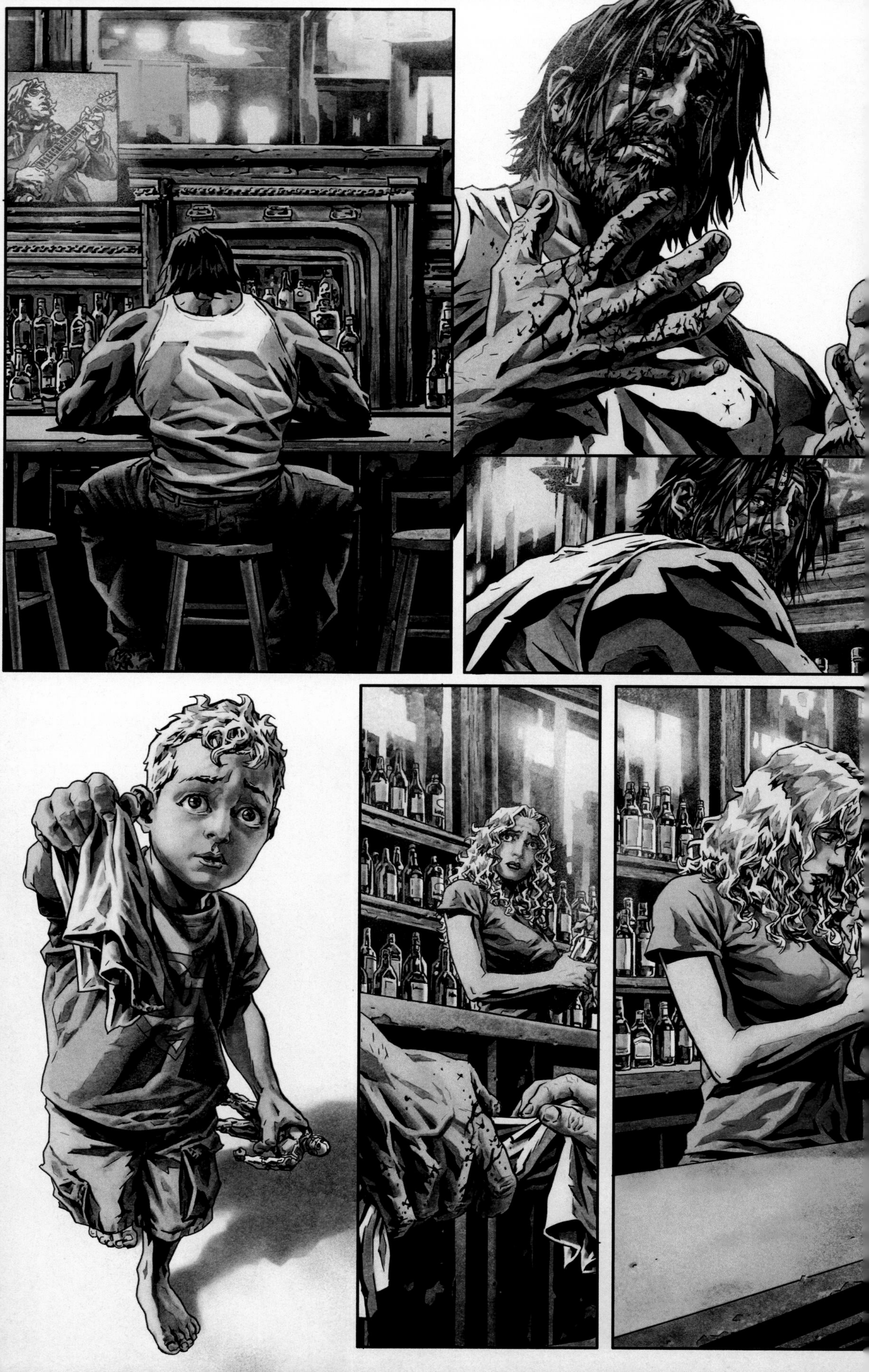

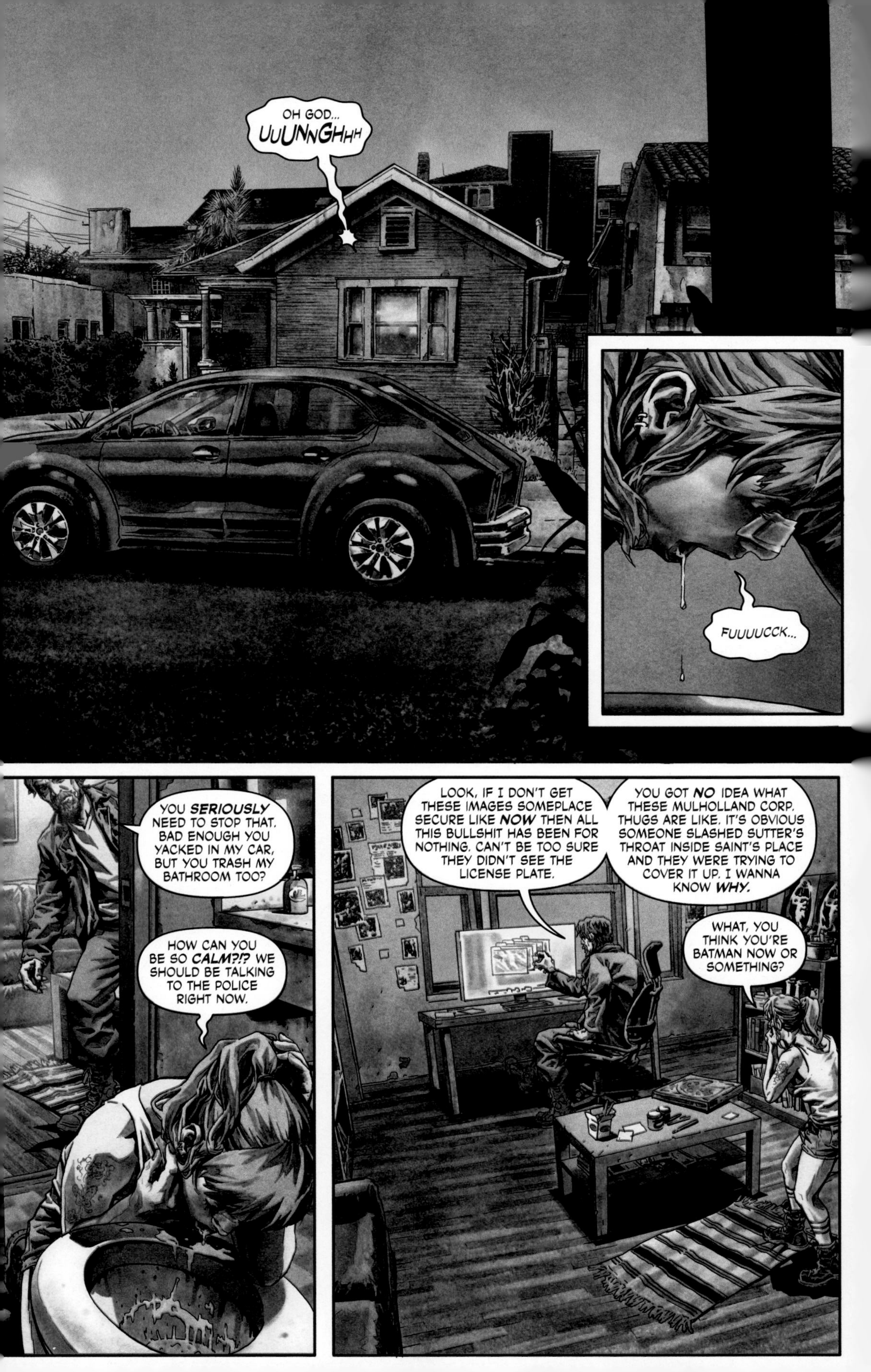
OH GOD... UUUNNGHHH
FUUUUCCK...
YOU SERIOUSLY NEED TO STOP THAT. BAD ENOUGH YOU YACKED IN MY CAR, BUT YOU TRASH MY BATHROOM TOO?
HOW CAN YOU BE SO CALM?!? WE SHOULD BE TALKING TO THE POLICE RIGHT NOW.
LOOK, IF I DON'T GET THESE IMAGES SOMEPLACE SECURE LIKE NOW THEN ALL THIS BULLSHIT HAS BEEN FOR NOTHING. CAN'T BE TOO SURE THEY DIDN'T SEE THE LICENSE PLATE.
YOU GOT NO IDEA WHAT THESE MULHOLLAND CORP. THUGS ARE LIKE. IT'S OBVIOUS SOMEONE SLASHED SUTTER'S THROAT INSIDE SAINT'S PLACE AND THEY WERE TRYING TO COVER IT UP. I WANNA KNOW WHY.
WHAT, YOU THINK YOU'RE BATMAN NOW OR SOMETHING?

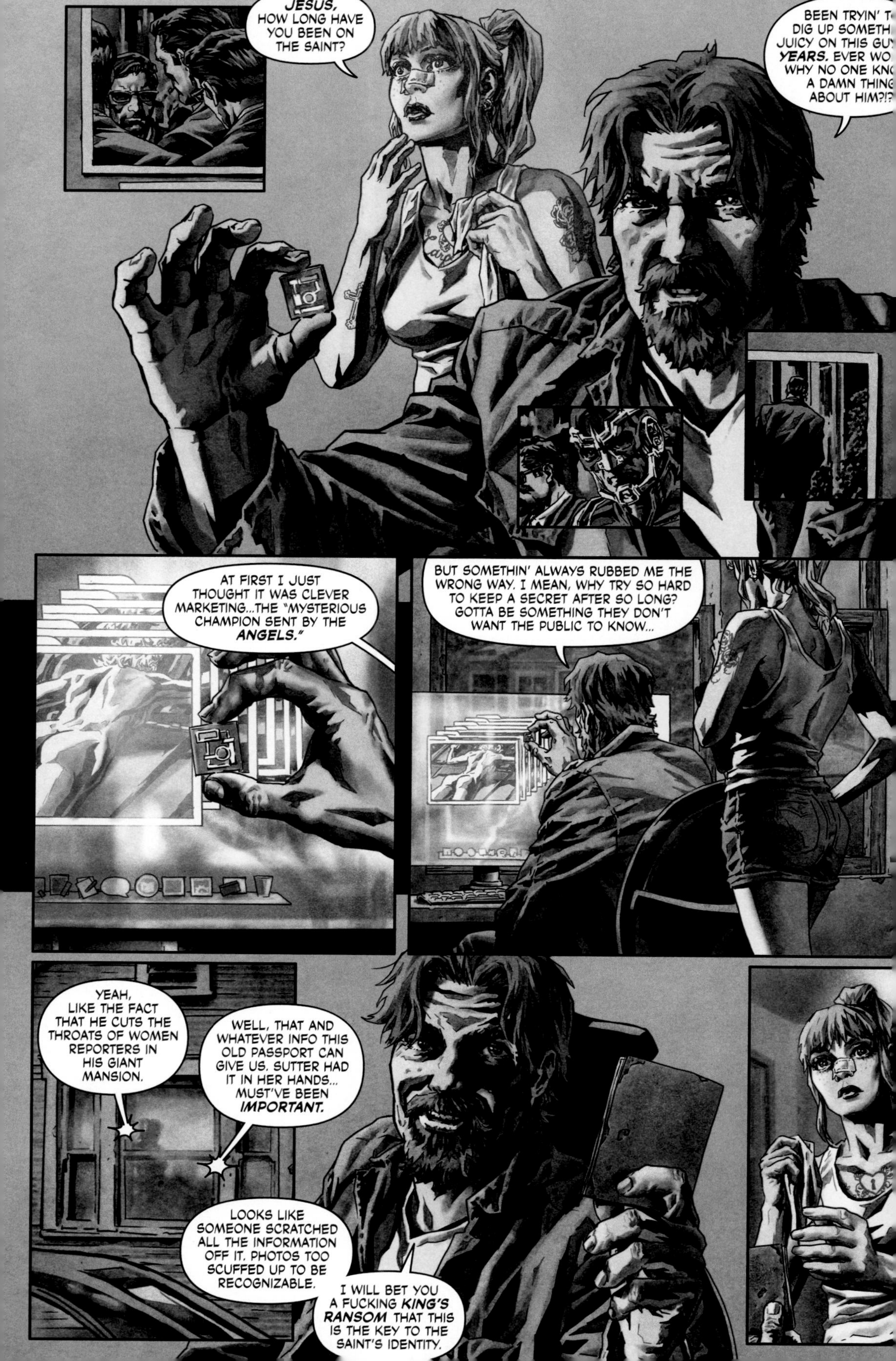
JESUS, HOW LONG HAVE YOU BEEN ON THE SAINT?
BEEN TRYIN' T DIG UP SOMETH JUICY ON THIS GU YEARS. EVER WO WHY NO ONE KN A DAMN THING ABOUT HIM?!?
AT FIRST I JUST THOUGHT IT WAS CLEVER MARKETING...THE "MYSTERIOUS CHAMPION SENT BY THE ANGELS."
BUT SOMETHIN' ALWAYS RUBBED ME THE WRONG WAY. I MEAN, WHY TRY SO HARD TO KEEP A SECRET AFTER SO LONG? GOTTA BE SOMETHING THEY DON'T WANT THE PUBLIC TO KNOW...
YEAH, LIKE THE FACT THAT HE CUTS THE THROATS OF WOMEN REPORTERS IN HIS GIANT MANSION.
WELL, THAT AND WHATEVER INFO THIS OLD PASSPORT CAN GIVE US. SUTTER HAD IT IN HER HANDS... MUST'VE BEEN IMPORTANT.
LOOKS LIKE SOMEONE SCRATCHED ALL THE INFORMATION OFF IT. PHOTOS TOO SCUFFED UP TO BE RECOGNIZABLE.
I WILL BET YOU A FUCKING KING'S RANSOM THAT THIS IS THE KEY TO THE SAINT'S IDENTITY.

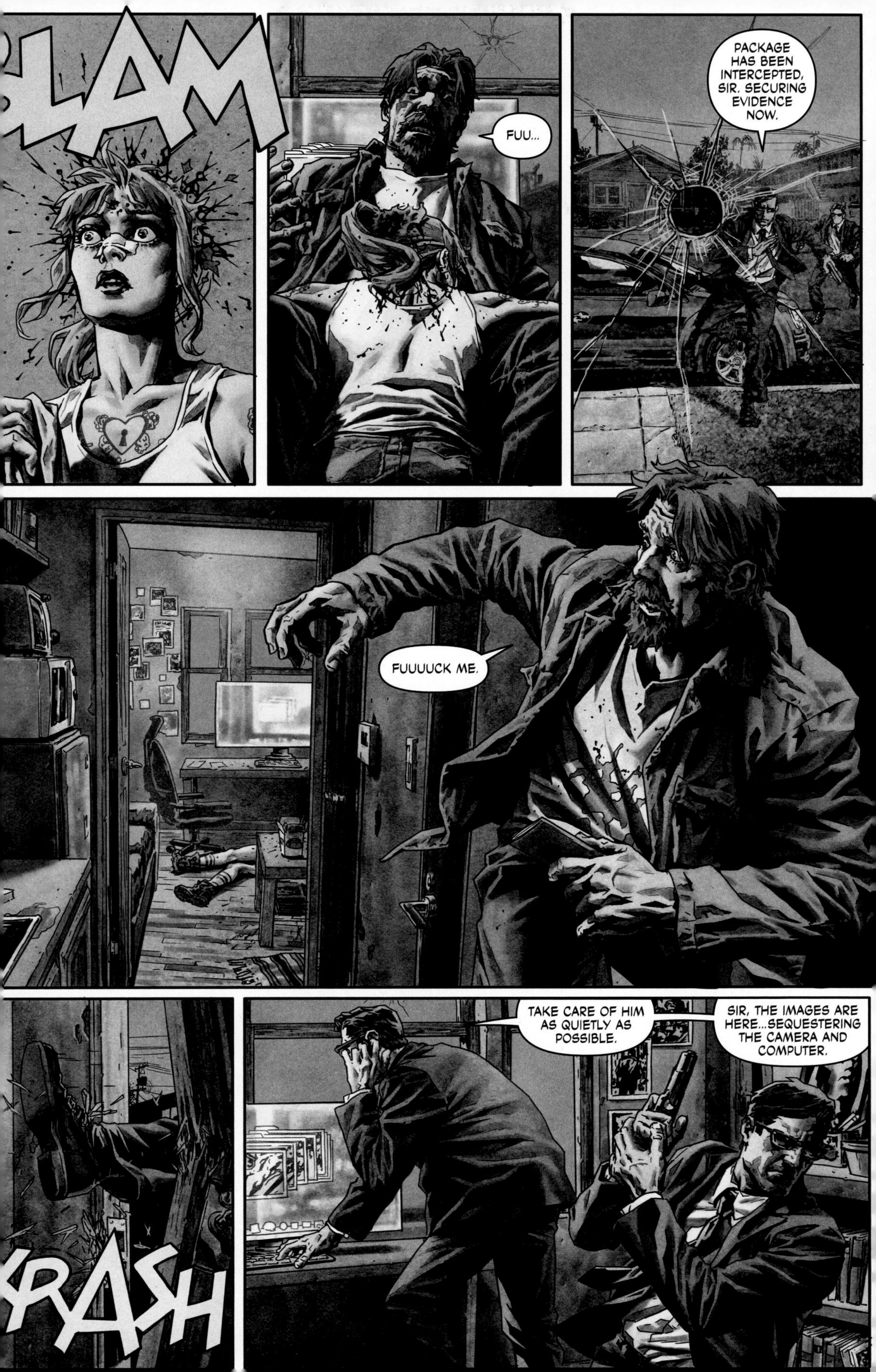
SLAM
FUU...
PACKAGE HAS BEEN INTERCEPTED, SIR. SECURING EVIDENCE NOW.
FUUUUCK ME.
KRASH
TAKE CARE OF HIM AS QUIETLY AS POSSIBLE.
SIR, THE IMAGES ARE HERE...SEQUESTERING THE CAMERA AND COMPUTER.

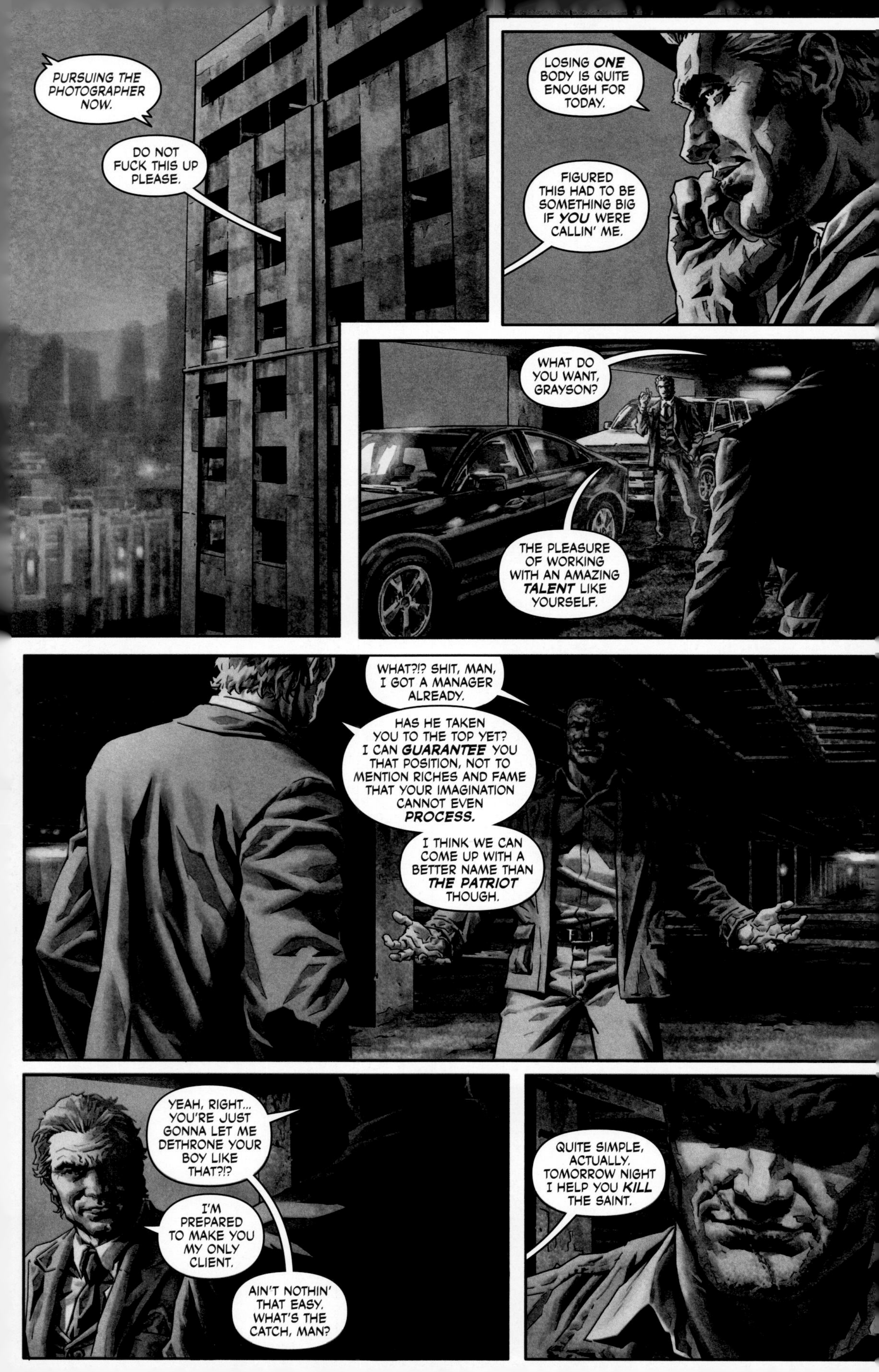
PURSUING THE PHOTOGRAPHER NOW.
DO NOT FUCK THIS UP PLEASE.
LOSING ONE BODY IS QUITE ENOUGH FOR TODAY.
FIGURED THIS HAD TO BE SOMETHING BIG IF YOU WERE CALLIN' ME.
WHAT DO YOU WANT, GRAYSON?
THE PLEASURE OF WORKING WITH AN AMAZING TALENT LIKE YOURSELF.
WHAT?!? SHIT, MAN, I GOT A MANAGER ALREADY.
HAS HE TAKEN YOU TO THE TOP YET? I CAN GUARANTEE YOU THAT POSITION, NOT TO MENTION RICHES AND FAME THAT YOUR IMAGINATION CANNOT EVEN PROCESS.
I THINK WE CAN COME UP WITH A BETTER NAME THAN THE PATRIOT THOUGH.
YEAH, RIGHT... YOU'RE JUST GONNA LET ME DETHRONE YOUR BOY LIKE THAT?!?
I'M PREPARED TO MAKE YOU MY ONLY CLIENT.
AIN'T NOTHIN' THAT EASY. WHAT'S THE CATCH, MAN?
QUITE SIMPLE, ACTUALLY. TOMORROW NIGHT I HELP YOU KILL THE SAINT.

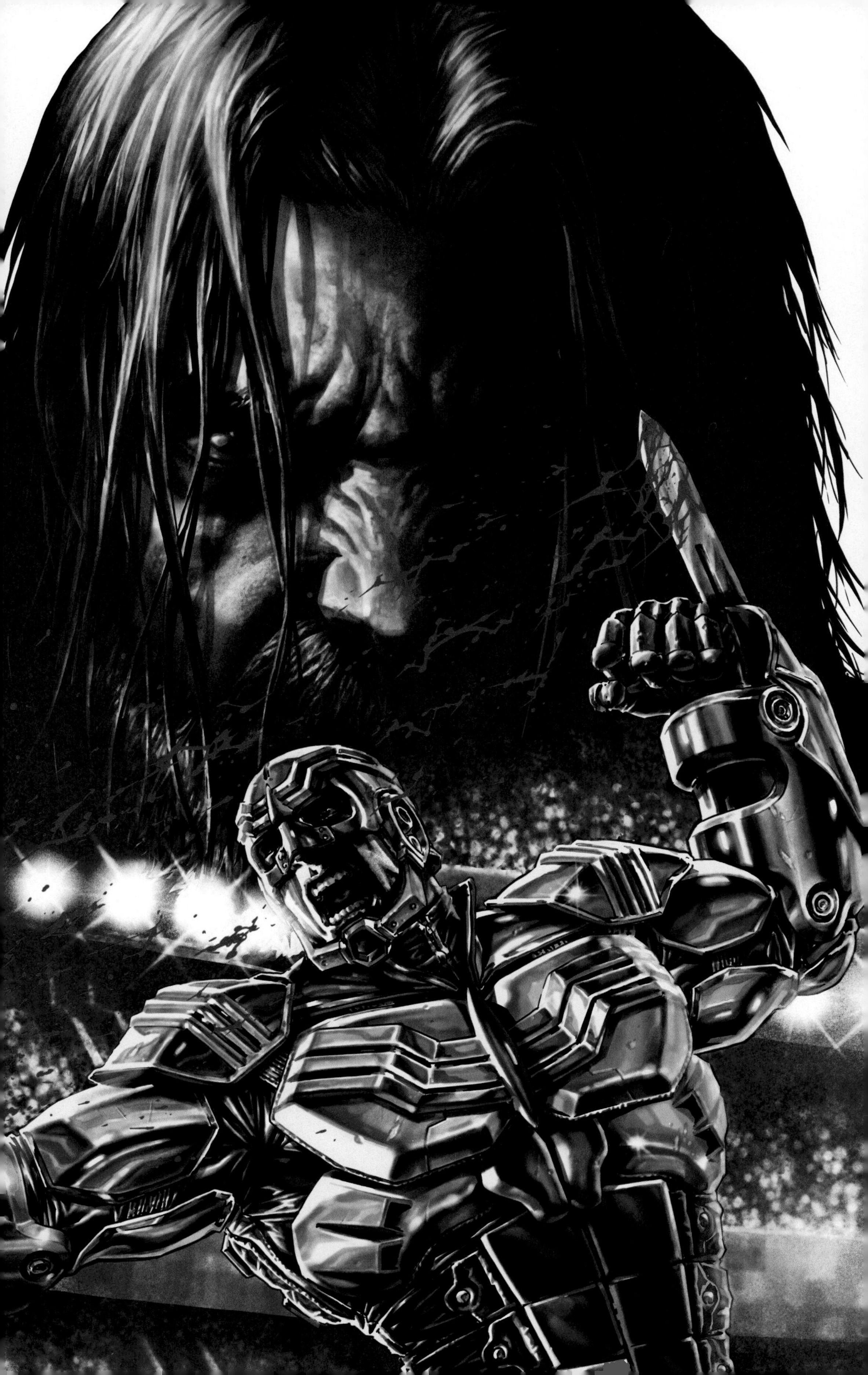

CHAPTER FOUR:
GOLDEN FIELDS
OF RAZOR WIRE

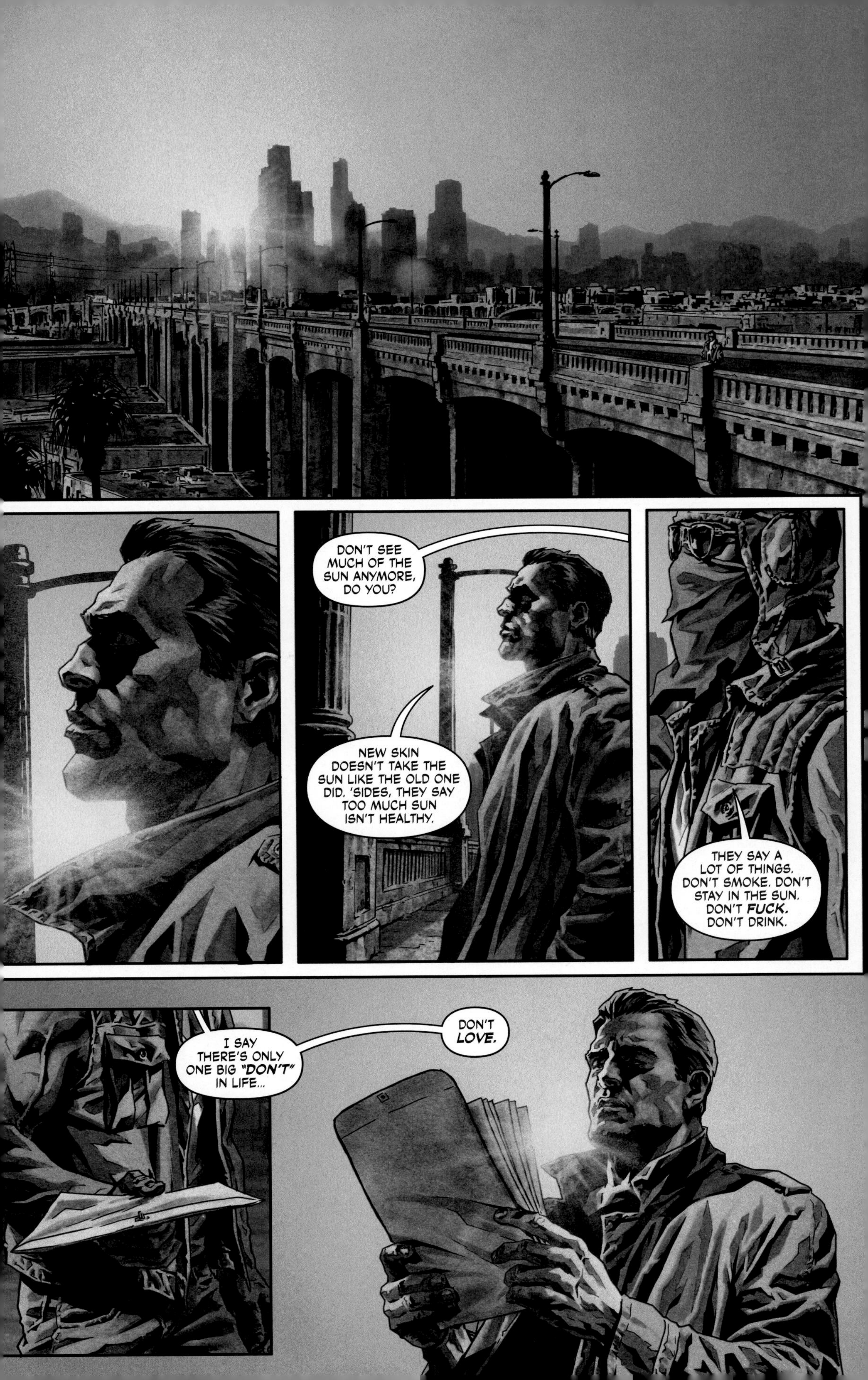
DON'T SEE MUCH OF THE SUN ANYMORE, DO YOU?
NEW SKIN DOESN'T TAKE THE SUN LIKE THE OLD ONE DID. 'SIDES, THEY SAY TOO MUCH SUN ISN'T HEALTHY.
THEY SAY A LOT OF THINGS. DON'T SMOKE. DON'T STAY IN THE SUN. DON'T *FUCK.* DON'T DRINK.
I SAY THERE'S ONLY ONE BIG *"DON'T"* IN LIFE...
DON'T *LOVE.*

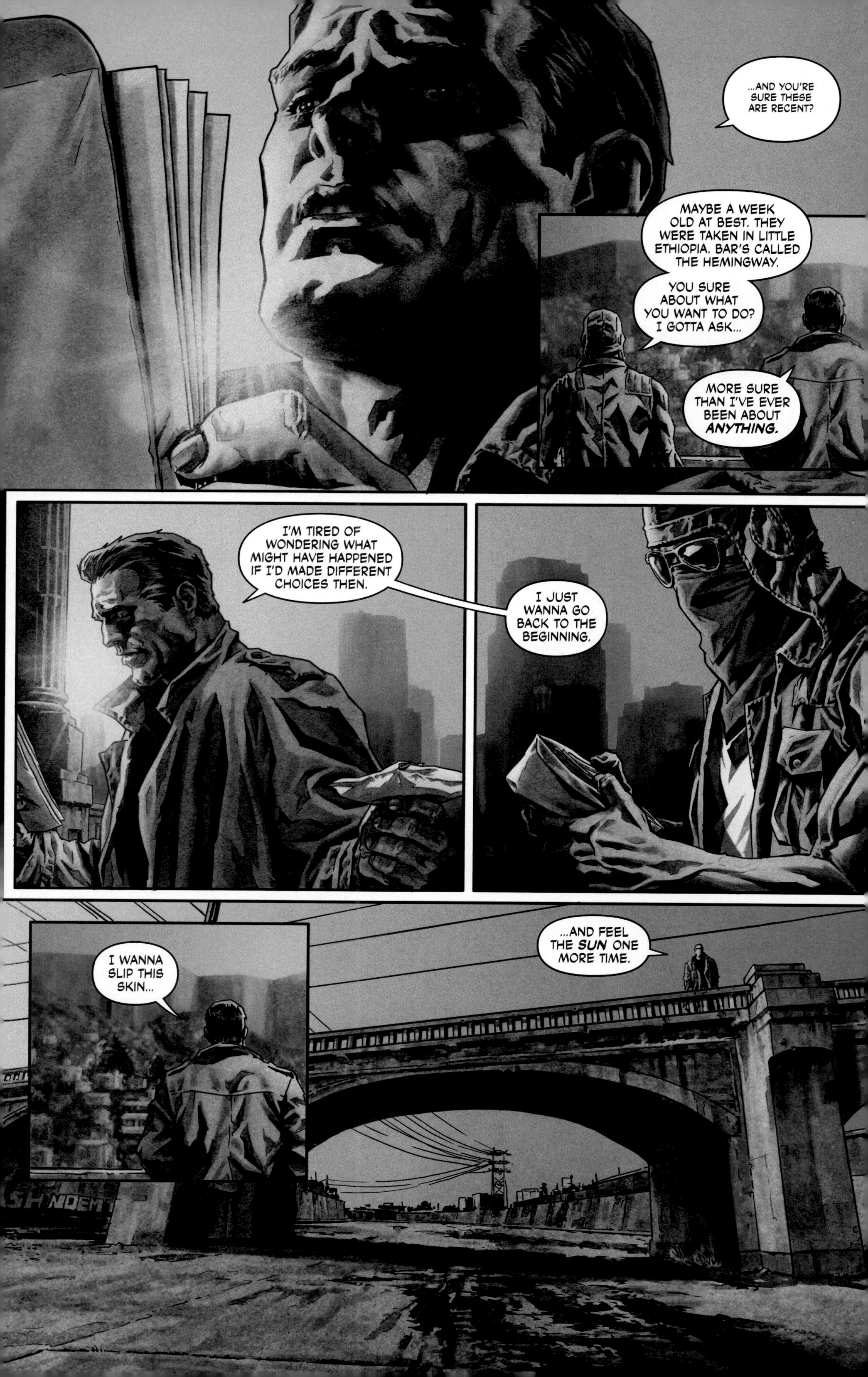
...AND YOU'RE SURE THESE ARE RECENT?
MAYBE A WEEK OLD AT BEST. THEY WERE TAKEN IN LITTLE ETHIOPIA. BAR'S CALLED THE HEMINGWAY.
YOU SURE ABOUT WHAT YOU WANT TO DO? I GOTTA ASK...
MORE SURE THAN I'VE EVER BEEN ABOUT *ANYTHING.*
I'M TIRED OF WONDERING WHAT MIGHT HAVE HAPPENED IF I'D MADE DIFFERENT CHOICES THEN.
I JUST WANNA GO BACK TO THE BEGINNING.
I WANNA SLIP THIS SKIN...
...AND FEEL THE *SUN* ONE MORE TIME.

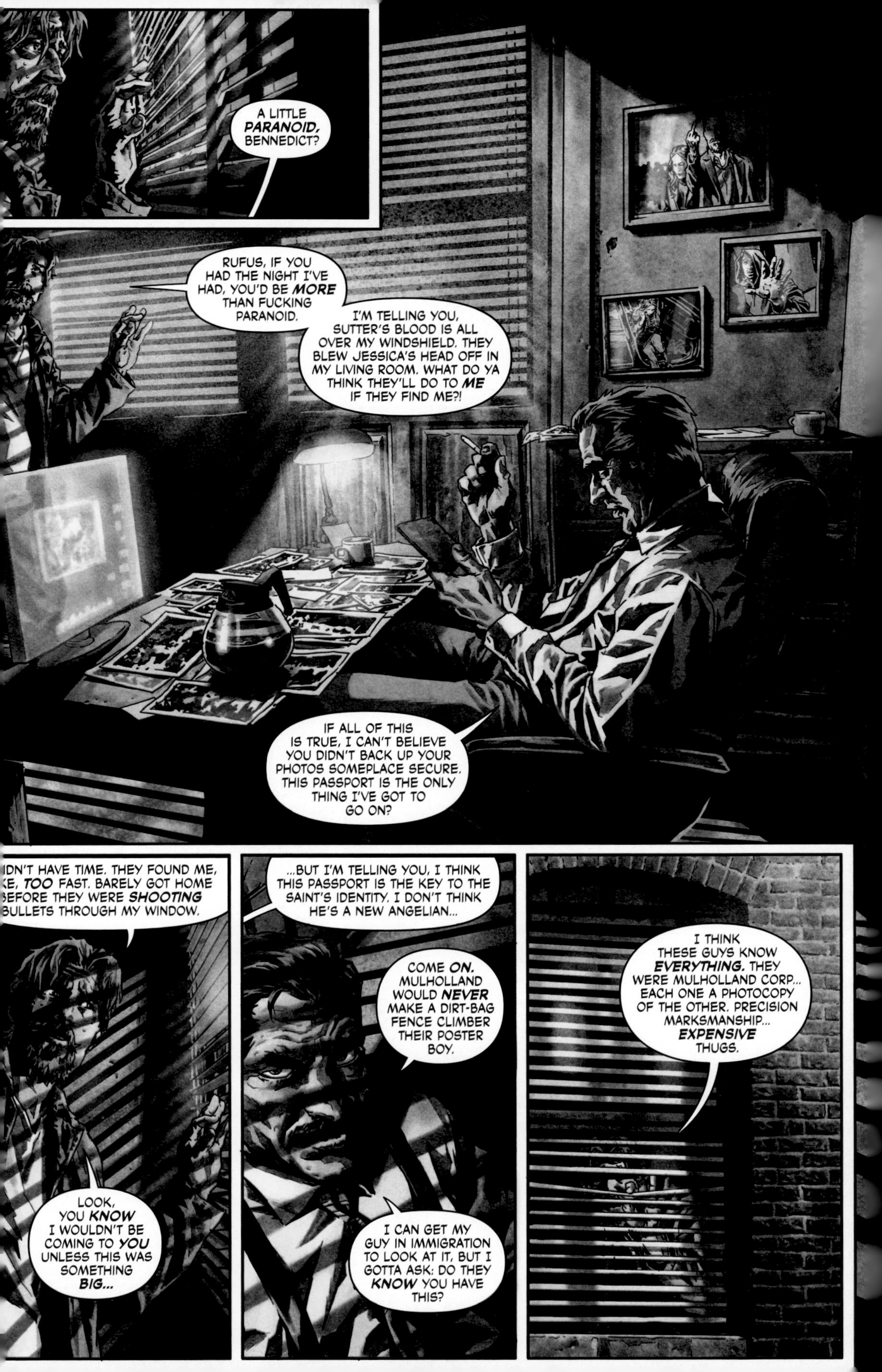

A LITTLE *PARANOID,* BENNEDICT?
RUFUS, IF YOU HAD THE NIGHT I'VE HAD, YOU'D BE *MORE* THAN FUCKING PARANOID.
I'M TELLING YOU, SUTTER'S BLOOD IS ALL OVER MY WINDSHIELD. THEY BLEW JESSICA'S HEAD OFF IN MY LIVING ROOM. WHAT DO YA THINK THEY'LL DO TO *ME* IF THEY FIND ME?!
IF ALL OF THIS IS TRUE, I CAN'T BELIEVE YOU DIDN'T BACK UP YOUR PHOTOS SOMEPLACE SECURE. THIS PASSPORT IS THE ONLY THING I'VE GOT TO GO ON?
IDN'T HAVE TIME. THEY FOUND ME, KE, *TOO* FAST. BARELY GOT HOME BEFORE THEY WERE *SHOOTING* BULLETS THROUGH MY WINDOW.
LOOK, YOU *KNOW* I WOULDN'T BE COMING TO *YOU* UNLESS THIS WAS SOMETHING *BIG...*
...BUT I'M TELLING YOU, I THINK THIS PASSPORT IS THE KEY TO THE SAINT'S IDENTITY. I DON'T THINK HE'S A NEW ANGELIAN...
COME *ON.* MULHOLLAND WOULD *NEVER* MAKE A DIRT-BAG FENCE CLIMBER THEIR POSTER BOY.
I CAN GET MY GUY IN IMMIGRATION TO LOOK AT IT, BUT I GOTTA ASK: DO THEY *KNOW* YOU HAVE THIS?
I THINK THESE GUYS KNOW *EVERYTHING.* THEY WERE MULHOLLAND CORP... EACH ONE A PHOTOCOPY OF THE OTHER. PRECISION MARKSMANSHIP... *EXPENSIVE* THUGS.

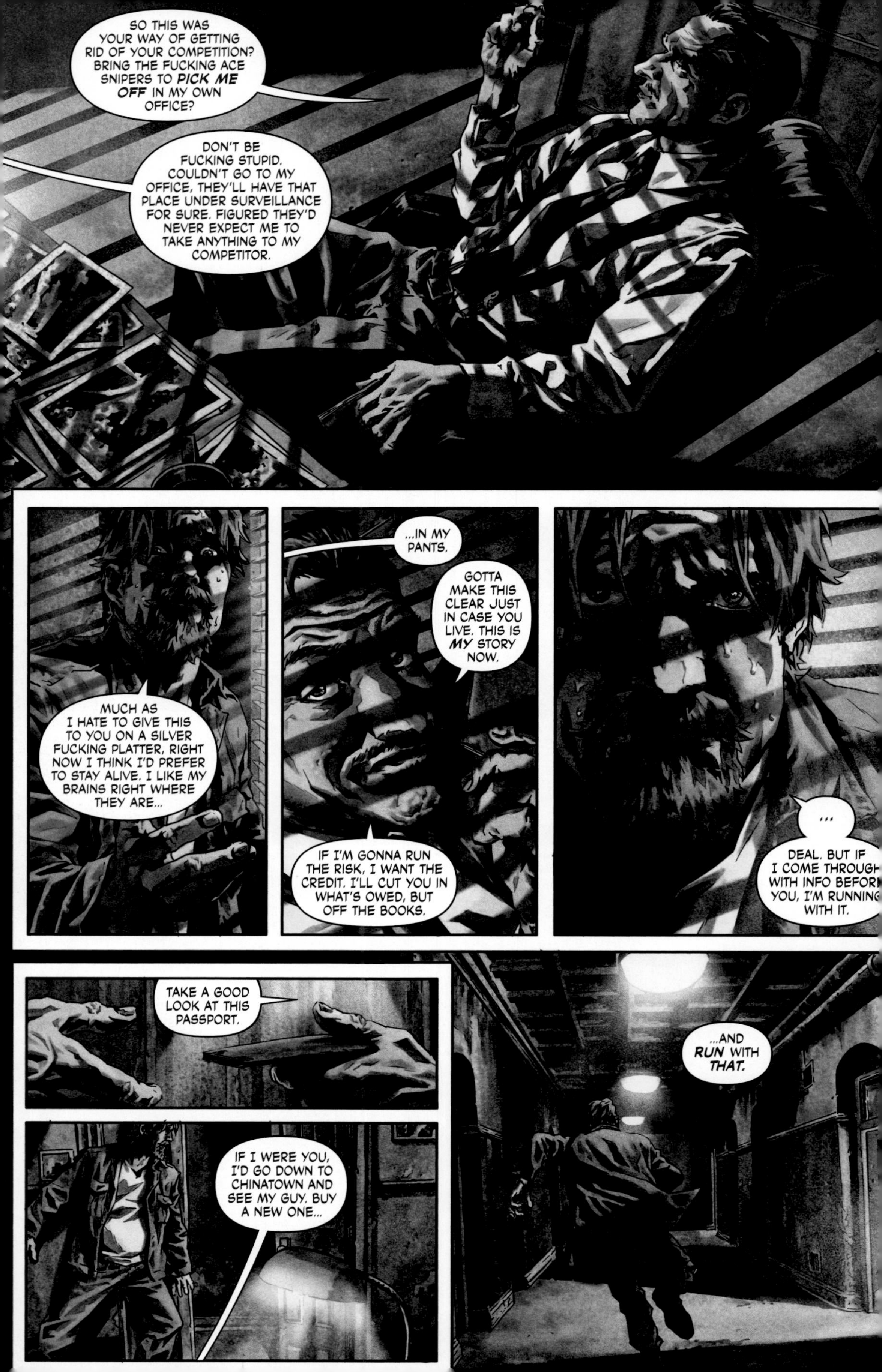
SO THIS WAS YOUR WAY OF GETTING RID OF YOUR COMPETITION? BRING THE FUCKING ACE SNIPERS TO PICK ME OFF IN MY OWN OFFICE?
DON'T BE FUCKING STUPID. COULDN'T GO TO MY OFFICE, THEY'LL HAVE THAT PLACE UNDER SURVEILLANCE FOR SURE. FIGURED THEY'D NEVER EXPECT ME TO TAKE ANYTHING TO MY COMPETITOR.
MUCH AS I HATE TO GIVE THIS TO YOU ON A SILVER FUCKING PLATTER, RIGHT NOW I THINK I'D PREFER TO STAY ALIVE. I LIKE MY BRAINS RIGHT WHERE THEY ARE...
...IN MY PANTS.
GOTTA MAKE THIS CLEAR JUST IN CASE YOU LIVE. THIS IS MY STORY NOW.
IF I'M GONNA RUN THE RISK, I WANT THE CREDIT. I'LL CUT YOU IN WHAT'S OWED, BUT OFF THE BOOKS.
...
DEAL. BUT IF I COME THROUGH WITH INFO BEFORE YOU, I'M RUNNING WITH IT.
TAKE A GOOD LOOK AT THIS PASSPORT.
IF I WERE YOU, I'D GO DOWN TO CHINATOWN AND SEE MY GUY. BUY A NEW ONE...
...AND RUN WITH THAT.

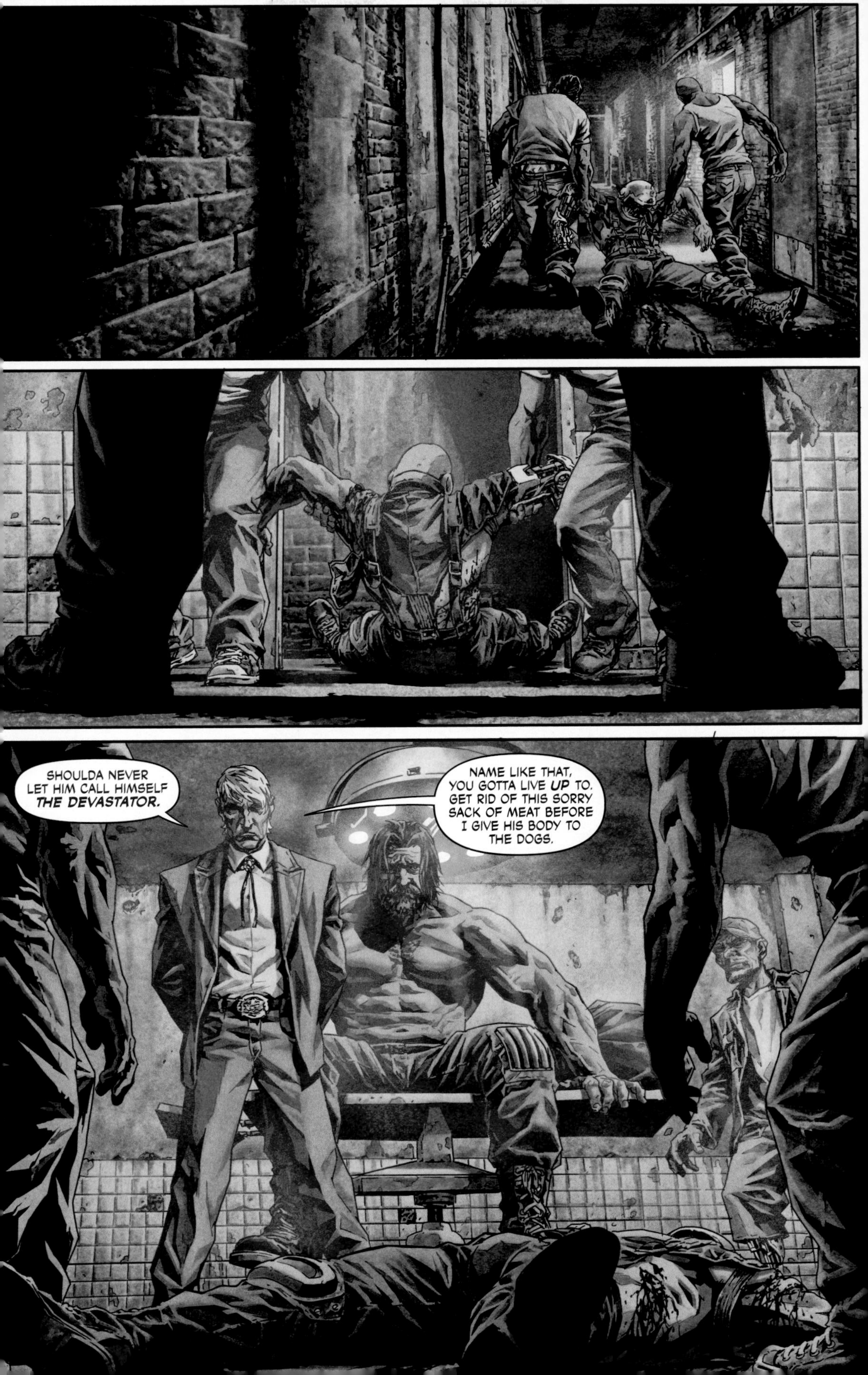
SHOULDA NEVER LET HIM CALL HIMSELF ***THE DEVASTATOR.***
NAME LIKE THAT, YOU GOTTA LIVE ***UP*** TO. GET RID OF THIS SORRY SACK OF MEAT BEFORE I GIVE HIS BODY TO THE DOGS.

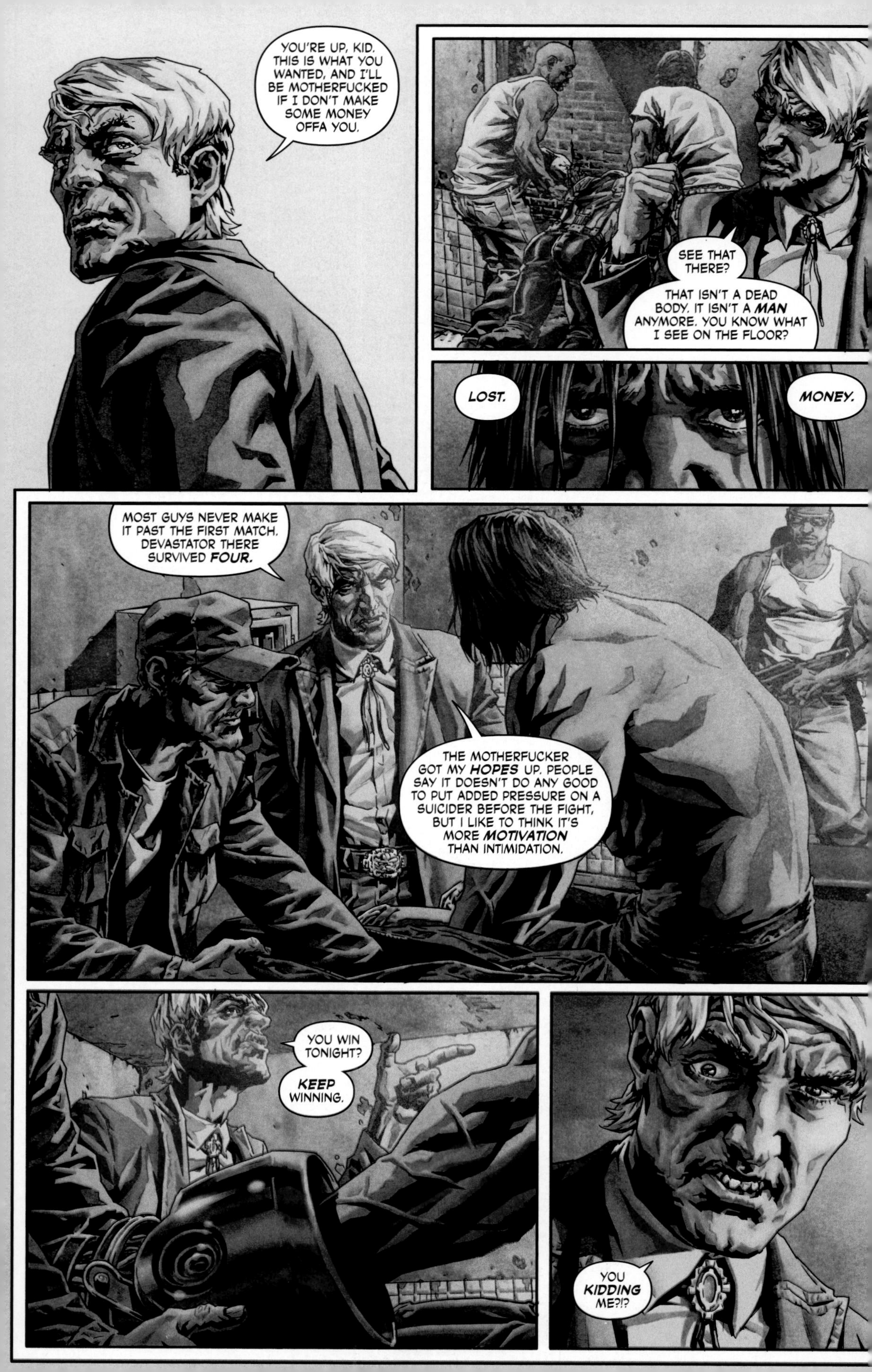
YOU'RE UP, KID. THIS IS WHAT YOU WANTED, AND I'LL BE MOTHERFUCKED IF I DON'T MAKE SOME MONEY OFFA YOU.
SEE THAT THERE?
THAT ISN'T A DEAD BODY. IT ISN'T A MAN ANYMORE. YOU KNOW WHAT I SEE ON THE FLOOR?
LOST.
MONEY.
MOST GUYS NEVER MAKE IT PAST THE FIRST MATCH. DEVASTATOR THERE SURVIVED FOUR.
THE MOTHERFUCKER GOT MY HOPES UP. PEOPLE SAY IT DOESN'T DO ANY GOOD TO PUT ADDED PRESSURE ON A SUICIDER BEFORE THE FIGHT, BUT I LIKE TO THINK IT'S MORE MOTIVATION THAN INTIMIDATION.
YOU WIN TONIGHT?
KEEP WINNING.
YOU KIDDING ME?!?

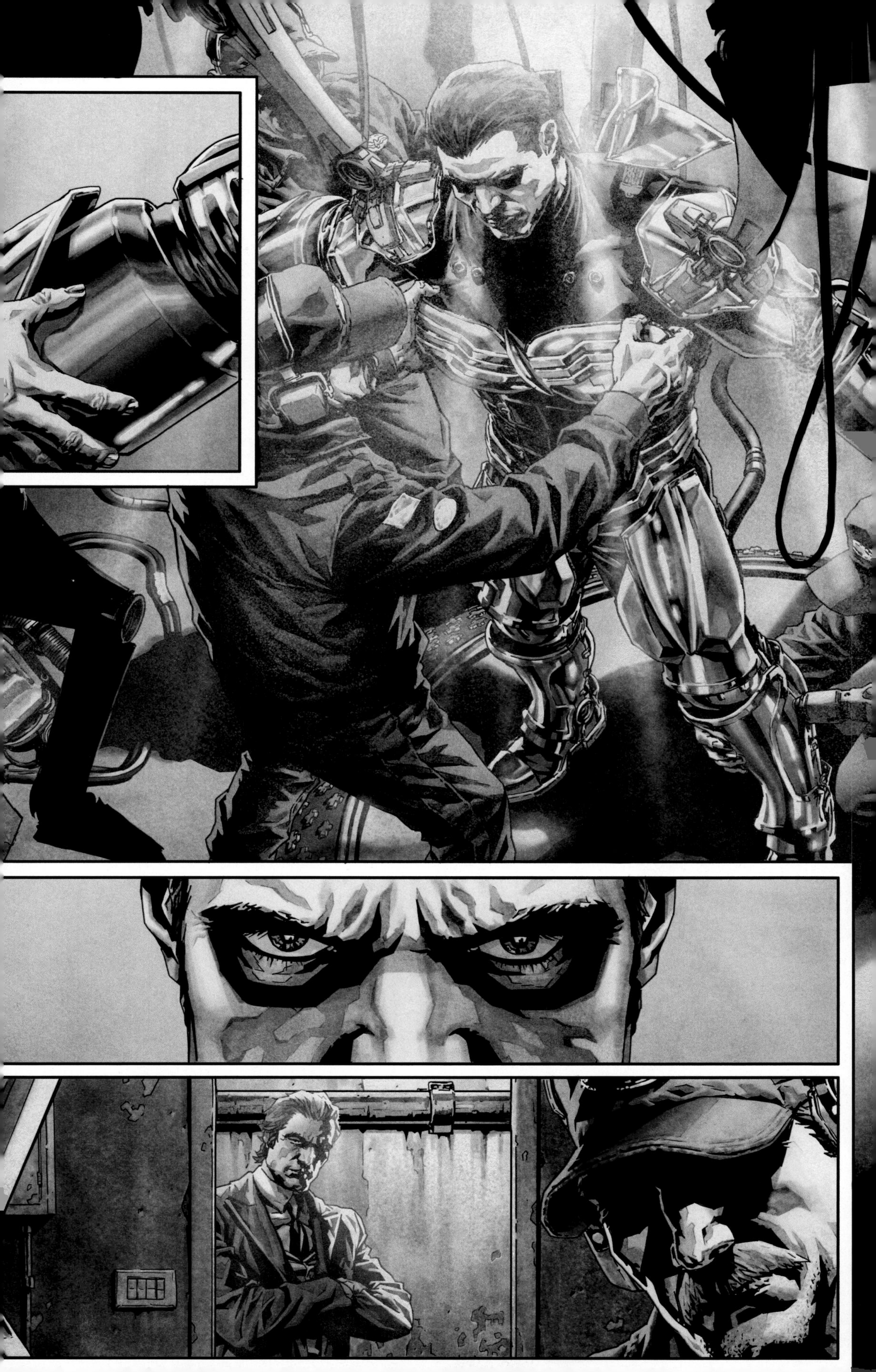

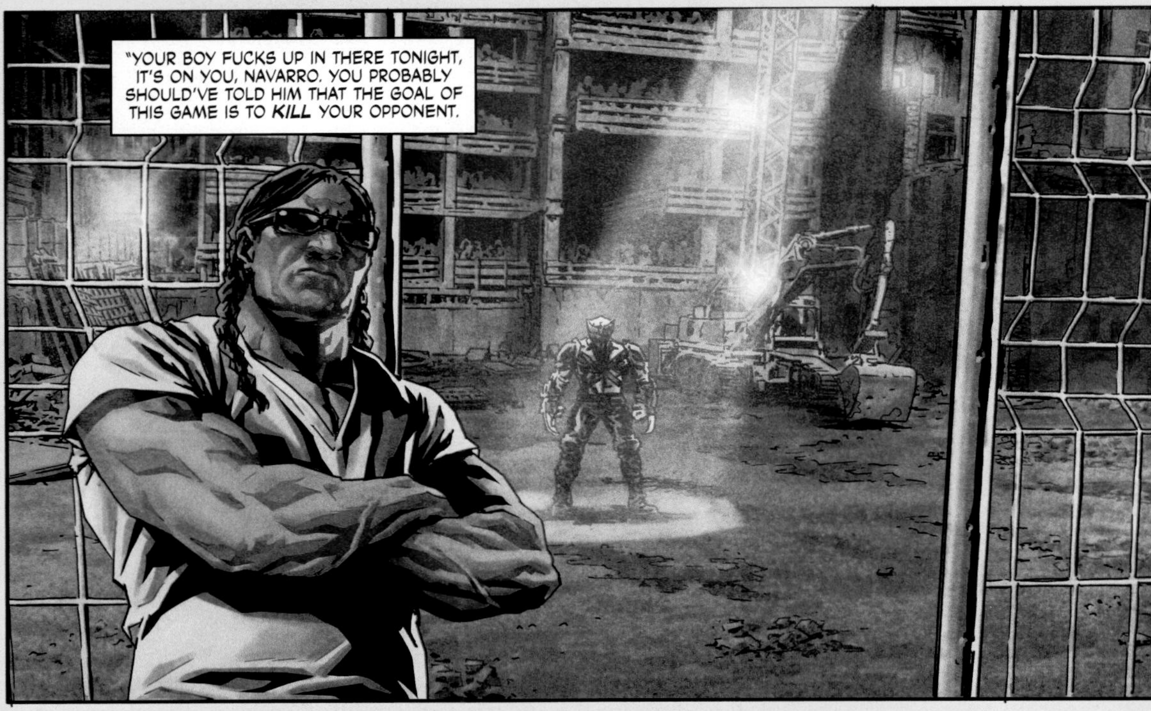
"YOUR BOY FUCKS UP IN THERE TONIGHT, IT'S ON YOU, NAVARRO. YOU PROBABLY SHOULD'VE TOLD HIM THAT THE GOAL OF THIS GAME IS TO *KILL* YOUR OPPONENT.

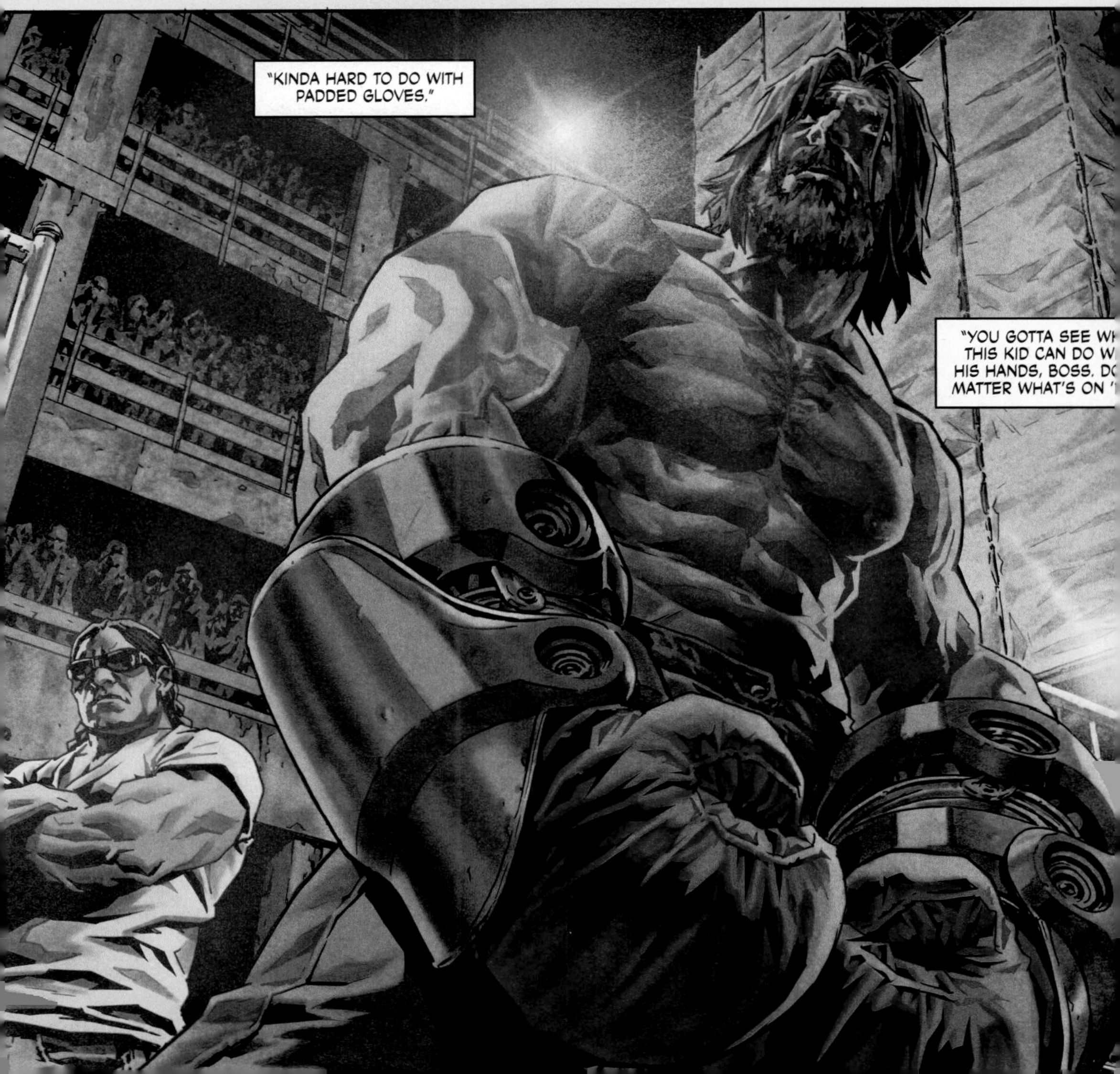
"KINDA HARD TO DO WITH PADDED GLOVES."
"YOU GOTTA SEE WH THIS KID CAN DO W HIS HANDS, BOSS. DO MATTER WHAT'S ON '

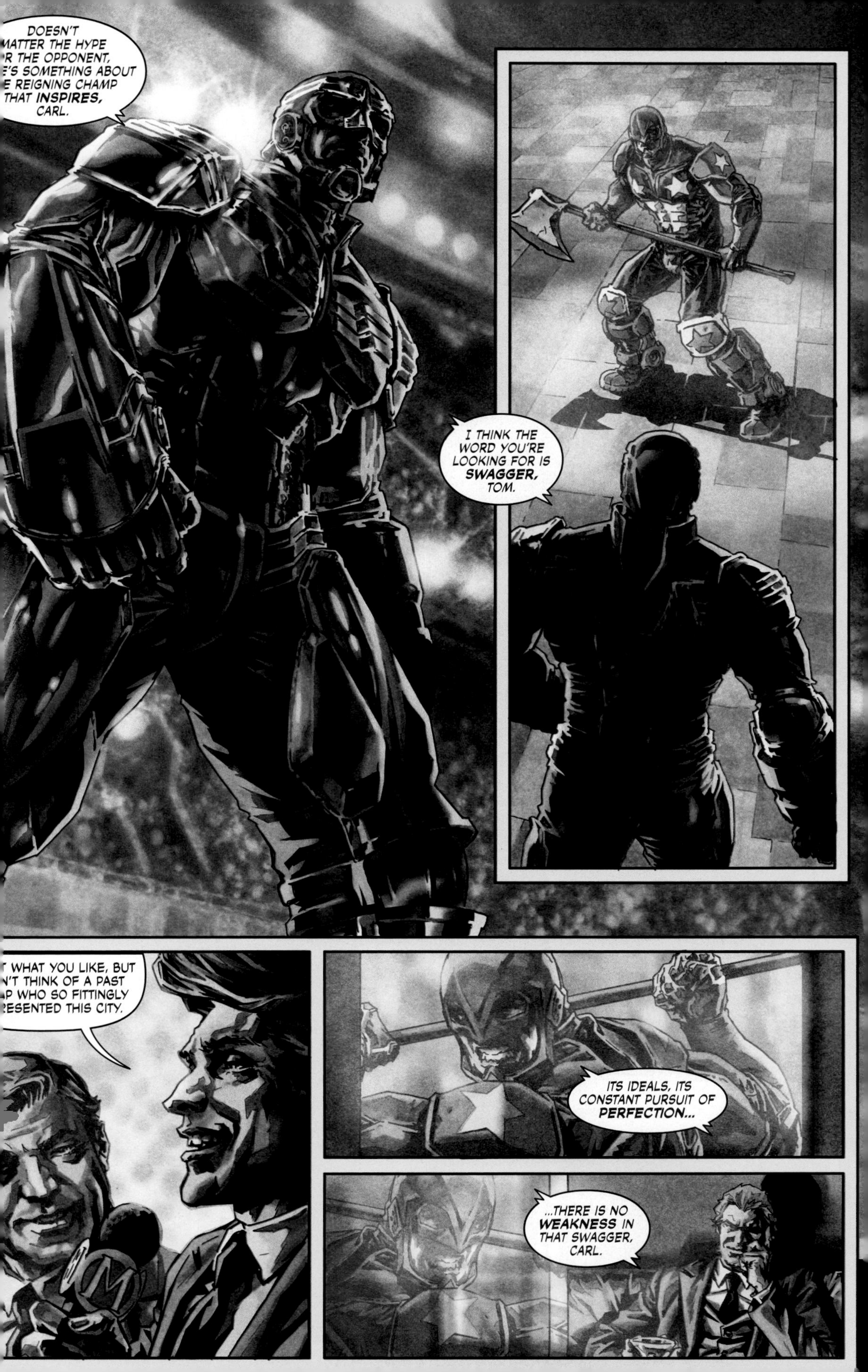

DOESN'T
MATTER THE HYPE
R THE OPPONENT,
E'S SOMETHING ABOUT
E REIGNING CHAMP
THAT INSPIRES,
CARL.
I THINK THE WORD YOU'RE LOOKING FOR IS SWAGGER, TOM.
T WHAT YOU LIKE, BUT N'T THINK OF A PAST P WHO SO FITTINGLY RESENTED THIS CITY.
ITS IDEALS, ITS CONSTANT PURSUIT OF PERFECTION...
...THERE IS NO WEAKNESS IN THAT SWAGGER, CARL.

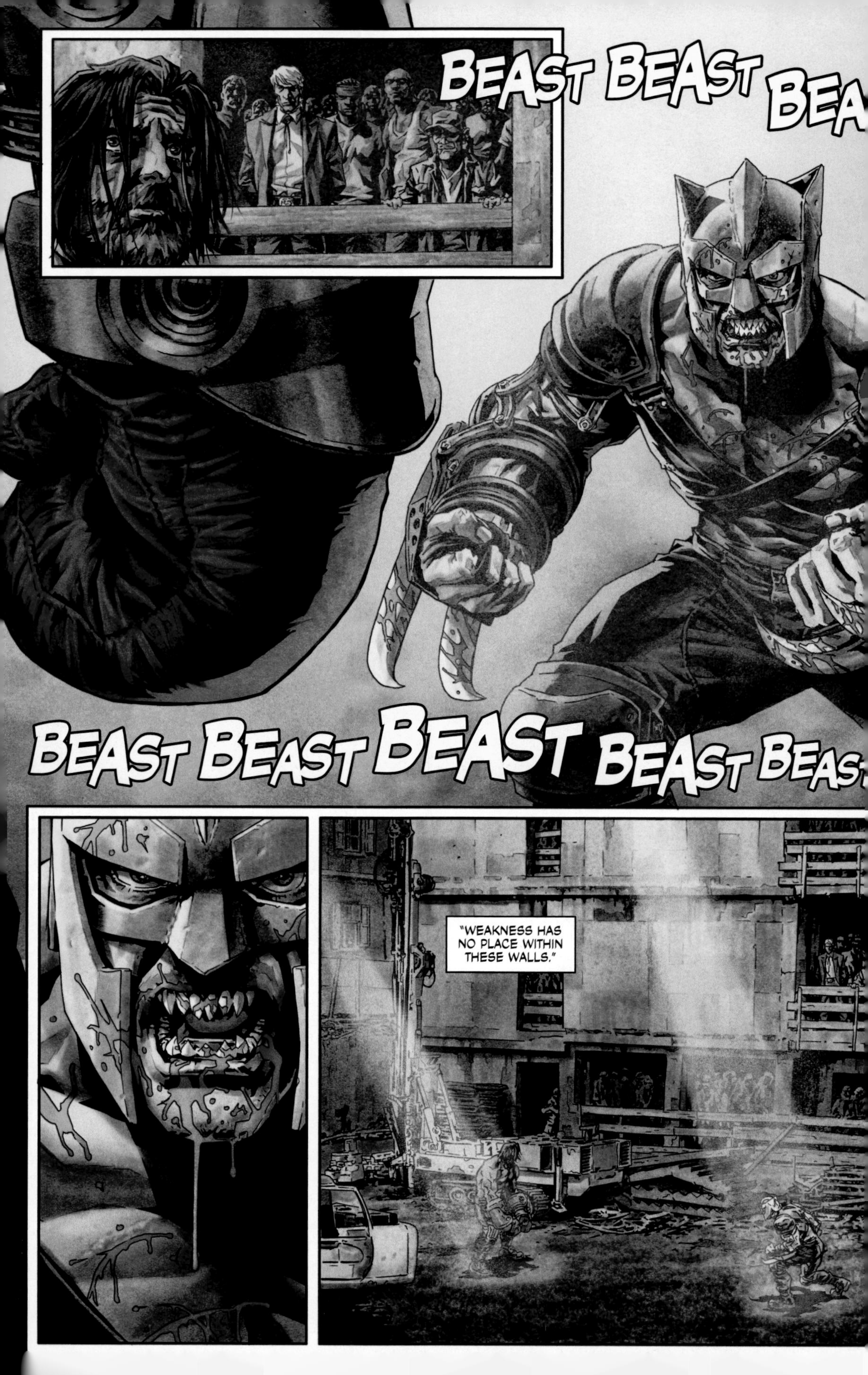
BEAST BEAST BEA
BEAST BEAST BEAST BEAST BEAS
"WEAKNESS HAS NO PLACE WITHIN THESE WALLS."

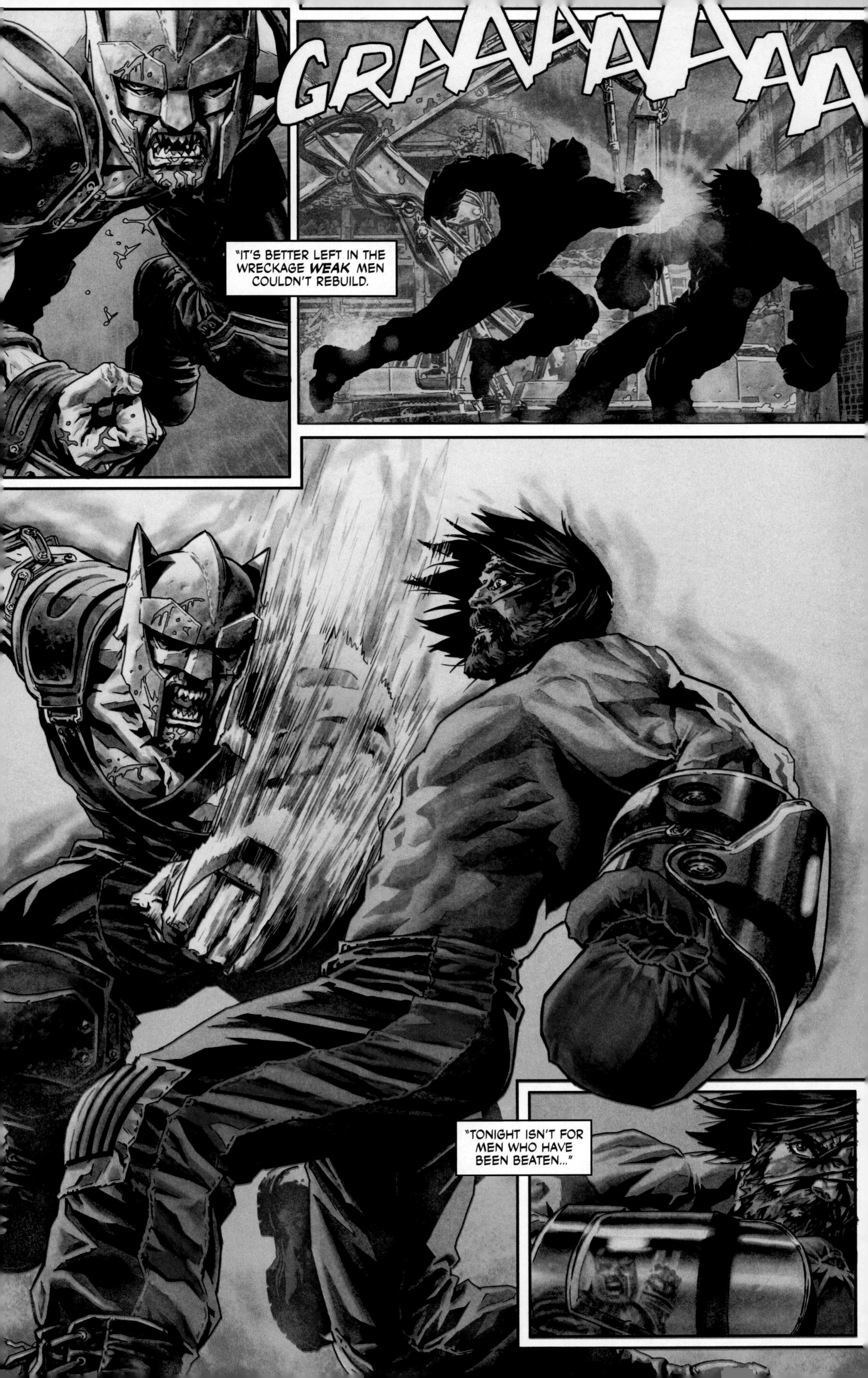
GRAAAAAAAA
"IT'S BETTER LEFT IN THE WRECKAGE WEAK MEN COULDN'T REBUILD.
"TONIGHT ISN'T FOR MEN WHO HAVE BEEN BEATEN..."

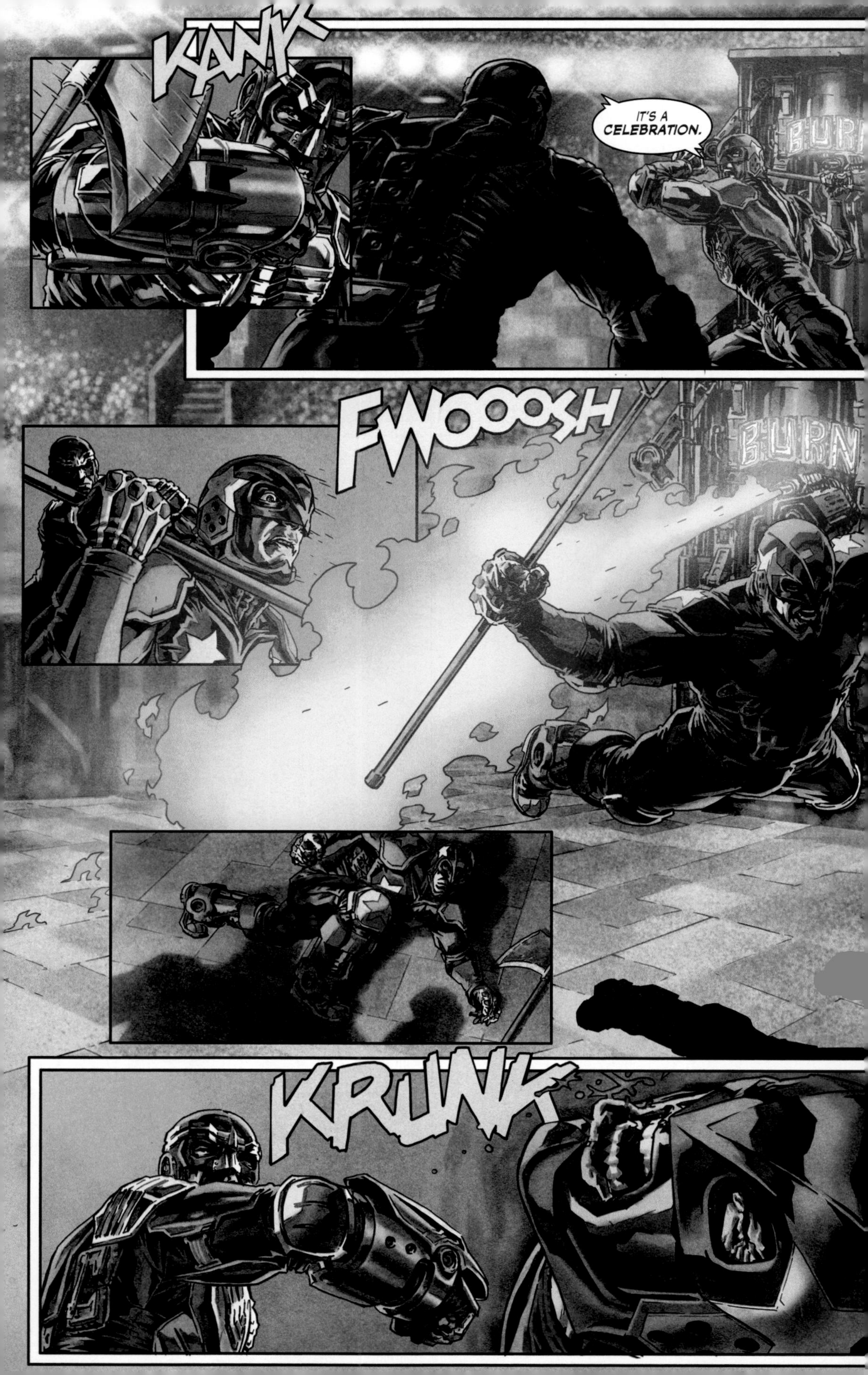
KANK
IT'S A CELEBRATION.
BURN
FWOOOSH
BURN
KRUNK

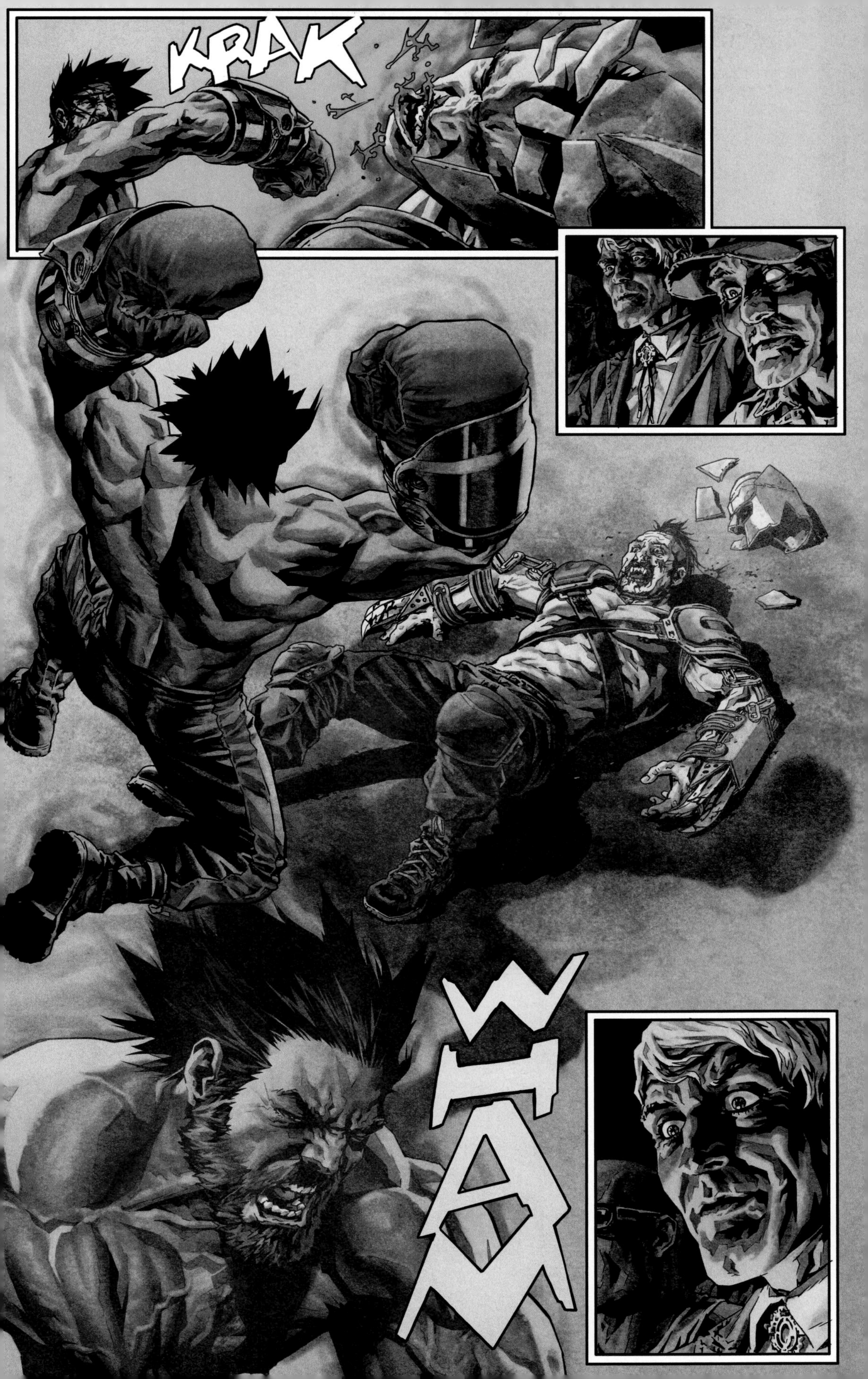
KRAK
WHAM

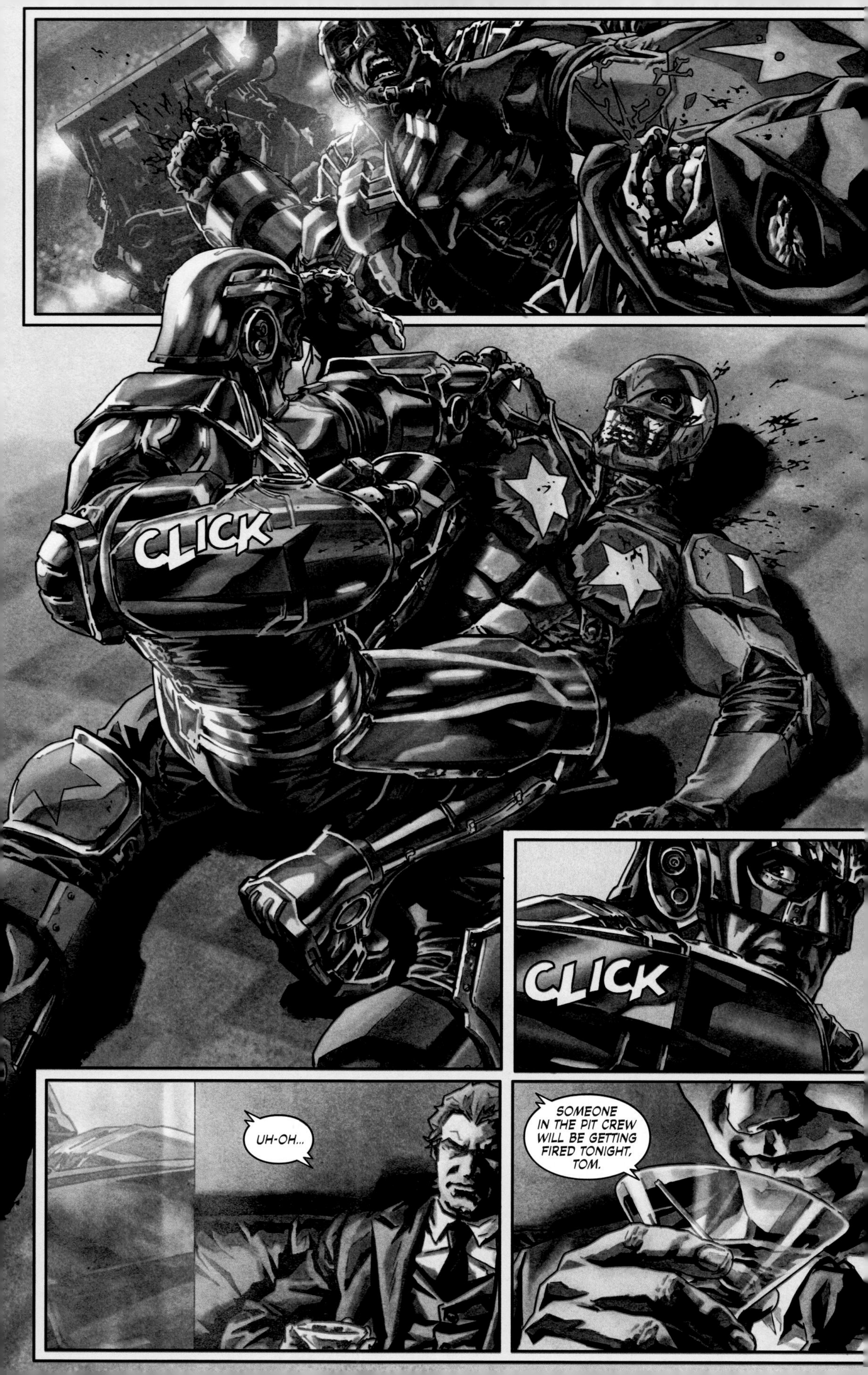
CLICK
CLICK
UH-OH...
SOMEONE IN THE PIT CREW WILL BE GETTING FIRED TONIGHT, TOM.

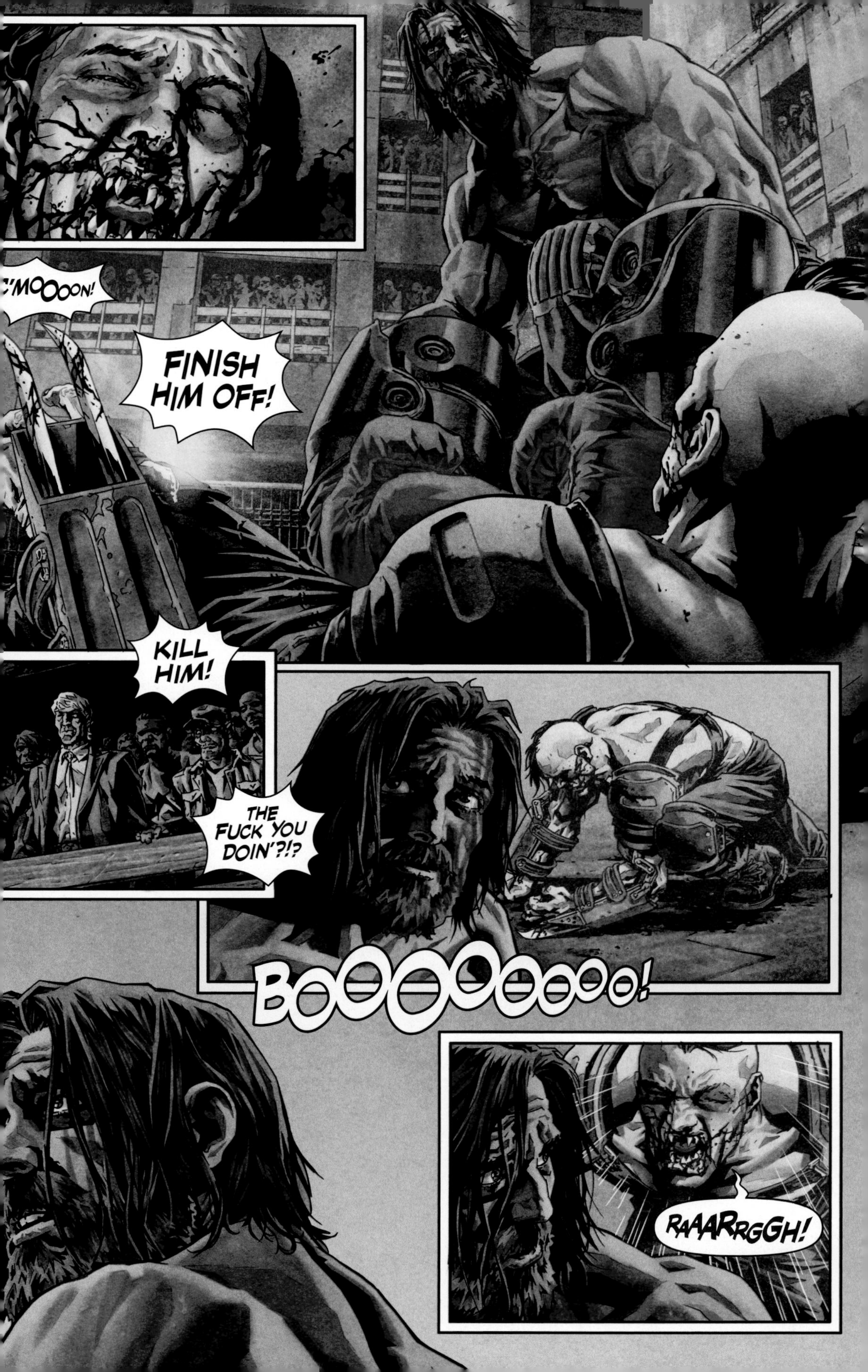
C'MOOOON!
FINISH HIM OFF!
KILL HIM!
THE FUCK YOU DOIN'?!?
BOOOOOOOOO!
RAAARRGGH!

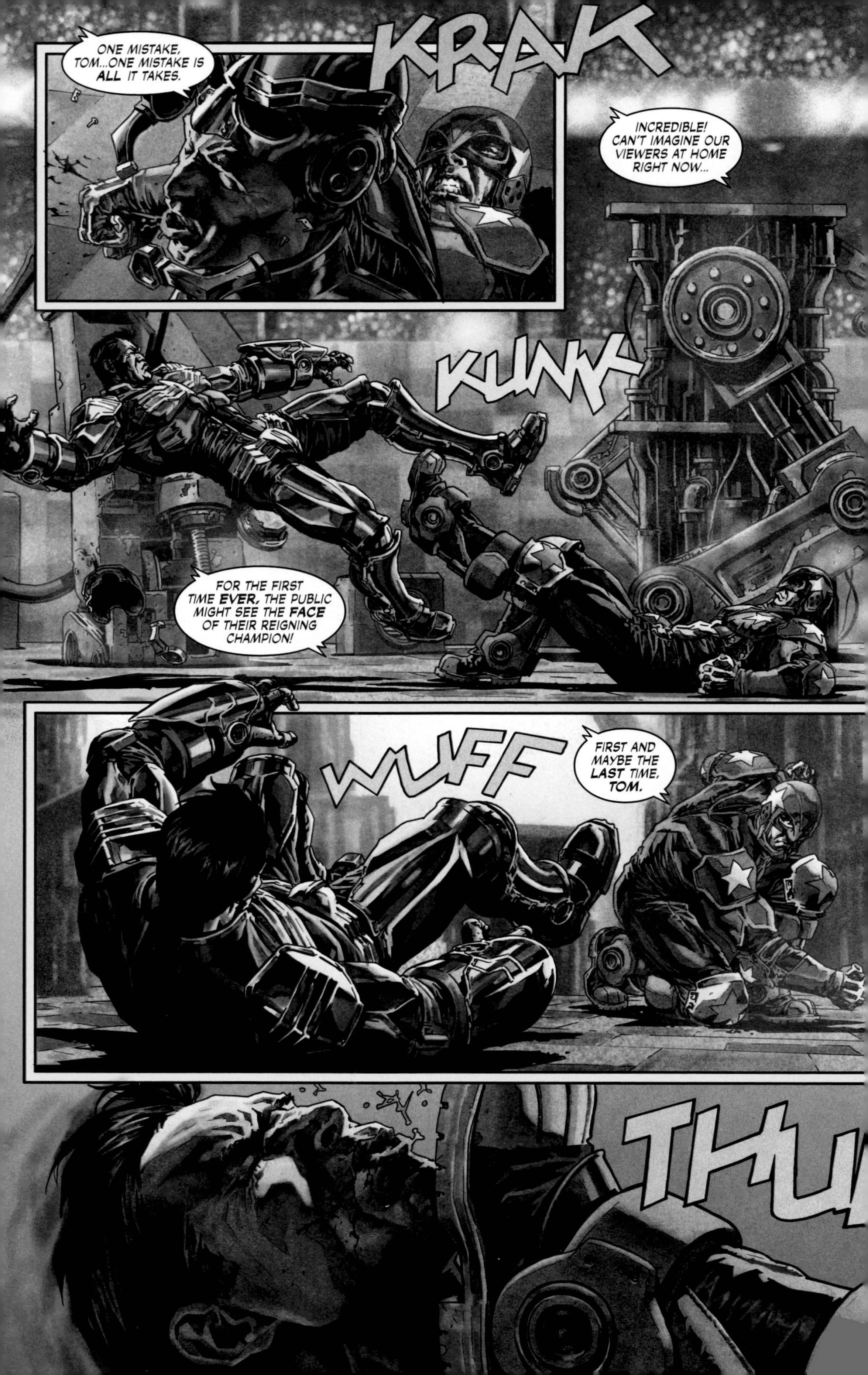
ONE MISTAKE, TOM...ONE MISTAKE IS ALL IT TAKES.
KRAK
INCREDIBLE! CAN'T IMAGINE OUR VIEWERS AT HOME RIGHT NOW...
KUNK
FOR THE FIRST TIME EVER, THE PUBLIC MIGHT SEE THE FACE OF THEIR REIGNING CHAMPION!
WUFF
FIRST AND MAYBE THE LAST TIME, TOM.
THU

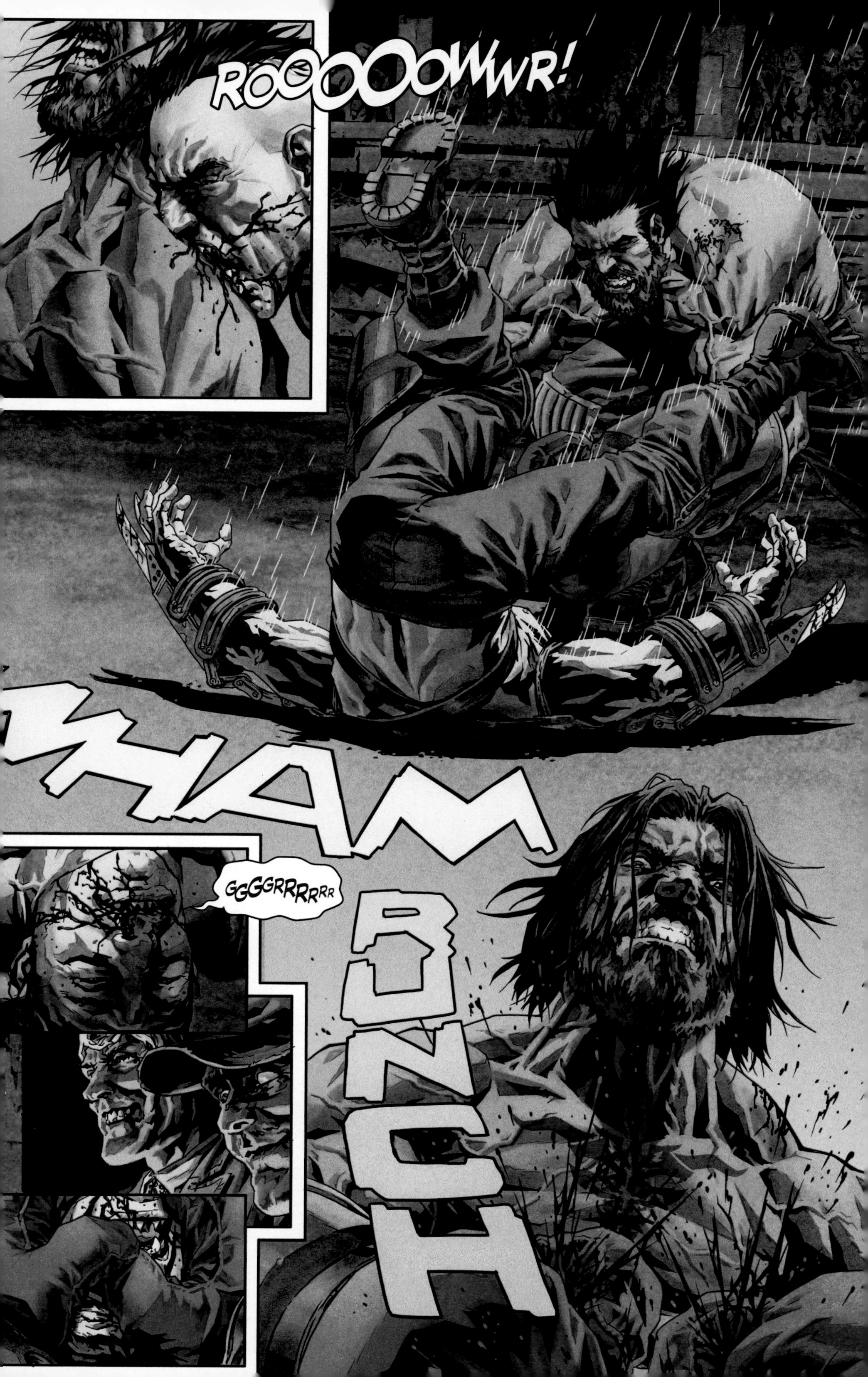
ROOOOOOWWR!
WHAM
GGGGRRRRRR
BUNCH

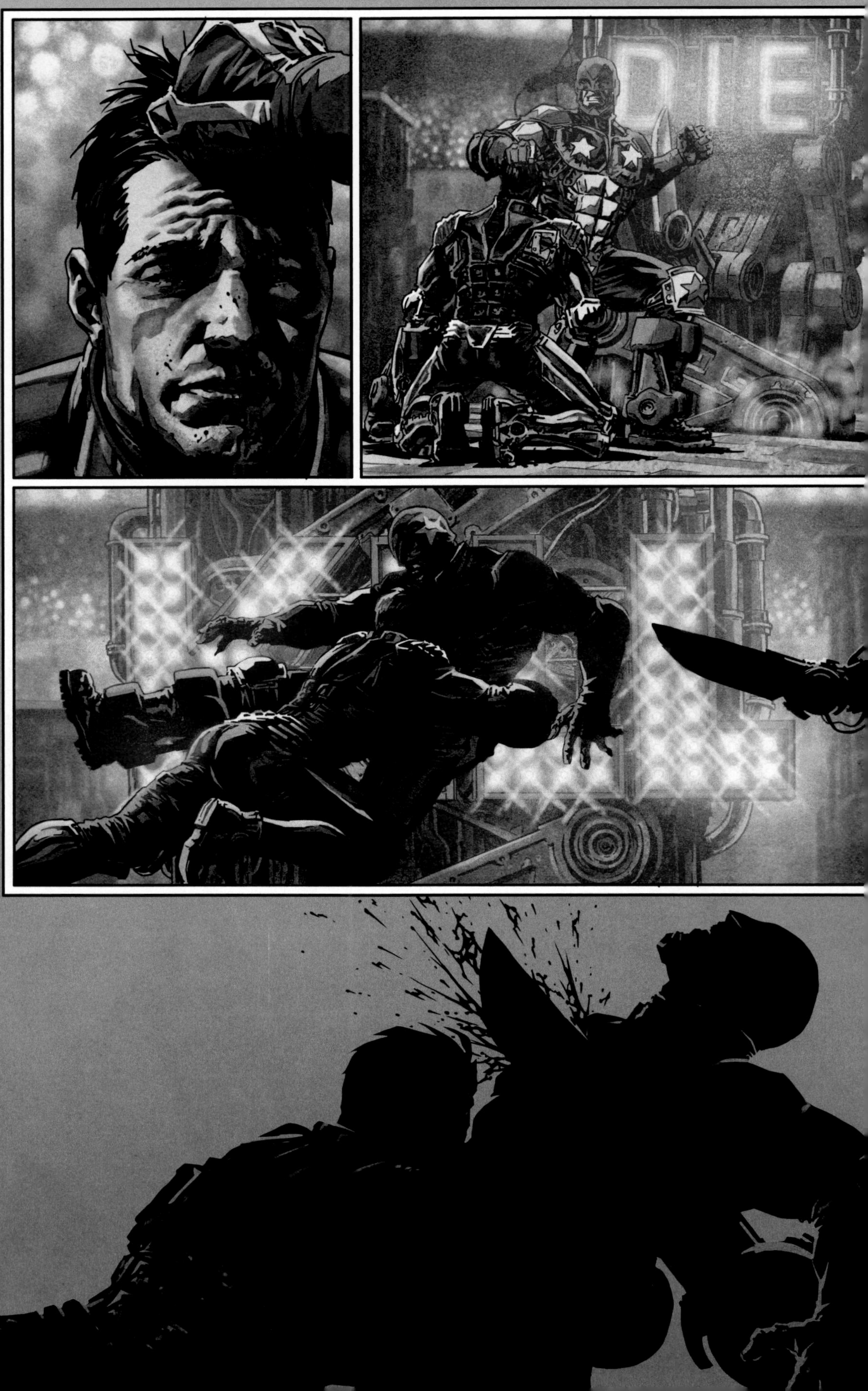
DIE

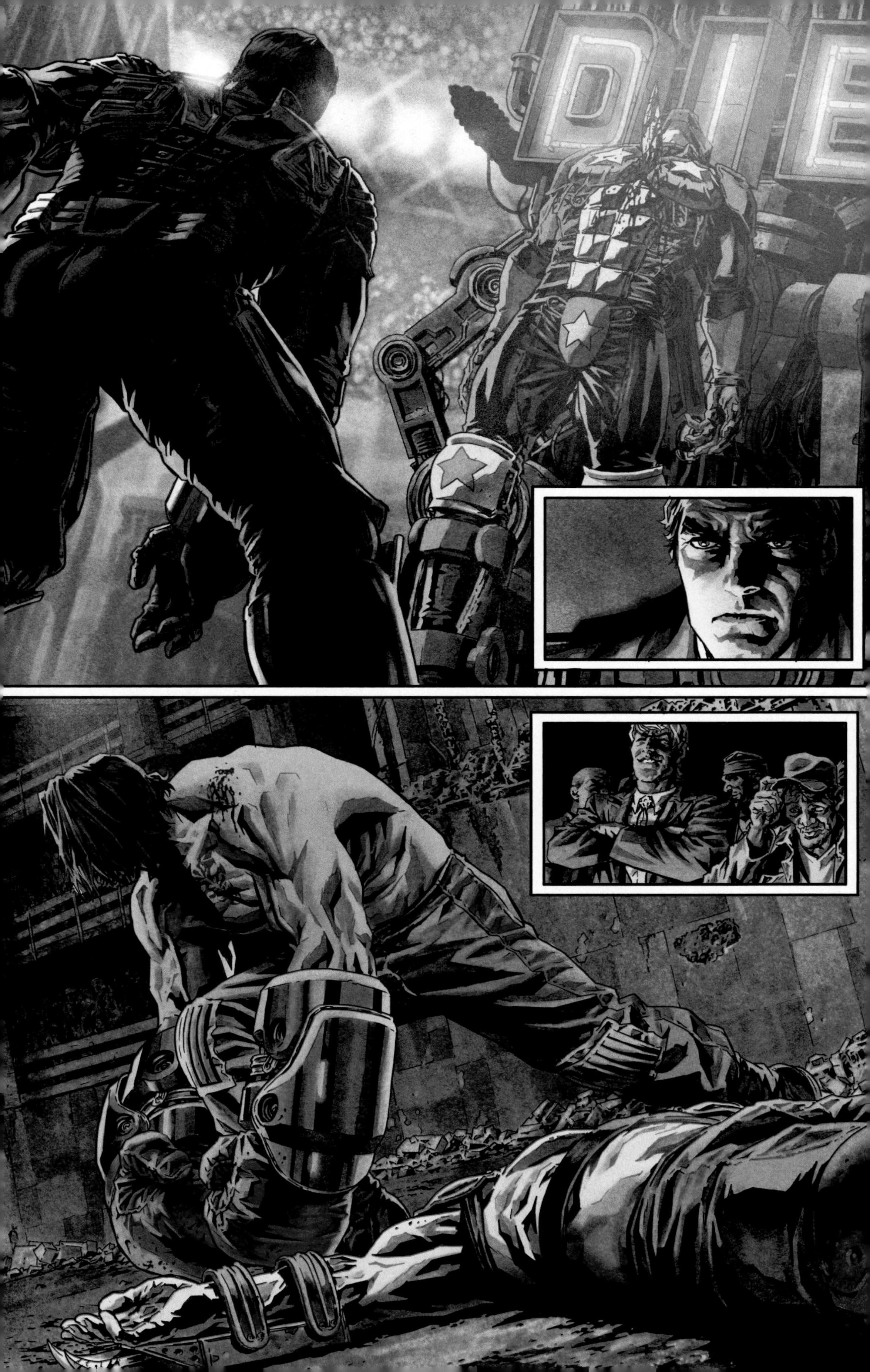
DIE

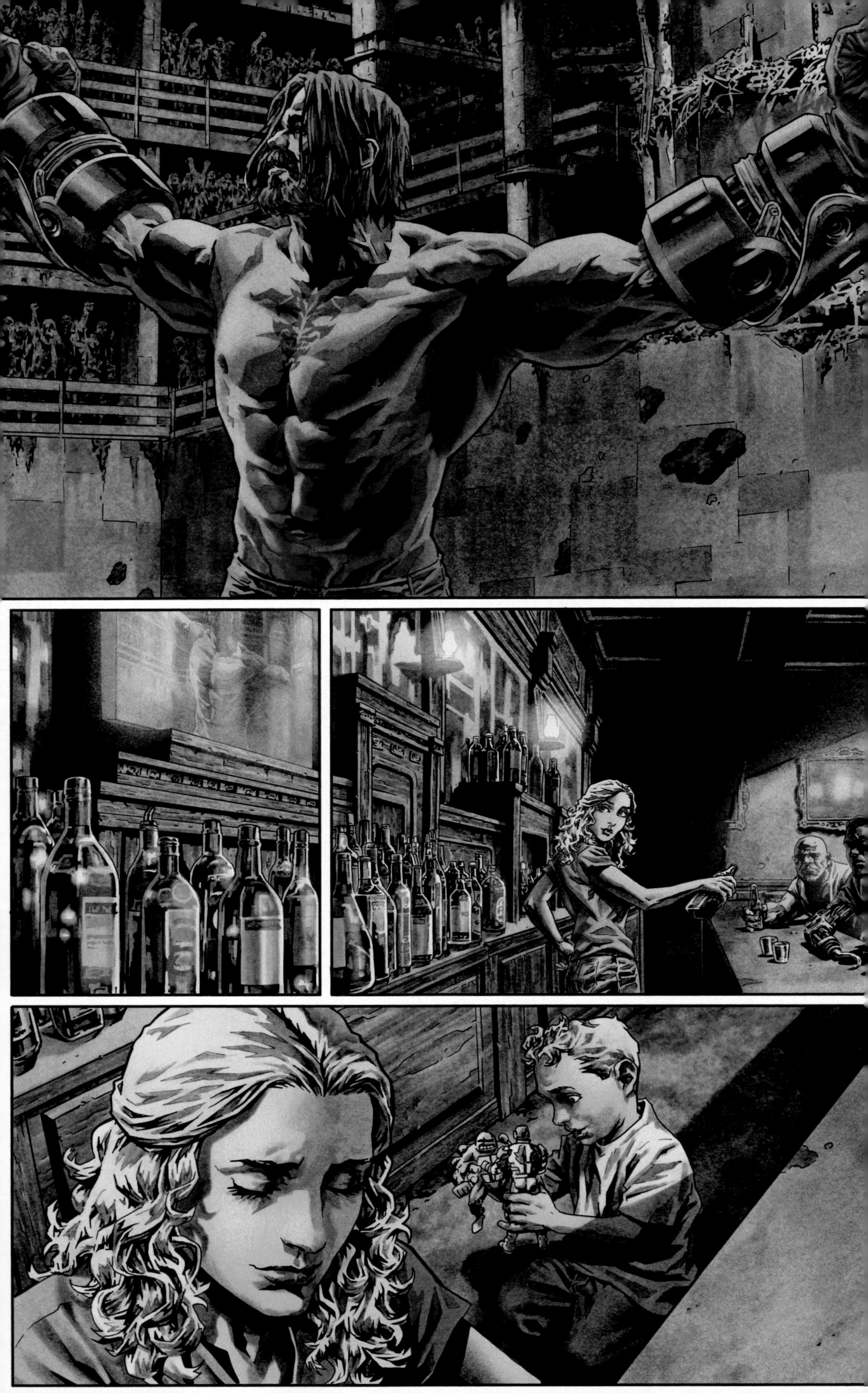

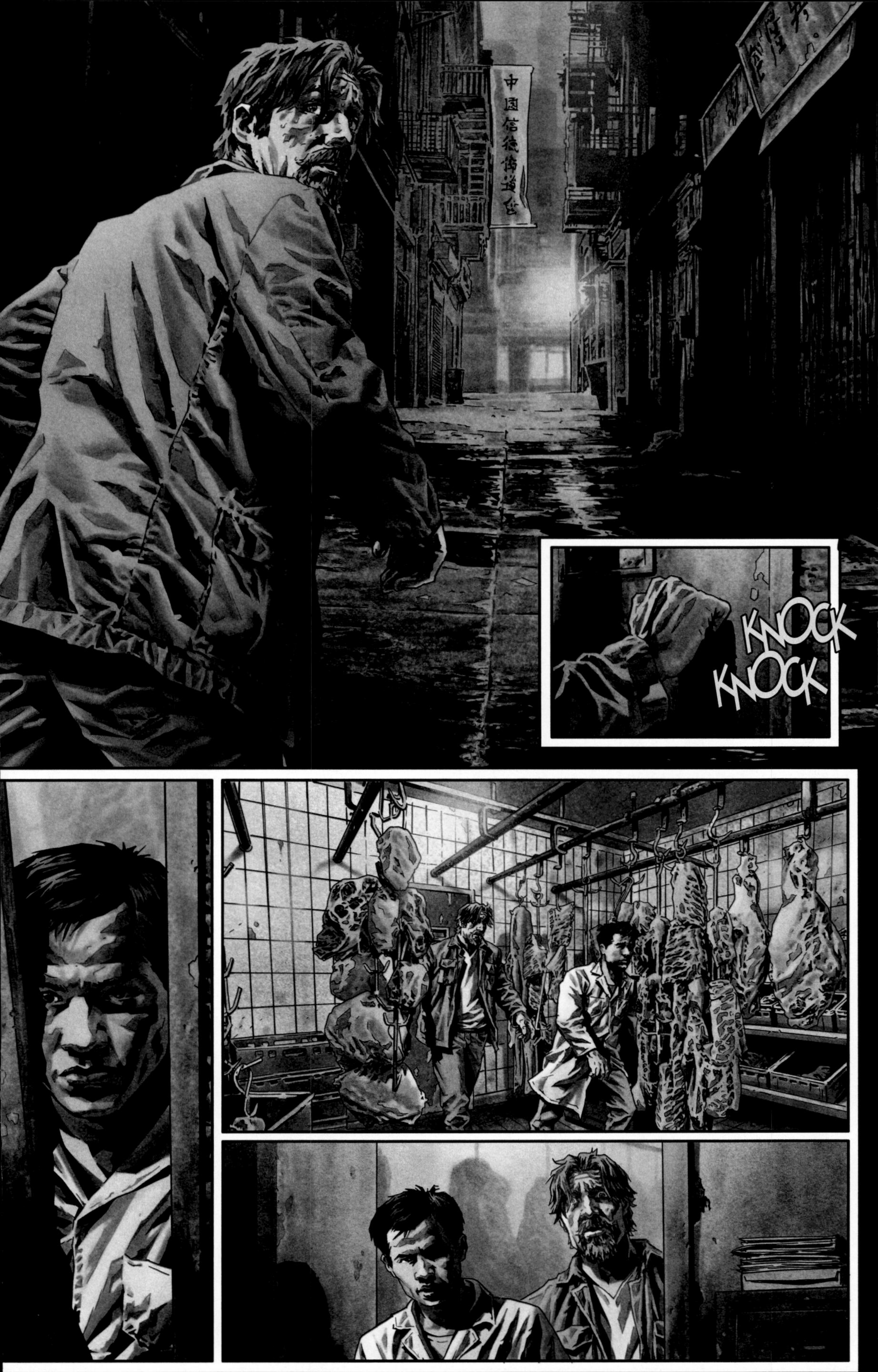
KNOCK
KNOCK

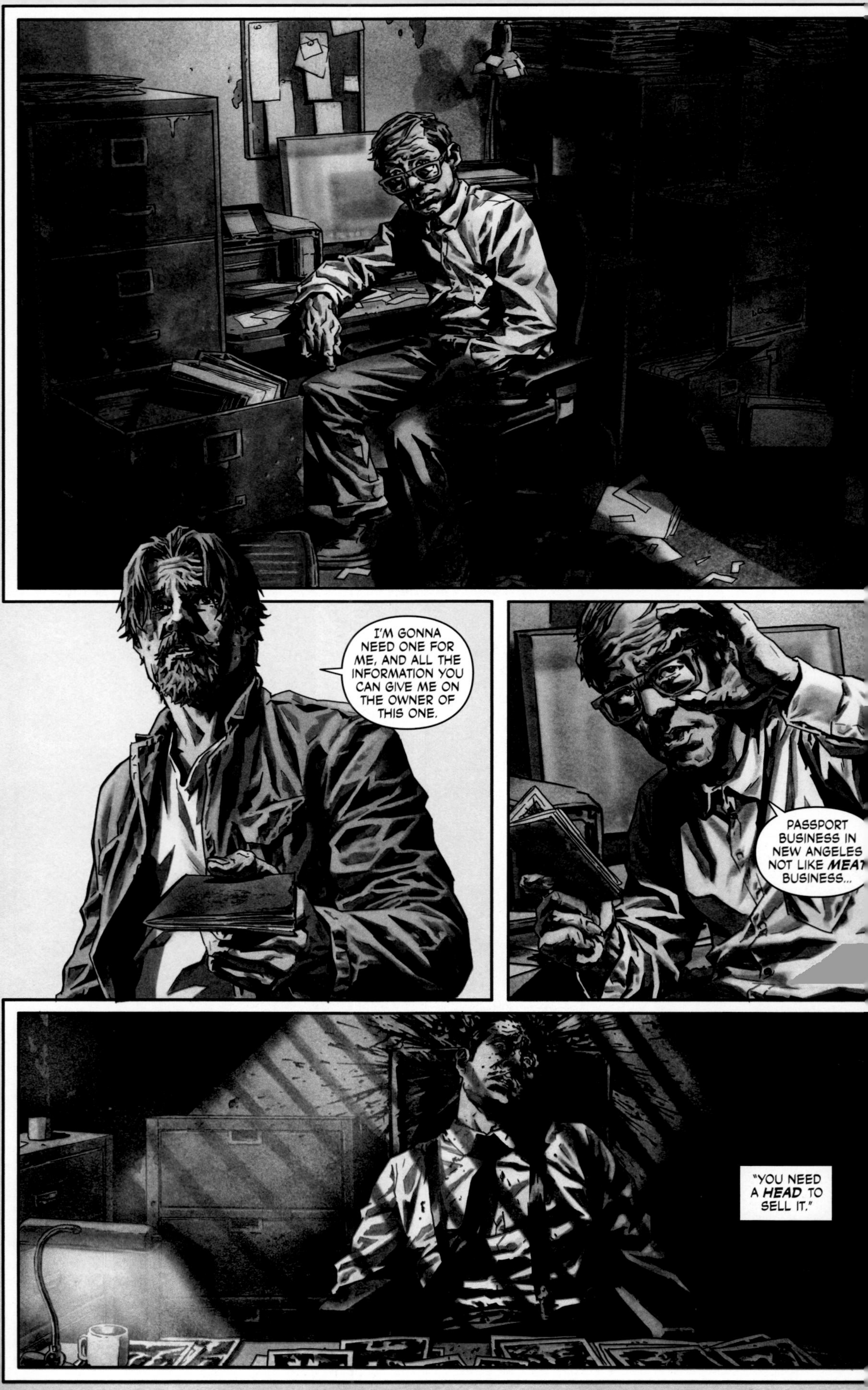
I'M GONNA NEED ONE FOR ME, AND ALL THE INFORMATION YOU CAN GIVE ME ON THE OWNER OF THIS ONE.
PASSPORT BUSINESS IN NEW ANGELES NOT LIKE MEAT BUSINESS...
"YOU NEED A HEAD TO SELL IT."

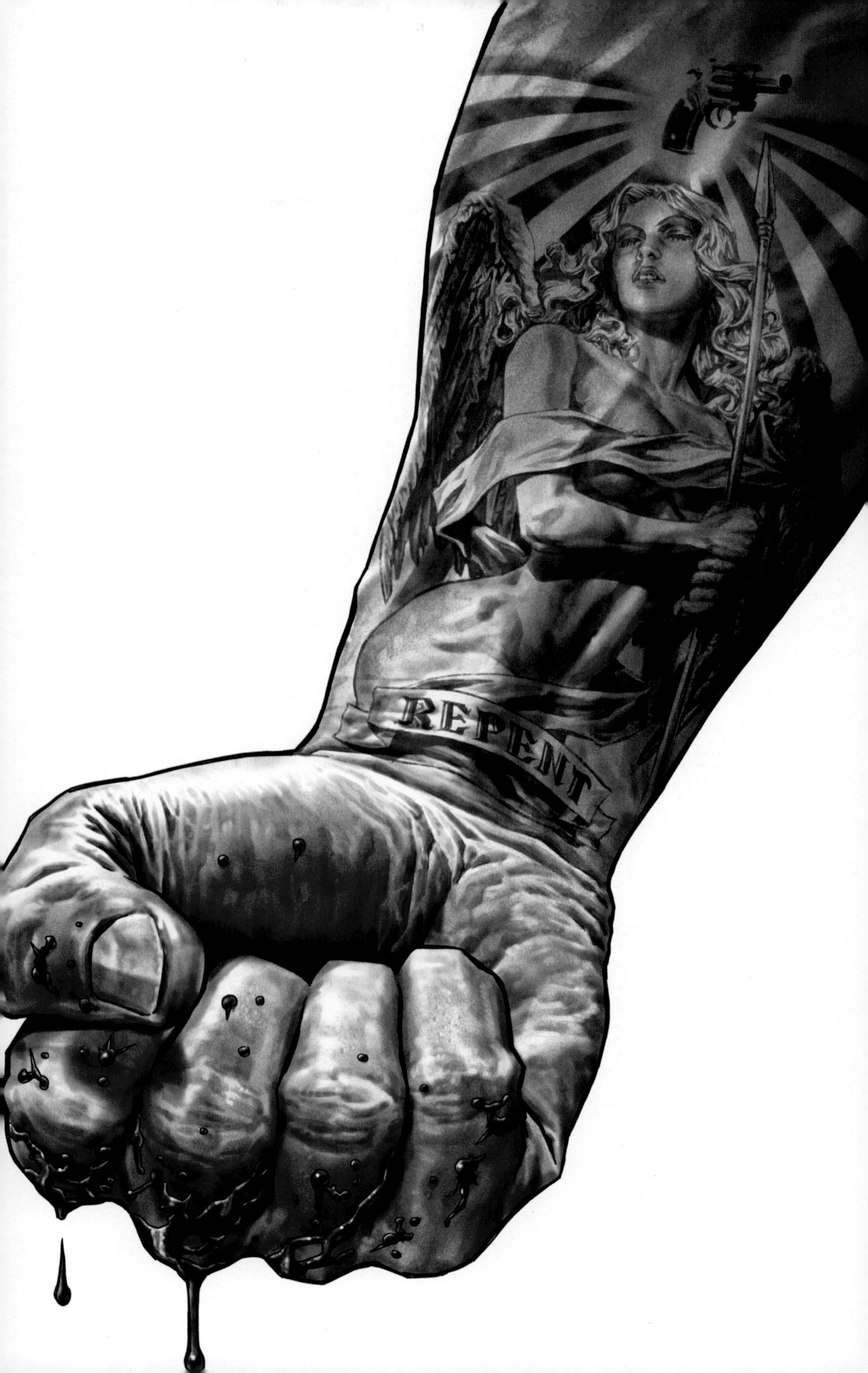
REPENT

CHAPTER FIVE:
MOONWALKER

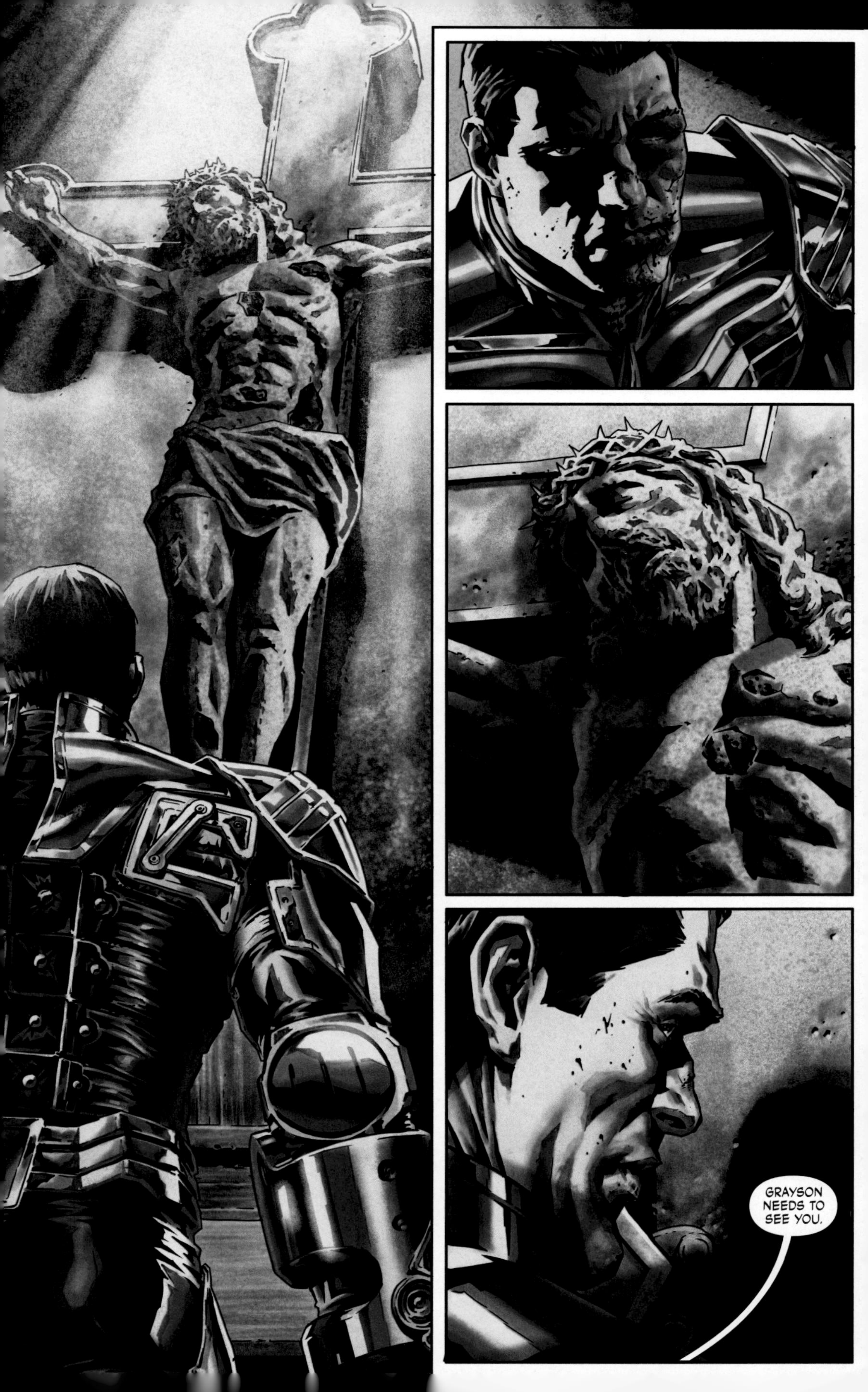
GRAYSON NEEDS TO SEE YOU.

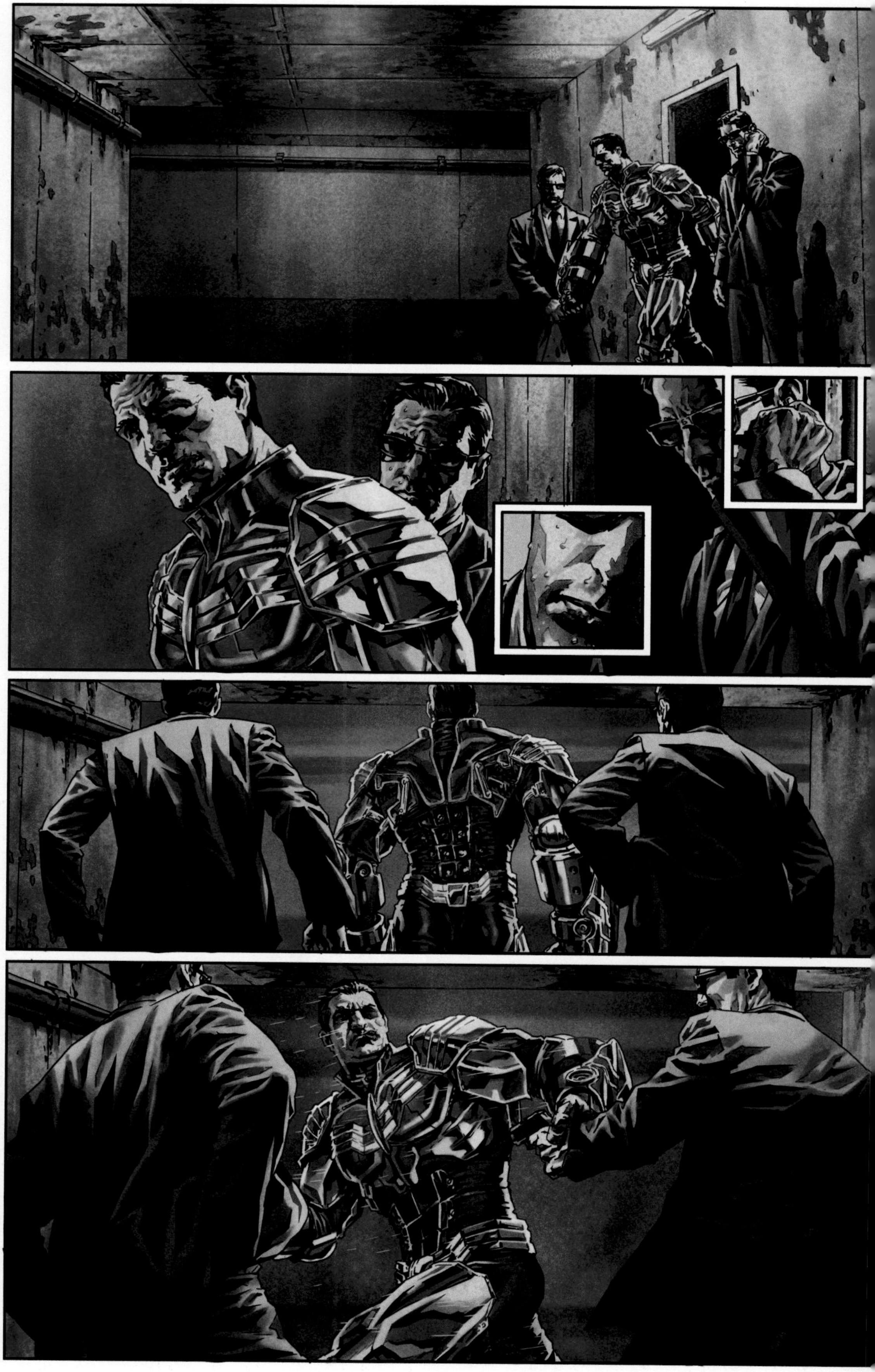

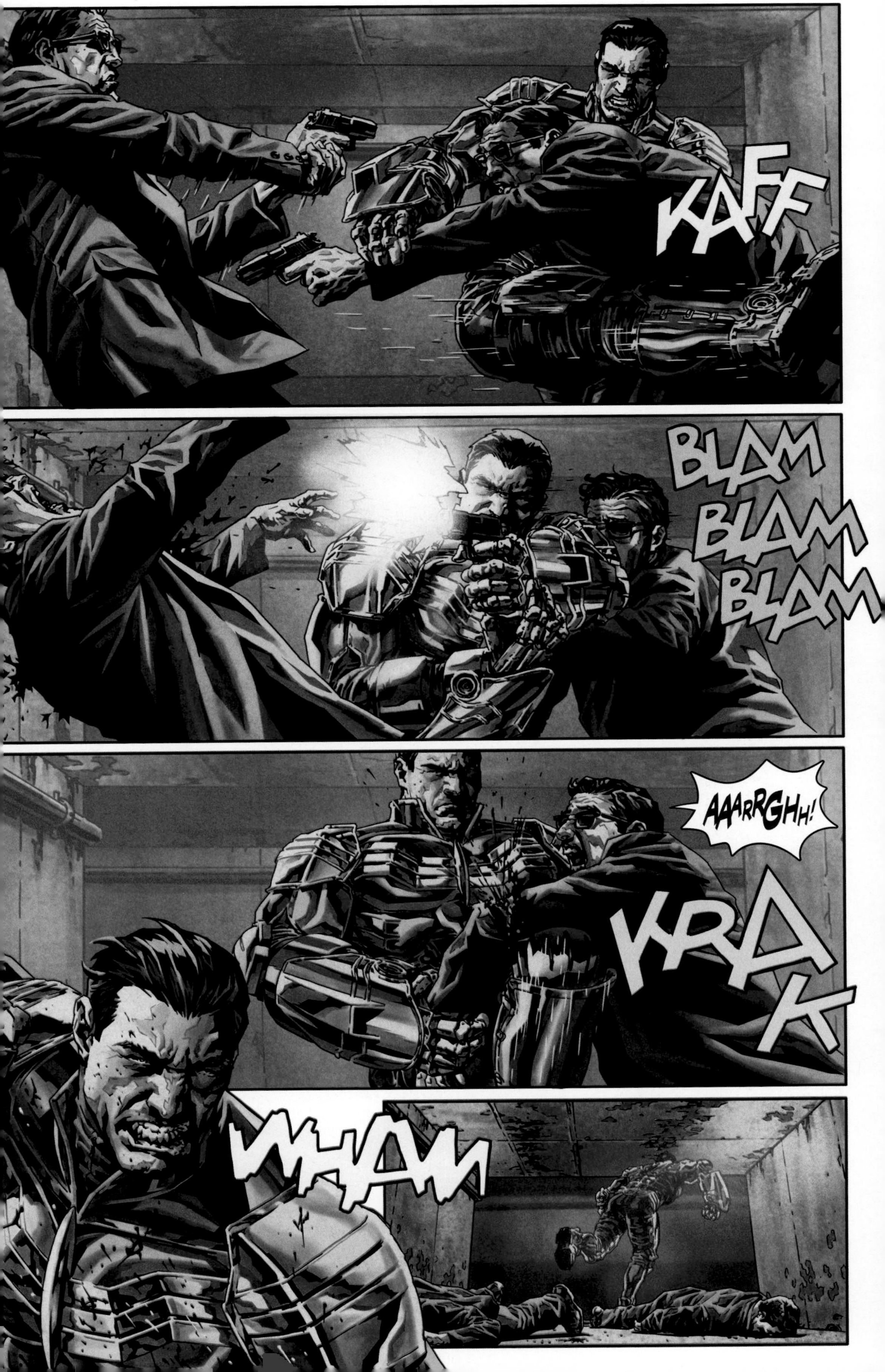
KAFF
BLAM
BLAM
BLAM
AAARRGHH!
KRAK
WHAM

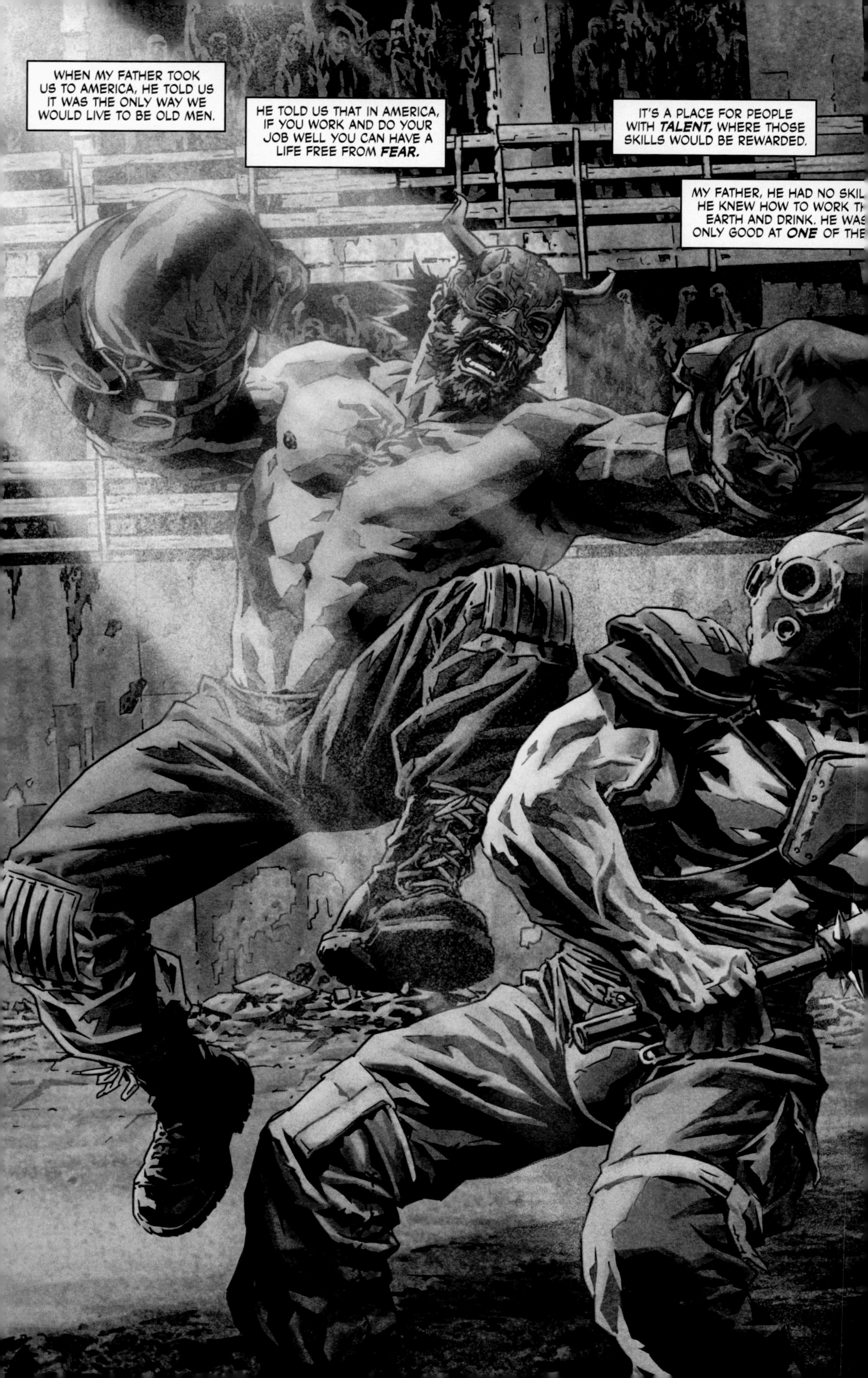
WHEN MY FATHER TOOK US TO AMERICA, HE TOLD US IT WAS THE ONLY WAY WE WOULD LIVE TO BE OLD MEN.
HE TOLD US THAT IN AMERICA, IF YOU WORK AND DO YOUR JOB WELL YOU CAN HAVE A LIFE FREE FROM FEAR.
IT'S A PLACE FOR PEOPLE WITH TALENT, WHERE THOSE SKILLS WOULD BE REWARDED.
MY FATHER, HE HAD NO SKIL HE KNEW HOW TO WORK TH EARTH AND DRINK. HE WAS ONLY GOOD AT ONE OF THE

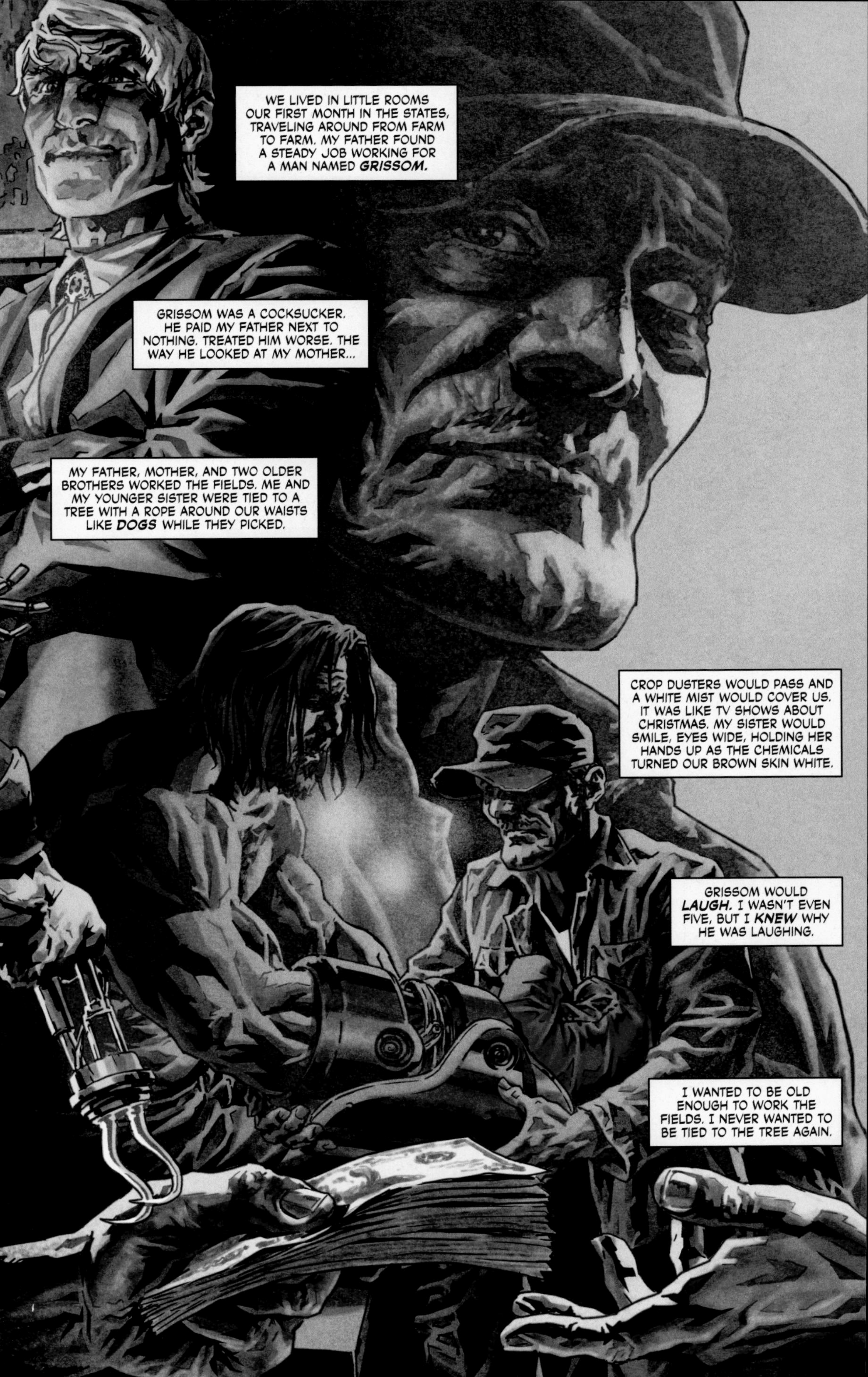
WE LIVED IN LITTLE ROOMS OUR FIRST MONTH IN THE STATES, TRAVELING AROUND FROM FARM TO FARM. MY FATHER FOUND A STEADY JOB WORKING FOR A MAN NAMED GRISSOM.
GRISSOM WAS A COCKSUCKER. HE PAID MY FATHER NEXT TO NOTHING, TREATED HIM WORSE. THE WAY HE LOOKED AT MY MOTHER...
MY FATHER, MOTHER, AND TWO OLDER BROTHERS WORKED THE FIELDS. ME AND MY YOUNGER SISTER WERE TIED TO A TREE WITH A ROPE AROUND OUR WAISTS LIKE DOGS WHILE THEY PICKED.
CROP DUSTERS WOULD PASS AND A WHITE MIST WOULD COVER US. IT WAS LIKE TV SHOWS ABOUT CHRISTMAS. MY SISTER WOULD SMILE, EYES WIDE, HOLDING HER HANDS UP AS THE CHEMICALS TURNED OUR BROWN SKIN WHITE.
GRISSOM WOULD LAUGH. I WASN'T EVEN FIVE, BUT I KNEW WHY HE WAS LAUGHING.
I WANTED TO BE OLD ENOUGH TO WORK THE FIELDS. I NEVER WANTED TO BE TIED TO THE TREE AGAIN.

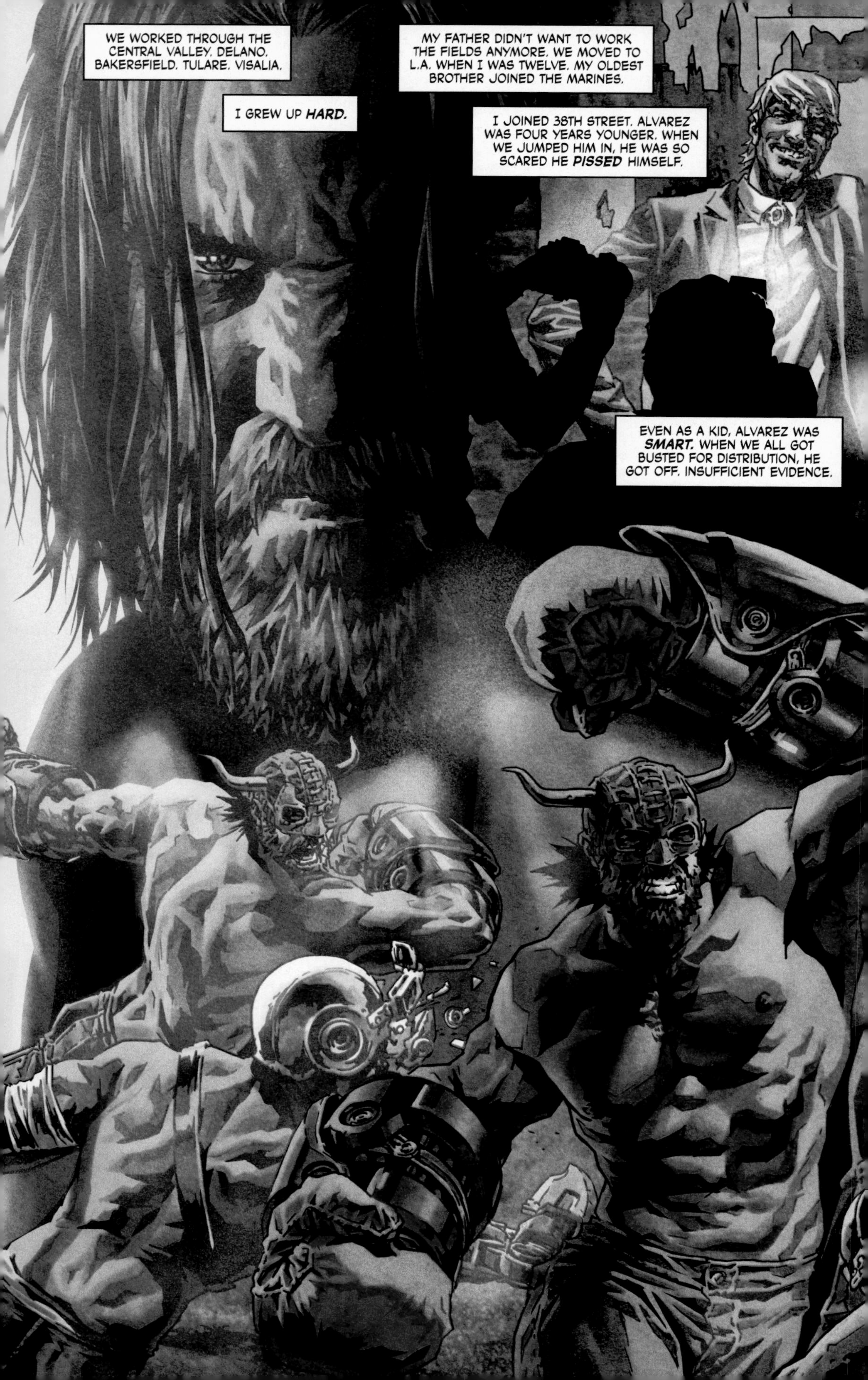

WE WORKED THROUGH THE CENTRAL VALLEY. DELANO. BAKERSFIELD. TULARE. VISALIA.
I GREW UP **HARD.**
MY FATHER DIDN'T WANT TO WORK THE FIELDS ANYMORE. WE MOVED TO L.A. WHEN I WAS TWELVE. MY OLDEST BROTHER JOINED THE MARINES.
I JOINED 38TH STREET. ALVAREZ WAS FOUR YEARS YOUNGER. WHEN WE JUMPED HIM IN, HE WAS SO SCARED HE **PISSED** HIMSELF.
EVEN AS A KID, ALVAREZ WAS **SMART.** WHEN WE ALL GOT BUSTED FOR DISTRIBUTION, HE GOT OFF. INSUFFICIENT EVIDENCE.

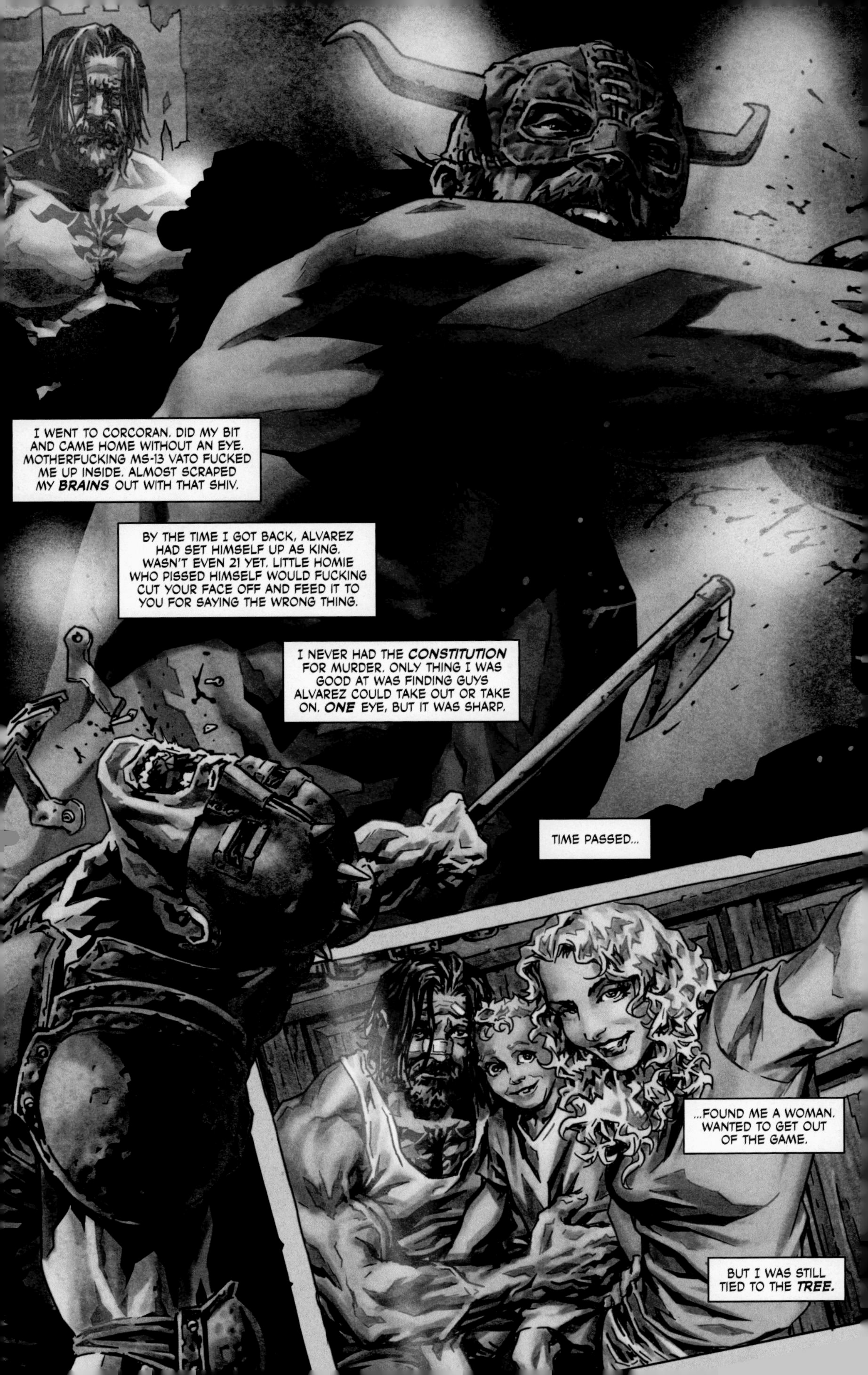
I WENT TO CORCORAN. DID MY BIT AND CAME HOME WITHOUT AN EYE. MOTHERFUCKING MS-13 VATO FUCKED ME UP INSIDE. ALMOST SCRAPED MY BRAINS OUT WITH THAT SHIV.
BY THE TIME I GOT BACK, ALVAREZ HAD SET HIMSELF UP AS KING. WASN'T EVEN 21 YET. LITTLE HOMIE WHO PISSED HIMSELF WOULD FUCKING CUT YOUR FACE OFF AND FEED IT TO YOU FOR SAYING THE WRONG THING.
I NEVER HAD THE CONSTITUTION FOR MURDER. ONLY THING I WAS GOOD AT WAS FINDING GUYS ALVAREZ COULD TAKE OUT OR TAKE ON. ONE EYE, BUT IT WAS SHARP.
TIME PASSED...
...FOUND ME A WOMAN. WANTED TO GET OUT OF THE GAME.
BUT I WAS STILL TIED TO THE TREE.

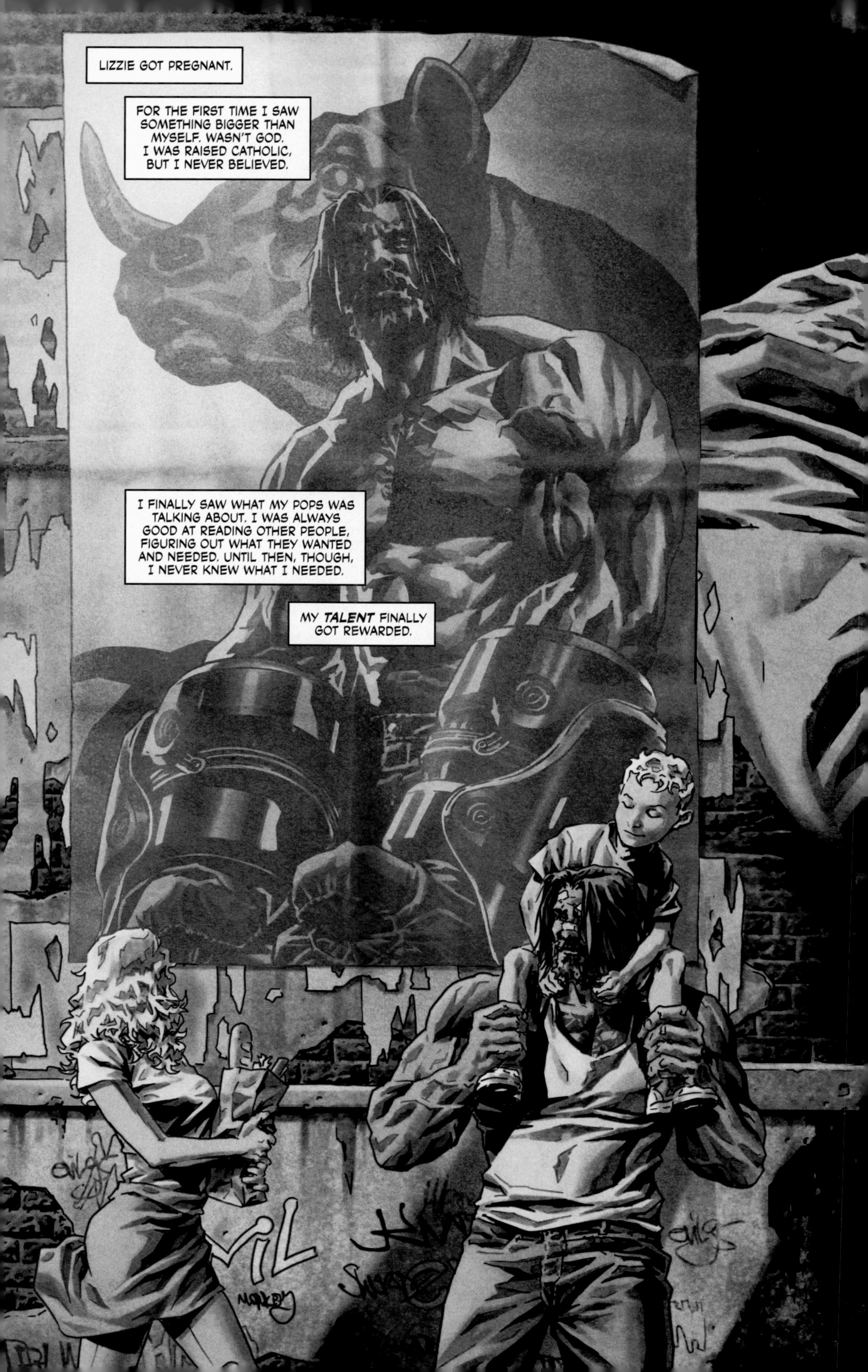

LIZZIE GOT PREGNANT.
FOR THE FIRST TIME I SAW SOMETHING BIGGER THAN MYSELF. WASN'T GOD. I WAS RAISED CATHOLIC, BUT I NEVER BELIEVED.
I FINALLY SAW WHAT MY POPS WAS TALKING ABOUT. I WAS ALWAYS GOOD AT READING OTHER PEOPLE, FIGURING OUT WHAT THEY WANTED AND NEEDED. UNTIL THEN, THOUGH, I NEVER KNEW WHAT I NEEDED.
MY *TALENT* FINALLY GOT REWARDED.

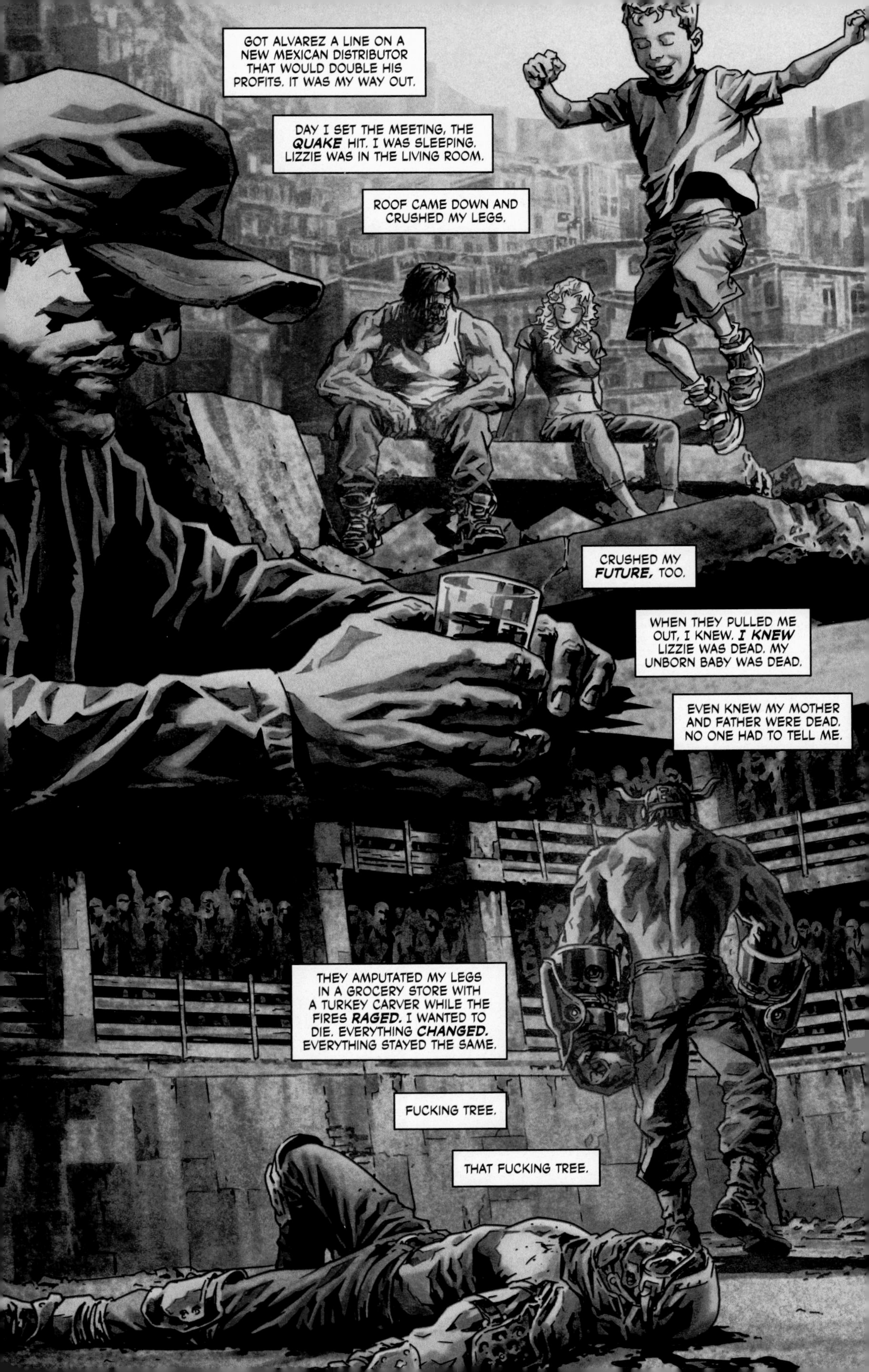
GOT ALVAREZ A LINE ON A NEW MEXICAN DISTRIBUTOR THAT WOULD DOUBLE HIS PROFITS. IT WAS MY WAY OUT.
DAY I SET THE MEETING, THE QUAKE HIT. I WAS SLEEPING. LIZZIE WAS IN THE LIVING ROOM.
ROOF CAME DOWN AND CRUSHED MY LEGS.
CRUSHED MY FUTURE, TOO.
WHEN THEY PULLED ME OUT, I KNEW. I KNEW LIZZIE WAS DEAD. MY UNBORN BABY WAS DEAD.
EVEN KNEW MY MOTHER AND FATHER WERE DEAD. NO ONE HAD TO TELL ME.
THEY AMPUTATED MY LEGS IN A GROCERY STORE WITH A TURKEY CARVER WHILE THE FIRES RAGED. I WANTED TO DIE. EVERYTHING CHANGED. EVERYTHING STAYED THE SAME.
FUCKING TREE.
THAT FUCKING TREE.

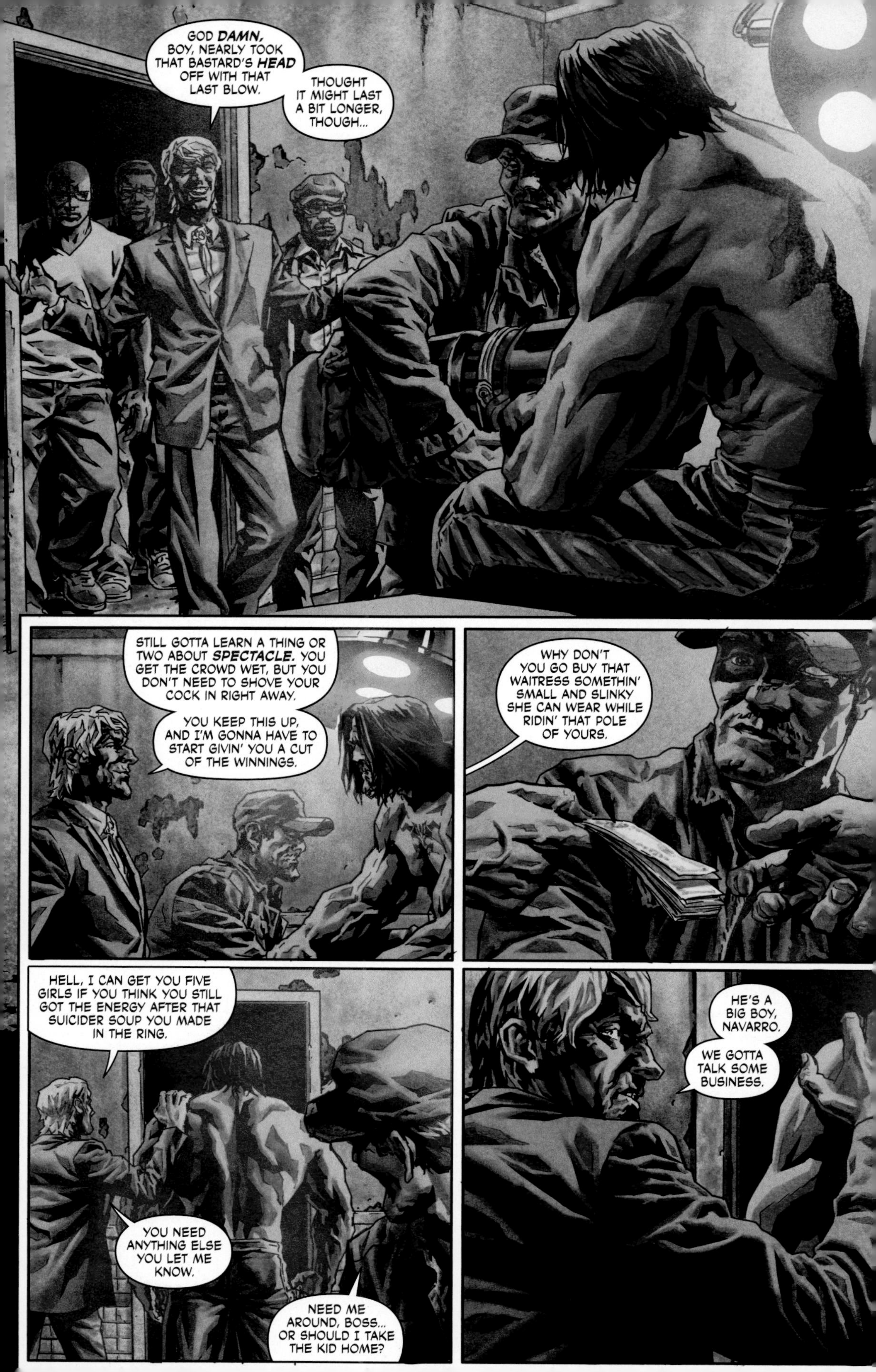
GOD DAMN, BOY, NEARLY TOOK THAT BASTARD'S HEAD OFF WITH THAT LAST BLOW.
THOUGHT IT MIGHT LAST A BIT LONGER, THOUGH...
STILL GOTTA LEARN A THING OR TWO ABOUT SPECTACLE. YOU GET THE CROWD WET, BUT YOU DON'T NEED TO SHOVE YOUR COCK IN RIGHT AWAY.
YOU KEEP THIS UP, AND I'M GONNA HAVE TO START GIVIN' YOU A CUT OF THE WINNINGS.
WHY DON'T YOU GO BUY THAT WAITRESS SOMETHIN' SMALL AND SLINKY SHE CAN WEAR WHILE RIDIN' THAT POLE OF YOURS.
HELL, I CAN GET YOU FIVE GIRLS IF YOU THINK YOU STILL GOT THE ENERGY AFTER THAT SUICIDER SOUP YOU MADE IN THE RING.
YOU NEED ANYTHING ELSE YOU LET ME KNOW.
NEED ME AROUND, BOSS... OR SHOULD I TAKE THE KID HOME?
HE'S A BIG BOY, NAVARRO.
WE GOTTA TALK SOME BUSINESS.

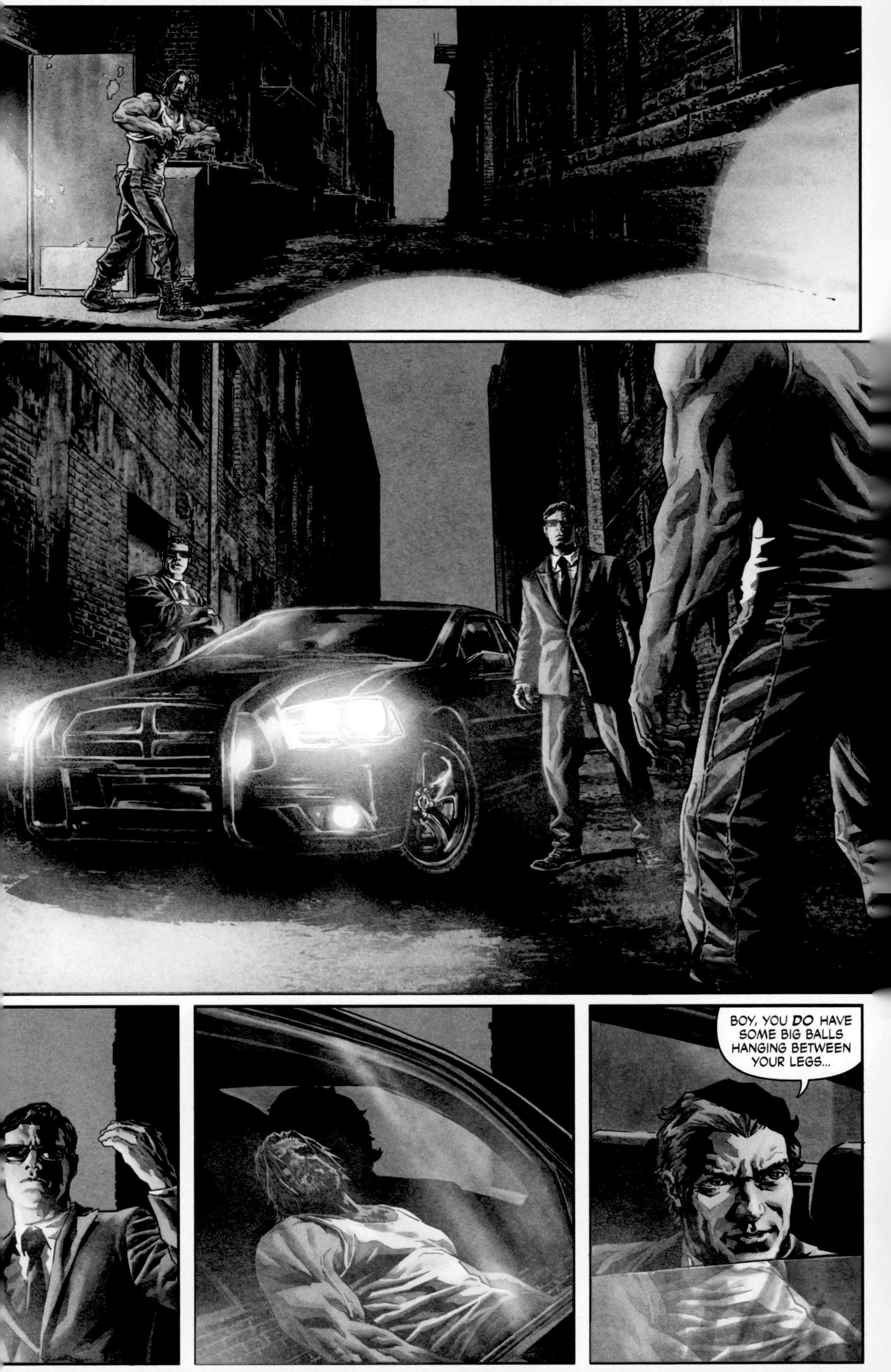
BOY, YOU DO HAVE SOME BIG BALLS HANGING BETWEEN YOUR LEGS...

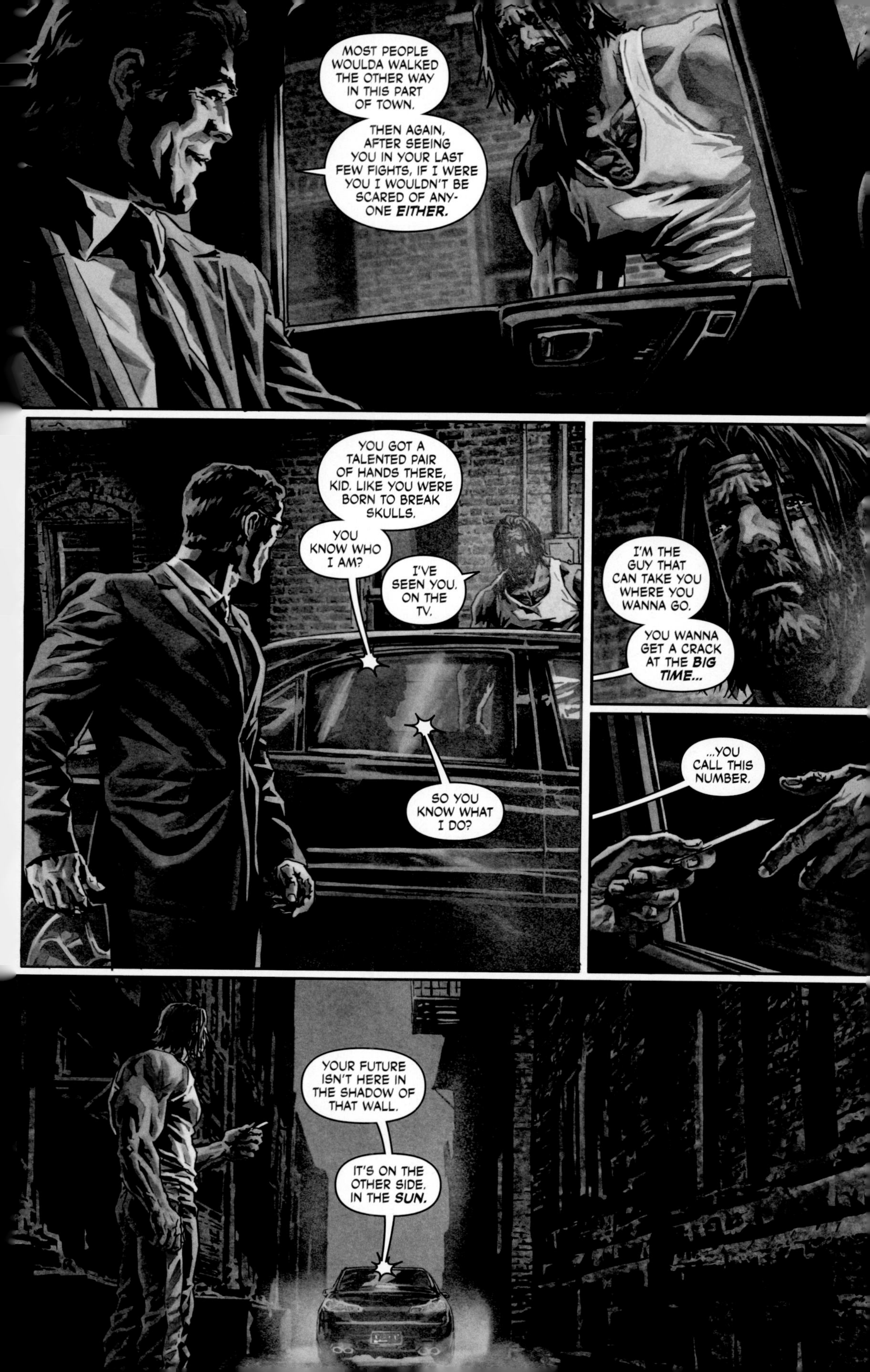
MOST PEOPLE WOULDA WALKED THE OTHER WAY IN THIS PART OF TOWN.
THEN AGAIN, AFTER SEEING YOU IN YOUR LAST FEW FIGHTS, IF I WERE YOU I WOULDN'T BE SCARED OF ANY-ONE *EITHER.*
YOU GOT A TALENTED PAIR OF HANDS THERE, KID. LIKE YOU WERE BORN TO BREAK SKULLS.
YOU KNOW WHO I AM?
I'VE SEEN YOU. ON THE TV.
SO YOU KNOW WHAT I DO?
I'M THE GUY THAT CAN TAKE YOU WHERE YOU WANNA GO.
YOU WANNA GET A CRACK AT THE *BIG TIME...*
...YOU CALL THIS NUMBER.
YOUR FUTURE ISN'T HERE IN THE SHADOW OF THAT WALL.
IT'S ON THE OTHER SIDE, IN THE *SUN.*

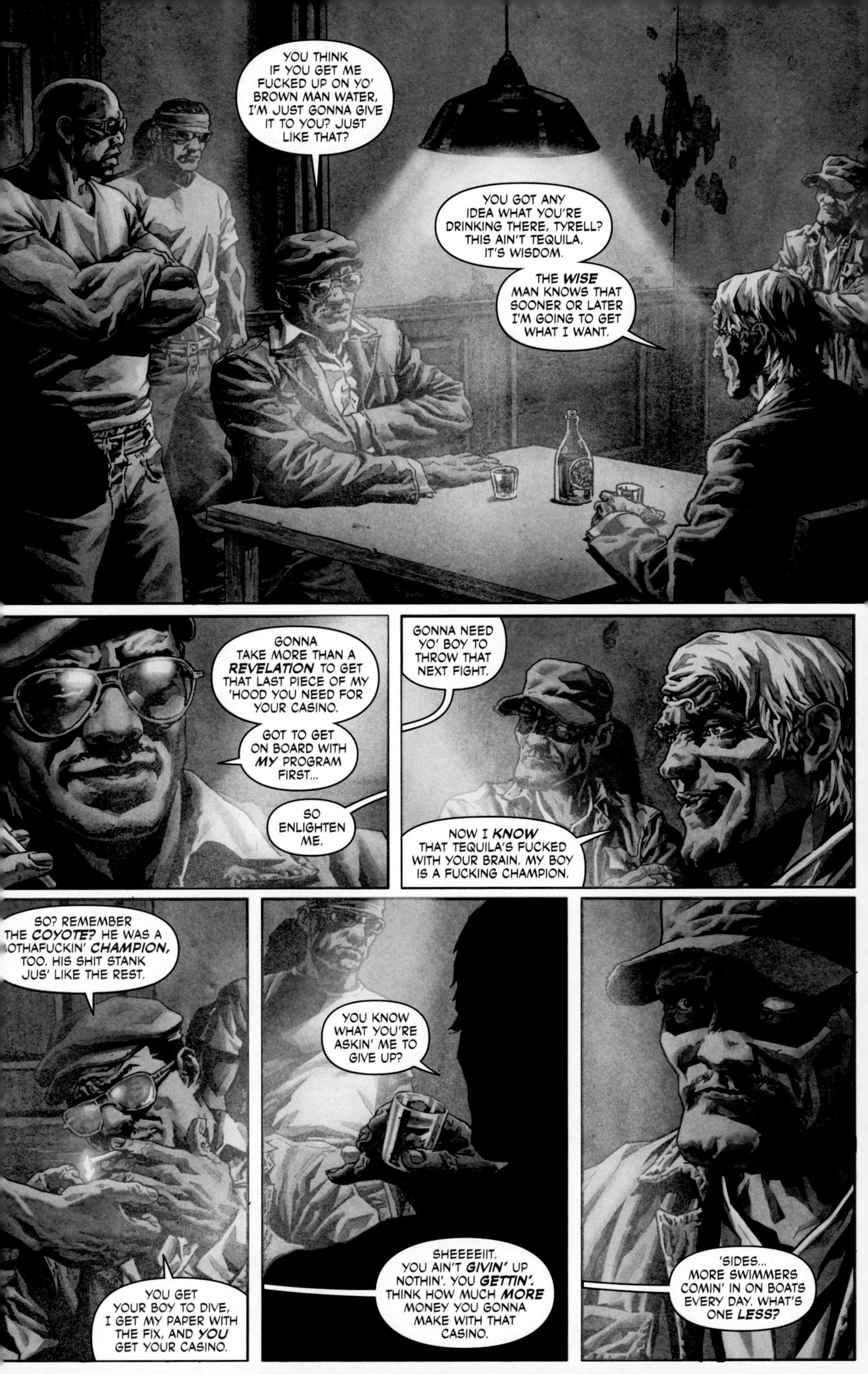
YOU THINK IF YOU GET ME FUCKED UP ON YO' BROWN MAN WATER, I'M JUST GONNA GIVE IT TO YOU? JUST LIKE THAT?
YOU GOT ANY IDEA WHAT YOU'RE DRINKING THERE, TYRELL? THIS AIN'T TEQUILA. IT'S WISDOM.
THE WISE MAN KNOWS THAT SOONER OR LATER I'M GOING TO GET WHAT I WANT.
GONNA TAKE MORE THAN A REVELATION TO GET THAT LAST PIECE OF MY 'HOOD YOU NEED FOR YOUR CASINO.
GOT TO GET ON BOARD WITH MY PROGRAM FIRST...
SO ENLIGHTEN ME.
GONNA NEED YO' BOY TO THROW THAT NEXT FIGHT.
NOW I KNOW THAT TEQUILA'S FUCKED WITH YOUR BRAIN. MY BOY IS A FUCKING CHAMPION.
SO? REMEMBER THE COYOTE? HE WAS A OTHAFUCKIN' CHAMPION, TOO. HIS SHIT STANK JUS' LIKE THE REST.
YOU GET YOUR BOY TO DIVE, I GET MY PAPER WITH THE FIX, AND YOU GET YOUR CASINO.
YOU KNOW WHAT YOU'RE ASKIN' ME TO GIVE UP?
SHEEEEIIT. YOU AIN'T GIVIN' UP NOTHIN'. YOU GETTIN'. THINK HOW MUCH MORE MONEY YOU GONNA MAKE WITH THAT CASINO.
'SIDES... MORE SWIMMERS COMIN' IN ON BOATS EVERY DAY. WHAT'S ONE LESS?

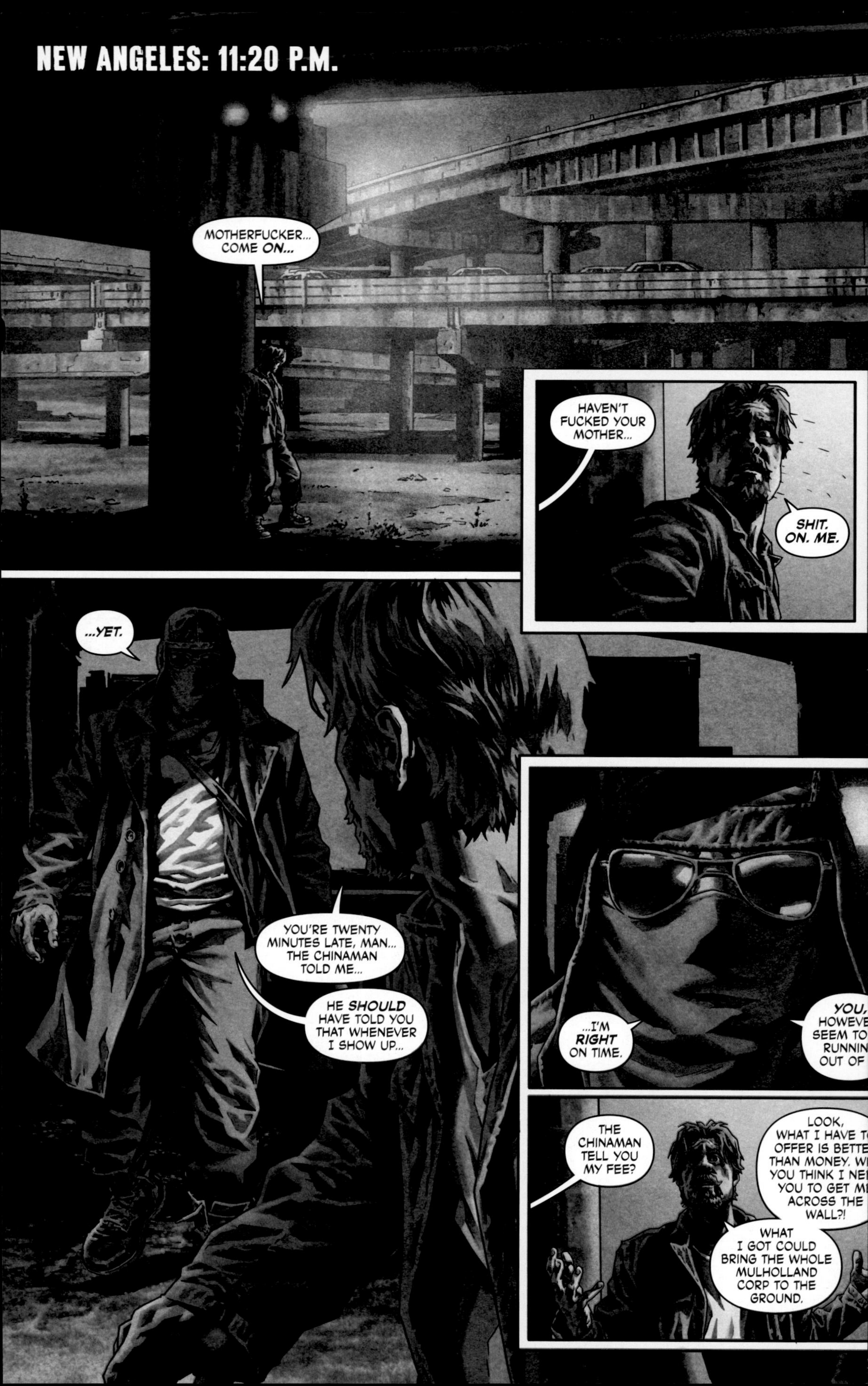
NEW ANGELES: 11:20 P.M.
MOTHERFUCKER... COME ON...
HAVEN'T FUCKED YOUR MOTHER...
SHIT. ON. ME.
...YET.
YOU'RE TWENTY MINUTES LATE, MAN... THE CHINAMAN TOLD ME...
HE SHOULD HAVE TOLD YOU THAT WHENEVER I SHOW UP...
...I'M RIGHT ON TIME.
YOU, HOWEVE SEEM TO RUNNIN OUT OF
THE CHINAMAN TELL YOU MY FEE?
LOOK, WHAT I HAVE T OFFER IS BETTE THAN MONEY. W YOU THINK I NE YOU TO GET M ACROSS THE WALL?!
WHAT I GOT COULD BRING THE WHOLE MULHOLLAND CORP TO THE GROUND.

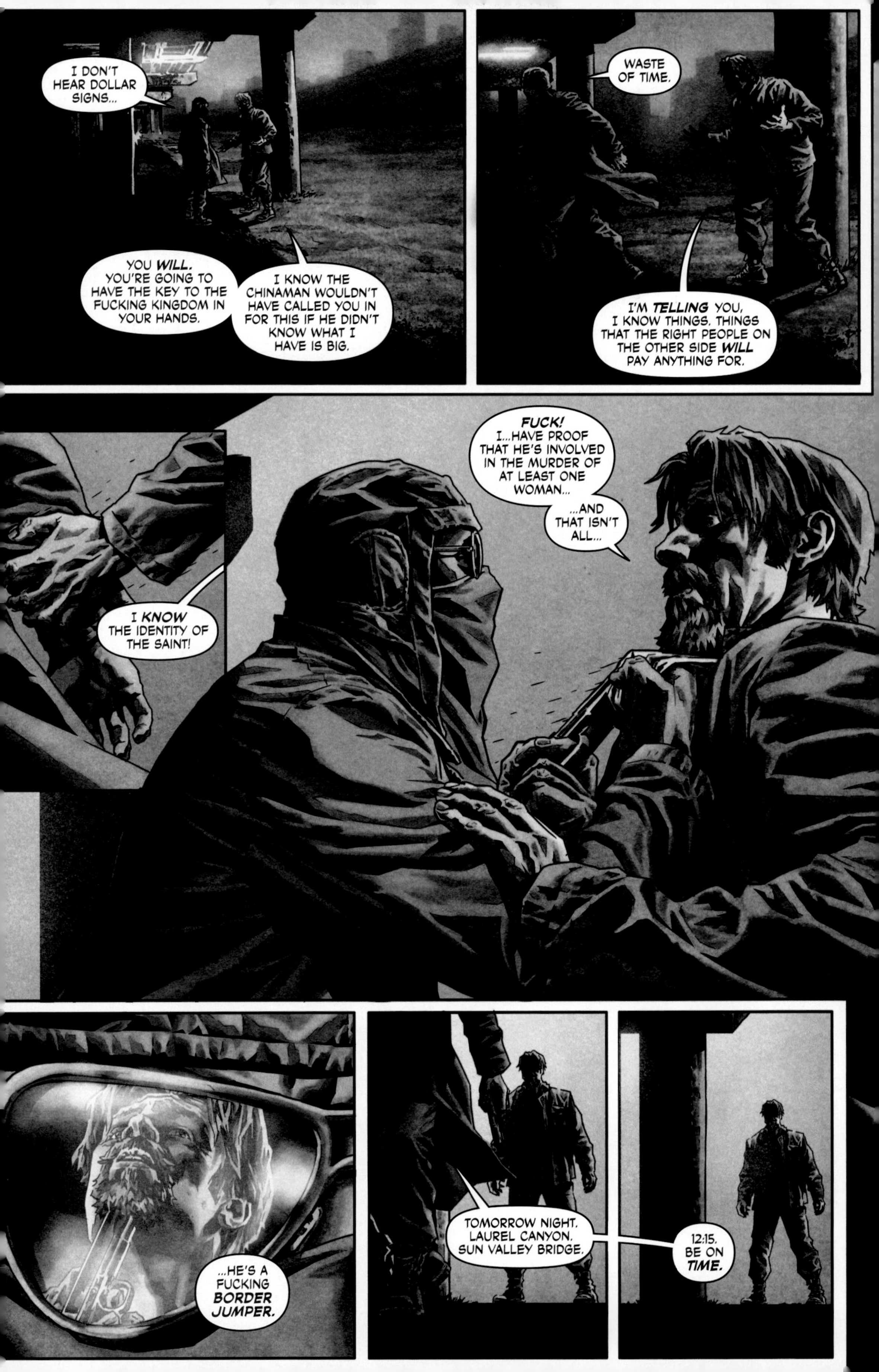
I DON'T HEAR DOLLAR SIGNS...
YOU *WILL.* YOU'RE GOING TO HAVE THE KEY TO THE FUCKING KINGDOM IN YOUR HANDS.
I KNOW THE CHINAMAN WOULDN'T HAVE CALLED YOU IN FOR THIS IF HE DIDN'T KNOW WHAT I HAVE IS BIG.
WASTE OF TIME.
I'M *TELLING* YOU, I KNOW THINGS, THINGS THAT THE RIGHT PEOPLE ON THE OTHER SIDE *WILL* PAY ANYTHING FOR.
FUCK! I...HAVE PROOF THAT HE'S INVOLVED IN THE MURDER OF AT LEAST ONE WOMAN...
...AND THAT ISN'T ALL...
I *KNOW* THE IDENTITY OF THE SAINT!
...HE'S A FUCKING *BORDER JUMPER.*
TOMORROW NIGHT. LAUREL CANYON. SUN VALLEY BRIDGE.
12:15. BE ON *TIME.*

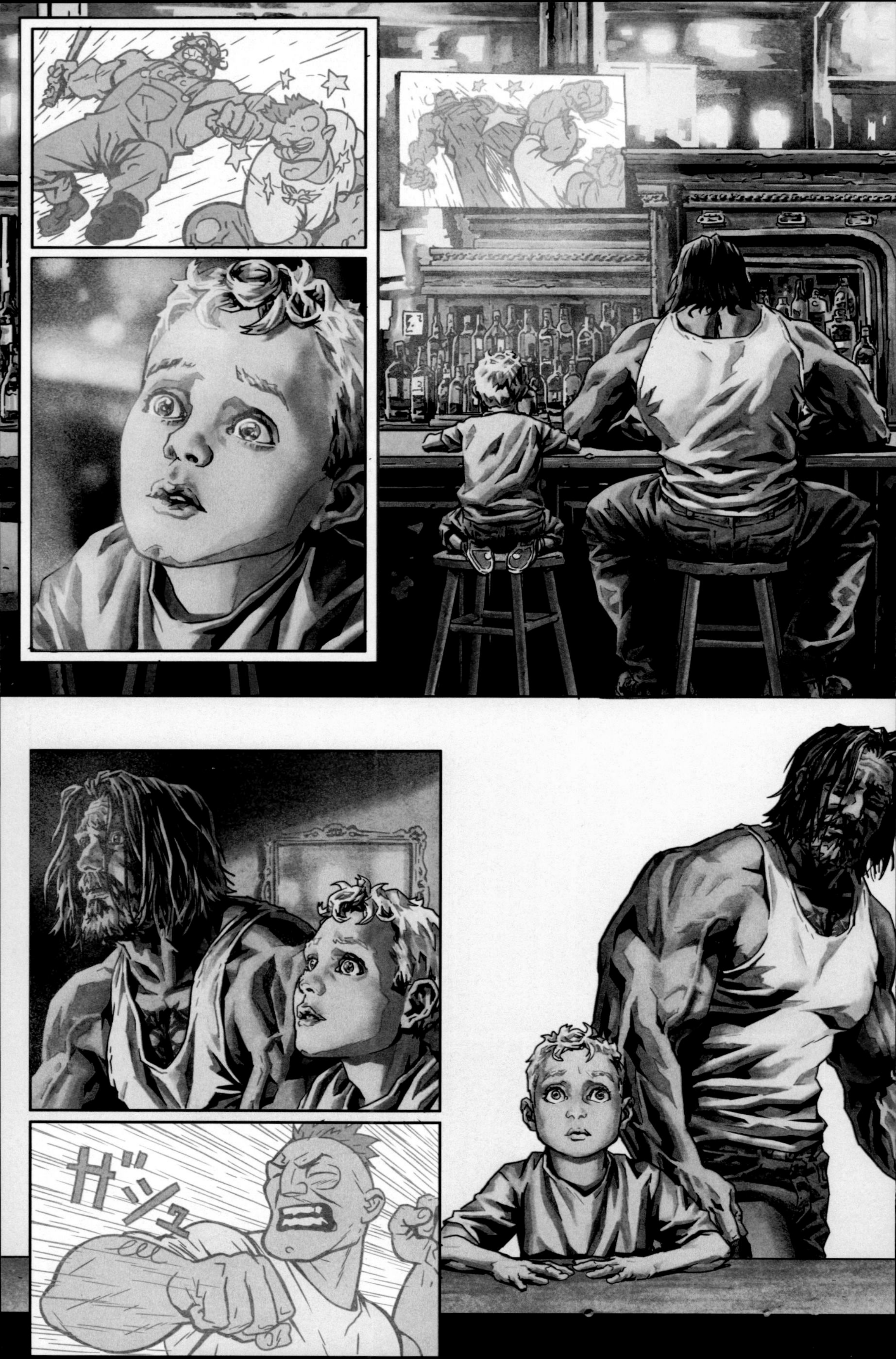
ザッシュ

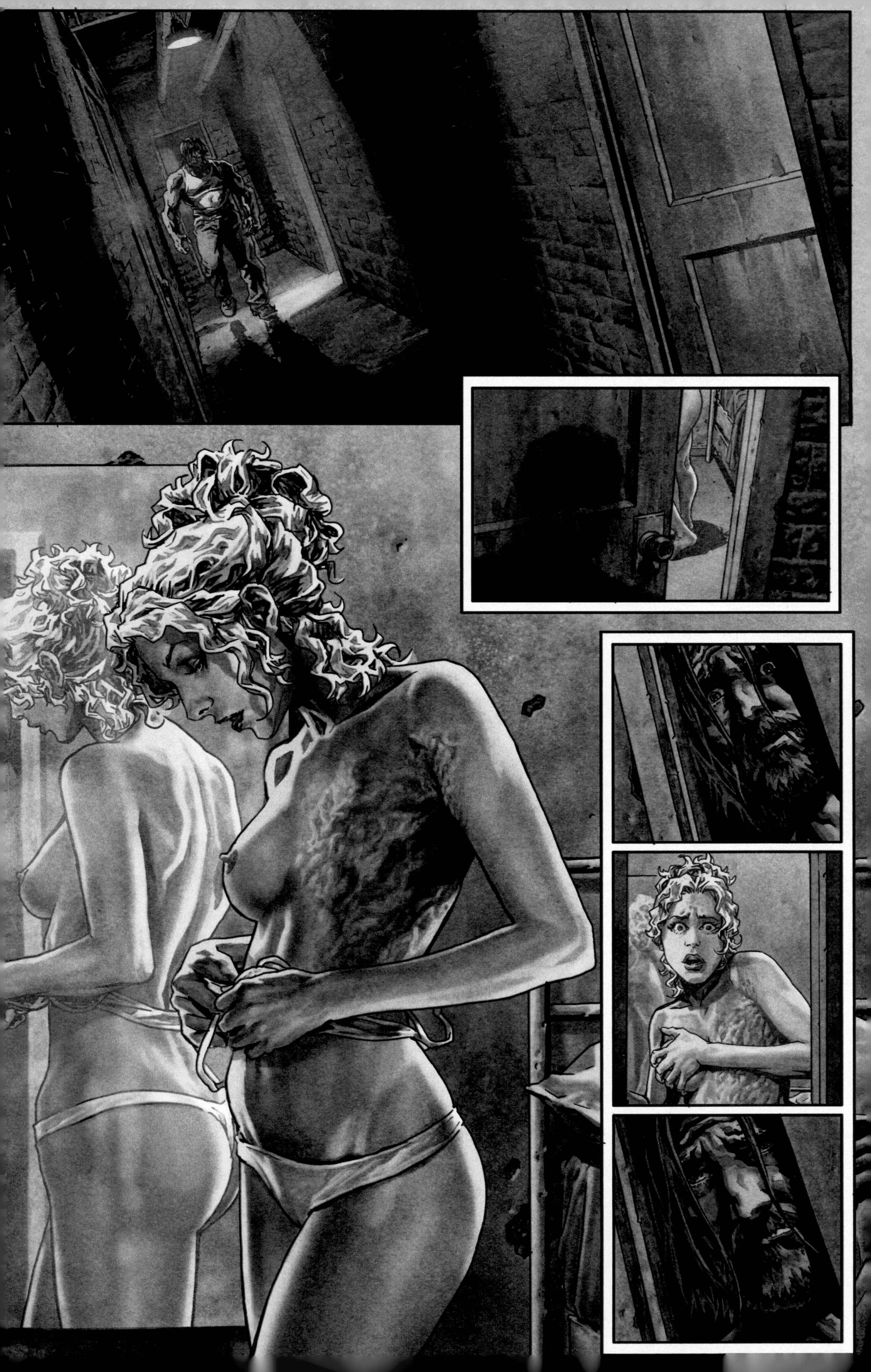

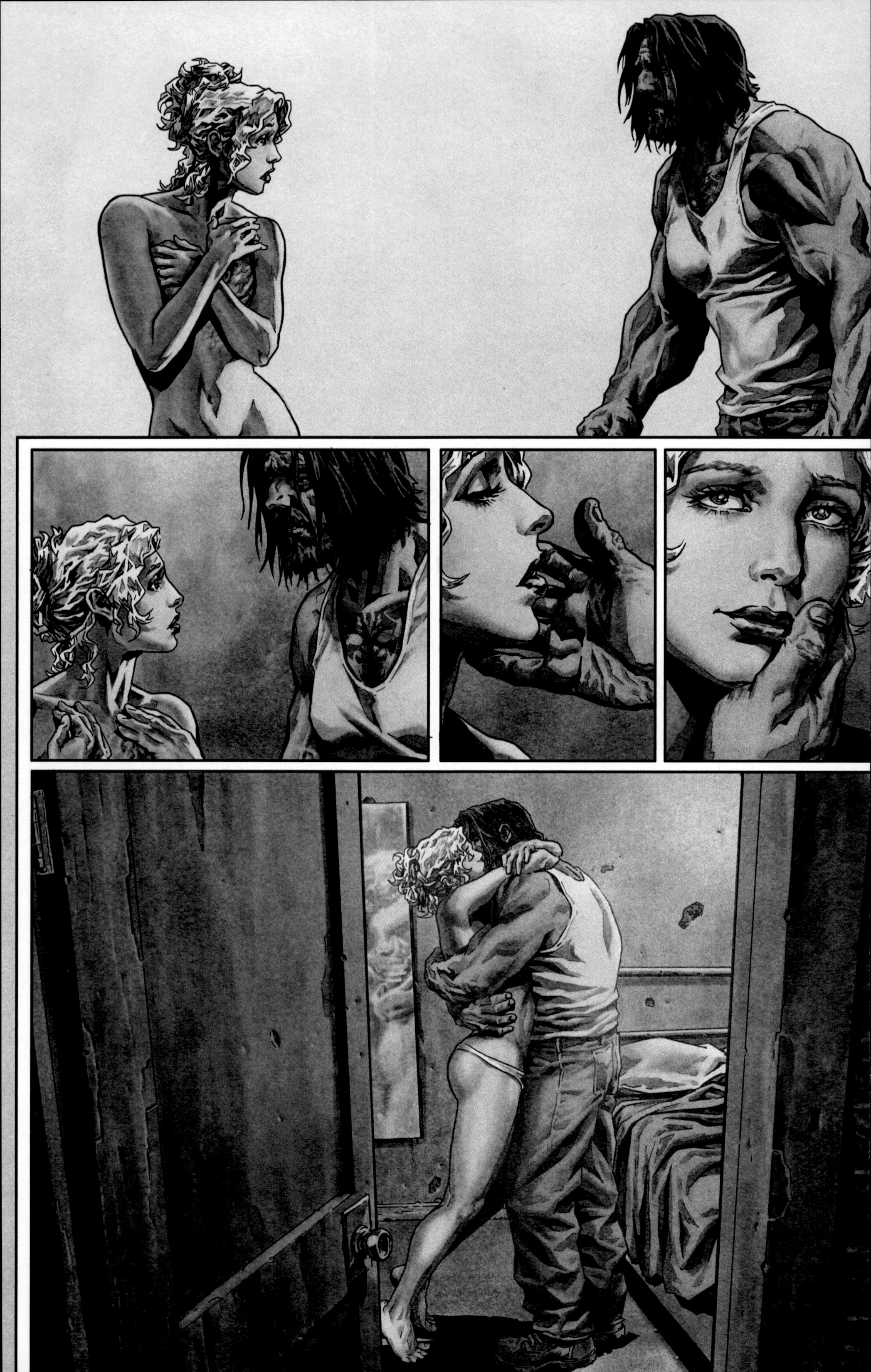

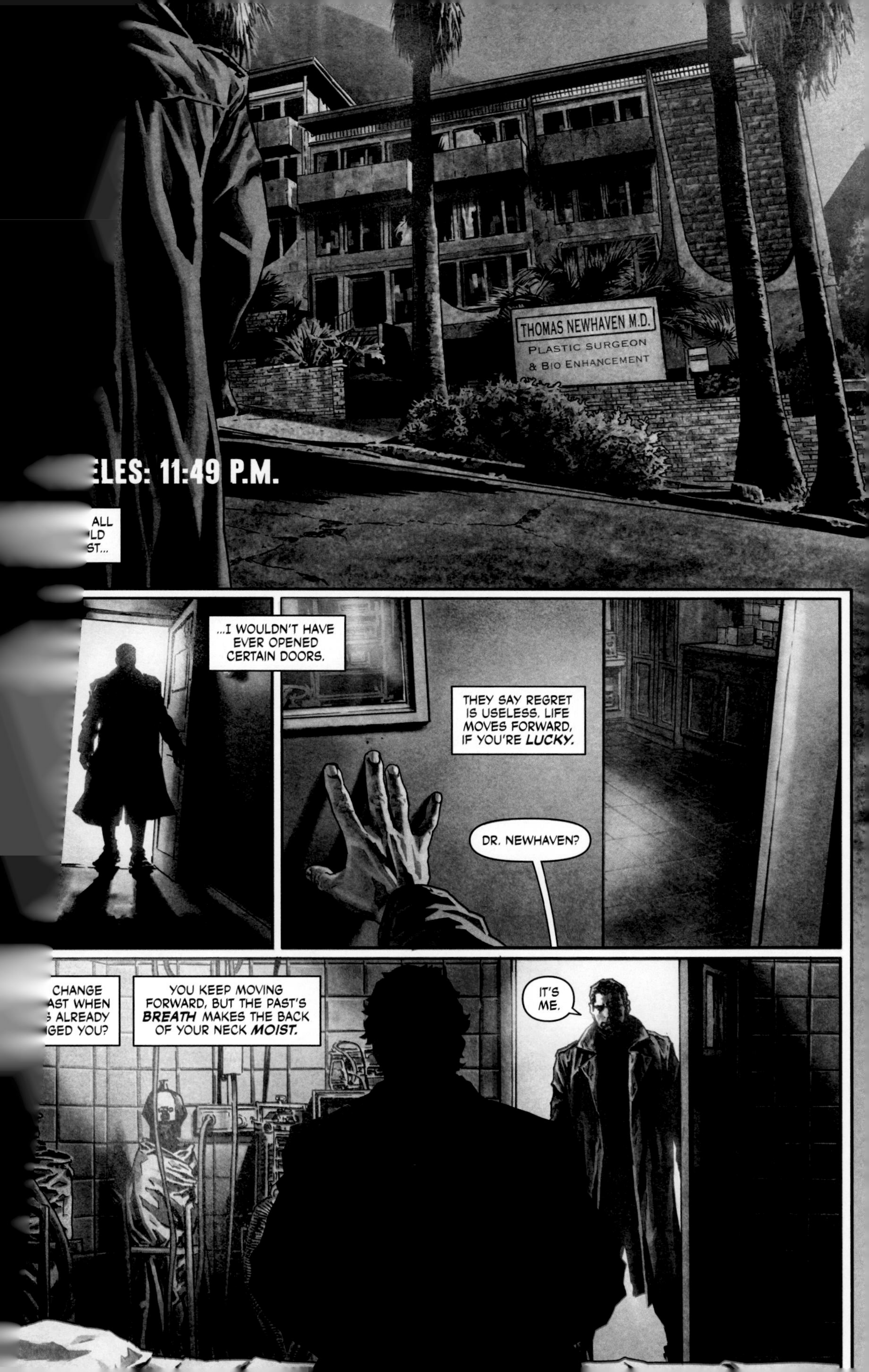
THOMAS NEWHAVEN M.D.
PLASTIC SURGEON
& BIO ENHANCEMENT
ELES: 11:49 P.M.
ALL
LD
ST...
...I WOULDN'T HAVE EVER OPENED CERTAIN DOORS.
THEY SAY REGRET IS USELESS. LIFE MOVES FORWARD, IF YOU'RE LUCKY.
DR. NEWHAVEN?
CHANGE
AST WHEN
S ALREADY
GED YOU?
YOU KEEP MOVING FORWARD, BUT THE PAST'S BREATH MAKES THE BACK OF YOUR NECK MOIST.
IT'S ME.

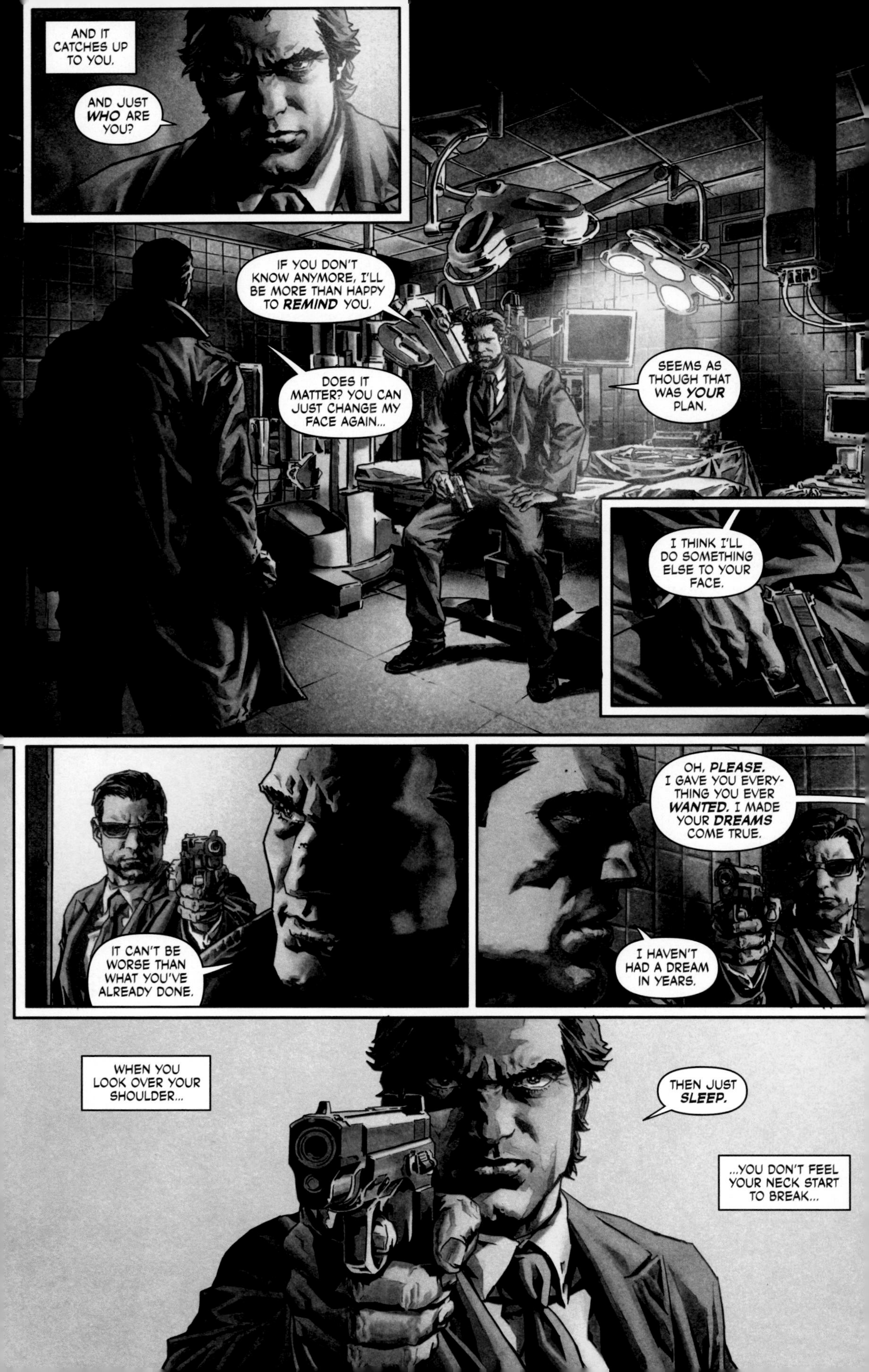
AND IT CATCHES UP TO YOU.
AND JUST WHO ARE YOU?
IF YOU DON'T KNOW ANYMORE, I'LL BE MORE THAN HAPPY TO REMIND YOU.
DOES IT MATTER? YOU CAN JUST CHANGE MY FACE AGAIN...
SEEMS AS THOUGH THAT WAS YOUR PLAN.
I THINK I'LL DO SOMETHING ELSE TO YOUR FACE.
IT CAN'T BE WORSE THAN WHAT YOU'VE ALREADY DONE.
OH, PLEASE. I GAVE YOU EVERYTHING YOU EVER WANTED. I MADE YOUR DREAMS COME TRUE.
I HAVEN'T HAD A DREAM IN YEARS.
WHEN YOU LOOK OVER YOUR SHOULDER...
THEN JUST SLEEP.
...YOU DON'T FEEL YOUR NECK START TO BREAK...

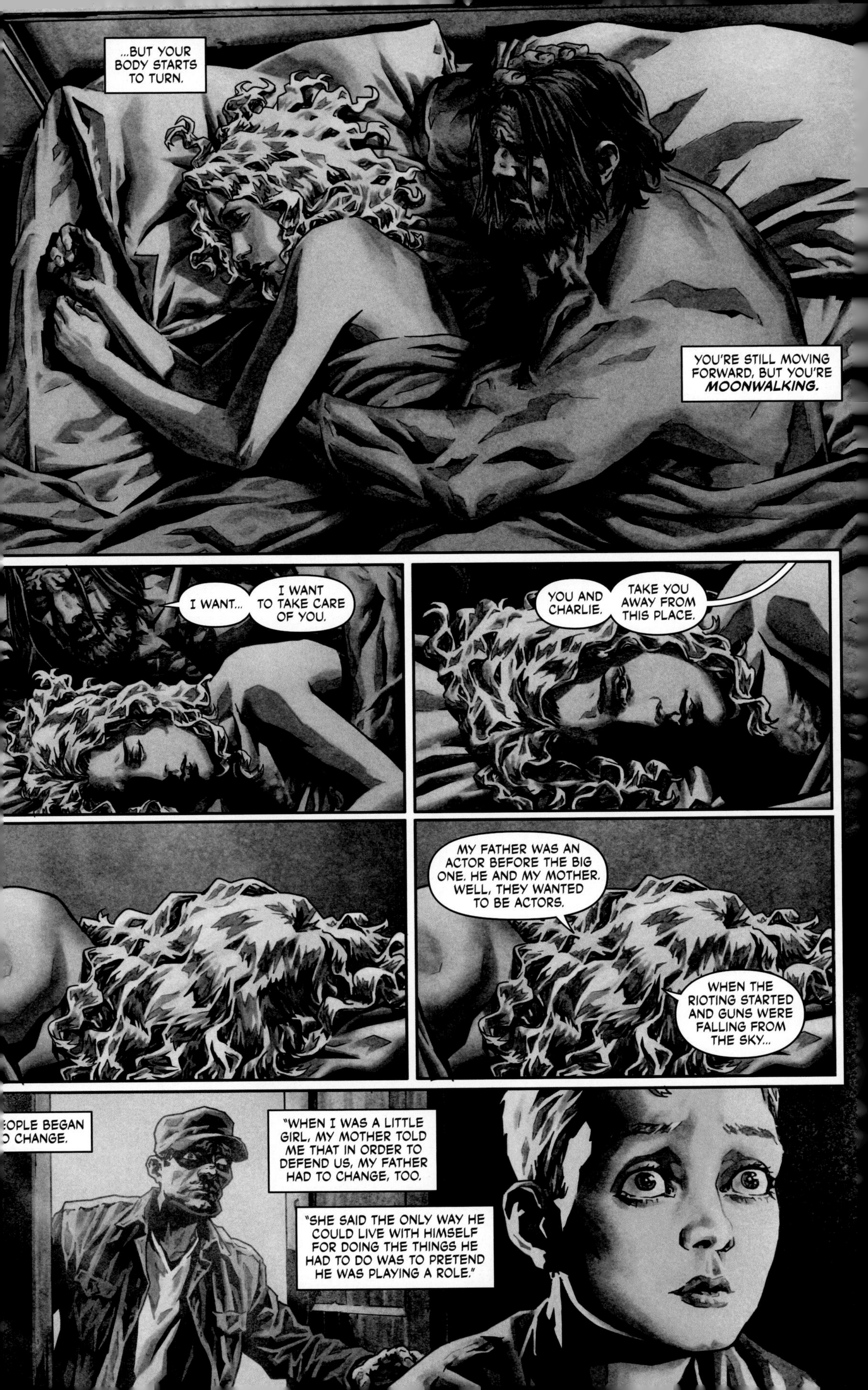

...BUT YOUR BODY STARTS TO TURN.
YOU'RE STILL MOVING FORWARD, BUT YOU'RE *MOONWALKING.*
I WANT...
I WANT TO TAKE CARE OF YOU.
YOU AND CHARLIE.
TAKE YOU AWAY FROM THIS PLACE.
MY FATHER WAS AN ACTOR BEFORE THE BIG ONE. HE AND MY MOTHER. WELL, THEY WANTED TO BE ACTORS.
WHEN THE RIOTING STARTED AND GUNS WERE FALLING FROM THE SKY...
EOPLE BEGAN
O CHANGE.
"WHEN I WAS A LITTLE GIRL, MY MOTHER TOLD ME THAT IN ORDER TO DEFEND US, MY FATHER HAD TO CHANGE, TOO.
"SHE SAID THE ONLY WAY HE COULD LIVE WITH HIMSELF FOR DOING THE THINGS HE HAD TO DO WAS TO PRETEND HE WAS PLAYING A ROLE."

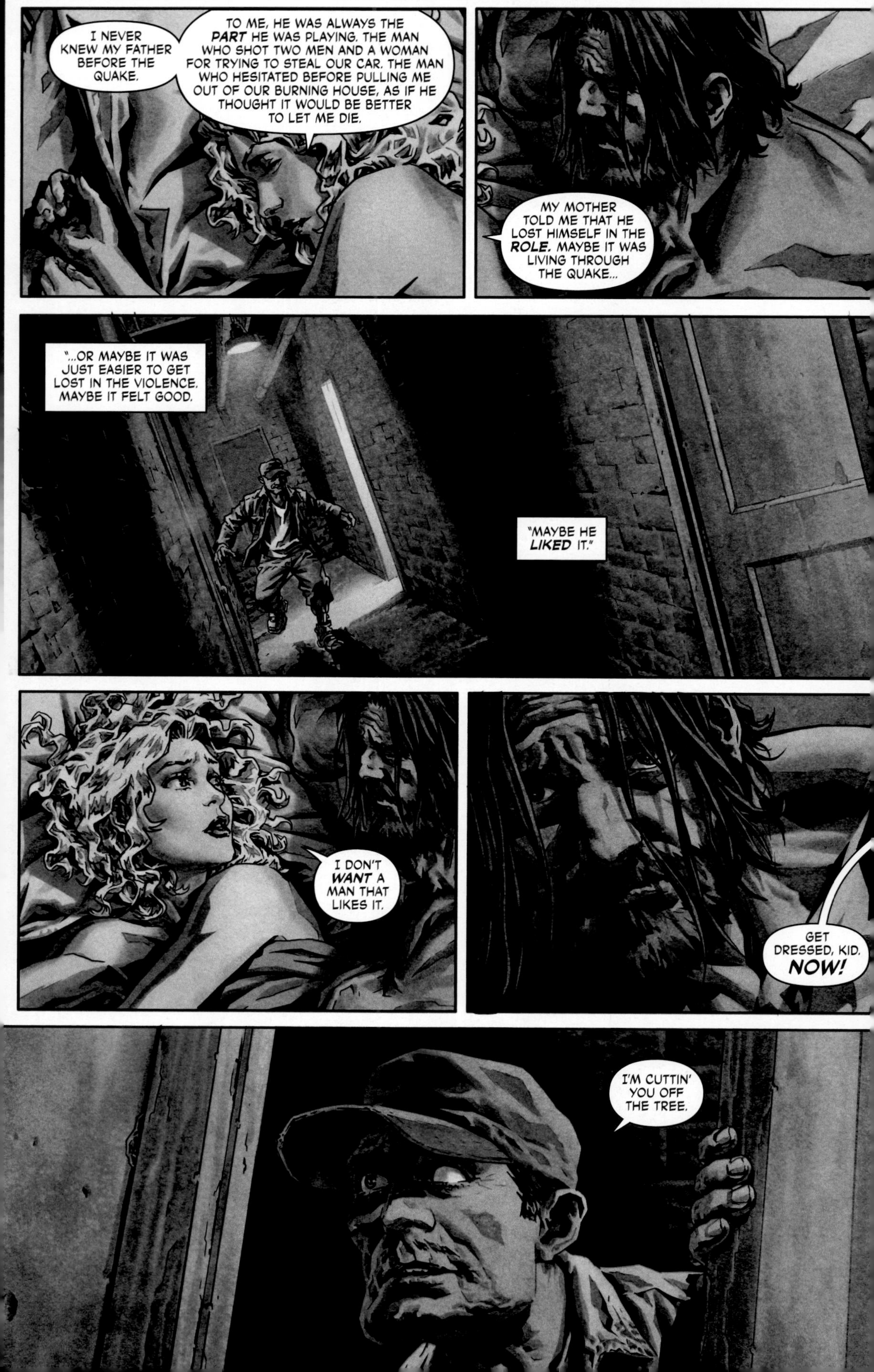

I NEVER KNEW MY FATHER BEFORE THE QUAKE.
TO ME, HE WAS ALWAYS THE *PART* HE WAS PLAYING. THE MAN WHO SHOT TWO MEN AND A WOMAN FOR TRYING TO STEAL OUR CAR. THE MAN WHO HESITATED BEFORE PULLING ME OUT OF OUR BURNING HOUSE, AS IF HE THOUGHT IT WOULD BE BETTER TO LET ME DIE.
MY MOTHER TOLD ME THAT HE LOST HIMSELF IN THE **ROLE.** MAYBE IT WAS LIVING THROUGH THE QUAKE...
"...OR MAYBE IT WAS JUST EASIER TO GET LOST IN THE VIOLENCE. MAYBE IT FELT GOOD.
"MAYBE HE *LIKED* IT."
I DON'T *WANT* A MAN THAT LIKES IT.
GET DRESSED, KID. **NOW!**
I'M CUTTIN' YOU OFF THE TREE.

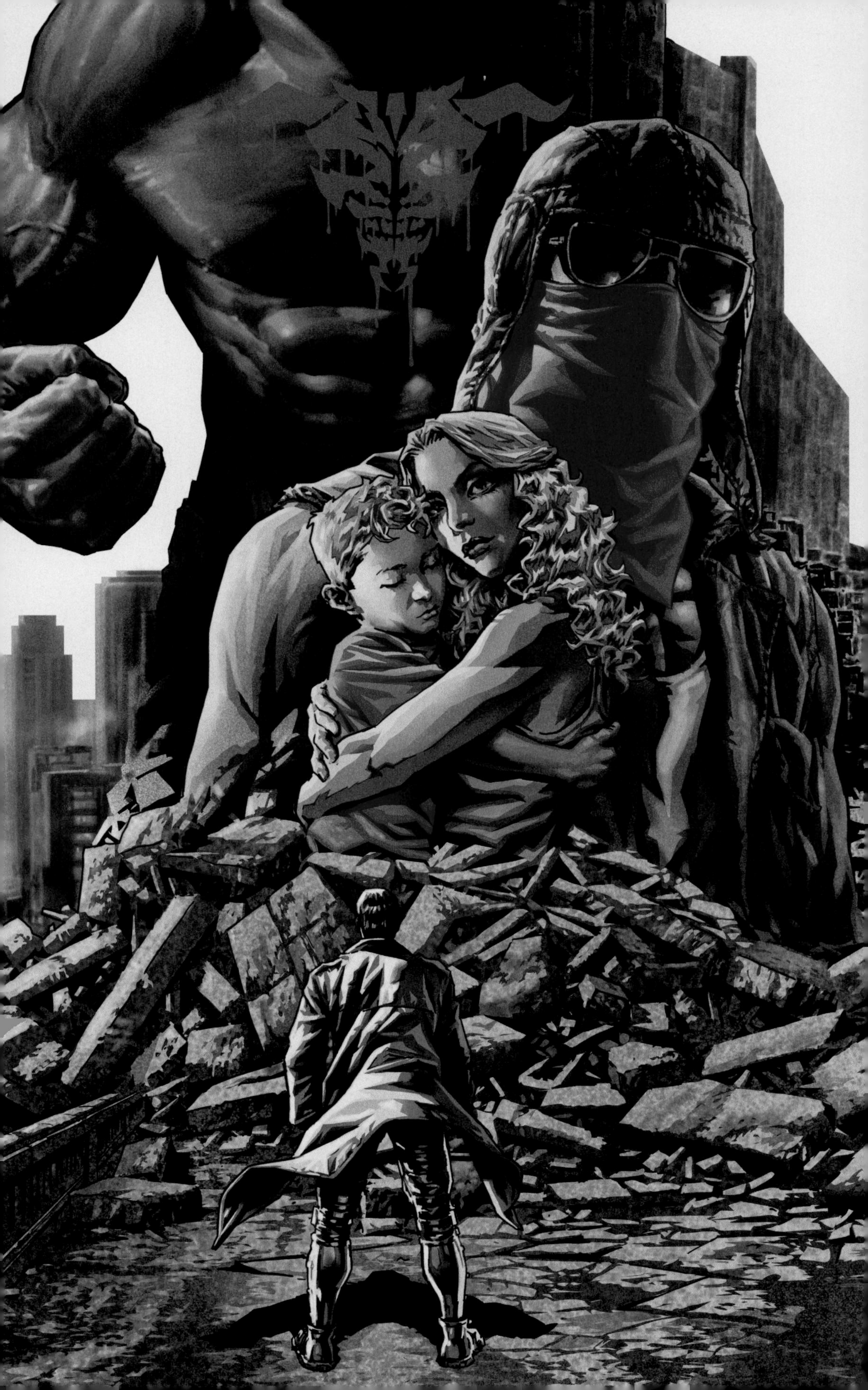

CHAPTER SIX:
WOLF AND MAN

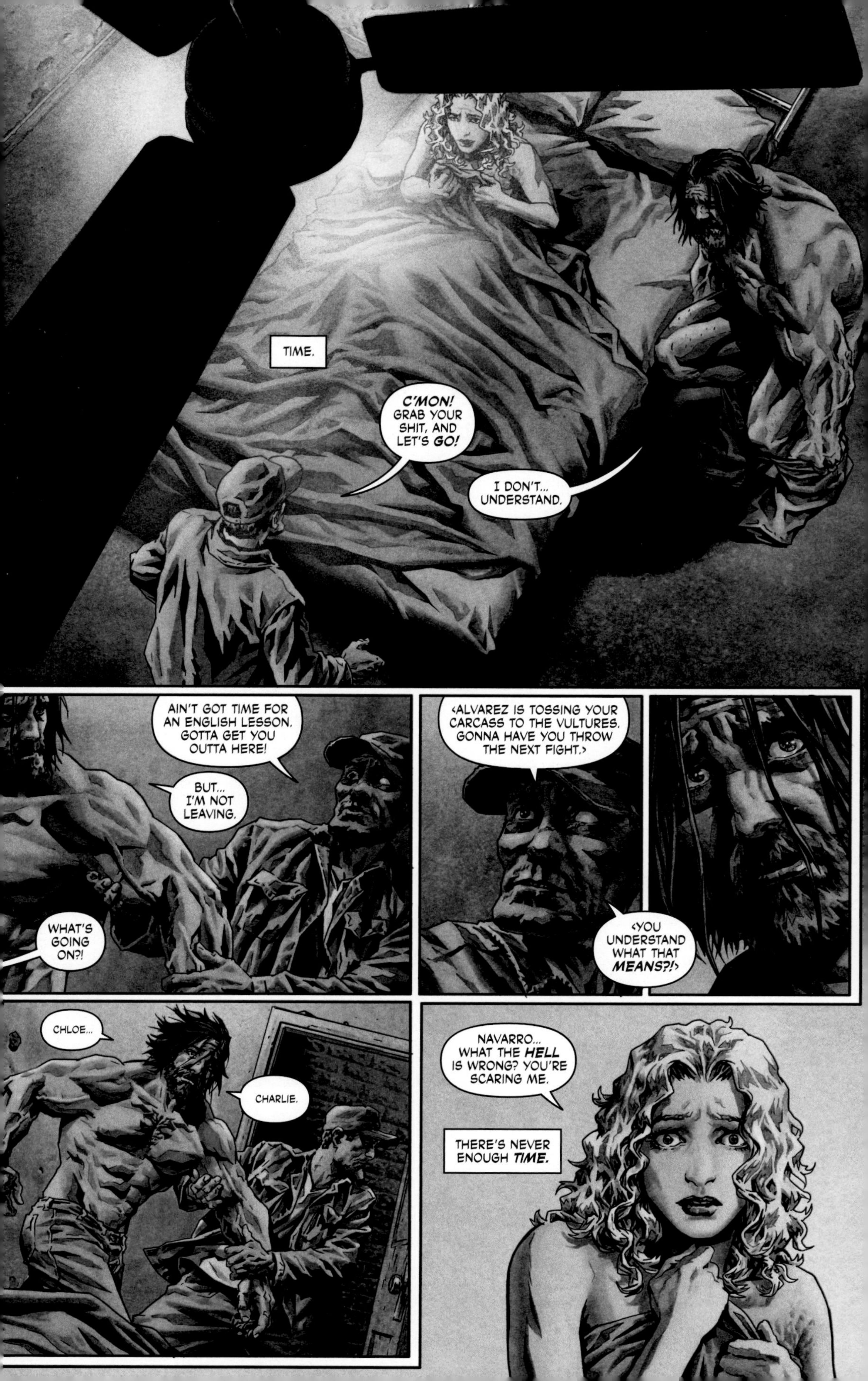
TIME.
C'MON! GRAB YOUR SHIT, AND LET'S GO!
I DON'T... UNDERSTAND.
AIN'T GOT TIME FOR AN ENGLISH LESSON. GOTTA GET YOU OUTTA HERE!
BUT... I'M NOT LEAVING.
WHAT'S GOING ON?!
‹ALVAREZ IS TOSSING YOUR CARCASS TO THE VULTURES. GONNA HAVE YOU THROW THE NEXT FIGHT.›
‹YOU UNDERSTAND WHAT THAT MEANS?!›
CHLOE...
CHARLIE.
NAVARRO... WHAT THE HELL IS WRONG? YOU'RE SCARING ME.
THERE'S NEVER ENOUGH TIME.

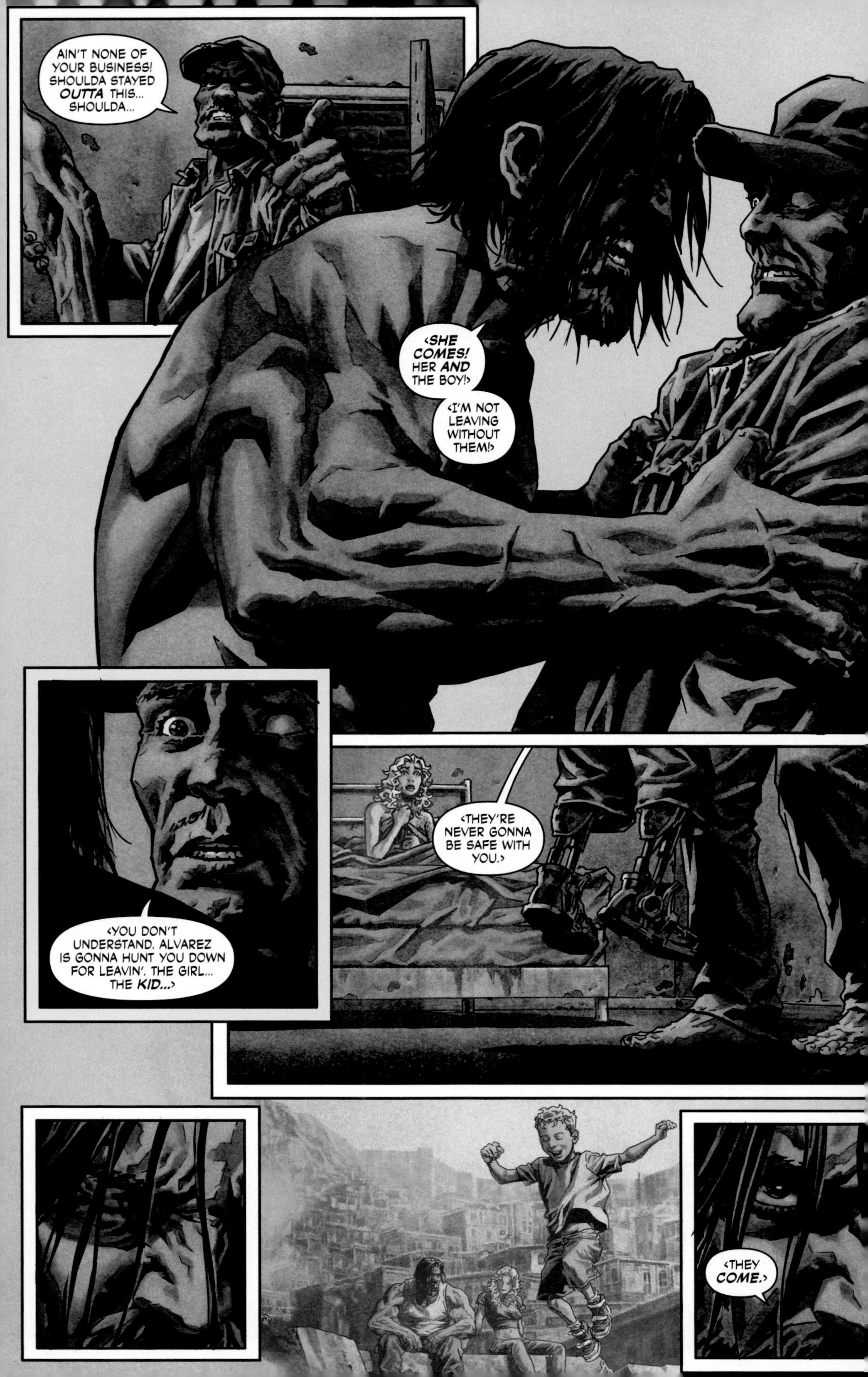
AIN'T NONE OF YOUR BUSINESS! SHOULDA STAYED OUTTA THIS... SHOULDA...
‹SHE COMES! HER AND THE BOY!›
‹I'M NOT LEAVING WITHOUT THEM!›
‹YOU DON'T UNDERSTAND. ALVAREZ IS GONNA HUNT YOU DOWN FOR LEAVIN'. THE GIRL... THE KID...›
‹THEY'RE NEVER GONNA BE SAFE WITH YOU.›
‹THEY COME.›

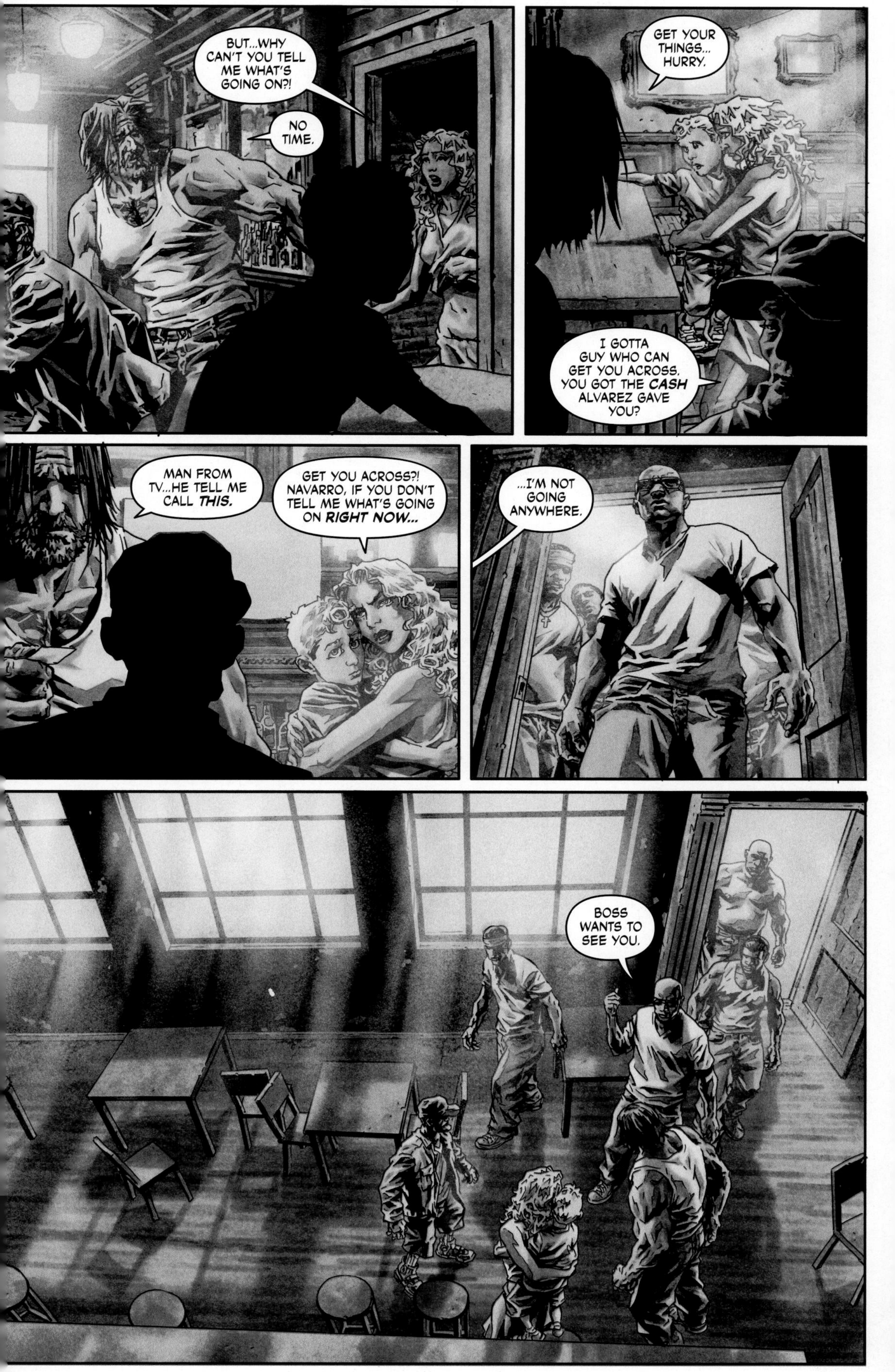
BUT...WHY CAN'T YOU TELL ME WHAT'S GOING ON?!
NO TIME.
GET YOUR THINGS... HURRY.
I GOTTA GUY WHO CAN GET YOU ACROSS. YOU GOT THE CASH ALVAREZ GAVE YOU?
MAN FROM TV...HE TELL ME CALL THIS.
GET YOU ACROSS?! NAVARRO, IF YOU DON'T TELL ME WHAT'S GOING ON RIGHT NOW...
...I'M NOT GOING ANYWHERE.
BOSS WANTS TO SEE YOU.

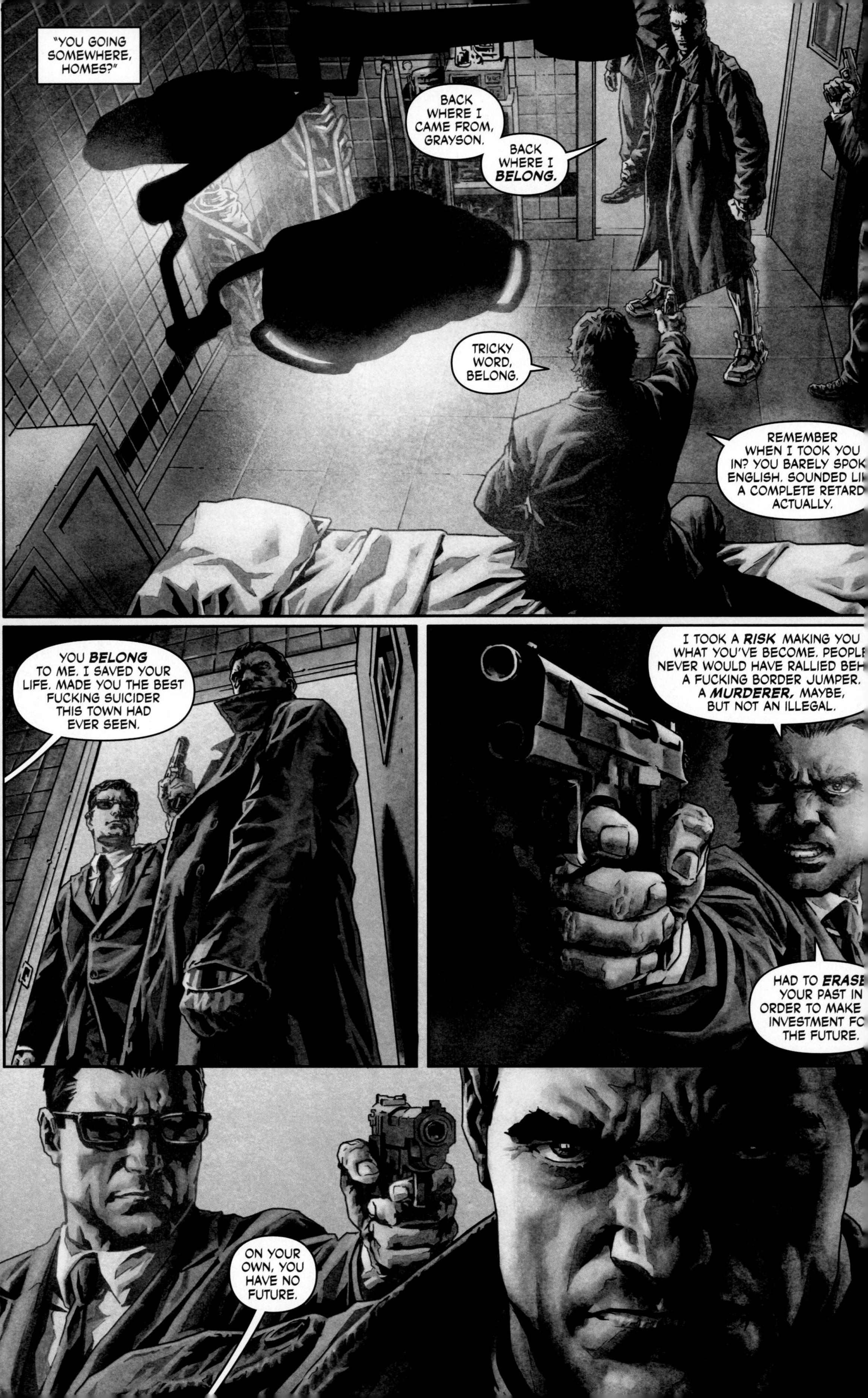
"YOU GOING SOMEWHERE, HOMES?"
BACK WHERE I CAME FROM, GRAYSON.
BACK WHERE I BELONG.
TRICKY WORD, BELONG.
REMEMBER WHEN I TOOK YOU IN? YOU BARELY SPOK ENGLISH. SOUNDED LI A COMPLETE RETARD ACTUALLY.
YOU BELONG TO ME. I SAVED YOUR LIFE. MADE YOU THE BEST FUCKING SUICIDER THIS TOWN HAD EVER SEEN.
I TOOK A RISK MAKING YOU WHAT YOU'VE BECOME. PEOPL NEVER WOULD HAVE RALLIED BEH A FUCKING BORDER JUMPER. A MURDERER, MAYBE, BUT NOT AN ILLEGAL.
HAD TO ERAS YOUR PAST IN ORDER TO MAKE INVESTMENT FO THE FUTURE.
ON YOUR OWN, YOU HAVE NO FUTURE.

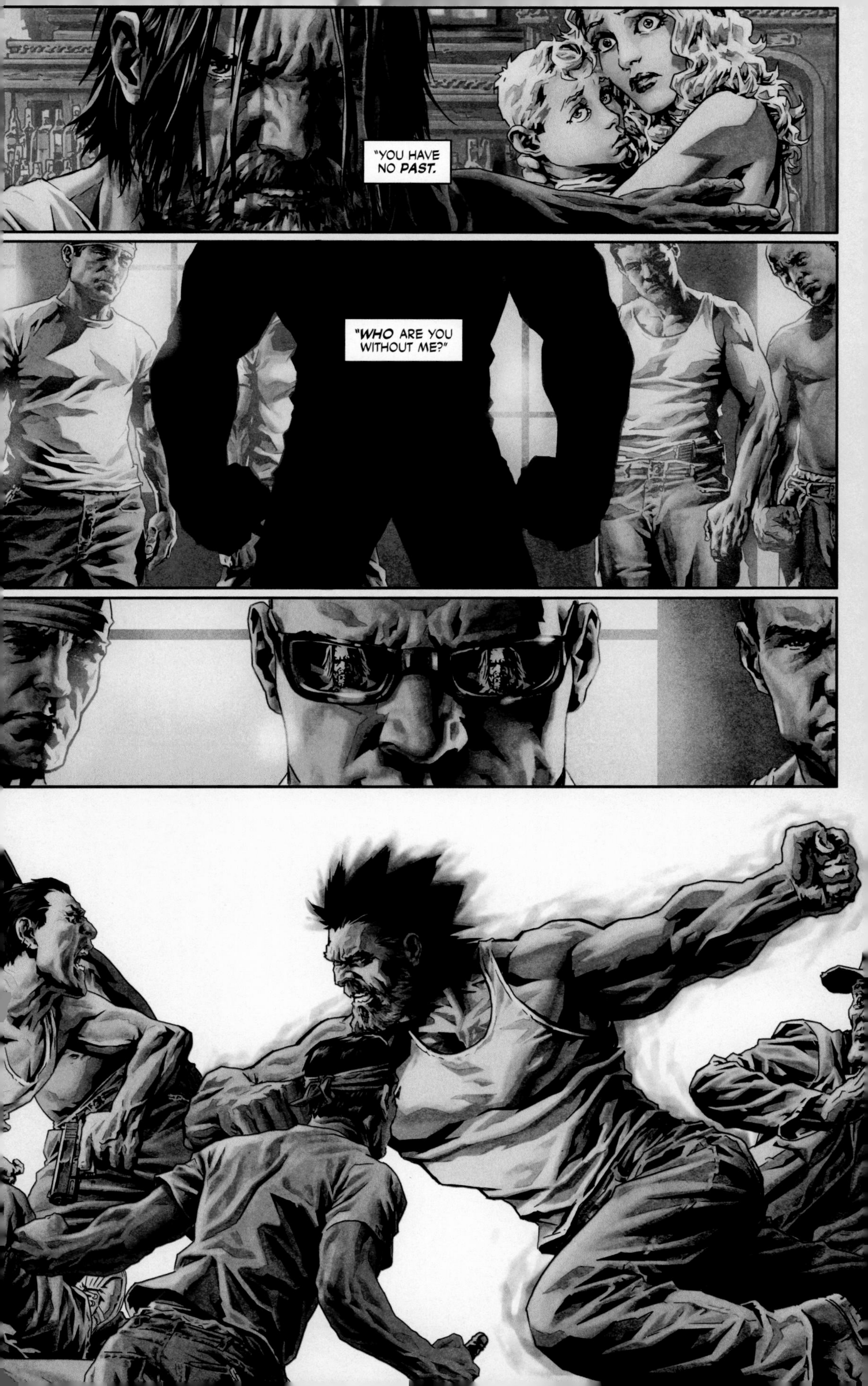
"YOU HAVE NO PAST.
"WHO ARE YOU WITHOUT ME?"

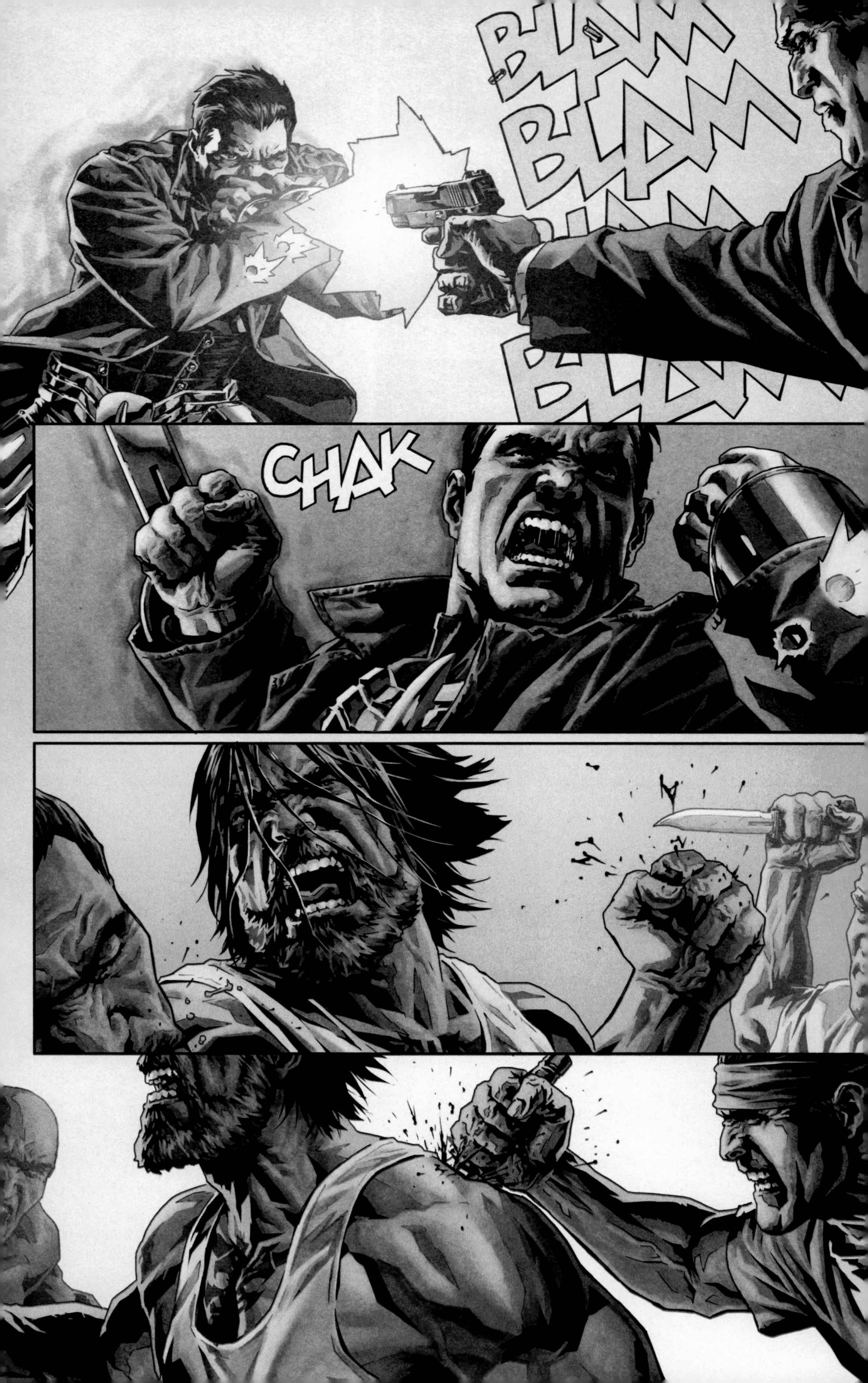
BLAM
BLAM
BLAM
BLAM
CHAK

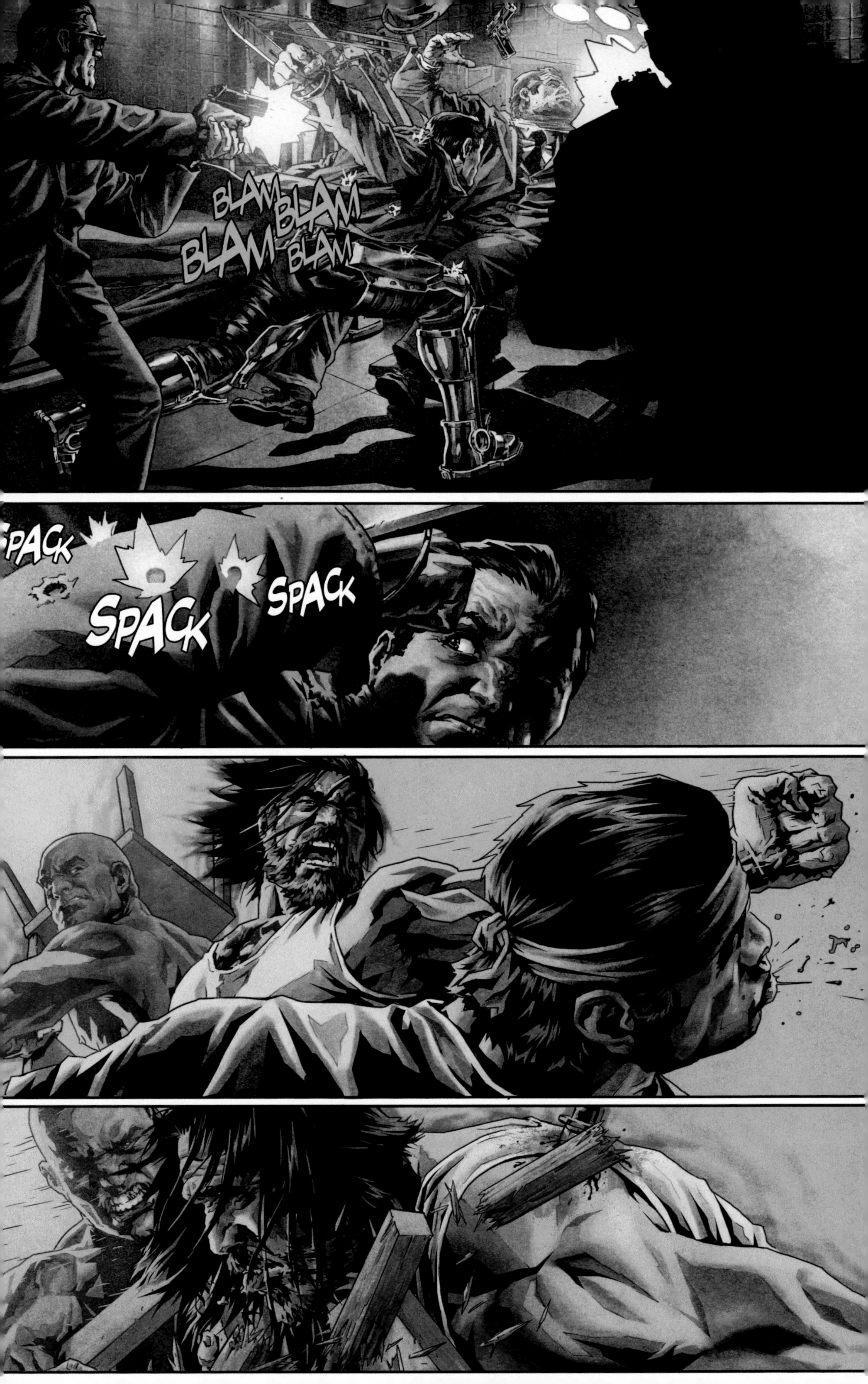
BLAM BLAM
BLAM BLAM
SPACK
SPACK
SPACK

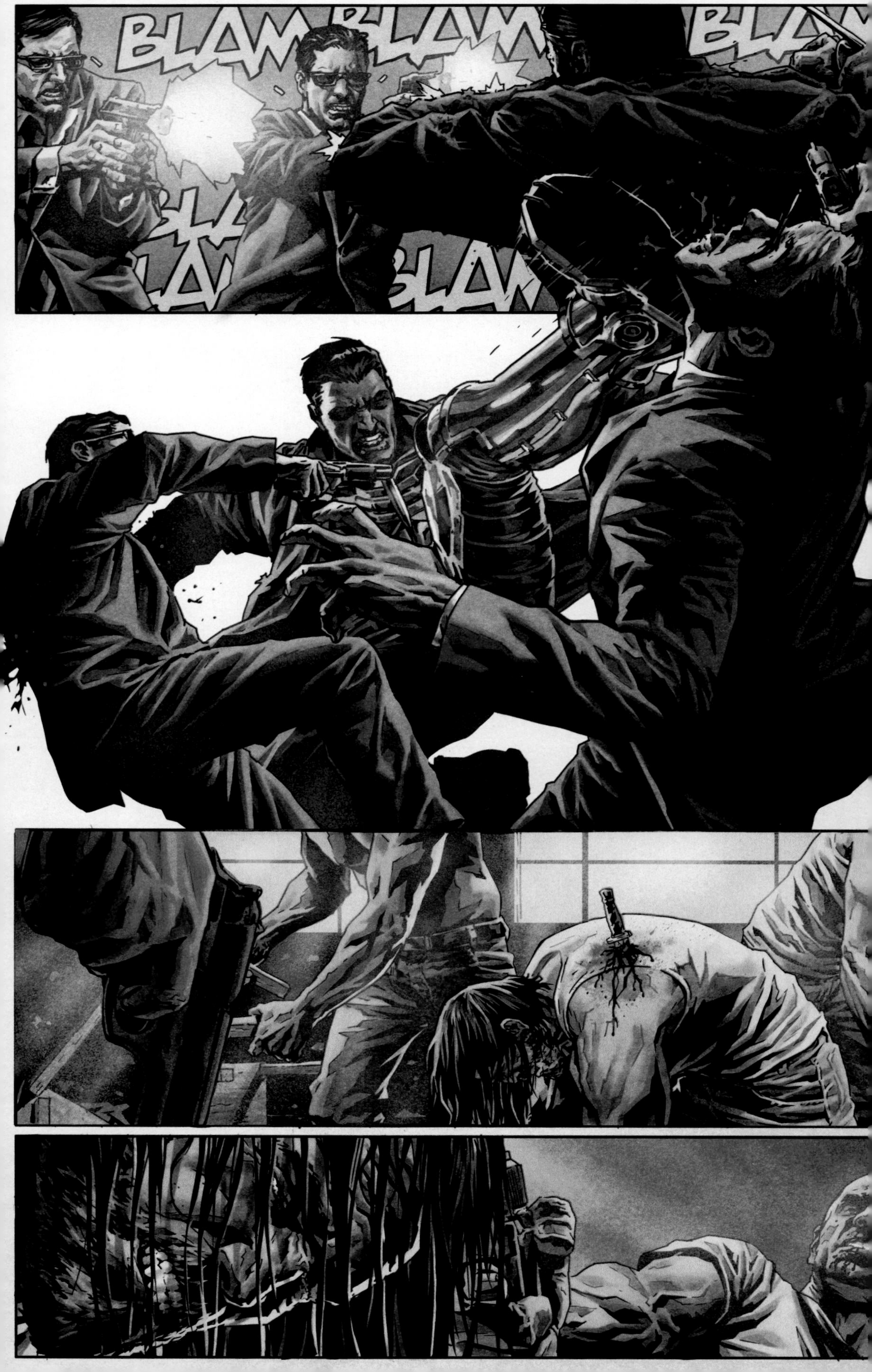
BLAM
BLAM
BLA
BLAM
BLAM

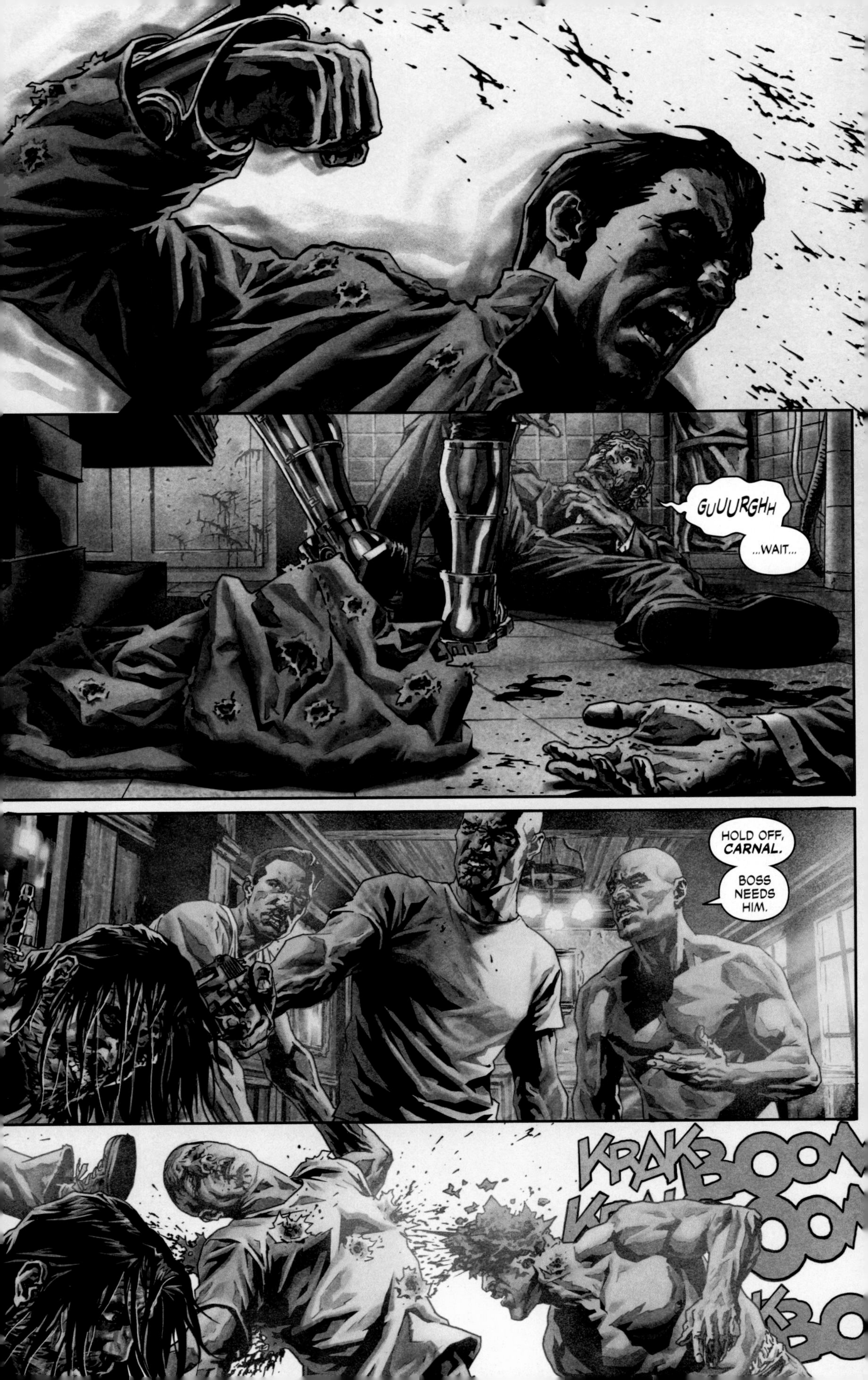
GUUURGHH
...WAIT...
HOLD OFF, CARNAL.
BOSS NEEDS HIM.
KRAKBOOM
BOOM
KBOO

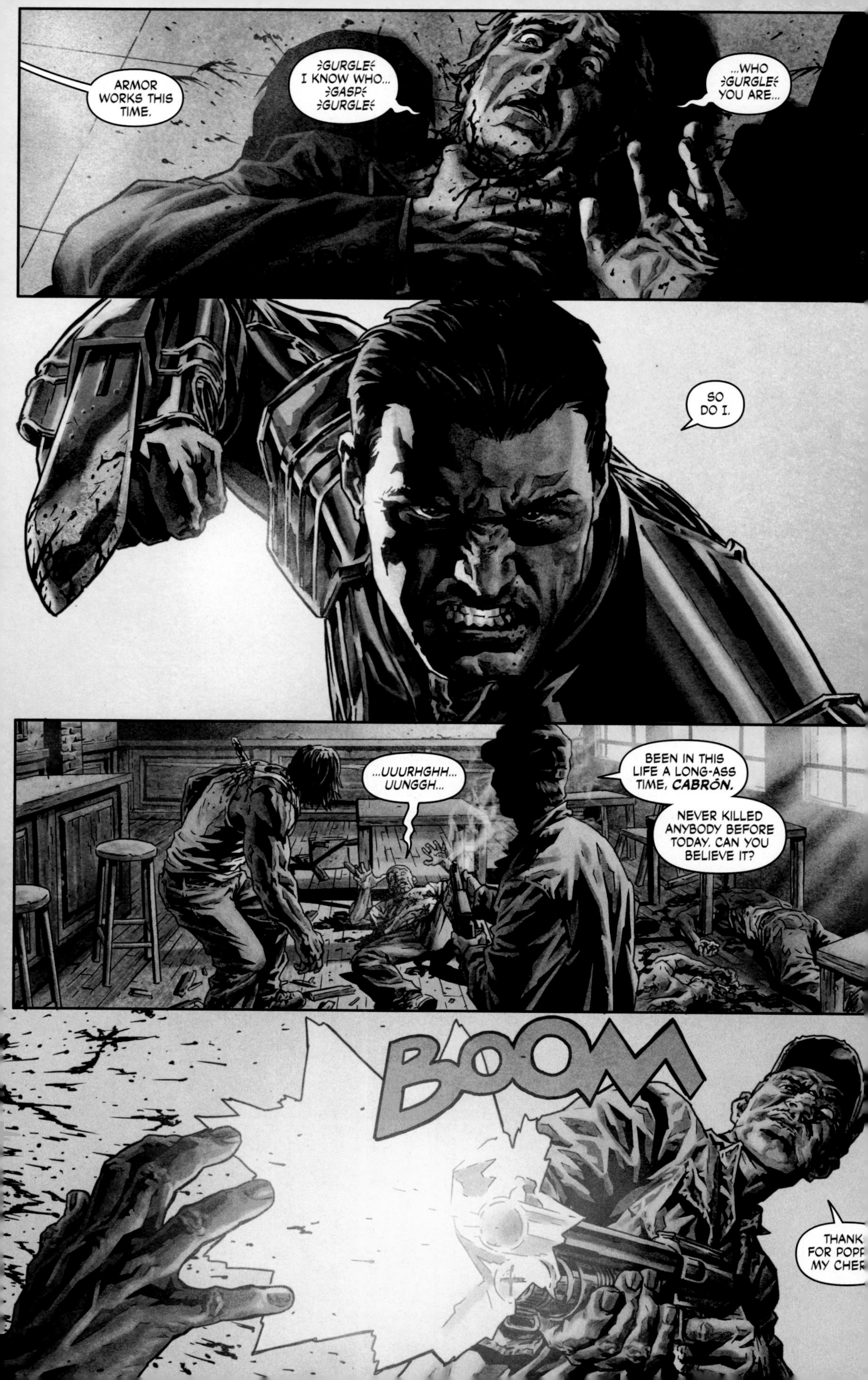
ARMOR WORKS THIS TIME.
⁂GURGLE⁂ I KNOW WHO... ⁂GASP⁂ ⁂GURGLE⁂
...WHO ⁂GURGLE⁂ YOU ARE...
SO DO I.
...UUURHGHH... UUNGGH...
BEEN IN THIS LIFE A LONG-ASS TIME, CABRÓN.
NEVER KILLED ANYBODY BEFORE TODAY. CAN YOU BELIEVE IT?
BOOM
THANK
FOR POPP
MY CHER

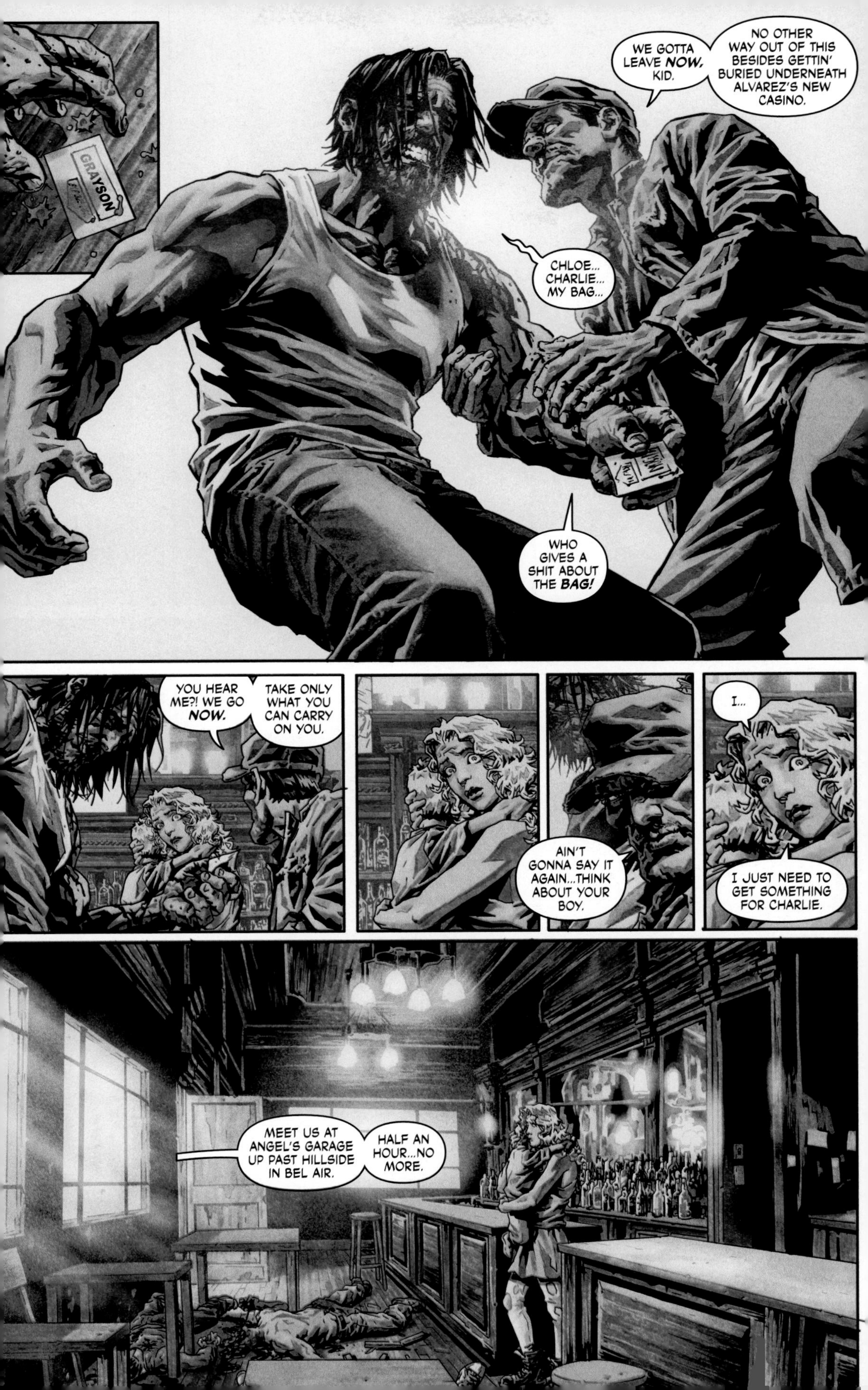
WE GOTTA LEAVE NOW, KID.
NO OTHER WAY OUT OF THIS BESIDES GETTIN' BURIED UNDERNEATH ALVAREZ'S NEW CASINO.
GRAYSON
CHLOE... CHARLIE... MY BAG...
WHO GIVES A SHIT ABOUT THE BAG!
YOU HEAR ME?! WE GO NOW.
TAKE ONLY WHAT YOU CAN CARRY ON YOU.
AIN'T GONNA SAY IT AGAIN...THINK ABOUT YOUR BOY.
I...
I JUST NEED TO GET SOMETHING FOR CHARLIE.
MEET US AT ANGEL'S GARAGE UP PAST HILLSIDE IN BEL AIR.
HALF AN HOUR...NO MORE.

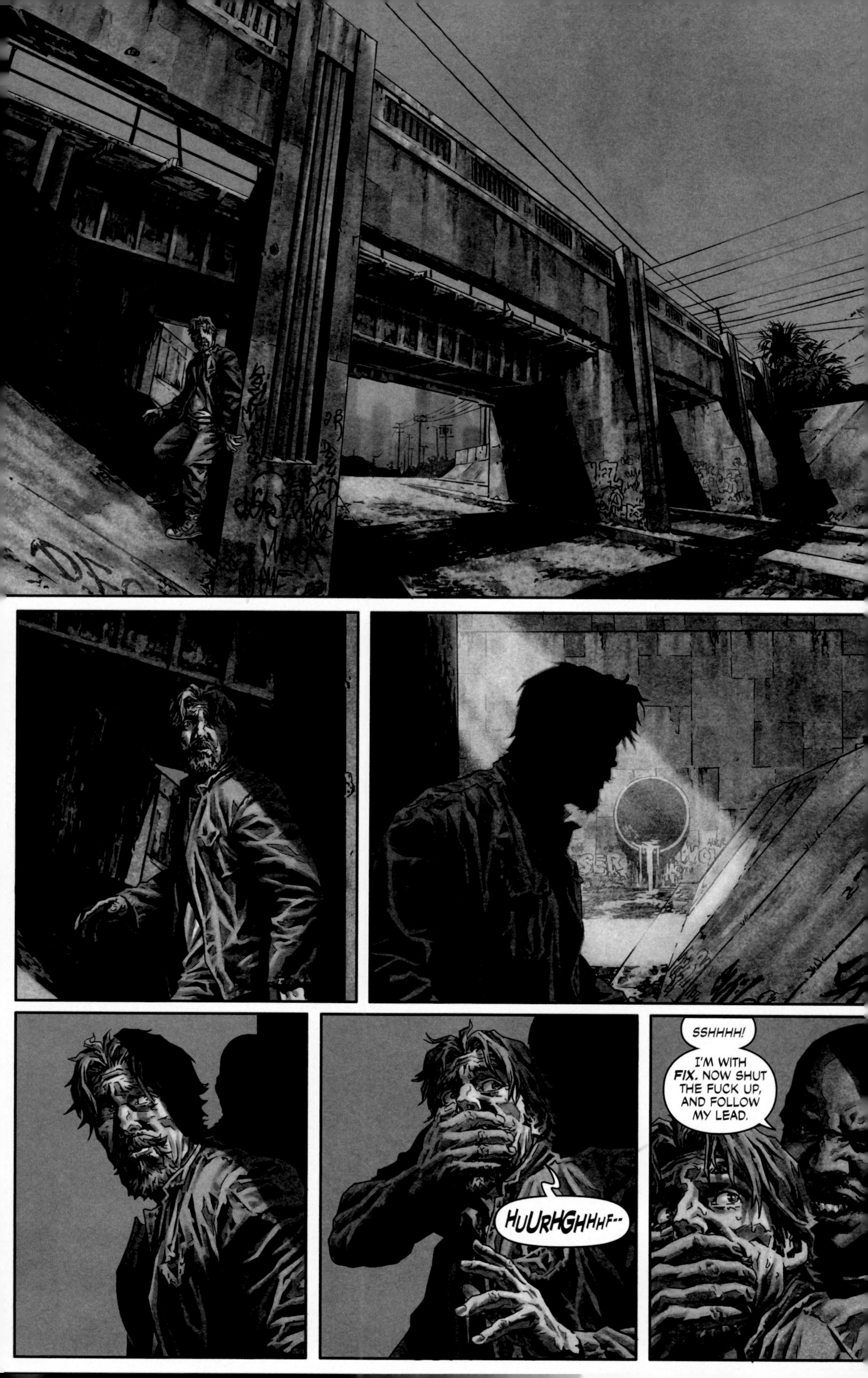

SSHHHH!
I'M WITH FIX. NOW SHUT THE FUCK UP, AND FOLLOW MY LEAD.
HUURHGHHHF--

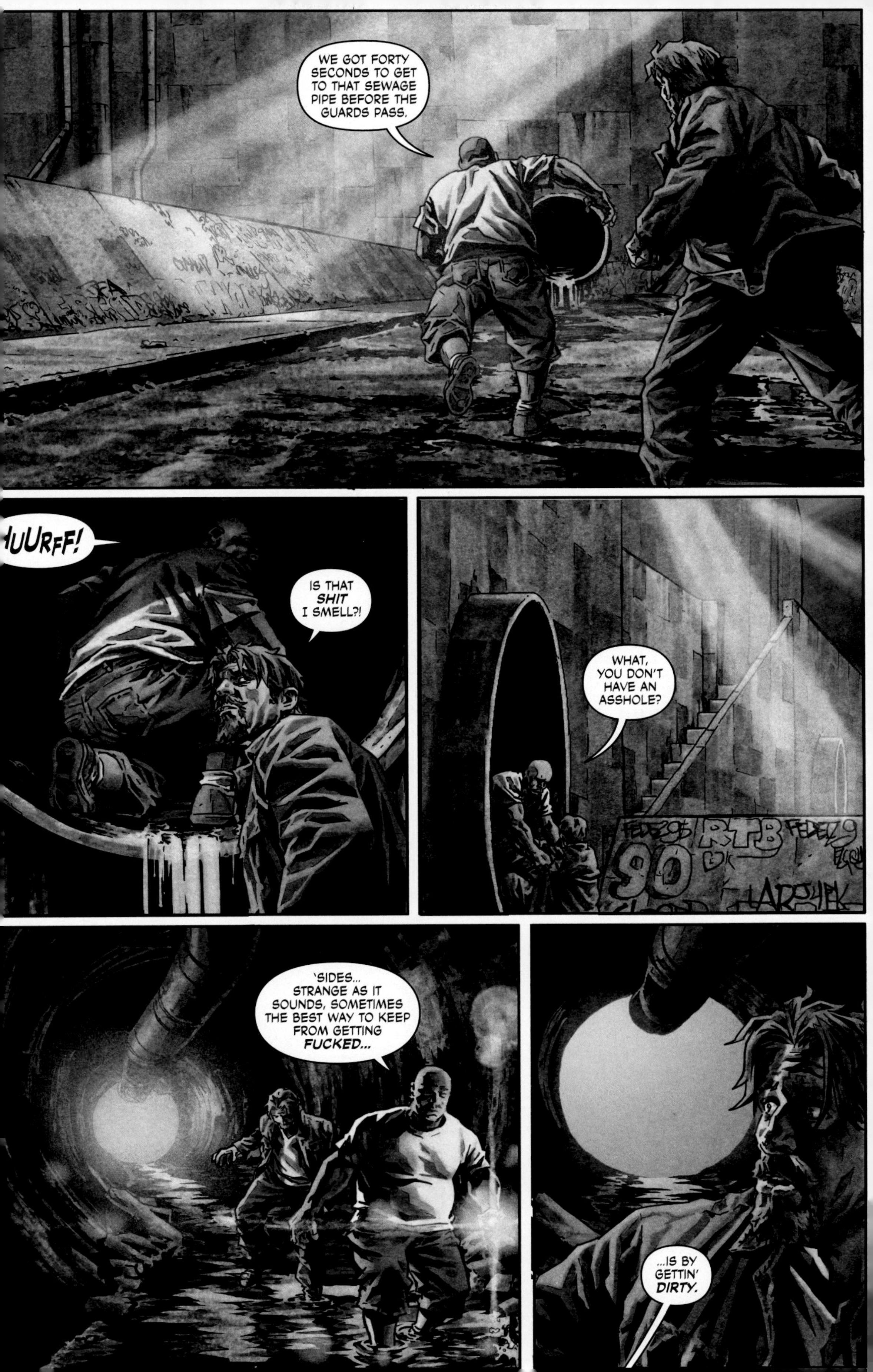
WE GOT FORTY SECONDS TO GET TO THAT SEWAGE PIPE BEFORE THE GUARDS PASS.
HUURFF!
IS THAT *SHIT* I SMELL?!
WHAT, YOU DON'T HAVE AN ASSHOLE?
'SIDES... STRANGE AS IT SOUNDS, SOMETIMES THE BEST WAY TO KEEP FROM GETTING *FUCKED*...
...IS BY GETTIN' *DIRTY*.

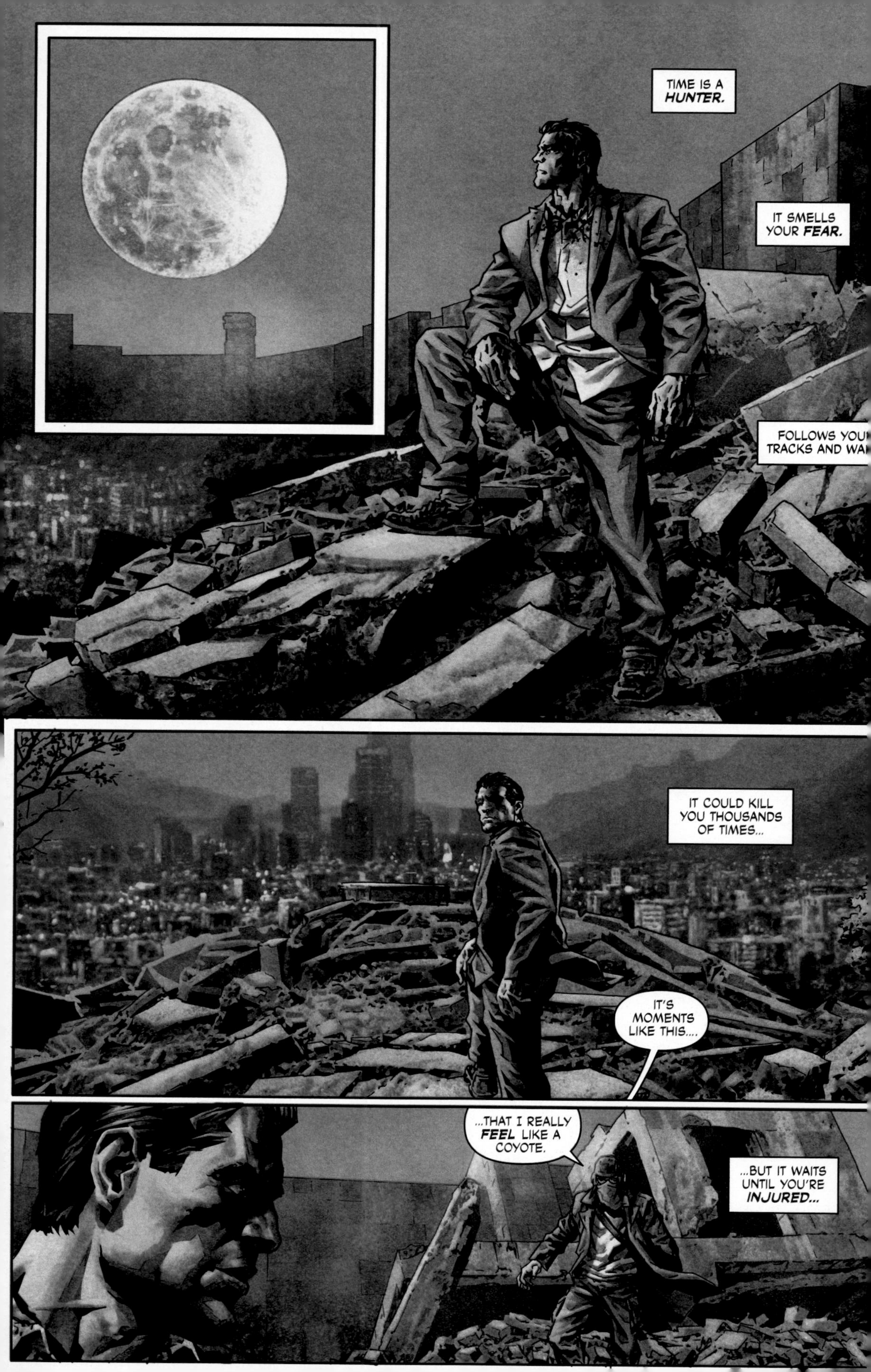
TIME IS A **HUNTER.**
IT SMELLS YOUR **FEAR.**
FOLLOWS YOU
TRACKS AND WA
IT COULD KILL YOU THOUSANDS OF TIMES...
IT'S MOMENTS LIKE THIS....
...THAT I REALLY **FEEL** LIKE A COYOTE.
...BUT IT WAITS UNTIL YOU'RE **INJURED...**

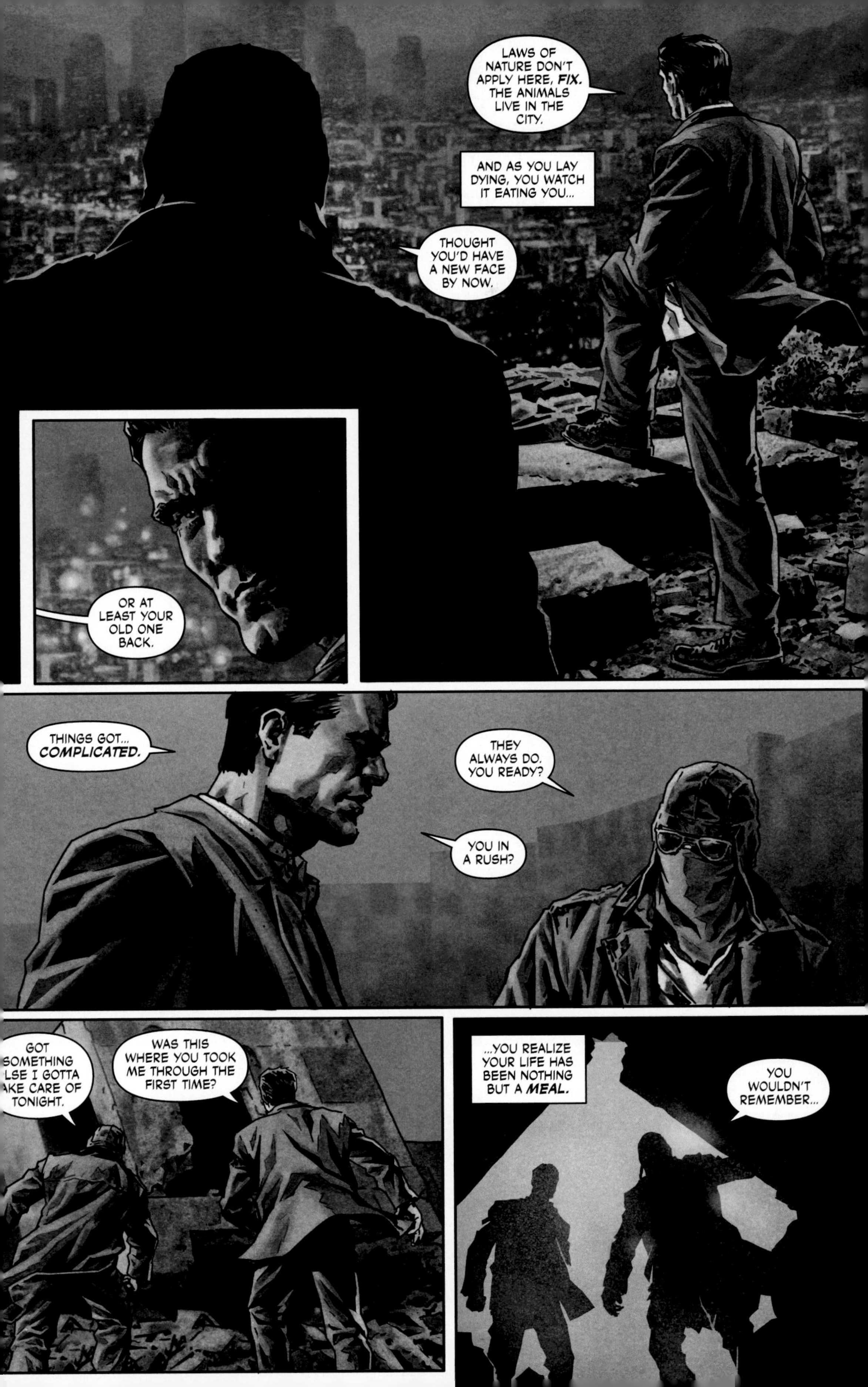
LAWS OF NATURE DON'T APPLY HERE, FIX. THE ANIMALS LIVE IN THE CITY.
AND AS YOU LAY DYING, YOU WATCH IT EATING YOU...
THOUGHT YOU'D HAVE A NEW FACE BY NOW.
OR AT LEAST YOUR OLD ONE BACK.
THINGS GOT... COMPLICATED.
THEY ALWAYS DO. YOU READY?
YOU IN A RUSH?
GOT SOMETHING LSE I GOTTA AKE CARE OF TONIGHT.
WAS THIS WHERE YOU TOOK ME THROUGH THE FIRST TIME?
...YOU REALIZE YOUR LIFE HAS BEEN NOTHING BUT A MEAL.
YOU WOULDN'T REMEMBER...

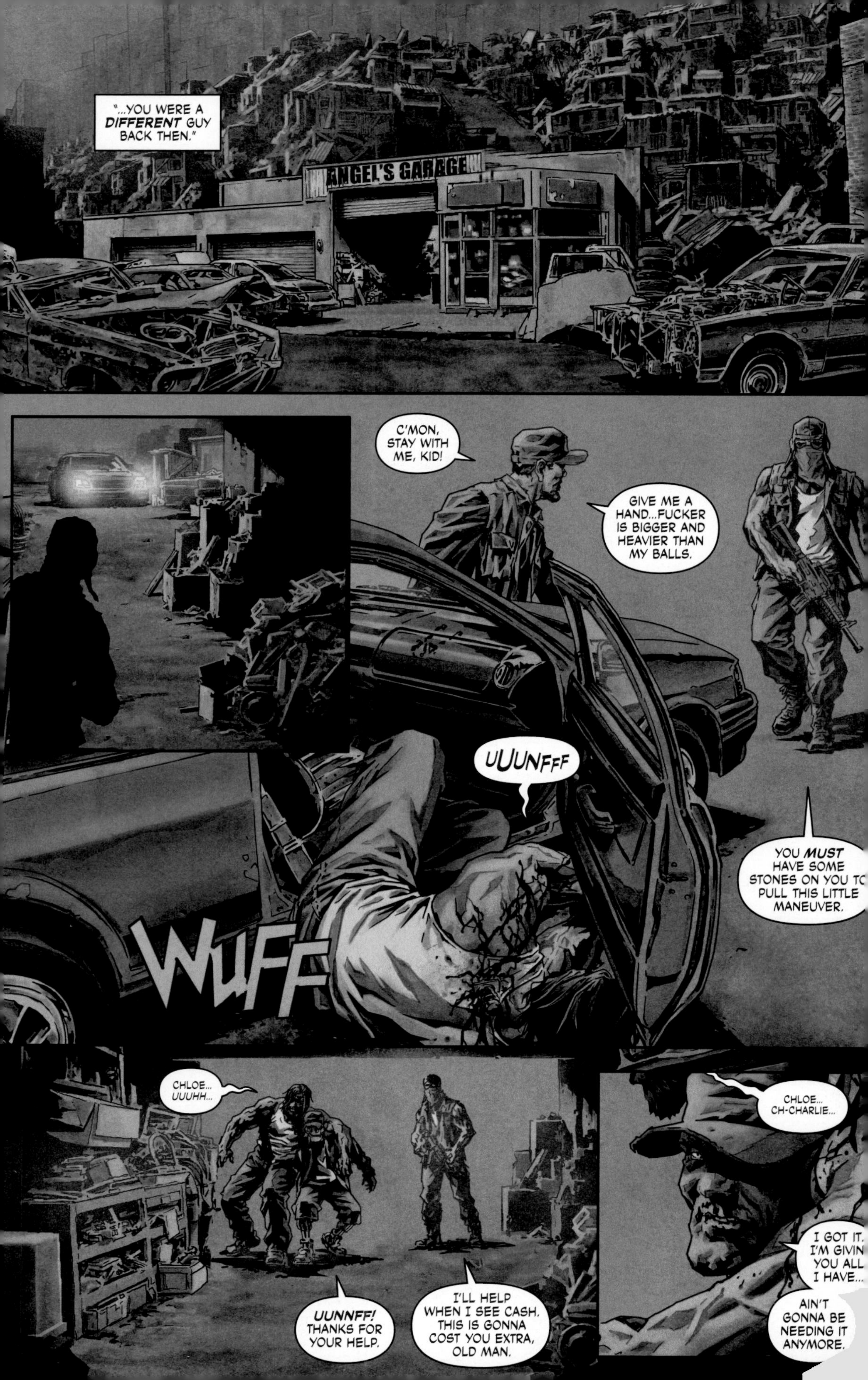
"...YOU WERE A DIFFERENT GUY BACK THEN."
ANGEL'S GARAGE
C'MON, STAY WITH ME, KID!
GIVE ME A HAND...FUCKER IS BIGGER AND HEAVIER THAN MY BALLS.
UUUNFFF
WUFF
YOU MUST HAVE SOME STONES ON YOU TO PULL THIS LITTLE MANEUVER.
CHLOE... UUUHH...
UUNNFF! THANKS FOR YOUR HELP.
I'LL HELP WHEN I SEE CASH. THIS IS GONNA COST YOU EXTRA, OLD MAN.
CHLOE... CH-CHARLIE...
I GOT IT. I'M GIVIN YOU ALL I HAVE...
AIN'T GONNA BE NEEDING IT ANYMORE.

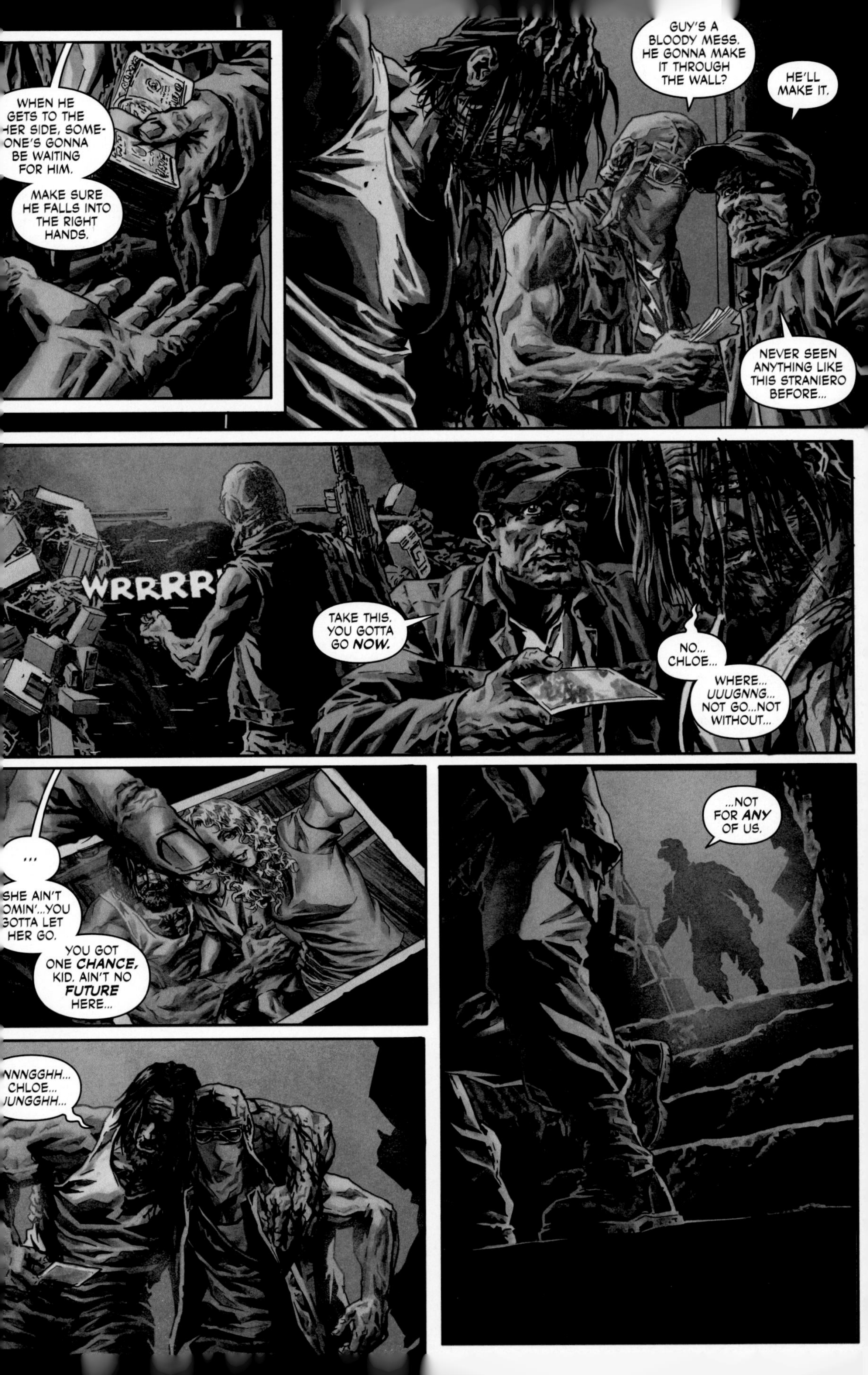
WHEN HE GETS TO THE -HER SIDE, SOME-ONE'S GONNA BE WAITING FOR HIM.
MAKE SURE HE FALLS INTO THE RIGHT HANDS.
GUY'S A BLOODY MESS. HE GONNA MAKE IT THROUGH THE WALL?
HE'LL MAKE IT.
NEVER SEEN ANYTHING LIKE THIS STRANIERO BEFORE...
WRRRR
TAKE THIS. YOU GOTTA GO *NOW.*
NO... CHLOE...
WHERE... *UUUGNNG*... NOT GO...NOT WITHOUT...
...
SHE AIN'T -OMIN'...YOU -GOTTA LET HER GO.
YOU GOT ONE *CHANCE,* KID. AIN'T NO *FUTURE* HERE...
...NOT FOR *ANY* OF US.
-NNNGGHH... CHLOE... -UNGGHH...

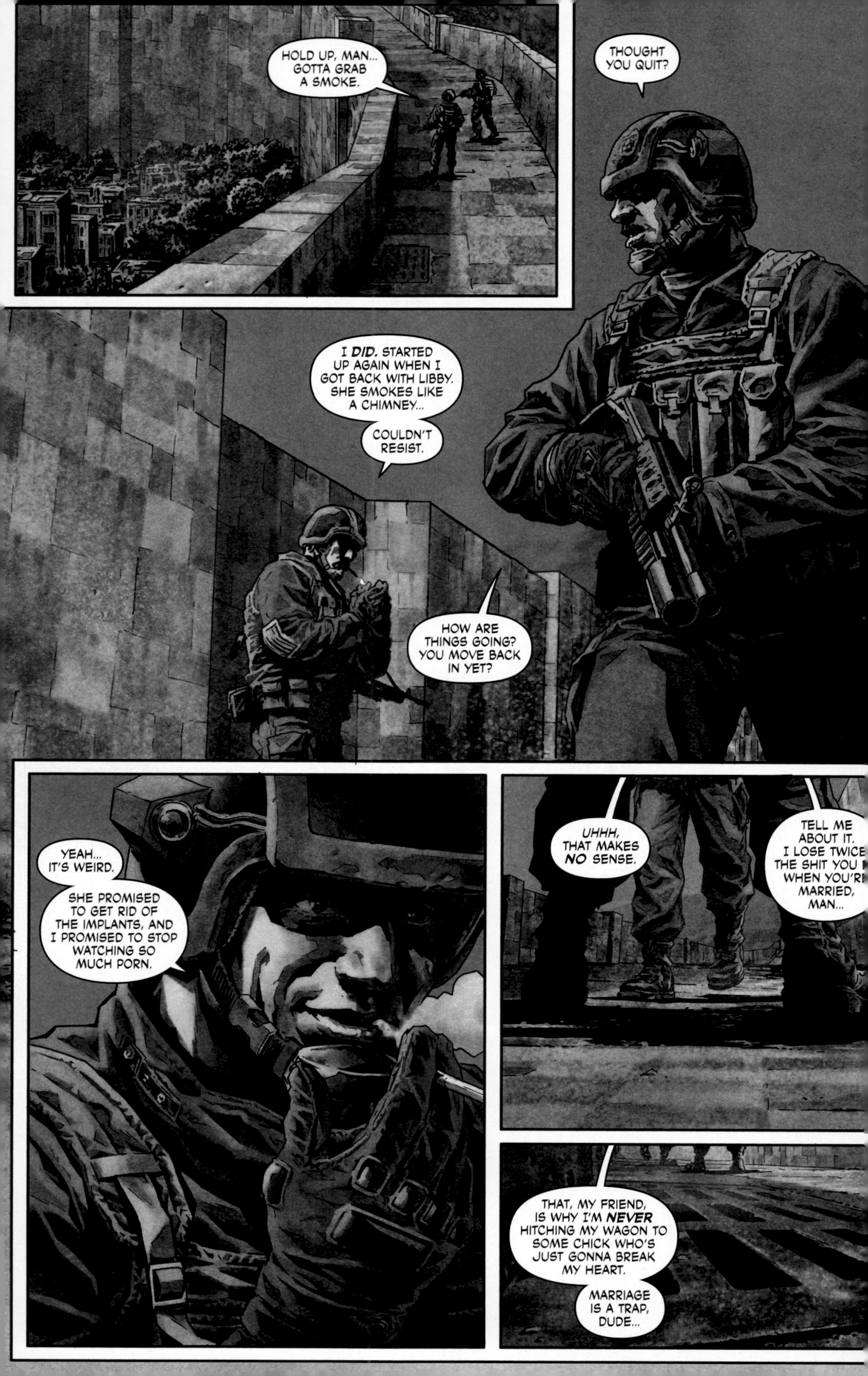
HOLD UP, MAN... GOTTA GRAB A SMOKE.
THOUGHT YOU QUIT?
I *DID.* STARTED UP AGAIN WHEN I GOT BACK WITH LIBBY. SHE SMOKES LIKE A CHIMNEY...
COULDN'T RESIST.
HOW ARE THINGS GOING? YOU MOVE BACK IN YET?
YEAH... IT'S WEIRD.
SHE PROMISED TO GET RID OF THE IMPLANTS, AND I PROMISED TO STOP WATCHING SO MUCH PORN.
UHHH, THAT MAKES ***NO*** SENSE.
TELL ME ABOUT IT. I LOSE TWICE THE SHIT YOU WHEN YOU'R MARRIED, MAN...
THAT, MY FRIEND, IS WHY I'M ***NEVER*** HITCHING MY WAGON TO SOME CHICK WHO'S JUST GONNA BREAK MY HEART.
MARRIAGE IS A TRAP, DUDE...

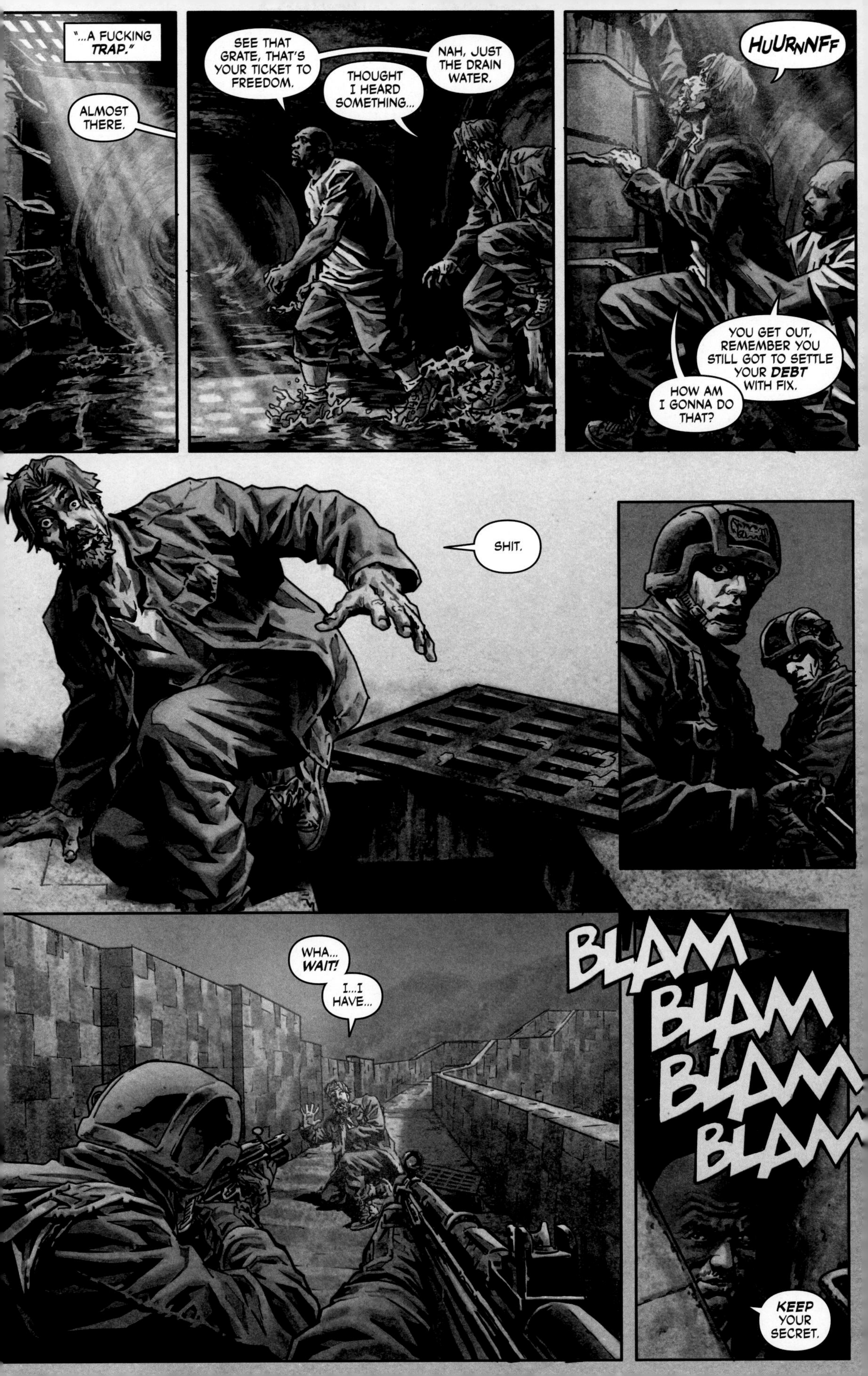
"...A FUCKING TRAP."
ALMOST THERE.
SEE THAT GRATE, THAT'S YOUR TICKET TO FREEDOM.
THOUGHT I HEARD SOMETHING...
NAH, JUST THE DRAIN WATER.
HUURNNFF
YOU GET OUT, REMEMBER YOU STILL GOT TO SETTLE YOUR DEBT WITH FIX.
HOW AM I GONNA DO THAT?
SHIT.
WHA... WAIT!
I...I HAVE...
BLAM
BLAM
BLAM
BLAM
KEEP YOUR SECRET.

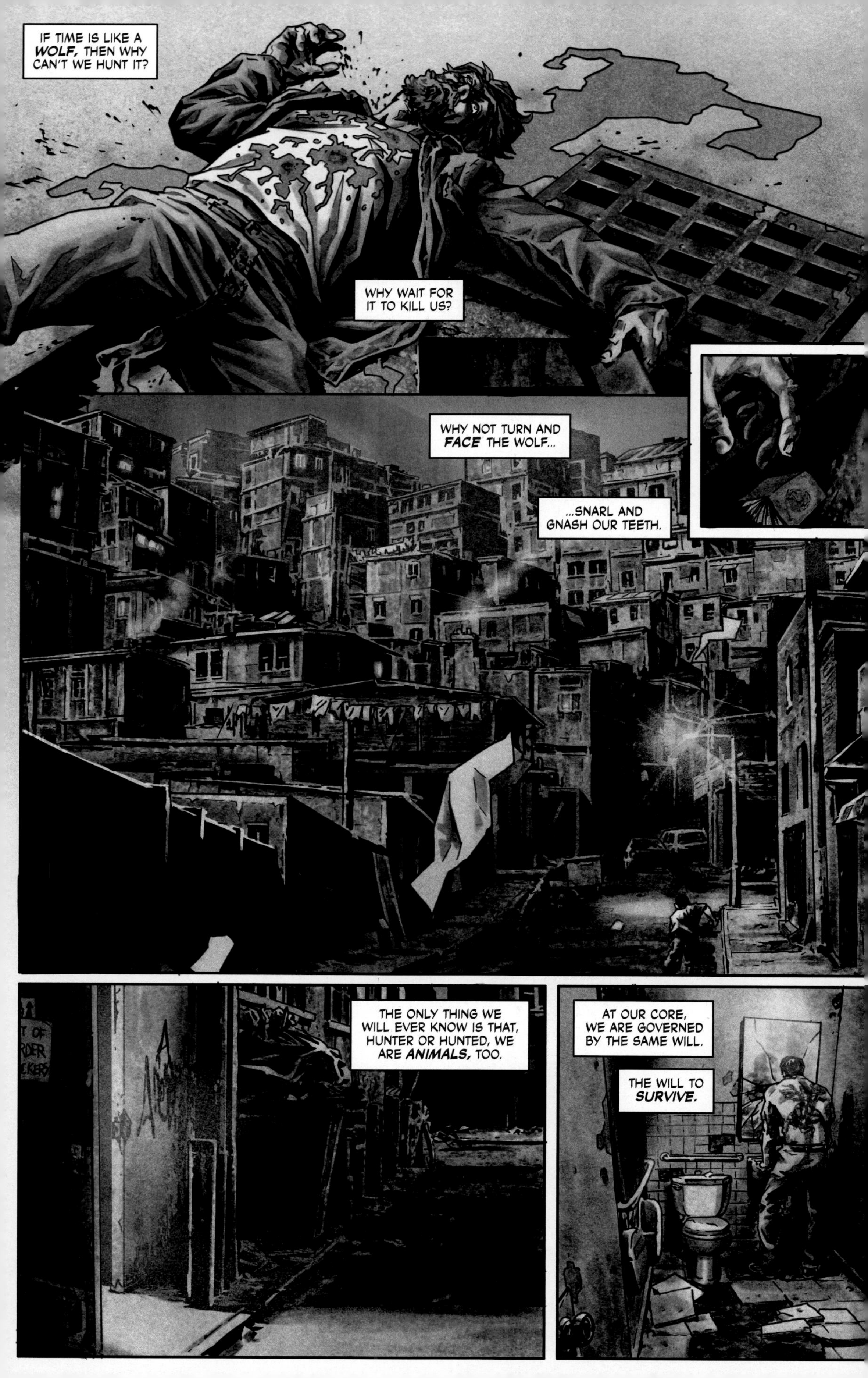
IF TIME IS LIKE A WOLF, THEN WHY CAN'T WE HUNT IT?
WHY WAIT FOR IT TO KILL US?
WHY NOT TURN AND FACE THE WOLF...
...SNARL AND GNASH OUR TEETH.
THE ONLY THING WE WILL EVER KNOW IS THAT, HUNTER OR HUNTED, WE ARE ANIMALS, TOO.
AT OUR CORE, WE ARE GOVERNED BY THE SAME WILL.
THE WILL TO SURVIVE.

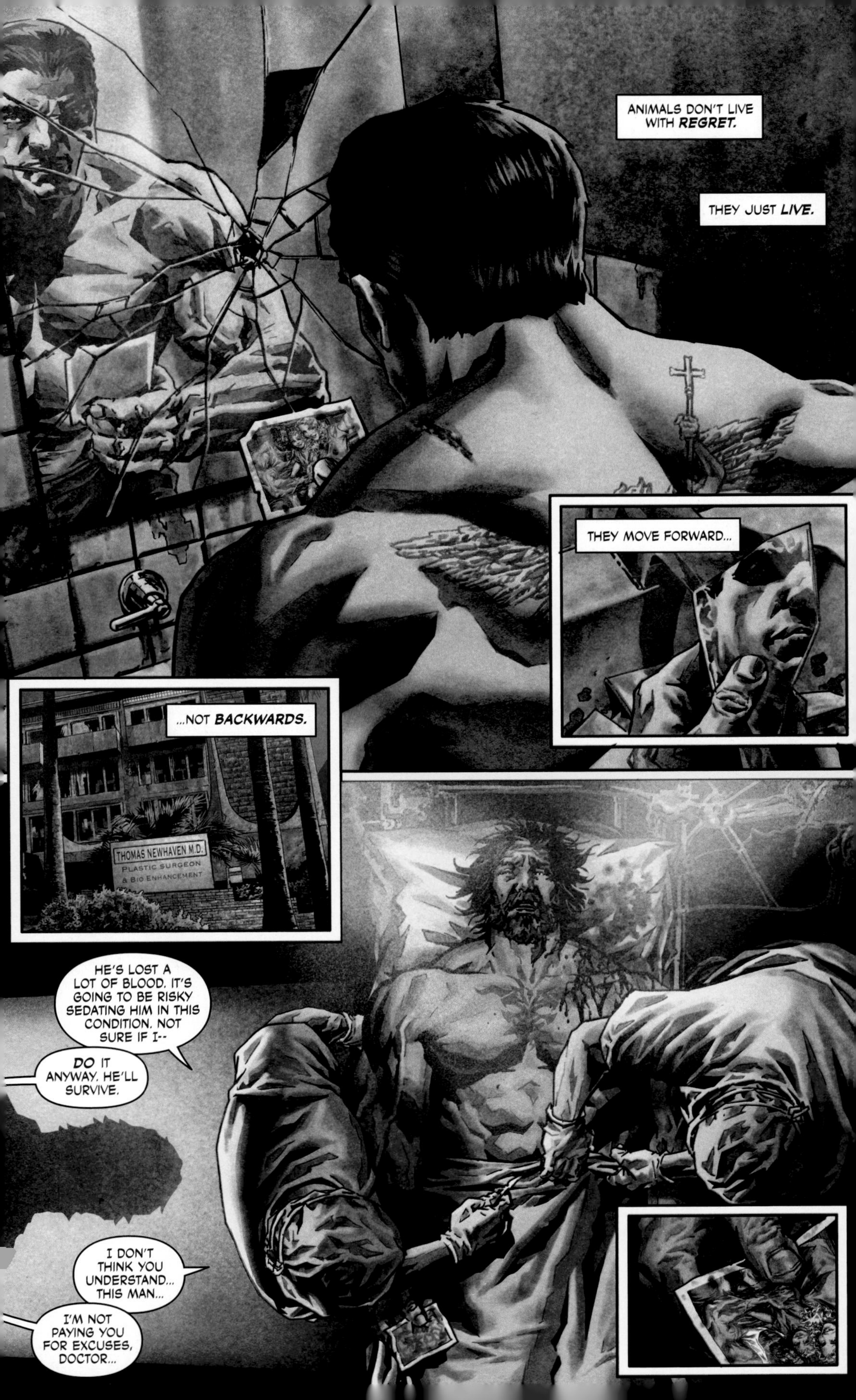
ANIMALS DON'T LIVE WITH REGRET.
THEY JUST LIVE.
THEY MOVE FORWARD...
...NOT BACKWARDS.
THOMAS NEWHAVEN M.D.
PLASTIC SURGEON
& BIO ENHANCEMENT
HE'S LOST A LOT OF BLOOD. IT'S GOING TO BE RISKY SEDATING HIM IN THIS CONDITION. NOT SURE IF I--
DO IT ANYWAY. HE'LL SURVIVE.
I DON'T THINK YOU UNDERSTAND... THIS MAN...
I'M NOT PAYING YOU FOR EXCUSES, DOCTOR...

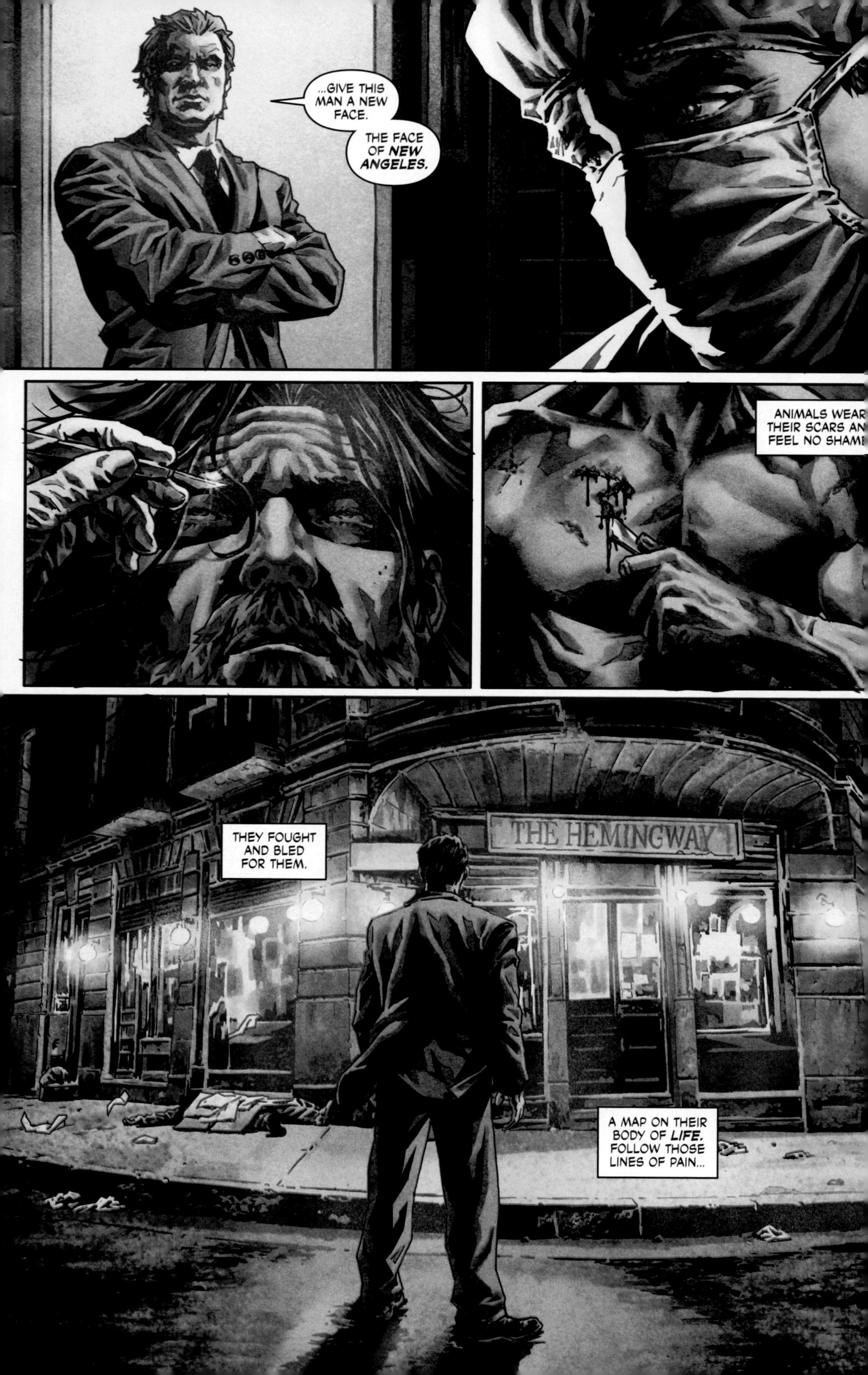
...GIVE THIS MAN A NEW FACE.
THE FACE OF NEW ANGELES.
ANIMALS WEAR THEIR SCARS AN FEEL NO SHAM
THE HEMINGWAY
THEY FOUGHT AND BLED FOR THEM.
A MAP ON THEIR BODY OF LIFE. FOLLOW THOSE LINES OF PAIN...

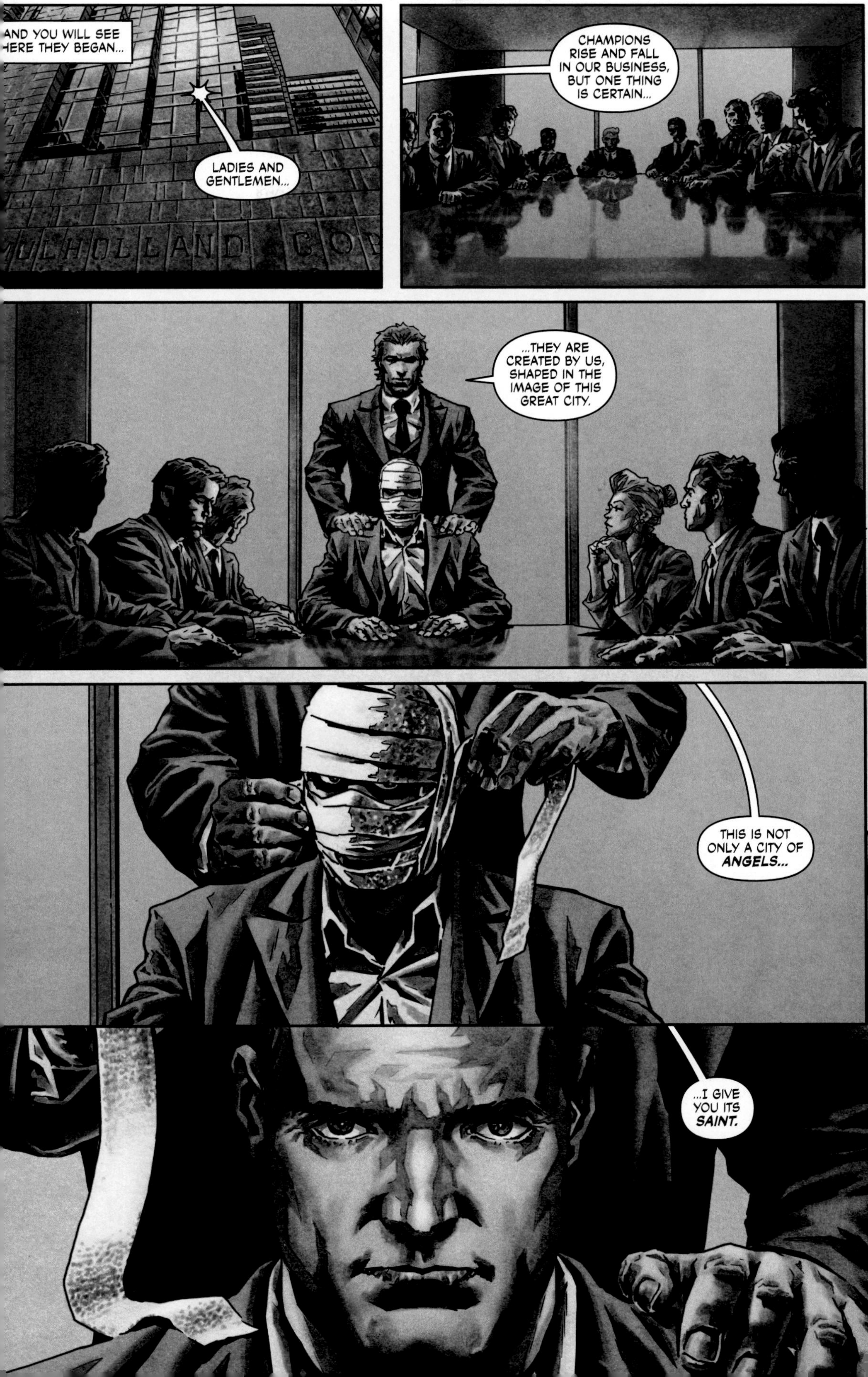

AND YOU WILL SEE
HERE THEY BEGAN...
LADIES AND GENTLEMEN...
CHAMPIONS RISE AND FALL IN OUR BUSINESS, BUT ONE THING IS CERTAIN...
...THEY ARE CREATED BY US, SHAPED IN THE IMAGE OF THIS GREAT CITY.
THIS IS NOT ONLY A CITY OF ANGELS...
...I GIVE YOU ITS SAINT.

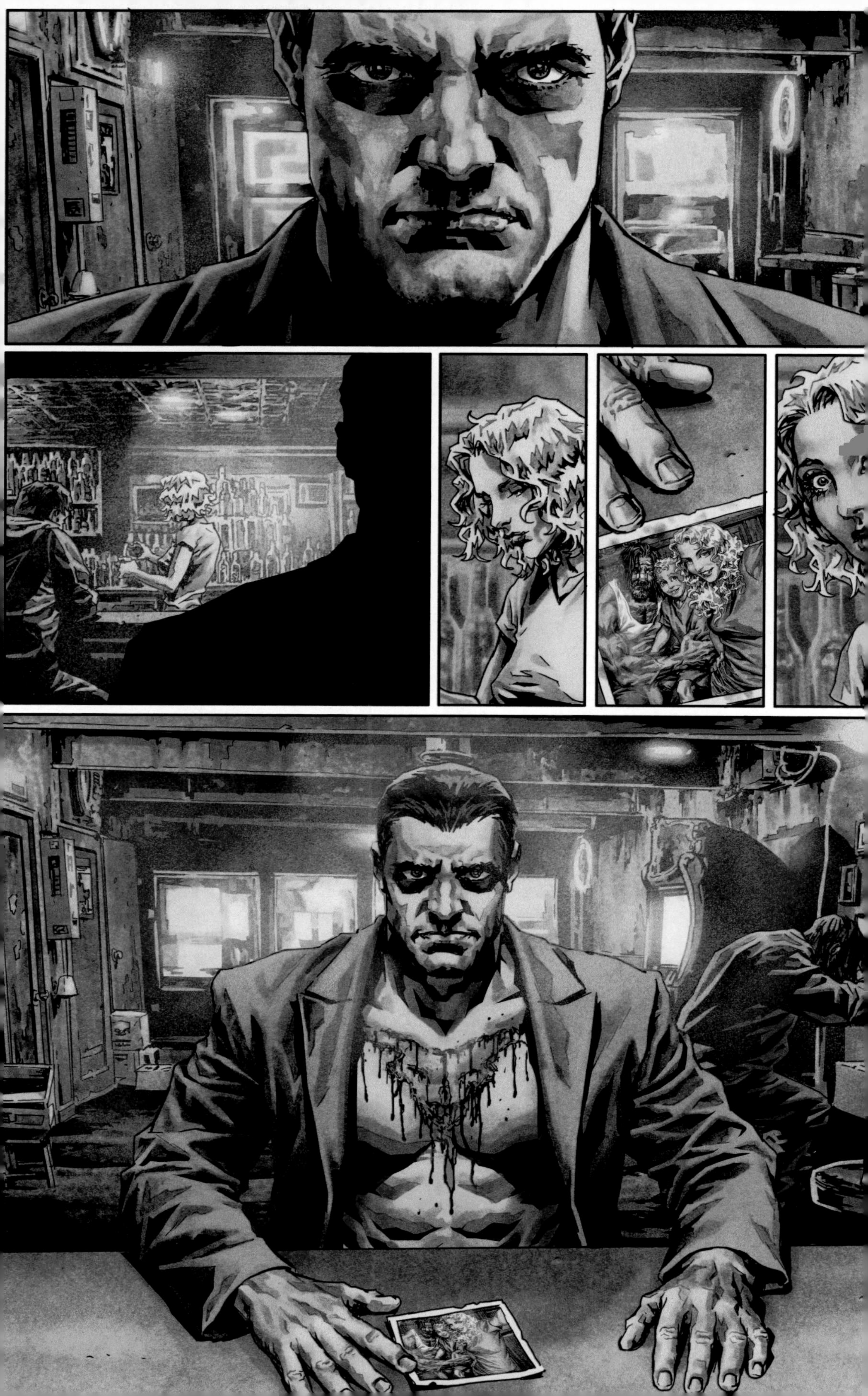

SUICIDERS #1 VARIANT COVER BY
JOCK

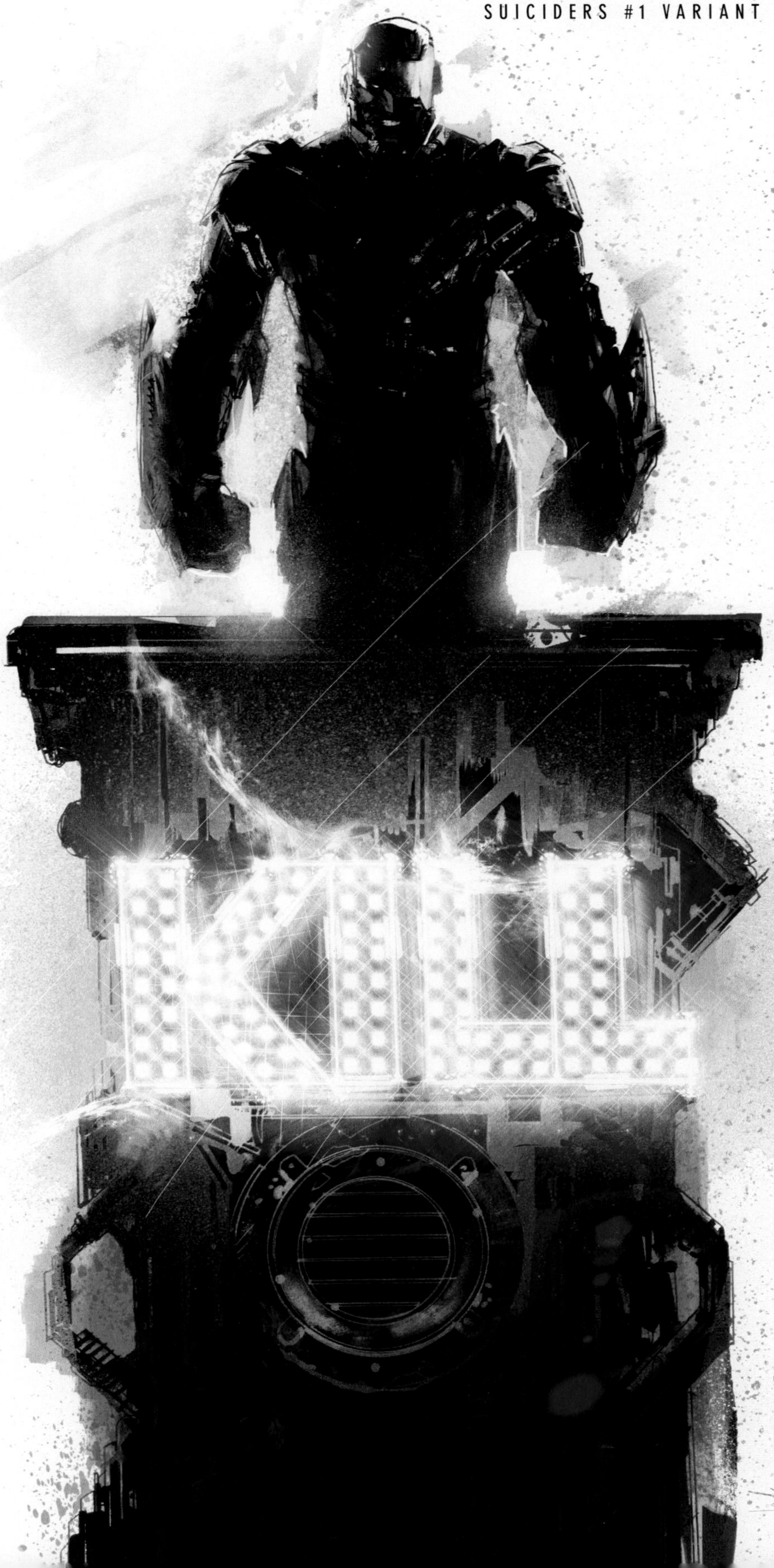
KILL

SUICIDERS promotional image,
the first piece of art done for the series.

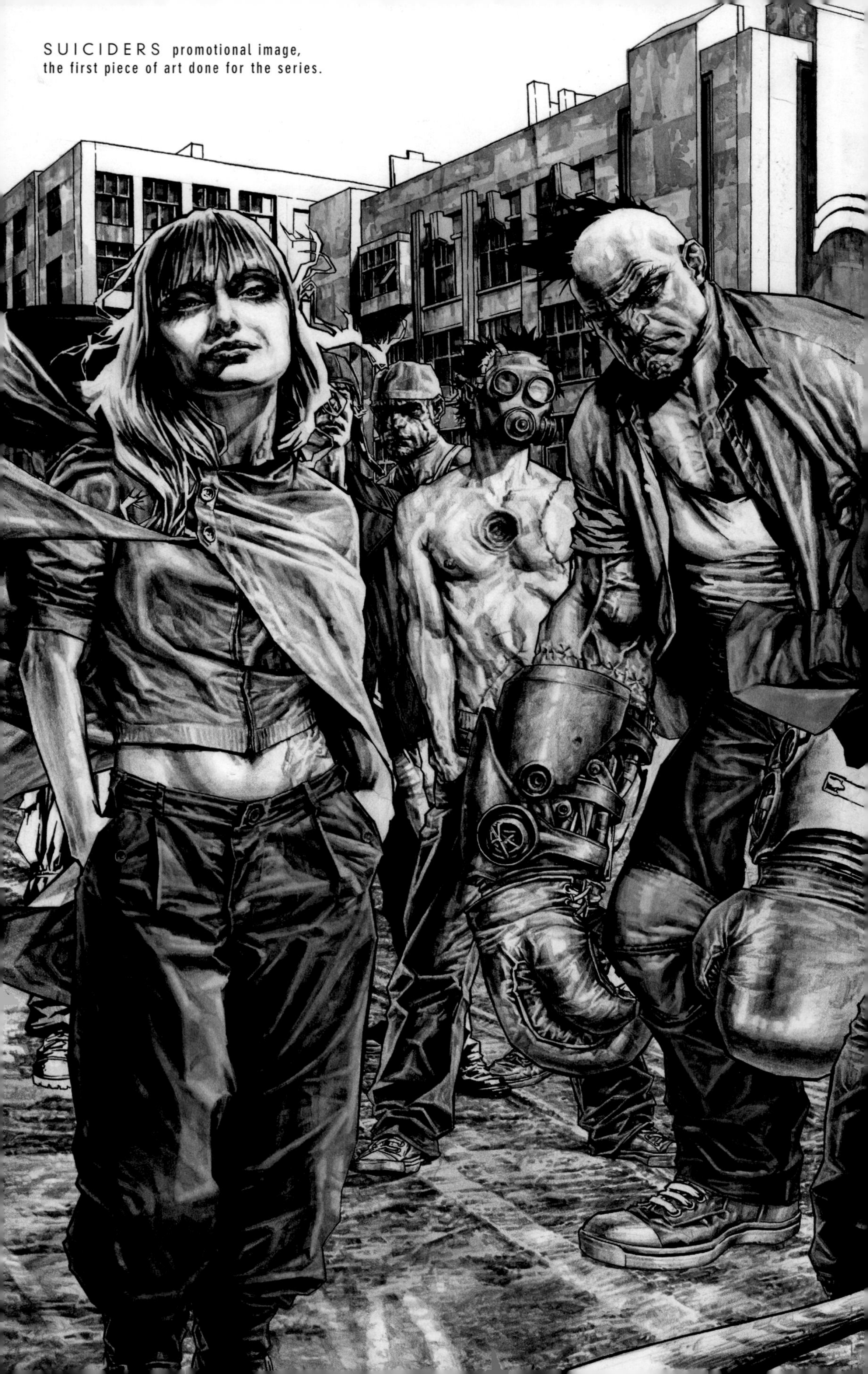

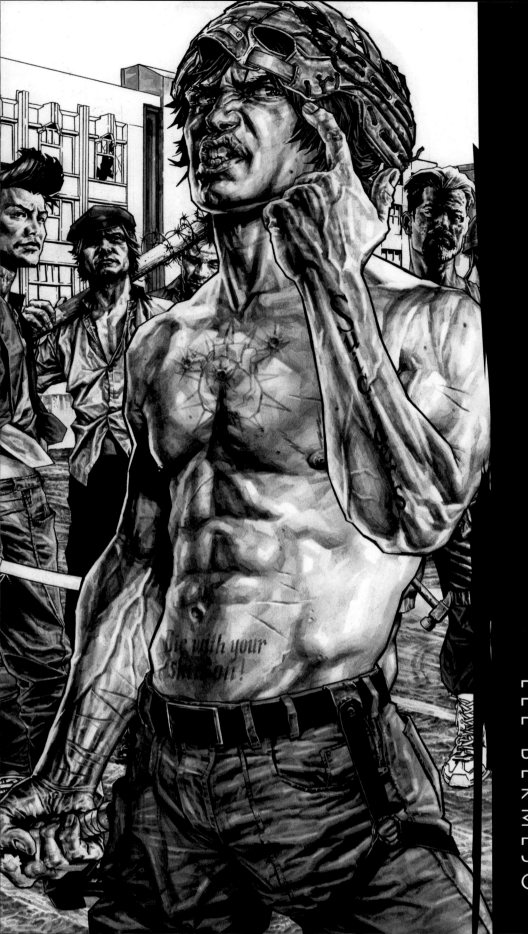

SUICIDERS SKETCHBOOK BY LEE BERMEJO

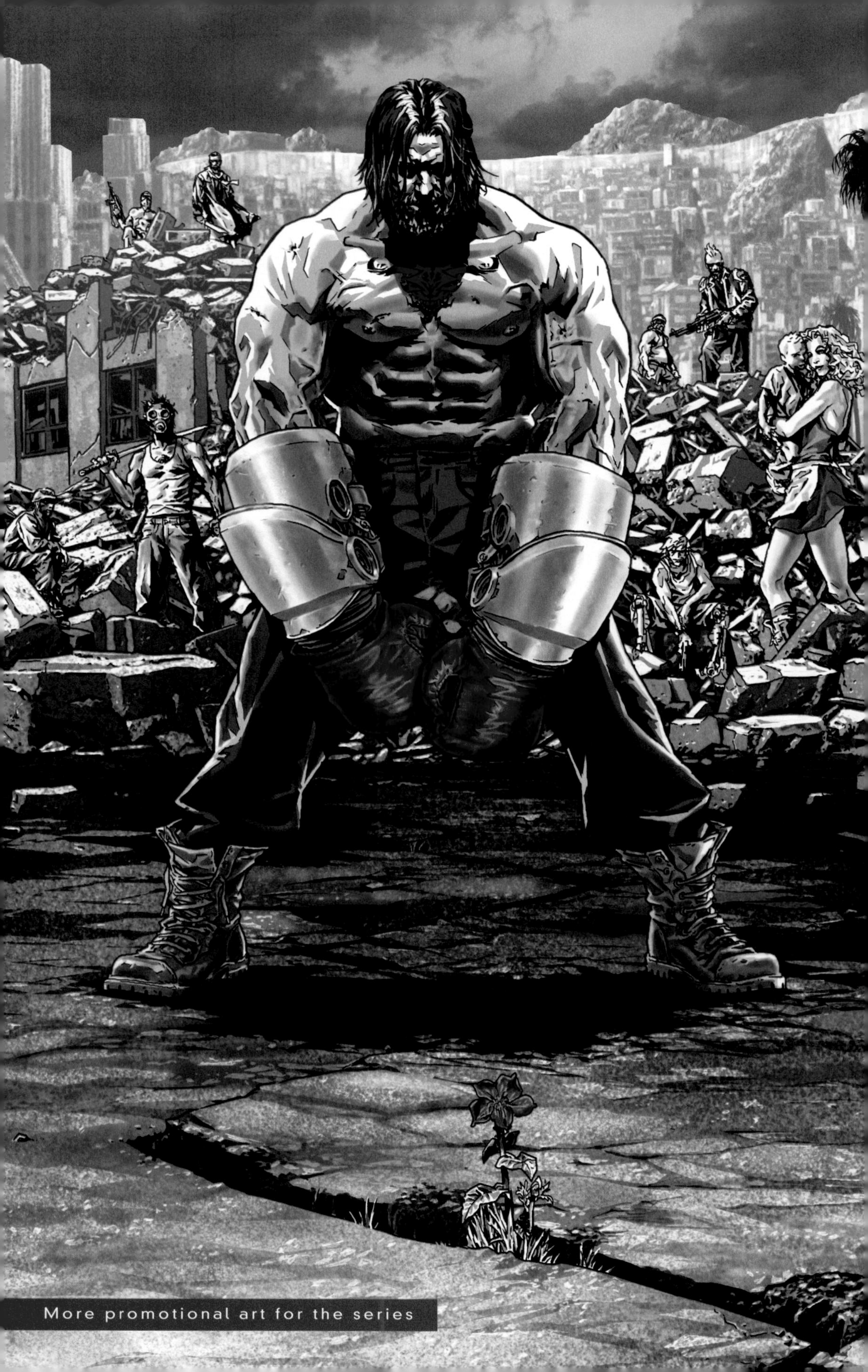

More promotional art for the series

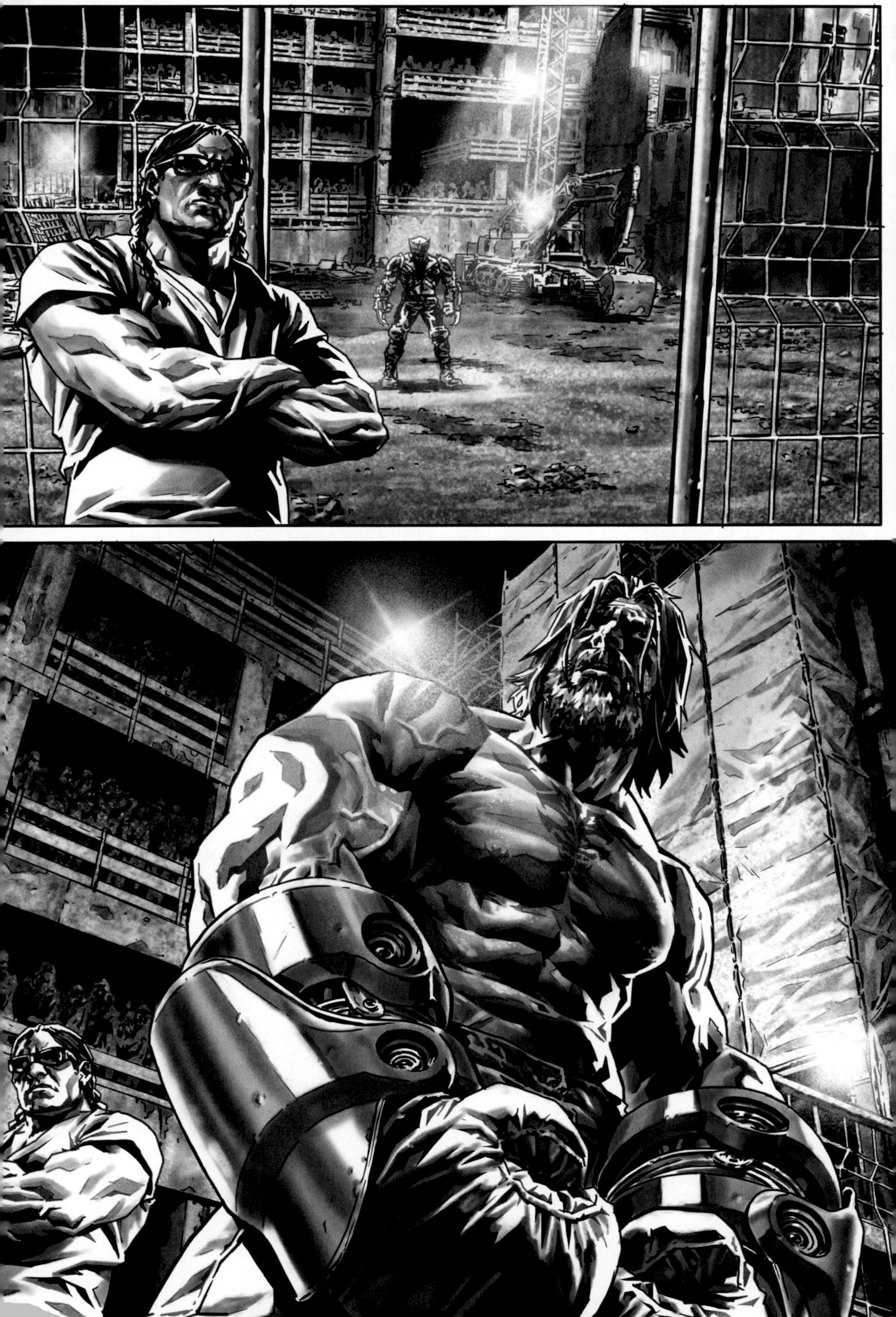

Pencils for SUICIDERS #4 page 8

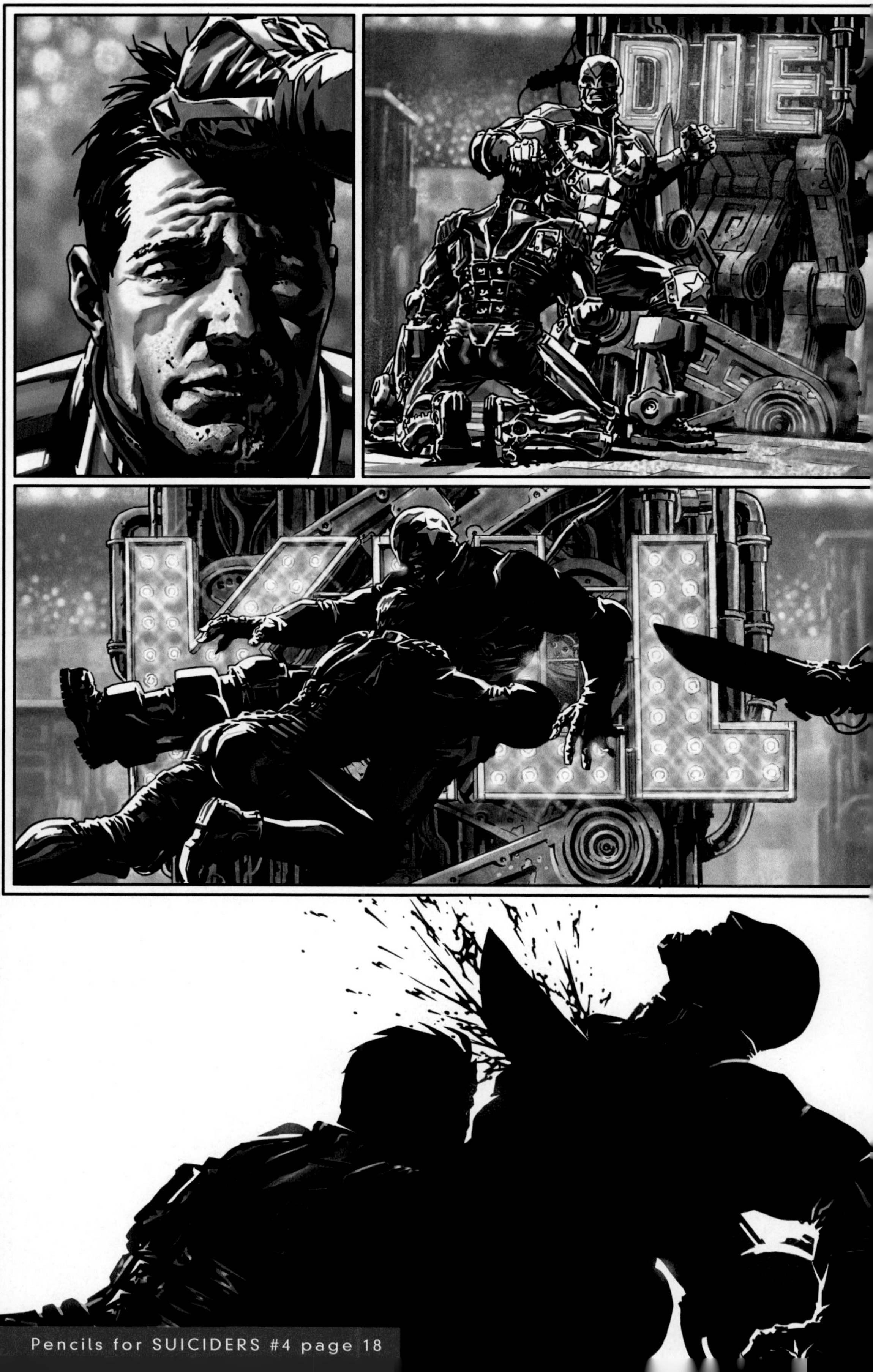
DIE

Pencils for SUICIDERS #4 page 18

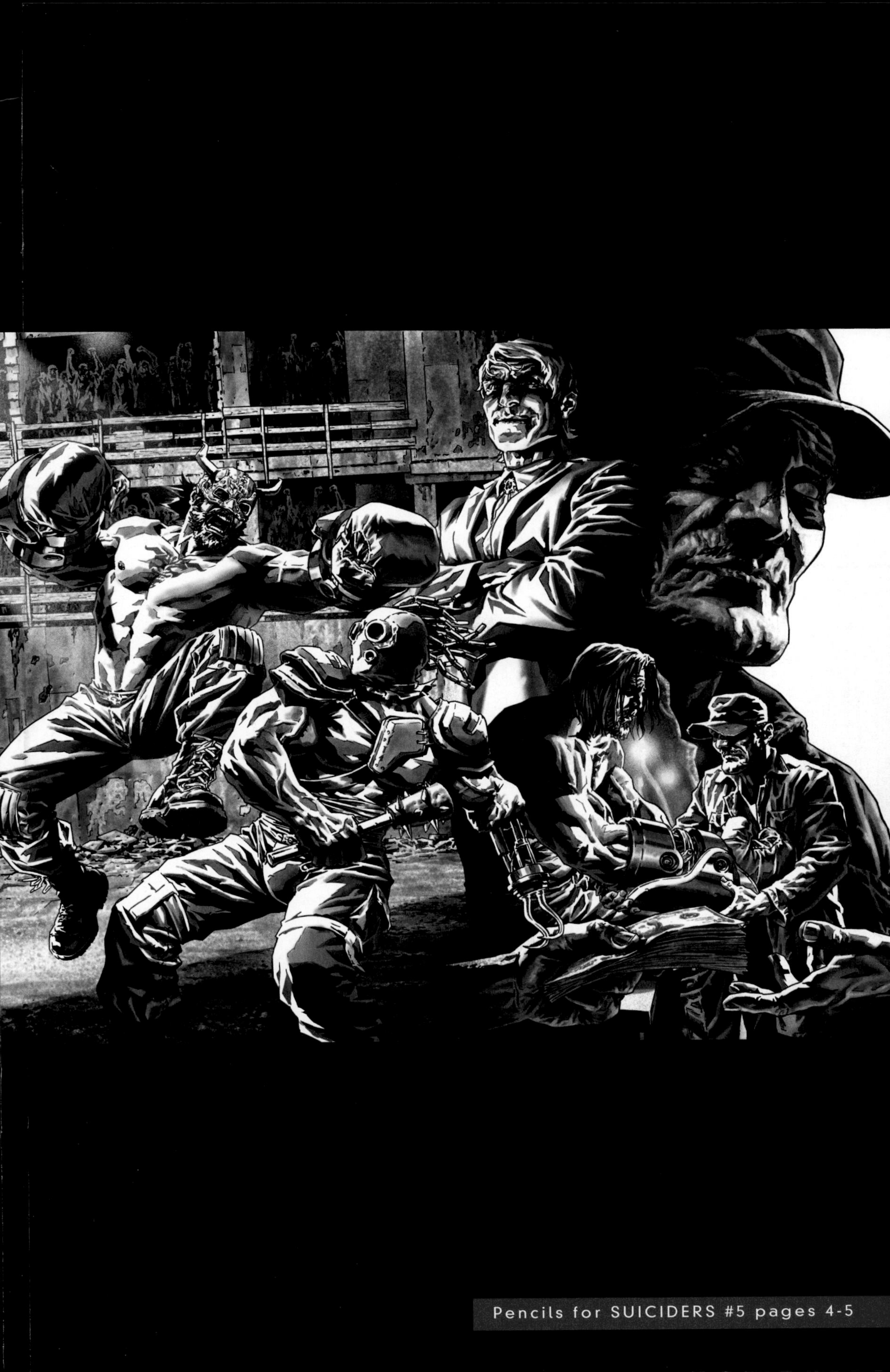

Pencils for SUICIDERS #5 pages 4-5

Award-winning artist **LEE BERMEJO** is the illustrator of the graphic novels BATMAN/DEATHBLOW, LUTHOR, BEFORE WATCHMEN: RORSCHACH and the *New York Times* best-selling JOKER, all of which were done in collaboration with writer Brian Azzarello.

Bermejo's other work for DC includes the titles GLOBAL FREQUENCY (with Warren Ellis), SUPERMAN/GEN 13 (with Adam Hughes) and HELLBLAZER (with Mike Carey), as well as several dozen painted covers and the best-selling graphic novel BATMAN: NOËL, which he wrote and illustrated. He currently lives with his wife Sara, in Italy, where he is hard at work writing WE ARE ROBIN and the second volume of his creator-owned Vertigo series SUICIDERS.

Born in southern California in 1968, **MATT HOLLINGSWORTH** began his comics career in 1991. Since then he has worked as a color artist for most of the major American comic book publishers, contributing to such titles as PREACHER, TOM STRONG, CATWOMAN, THE FILTH, *Hellboy, Iron Fist, Alias* and *Daredevil*. In 2004, while living in Los Angeles, he embarked on a two-year stint in the world of visual effects that led to assignments on seven feature films, including *Sky Captain and the World of Tomorrow*, *Serenity*, and his personal favorite, *Surf's Up*. In addition to rebuilding his home brewery, Hollingsworth spends his free time consuming massive quantities of beer, playing drums, studying genealogy and wandering the countryside in Croatia where he lives with his fiancée and two cats.

JARED K. FLETCHER grew up sailing around the waters of his native Rhode Island. After graduating from the Kubert School in 2003, he began working at DC Comics as part of their new in-house lettering department. In 2007 he left DC to pursue his freelance career as the proprietor of Studio Fantabulous. He spends long days there designing logos and type treatments, art directing covers, cartooning, designing T-shirts and lettering comic books like BATMAN, EX MACHINA, THE SPIRIT, WONDER WOMAN and *Spider-Man*.

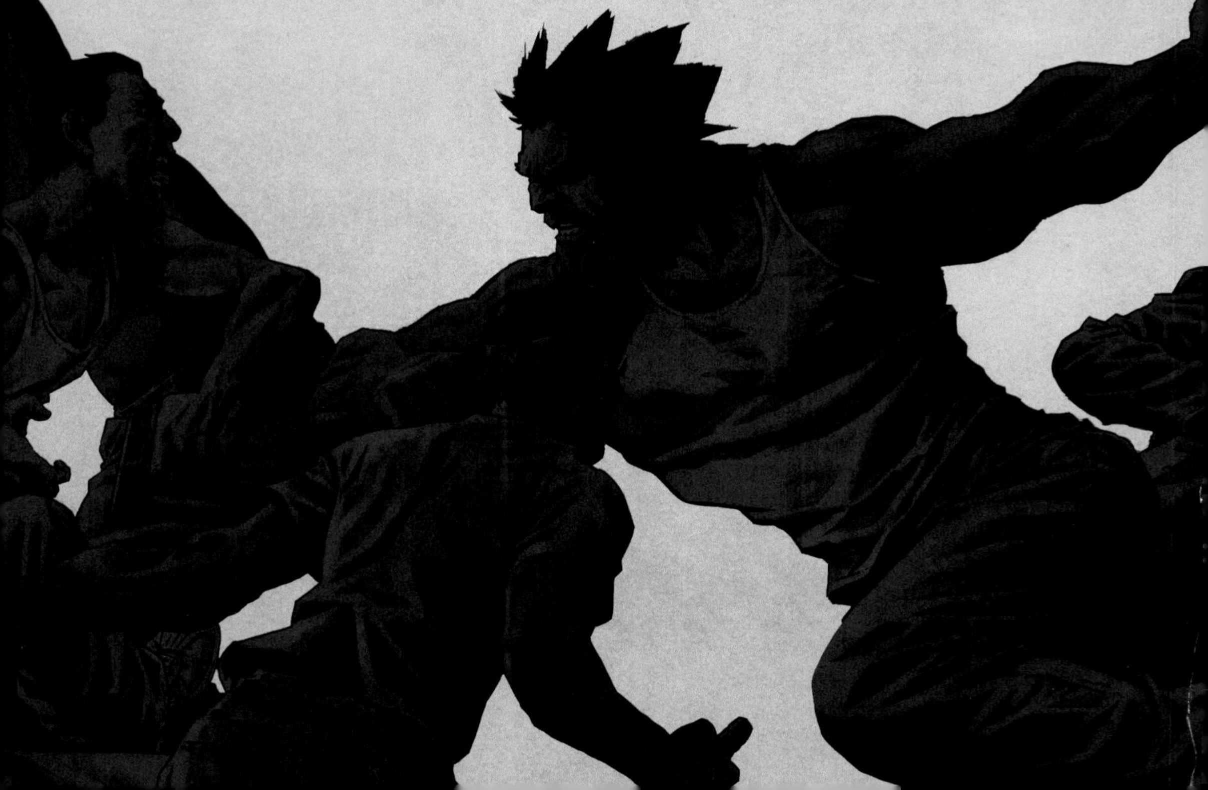